Metropolitan Lovers

Metropolitan Lovers

The Homosexuality of Cities

Julie Abraham

UNIVERSITY OF MINNESOTA PRESS

MINNEAPOLIS · LONDON

Published with assistance from the
Margaret S. Harding Memorial Endowment
honoring the first director of the
University of Minnesota Press.

Published by the University of Minnesota Press
111 Third Avenue South, Suite 290
Minneapolis, MN 55401-2520
http://www.upress.umn.edu

Library of Congress Cataloging-in-Publication Data

Abraham, Julie.
    Metropolitan lovers : the homosexuality of cities / Julie Abraham.
        p. cm.
    Includes bibliographical references and index.
    ISBN 978-0-8166-3818-5 (hc : alk. paper) — ISBN 978-0-8166-3819-2
(pb : alk. paper)
    1. Homosexuality in literature. 2. American literature—History and
criticism. 3. Lesbianism in literature. 4. Cities and towns in literature.
5. City and town life in literature. 6. Homosexuality—History.
7. City and town life—United States—History. 8. Gays—United States—
Social conditions. I. Title.
    PS169.H65A37   2008
    809´.93352664—dc22

                                        2008037977

Printed in the United States of America on acid-free paper

The University of Minnesota is an equal-opportunity educator and
employer.

15 14 13 12 11 10 09   10 9 8 7 6 5 4 3 2 1

FOR HAZEL ADELINE HANNAFORD
(1903–1973)
who rarely left Adelaide

FOR SIMON JOSEPH ABRAHAM
(1900–1973)
who traveled from Gray Street to Lebanon and back again

TO NEW YORK CITY
where I have found my home

I will make inseparable cities with their arms about each other's necks,
By the love of comrades,
By the manly love of comrades.

—WALT WHITMAN, "For You, O Democracy"

Contents

Preface: The Lives of Homosexuals in the Idea of the City   xiii

Acknowledgments   xxi

Part I. Setting Terms

1. *Les Lesbiennes,* or The City in History   3
     Femmes damnées   3
     The Vice of Whores   10
     The Victims of Capital   14
     The Heroines of Modernism   24

2. Oscar Wilde in Los Angeles   37
     Reading Lessons   37
     The Legible City   44
     The Genius of Criminals   50
     Ernest in Town   59
     Socialism and Interpretation   68

Part II. Claiming Residence

3. Perverts in Groups   83
     The Social Evil in Chicago   83
     Modern Nervousness   91
     La Ville invisible   98

4. City of Women   111
   The Social Claim and the Industrial City   111
   At Home on Halsted Street   125

5. Radclyffe Hall at the Chicago School   141
   The Criminal, the Defective, and the Genius   141
   Communal Lives   155

Part III. The Fear and Hope of Great American Cities

6. Paris, Harlem, Hudson Street—1961   169
   Are Cities Un-American?   169
   History in the City   181
   Children and Strangers   194
   Neighborhoods and Slums   208

7. City of Feeling   221
   The Culture of Cities   221
   Into the Streets   230
   Ghetto Gentry   242
   Making Urban Meaning   253

Afterword: Queer in the Great City   273
   Somewhere   273
   A Place for Us   279
   The Future of Cities   287

Notes   301

Index   351

Honoré Daumier (1808–1879), *The Destruction of Sodom*, ca. 1850. Watercolor and gouache on paper. Copyright Ashmolean Museum, University of Oxford, U.K. / The Bridgeman Art Library.

Preface

The Lives of Homosexuals in the Idea of the City

Homosexuals and cities even share a name. "Sodom" has been, in Western religion and law, one of the most enduring signs of same-sex desire. "Sodom" has also been, simultaneously, one of the "ruling metaphors" of the city.[1] In the opening pages of *Cities of the Plain* (1921), Marcel Proust's narrator describes his initial recognition of homosexual desire—in the "reciprocal glances" of the Baron de Charlus and the tailor Jupien—by observing "[i]n the eyes of both of them . . . the sky . . . of some Oriental city . . . reflected." He goes on to refer to contemporary homosexuals as simultaneously "inhabitants" of Sodom and Gomorrah (the inhabitants of Gomorrah being lesbians), Sodomites themselves, and "descendants of the Sodomites," all of whom he imagines as living either in flight or in exile from their city. Their modern efforts to assert their rights he represents as a movement to rebuild that city. In the meantime, they are most happy in "London, Berlin, Rome, Petrograd, or Paris."[2]

Whether a city or a person is identified with Sodom, the associations are grim. The original Sodom was annihilated by an angry God for the sins of its citizens. The city as Sodom is a site of "depravity," of the "failure" of "human faith and aspirations," a bitter alternative to the hopes represented by Augustine's *City of God* or Blake's "New Jerusalem."[3] Lesbians and gay men called out as sodomites are identified as the source of that depravity and marked for punishment. As recently as *Bowers v. Hardwick* (1986), the United States Supreme Court read Georgia's "sodomy law" (which prohibited a range of nonprocreative sexual practices, regardless of the genders of the actors) as referring specifically and only to homosexuals, going on to

xiii

conclude that lesbians and gay men had no constitutional right to their sexuality or their privacy—that is, no right to be recognized as other than "sodomites."[4] That legal decision would stand until 2004.

The hostile identification of homosexuality with the city encapsulated in this shared name persists, at least in those parts of the United States clinging to their other-than-urban status. In July 1998 Mark S. McBride became mayor of Myrtle Beach, South Carolina, on the strength of his opposition to homosexuality, after he vowed to defend his people against "all the progressiveness, all the sophistication, all the enlightenment of big-city life."[5] In response to Vermont's spring 2000 institution of "civil unions" for same-sex couples, a Take Back Vermont campaign agitated to vote out of office the politicians responsible for the new law and save Vermont from the city. "Vermonters have been divided: native against newer Vermonters, rural against urban," a newspaper columnist explained.[6] As one of the campaign's supporters declared, "We're losing our values. . . . We were an agricultural state."[7] After the 2004 U.S. elections, Pastor Russell Johnson established the Ohio Restoration Project, because, he insisted, "the Ohio Republican Party" was insufficiently hostile to same-sex marriage: the party "acts as if it lives" not just in the permissive state of Massachusetts, where lesbian and gay couples have been allowed to marry since 2003, but "in Boston, Mass."[8] To denounce the city is still to denounce homosexuality, and to denounce homosexuality is still to denounce the city.

But the identification of homosexuality with the city also remains vivid, and vivid with promise, within contemporary lesbian/gay/queer cultures—and not only in the United States, as witnessed by the many young men and women from the provinces who still travel to San Francisco and New York, but also around the world by those who travel to London, Harare, Beijing, and Rio to pursue their same-sex desires. Although he was in fact writing about post–World War II gay life throughout the United States, journalist Charles Kaiser named his subject "the gay metropolis" (1997). With a conviction as absolute as that of Mayor Mark McBride or the more recent defenders of Vermont and Ohio, he blithely announced as self-evident that wherever there are gay people, there is the city: "In the postwar period, New York City became the literal gay metropolis for hundreds of thousands of immigrants from within and without the United States . . . where they chose . . . to live openly, honestly and without shame." "But the figurative gay metropolis," he continued, "encompasses every place on every continent where gay people have found the courage and dignity to be free."[9] Even heterosexuals now share this faith in the capacity of queers to make metropolises. In the past decade mayors from Memphis to Madrid have publicized their gay neighborhoods as proof of their cities' urbanity.[10] To embrace homosexuality, then, is still to embrace the city, and to embrace the city is still to embrace homosexuality.

TO SAY THAT homosexuals and cities go together, as it were, is not, then, to say anything new. We have Walt Whitman's quite literal promise, from 1860: "I will make inseparable cities with their arms about each other's necks, / By the love of comrades, / By the manly love of comrades."[11] I want us to think again, however, about what we think we already know. Consequently, I have organized my discussion of the union of homosexuals and cities around the familiar: famous homosexuals (Oscar Wilde, Jane Addams, Radclyffe Hall, James Baldwin); often-cited city commentators (Georg Simmel, Walter Benjamin, Robert Park, Richard Sennett); well-known texts (from Émile Zola's late nineteenth-century novel *Nana* to Jane Jacobs's classic of twentieth-century urban planning, *The Death and Life of Great American Cities*); frequently invoked metropolitan types (the prostitute, the flaneur, the delinquent, the drag queen); and the standard subjects and language of urban analysis (from "capital" and "vice" to "ghettos" and "gentrification").

I most often use the term "homosexual" to indicate my interest in the whole complex of cultural clichés that have accompanied that term for most of its existence.[12] I wanted also to encompass the widest possible range of modern references to, names for, and identifications with same-sex desire. But although I discuss the lives and work of many individuals, this book is a cultural, not a social, history.

The urban studies I consider are often based on particular cities: Friedrich Engels was writing about London and Manchester in 1845; Samuel Delany about New York City in 1999. Specific cities have also served as points of reference for "classic" works: Berlin for Georg Simmel's "The Metropolis and Mental Life" (1903), or Chicago for Robert Park's "The City: Suggestions for the Investigation of Human Behavior in the Urban Environment" (1916). But the urban studies literature most often relies on a generalized metropolis. American sociologist Richard Sennett, for example, treats specific cities chapter by chapter in such later works as *Flesh and*

Stone (1994), but his analysis begins with the "simplest" definition of a city, the one he offers in *The Fall of Public Man* (1978): "[A] city is a human settlement in which strangers are likely to meet."[13]

The closest the authors of these various urban studies get to agreeing is in their focus on "great cities." But, then, the "great cities" that the various contributors to this literature describe are remarkably similar. In the past three decades, as the proportion of the world's population that lives in cities has shifted from two-thirds to one-half, the most dramatic urban growth has occurred in places like Mexico City, São Paulo, and Mumbai.[14] Yet the premise of much recent urban commentary remains, in British cultural critic Raymond Williams's words, "the metropolis of the second half of the nineteenth century and of the first half of the twentieth century. . . . the place where new social and cultural relations, beyond both city and nation in their older senses, were beginning to be formed."[15] That "great city" is also, therefore, the paradigmatic city of my discussion.

Gay life in New York City. Still from *Advise and Consent*, Otto Preminger, director, 1962. Copyright Columbia Pictures, Columbia Pictures/Photofest.

I begin in western Europe, in the first half of the nineteenth century, and conclude in the United States, at the beginning of the new millennium, following the path of the modern history of urbanization and the shifting centers of modern lesbian and gay culture and politics. By the end of the twentieth century in the United States, the threat of homosexuality could represent the threat of urbanization. But internationally, the threat of homosexuality represented the threat of Americanization.

The structure of this book is cumulative—as is the history of modern understandings of homosexuality and of the city. The language, the paradigms for analyses, and the questions that have driven debates about the modern great city developed in the early nineteenth century. They were drawn from earlier models, and they have been drawn on by urban commentators ever since. Conditions change, new claims are made, but nothing is lost. And the fundamental terms of dominant (Western) understandings of same-sex desire have been equally consistent.

Likewise, particular cities have consistently served as cultural touchstones, albeit at different moments, over the past century and a half. Those cities also serve as touchstones in this study: Paris, London, Manchester, and Los Angeles, in the first part; Chicago and Paris, in the second part; New York, Paris, and San Francisco, in the third.

Nonetheless, this study challenges a recent and powerful assumption about the union of homosexuals and cities, namely, that the homosexuality of the city is always male. For reasons I will explore here, in different cities, at different moments, lesbians or gay men have been in turn more or less salient figures—more or less useful to the construction and maintenance of central understandings of the great city.

METROPOLITAN LOVERS: *the Homosexuality of Cities* is a study of the modern history—the forms, the contents, and the consequences—of the cross-identifications of homosexuality with the city and of the city with homosexuality. It maps the convergences, the exchanges of meaning, the transfers of value, and the intertwined fates of understandings of homosexuality and the city that have in turn shaped our comprehension of modernity.

The city, as imagined around imaginary homosexuals by straight and gay commentators, has historically been inseparable from "the city" as it has been imagined by everyone since modern cities, and modern homosexuals, emerged. My fundamental assertion is that homosexuals became,

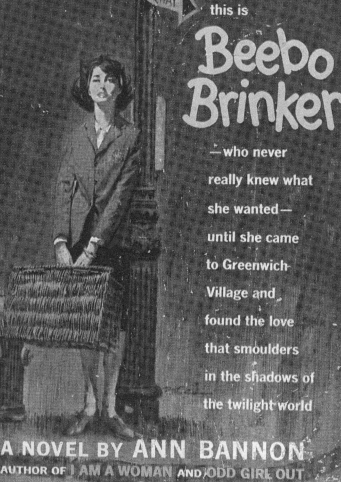

The women of the twilight world. Cover of *Beebo Brinker,* by Ann Bannon (Greenwich, Conn.: Fawcett, 1962).

over the course of the past two centuries, simultaneously model citizens of the modern city and avatars of the urban; that is, models of the city itself. More familiar claims—that cities produce homosexuals or their identities, or, conversely, that cities are produced by homosexuals; that cities have been the salvation of gays, or that gays might be the saviors of cities—have been derived from and supported those developments. Understandings of historical change, fears of illegible persons and places, convictions about the workings of social groups, conflicts over divisions between public and private lives, and assumptions about the street and the home have all been worked out within this framework. Straight as well as gay commentators have used ideas about homosexuals to negotiate their own places in "the city," from the mid-nineteenth century to the present. Most recently, gay as well as straight commentators have used the identification of homosexuals with cities as a means of talking about place itself. What we think of cities, and who we think of as homosexual, has been determined by these processes. The consequences for homosexuals have been great, yet the consequences for cities might have been greater.

   Metropolitan Lovers is an exploration of how we arrived here.

Acknowledgments

I thank the colleagues and students who listened and generously responded to early versions of this work—at Sarah Lawrence College, at the conference "The Future of the Queer Past" at the University of Chicago in September 2000, and at New York University's 1999–2000 International Center for Advanced Studies (ICAS) seminar "Cities and Urban Knowledge." I am particularly grateful to Thomas Bender and the members of the ICAS seminar for allowing me to join them. Columbia University Press graciously granted me permission to reprint an earlier version of chapter 4, which appeared as "Great Cities: Radclyffe Hall at the Chicago School" in Laura Doan and Jay Prosser's *Palatable Poison: Critical Perspectives on "The Well of Loneliness."* Sarah Lawrence College provided me with a much-needed release-time grant in 2003 and a sabbatical in 2005, and helped defray the cost of the images in this volume.

My students at Emory University and at Sarah Lawrence worked through with me many different versions of my course "The City of Feeling: Sexuality and Space" over the past decade. I am indebted to my hardworking Sarah Lawrence research assistants, especially Jeremy Ravdin, Ben Sher, Erin Boyle, and Kara Elverson. I offer special thanks to Lisa Andrews for her invaluable assistance at the last.

Many thanks to Judith Rohrer for her first suggestions, and to Cynthia Enloe, Jennifer Leighton, Ellen Marakowitz, Esther Newton, Jane Queller, Joni Seager, Elaine Sexton, and Carole Vance for their encouragement and advice along the way. Robin Becker cheered on this project in the ways every author most wants and helped at many key moments. John D'Emilio and Glen Elder read the manuscript and offered their insights at a crucial stage. To James Saslow, Steve Cohan, Roger Hallas, and Ellen Neskar, my thanks for their assistance with illustrations.

My great thanks to Moreen and Brian McGee, intrepid world-traveling Australians, for visiting my city. To Daniel and Emma Lang, for their steady interest in my work and for not asking when I would be done. And to Amy Schrager Lang, who has seen me through the entire project and still cares.

PART I

Setting Terms

Henri de Toulouse-Lautrec (1864–1901), *At the Moulin Rouge: The Two Waltzers*, 1892. Board. Copyright Narodni Galerie, Prague, Czech Republic/The Bridgeman Art Library.

1

Les Lesbiennes, or
The City in History

FEMMES DAMNÉES

"Les Lesbiennes" was Charles Baudelaire's first choice for the title of the collection of poems that he eventually published, in Paris, in June 1857, as *Les Fleurs du mal*.[1] That collection would eventually be hailed as not only the point of origin of modern literature but also the quintessential poetic portrait of modern urban life.[2] But immediately *Les Fleurs du mal* was seized by the public prosecutor. And although we did not in the end lend our name to his book, lesbians were central to the scandal it produced.

According to the Sûreté publique of the French Ministry of the Interior, Baudelaire's collection was "an act of defiance in contempt of the laws which safeguard religion and morality." The essence of that defiance was his inclusion of poems "express[ing] the most repugnant lubricity," poems such as "'Les Femmes Damnées' . . . a paean of praise for the shameful love of women for other women." Despite strenuous efforts to induce various well-known writers, faintly well-disposed officials, and the occasional society lady to intervene on his behalf—and despite the state's abandonment of its complaint on behalf of religion—Baudelaire was convicted in August 1857 on the charge that the book contained "obscene and immoral passages or expressions."[3] Though spared imprisonment, he was fined three hundred francs and ordered to suppress six of his poems, including the triptych that would seem to have been the basis for his original title: "Lesbos," "Delphine et Hippolyte," and "Femmes damnées."

It is, in retrospect, difficult to read Baudelaire's poems as either a cultural breakthrough or a cultural threat. Rather, they fit tidily into a hoary

3

tradition that can be traced back through the early modern period—the drama of John Lyly, John Donne's "Sappho to Philaenis"—to "classical idioms, rhetorics, tropes, and illustrative examples" (Ovid's *Metamorphoses* provided a model for many): a tradition of male artists fantasizing about women together.[4] The key term in the court's verdict was "realism." Baudelaire's prosecutor denounced "this unhealthy fever which induces writers to portray everything, to describe everything, to say everything." But "realism" here seems to be a synonym for sex. The judge declared that nothing "could dissipate the harmful effect of the images he presents to the reader, and which, in the incriminated poems, inevitably lead to the arousal of the senses."[5] Whatever effect they may have had on his contemporaries, Baudelaire's elaborate descriptions of his *lesbiennes*' fevered caresses faithfully reiterate the two assertions central to the tradition of which they are a part. They highlight his own authority as an observer, the poet whom "Lesbos has chosen . . . among all men / to sing the secrets of her budding grove."[6] And they confirm the superiority of heterosexuality. "[Y]ou whom my soul has followed to your hell," he declares, "Sisters! I love you as I pity you / for your bleak sorrows, for your unslaked thirsts."[7] These women are in hell, tormented by "unslaked thirsts," because as women they are supposedly unable to satisfy each other.

Baudelaire had declared himself in no uncertain terms, both in his analyses of the art of others and in his own writings, to be in pursuit of the contemporary, of what he labeled "modernity." "By 'modernity,'" he wrote, famously, in "The Painter of Modern Life," "I mean the ephemeral, the fugitive, the contingent"; that is, "present-day beauty."[8] This modernity could be represented by "the gesture and bearing of the woman of today [that] give to her dress a life and a special character which are not those of the woman of the past" (13). But above all, the painter of modern life—represented in his essay by Constantin Guys—was concerned with "the landscapes of the great city" (10). Why, then, did Baudelaire ever consider, as representatives of his modern art, these thoroughly conventional *lesbiennes*? Their name alone invokes classical models. And, far from city streets, his *femme damnées* are to be found only on beaches and in boudoirs, in a universe most oddly composed of cascades and scented couches.

Nevertheless, as the history of *Les Fleurs du mal* indicates, fantasies of lesbianism were fundamental to some of the most influential efforts to represent modern cities. As Walter Benjamin would later observe, "Baudelaire by no means discovered the lesbian for art," not even in Paris in the nineteenth century.[9] Nor did he discover the lesbian for the city. Among the writers whose images of women together Baudelaire's lawyer tried to invoke in his defense—Alfred de Musset, Pierre Jean de Béranger, Théophile Gautier (for *Mademoiselle de Maupin*), George Sand (for *Lélia*), Jean de La Fontaine, Alphonse Lamartine, and others—was Honoré de Balzac, cited for his *The Girl with the Golden Eyes*.[10] When Baudelaire began to champion contemporary urban life as the proper subject of modern artists, in "The Salon of 1846," he cited Balzac's characters as proof that the "life of our city is rich in poetic and marvelous subjects."[11] Twenty years before Baudelaire published *Les Fleurs du mal*, Balzac had located lesbianism at the heart of Paris in *The Girl with the Golden Eyes*, the culminating novella in his triptych *History of the Thirteen* (1837). Those stories became in turn the basis for his life's greatest work, his subsequent series "Scenes of Parisian Life." *The Girl with the Golden Eyes* also established the frame within which Baudelaire's *lesbiennes* are intelligible as urban types. Although Balzac prepared the ground for Baudelaire's *lesbiennes*, it was Émile Zola who completed their career with his notorious *Nana*, published twenty years after *Les Fleurs du mal*. *Nana* culminates in its prostitute heroine, the cynosure of a completely corrupted Paris social elite, abandoning herself to the love of another woman.

My goal is not to argue that these writers succeeded in installing lesbianism, or fantasies of lesbianism, at the heart of the modern city—though they did do that. I am most interested in what their uses of such fantasies reveal about nineteenth- and twentieth-century efforts to think about the modern city, and at the same time, in the ways in which modern fantasies about lesbianism were shaped by their urban analyses.

The fantasies of lesbianism produced by Baudelaire and by other representative nineteenth-century French writers on the modern city, such as Balzac and Zola, became embedded within efforts to represent the modern city because of the particular accounts of that city they facilitated, and the particular understandings of that city's relationship to history those accounts facilitated. Such fantasies made possible efforts to subsume an industrial and political modernity within a sexual modernity, an industrialized and politicized city within a sexualized city. They also made it possible for these "modern" writers to attach their modern city to a more congenial past. These *lesbiennes*, and the rhetorical tactics they enabled, were consequently also of use to nineteenth-century urban observers intent on negotiating their own relations to the city, relations shifting under the pressures of the explosive changes occurring in modern cities. Further, their influence was extended by early twentieth-century urban observers such as Benjamin, whose commentary on Baudelaire was central to his own account of the modern metropolis, as well as by more recent generations of urban scholars who routinely take Baudelaire's and Benjamin's writings as their point of origin.

BALZAC'S THE GIRL *with the Golden Eyes,* which he concluded, very specifically, with its urban location and dates ("Paris, March 1834–April 1835"), is a radically divided work. Balzac simultaneously yokes the city to lesbianism and social history to fantasy. The first third of the text, a chapter titled "Parisian physiognomies," is not a story at all but an extraordinarily detailed account of the social structures and pressures of Parisian life. Balzac describes every level of the city's class hierarchy, myriad types within each level, many representative daily rounds, and everyone and their children's opportunities for failure or for advancement. But his sociological disquisition is the prelude to a melodrama of aristocratic power and decadence featuring false identities, masked journeys, hidden chambers, uncontrollable passions, and murderous revenge, pivoting on the mysteries created by one woman's desire for another.

In the opening of his novella, Balzac lays out what came to be the key terms, and pairings, of subsequent accounts of the modern city: gold and pleasure, nature and artifice, secrets and knowledge. "Parisian physiognomies" is still being mined by urban commentators from British geographer David Harvey to American novelist Edmund White, as a source of accurate descriptions of modern Paris.[12] The story to which Balzac's sociology is attached is, however, most often overlooked by readers seeking in his fiction a study of urban life. Nevertheless, whether far-fetched fantasy or not, Balzac's lesbians are not separable from his city. They and their melodrama enact all of the terms he lays out in his sociological study. They enact these terms, moreover, in such a way as to mitigate the most fundamental threats of this new city life.

Setting out to assess "Paris as a moral entity" in *The Girl with the Golden Eyes,* Balzac likens the social circles of the city he is describing to the circles of Dante's inferno.[13] This city is a hell because "[a]ll passion in Paris is resolved into two terms: gold and pleasure" (322). These ruling terms have vitiated any emotional connection the city's citizens might have had to one another: "Love is reduced to desire, hate to a whimsy. The only family link is with the thousand-franc note, one's only friend is the pawnbroker" (310). And as its citizens' pursuit of gold and pleasure has vitiated emotional connections, in this city the natural has become fatally enmeshed in the artificial. Balzac describes Paris, in terms simultaneously natural and artificial, as a "field" or a "sea," "not so much [of] faces as masks: masks of weakness or strength, masks of misery or joy or hypocrisy, all of them drained of vitality, all of them bearing the ineffaceable mark of panting avidity" (309). Such a field of masks, in turn, is not only a field of artificial forms. A field of masks also embodies Balzac's vision of the city as a universe of secrets, founded in careful efforts to manage knowledge and, to complete his circle, revealing only avidity itself, for pleasure and for gold.

Women are exemplary of Balzac's urban hell, the "privileged beings who draw profit from this perpetual to-and-fro of manufacturers, interests,

Baudelaire's "painter of modern life." Constantin Guys (1802–1892), *Scene in Café Interpole (a Bordello),* Louvre, Paris, France. Réunion des Musées Nationaux/ Art Resource, New York.

affairs, arts and affluence" (326). They "profit" even though, or perhaps because, "a thousand secret causes operate on them" (326), because they are most completely enmeshed in the city's secrets. The center of Balzac's subsequent story is a most carefully masked *Parisienne,* Paquita, the most desirable young woman in the city, "of whom . . . all the elegant young men of Paris were enamored" (372). She rarely appears in public, and then only to quickly vanish. She has to be tracked to the mansion in which she is hidden, in the city's most fashionable quarter.

Balzac's narrative is about the pursuit of Paquita by the most desirable young man in Paris, Henri de Marsay, who because of his own wealth as well as his beauty has experienced so many pleasures that "nothing was left to him but extravagant whims [and] fantasies" (346). He is drawn to Paquita partly because she is hidden. And his pursuit of such an inaccessible beauty reveals to him a new source of pleasure, in the possibility of masking sexual desire offered by the city. "[H]ow diverting it is to make fun of society by concealing from it the secret of our affections," he declares (375).

Balzac's novella turns on a particular set of ideas about lesbianism, which he draws on to express most fully—most personally—the threat of his hellish Paris and the ultimate baselessness of that threat. Lesbianism is the emblematic secret of Balzac's Paris. The Paquita whom de Marsay discovers is the embodiment of a "mystery" (359), "a flesh and blood enigma" (369), because of her combination of "purely physical innocence" and "voluptuousness" (376). Only after he has won her favors does de Marsay realize, to his chagrin, that she is in fact both "innocent" and experienced, because her previous lover was a woman.

This lesbianism allows Paquita not only to embody the secret of the city but also to join its fundamental elements, nature and artifice, gold and pleasure. Paquita is relentlessly naturalized as a woman. De Marsay describes her as "the very essence of woman . . . the ideal woman" (339), as "the richest organization that Nature had ever been pleased to create for love" (359). She is also racialized as a woman—identified with both Asia and Africa—in ways that further naturalize her.[14] "[L]inked through her mother to the houris of Asia" (372), she is "a girl who . . . completely embodied the most luminous ideas on women expressed in Oriental poetry" (342). At the same time, Paquita's mother is a "savage" (360), "a slave sold in Georgia" (358) who has in turn "sold" her daughter, as a "slave girl" (368) to her mistress. In the center of Paris, Paquita is kept closely confined and fiercely guarded not only by her "savage" mother but also by a "mulatto," her "foster-brother," Christemio (364).

But the lesbianism in which this paragon of the natural has indulged is an "artificial love" (382). The artificiality of that love is reflected in the boudoir at the center of the story's city, in Paquita's home, a symphony of luxury. Balzac rhapsodizes for pages about "a genuine Turkish divan . . . fifty feet in circumference, of white cashmere offset by black and poppy-red rosettes," hanging "red fabric overlaid with Indian muslin," "silver-gilt" sconces and chandeliers, and oriental carpets (365–66).

Nature and artifice have been joined in Paquita's person, because of the power of gold to purchase pleasure. De Marsay's pursuit of Paquita reveals another woman, otherwise completely hidden, at the heart of the city, the Marquise de San-Real. Her gold made it possible for her to buy the girl from her mother and then hide the girl from the world. She could thus ensure her complete control over the girl and the girl's ignorance of men, which together in this fantasy of lesbianism are necessary to explain a mystery even more fundamental than that of Paquita's physical combination of innocence and experience: her response to the marquise's sexual desires.[15]

Lesbianism not only allows Balzac to represent secrets and knowledge at the heart of the city, to enact a complete merger of nature and artifice, and to confirm the threatening power of gold over pleasure, it also allows him to join all these terms in an expression of the danger this urban hell poses to male authority, as a sexual threat. Paquita's artificial love is threatening because of the rejection of men and masculinity it represents. Balzac even elaborates on this threat. When Paquita meets de Marsay—when she learns that she might have a male rather than a female lover—he immediately replaces the marquise as the object of her desire. But she persuades him to let her put him into a dress: he first makes love to her in the guise of a woman, so that it is unclear which, heterosexuality or lesbianism, is being enacted. That confusion is compounded when she reveals her secret by calling out her mistress's name while clutched in his arms.

But lesbianism also allows Balzac to negate this threat, to set a limit to the urban hell of Paris for the city's male citizens. The benefit of any fantasy is that crises can be easily resolved. Soon after Paquita's secret, her lesbian history, is revealed, she is brutally murdered, bloodied in her blood-red boudoir by her mistress, who has been enraged by her sexual betrayal. The marquise, defeated by the loss of the lover she has destroyed, then exiles herself from the city. The fantasies of lesbianism that Balzac drew on and honed in *The Girl with the Golden Eyes,* those fantasies taken up and elaborated through nineteenth-century French literature on the city, have a very particular added value even beyond the degree to which they allow their proponents to join nature and artifice, and pleasure and gold, in a figure who embodies secrets. This lesbianism—and thus the threat of the modern city it has been made to bear—can simply be erased.

Balzac's final revelation is that Paquita's two lovers, de Marsay and the marquise, are an almost identical pair, brother and sister, both extraordinarily beautiful, powerful, and amoral illegitimate children of the aristocracy. Unaware of each other's existence, both equally ruthlessly pursue their own pleasure with their own inherited fortunes. So Paquita's desire for the woman is revealed to have been really desire for her male counterpart all along. De Marsay comes to view the entire episode ironically and goes on to a long career in later volumes of Balzac's scenes of Parisian life, as if his primacy had never been threatened.

THE VICE OF WHORES

The city's scandal sheets responded to the romance of the novelist George Sand (Aurore Dupin) and the actress Marie Dorval in the mid-1830s.[16] A "frequently expanded poem *Les Lesbiennes de Paris* . . . circulated in Paris around 1845 with the goal of denouncing the well-known women of the day suspected of having homosexual liaisons," including "all the women important in Baudelaire's early amorous life, notably his long-term mistress Jeanne Duval."[17] Gustave Courbet attributed both of his notorious paintings of female couples, *Femmes damnées* (1864) and *Le Sommeil, ou Les Dormeuses* (1866), in part to the influence of Baudelaire's "Delphine et Hippolyte."[18] But at the nexus of pleasure and gold that Balzac insisted defined nineteenth-century Paris, lesbianism was most consistently identified with prostitution.

Alexandre Parent-Duchâtelet produced his landmark "scientific study," *La Prostitution a Paris au XIXe siecle,* in 1836, just after the first appearance of Balzac's *Girl with the Golden Eyes.*[19] For Parent-Duchâtelet lesbianism was the extremity of vice ("Lesbians have fallen to the last degree of vice to which a human creature can attain"), a result of the sexual insatiability that produces and is produced by prostitution in women.[20] "Lesbian love," he explains, is the final step taken by "prostitutes of great sensuality . . . unsatisfied with intercourse with impotent or perverse men."[21] Parent-Duchâtelet's "findings" about the intrinsic connection between prostitution and lesbianism were replicated across the century in the volumes of a series of dedicated followers, from Ambroise Tardieu in the 1850s, who also recorded male homosexual subcultures, to Leo Taxil in *La Prostitution contemporaine* (1884), Louis Martineau in *La Prostitution clandestine* (1885), and Louis Fiacre in *Les Maisons de tolérance* (1892). The association of prostitution and lesbianism was further reinforced in a series of highly visible memoirs of prostitutes (Celeste Mogador in the 1850s, Marguerite Bellanger in the 1880s) and police chiefs (Louis Canler, *Mémoires de Canler* [1862], and M. Claude [1881–1883]).[22]

Lesbians also invariably appeared among prostitutes in the urban underworld of late nineteenth-century guides to the city and other journalistic exposés of the secrets of Parisian life, such as Catulle Mendes's *Monstres Parisiens* (1882; Paris, 1902), Ali Coffignon's *Paris vivant: La Corruption á Paris* (1889), and Jules Davray's *L'Amour a Paris* (1890). The most widely

Gustave Courbet (1819–1877), *The Two Friends,* or *Sleep,* 1866. Musée du Petit Palais, Paris, France. Erich Lessing/Art Resource, New York.

known visual representations of lesbianism in the later part of the century were the female couples Toulouse-Lautrec painted in his Paris brothel scenes.

The most famous portrait of Parisian prostitution, however, and the apotheosis of Parent-Duchâtelet's vision of lesbianism as the vice of whores, was Émile Zola's scandalous, and scandalously successful, novel *Nana* (1880). Four decades after Balzac's *Girl with the Golden Eyes,* Nana is born, lives, and dies at the center of a city in which even the exchange of gold for pleasure can no longer be relied upon as an organizing principle of urban life. Here, lesbianism as the vice of whores, sexuality at its most abandoned, does not simply confirm the utter degradation of prostitutes but represents the fundamental threat of vice itself to the social world of the city, which is the possibility that even gold might cease to control pleasure.

Nana is a natural force, "a superb, mindless animal, oblivious of what she'd done, never anything but a 'good sort of a girl,' a big, fat wench bursting with health and the joy of life."[23] When she is first taken to view the Paris lesbian scene by Satin, a friend and fellow prostitute, she looks down on the habitués of Laure's restaurant "disgustedly": "She still couldn't understand that sort of thing" (225).[24] But as she philosophically concludes, "in her sensible way, . . . there was no accounting for tastes and you could never know what you might come to like one day" (225). Nature ("her animal health") does not defend her from this artificial love. After many heterosexual adventures, she "come[s] to like" what she did not before. Paris and prostitution provide her with not only sexual and financial opportunities but also a sexual education. Satin becomes her lover.

Nana establishes Satin in her life "on the same footing" as her male lovers yet insists that the women's relationship is "nothing that concerns" the men, no challenge to their positions (291). Assuming the inconsequence of women's desires, the men see no contradiction here and accept Nana's proposition. Zola does not. Nana is "ecstatic and devastated" when her affair with Satin begins (289). Satin becomes "an absorbing passion . . . her vice" (289). She who collects male lovers effortlessly willingly competes for Satin, fighting both against the lure of the streets (to which Satin repeatedly retreats when bored with the luxurious setting Nana has finally achieved for herself) and against another woman with a prior claim, the very respectable-looking Mme Robert. (Mme Robert is herself securely kept "by older, highly respectable men" in middle-class gentility [223]).

Despite the vigorous efforts of each of her male lovers, only another woman can gain control over Nana: Satin "at last succeeded in completely dominating Nana, who respected her" (390). But because of Satin's control over her lover, Nana loses all control over her own sexuality, and consequently over her life. She has moved from man to man, and managed these men so successfully that she has established the preeminence of her desirability and has achieved wealth and luxury. Her feeling for Satin inaugurates the final phase of her career, when her "star blazed with ever increasing brilliance and her vicious life loomed even larger on the horizon of vice of Paris" (367). Yet even as she finally has "the capital at her feet," Nana becomes sexually insatiable (367). She cannot be faithful even to Satin. She "pick[s] up tarts from the street" (390). And although she is described throughout the novel as the essence of femininity, she is driven by lesbianism to gender-crossing, "disguis[ing] herself as a man and [attending] orgies in brothels" (390).

The degree to which Nana's lesbianism threatens the social order is underlined when she defends her desire for Satin by insisting that women's desire for one another is not only ubiquitous among prostitutes but ubiquitous across class lines. "It was happening everywhere. She mentioned the names of her friends and assured" one of her most persistent male suitors, Count Muffat, "that society ladies did it. According to her there was nothing more common or more normal" (291). This assertion echoes her frequent declarations that all women have sexual desires and are unfaithful to their men, even the "ladies" to whom her male lovers are married. Nana's claims clarify Zola's portrait of a treacherous female sexuality within which lesbianism is an extreme and extremely destructive aspect of "normal" desire.

Zola would later claim, "An invert is a disorganizer of the family, of the nation, of humanity," because "in the end everything which touches on sex touches social life itself."[25] Lesbianism becomes emblematic of the danger of Nana's sexuality, because it takes her beyond the reach of calculated exchanges of pleasure for gold. Zola describes Nana as feeling most "deeply the immense force of her sexuality" when her desire for Satin triumphs over class hierarchies and financial considerations alike (305). During a long evening spent with a cadre of male lovers, "men bearing great names, of old and honorable families," who pay and pay for Nana's company, Nana and Satin exchange "tender glances, imposing their will on [these men], calmly exploiting their sex in undisguised contempt" (297). At the end of this evening, Satin persuades Nana to send all of the men away, so that they can spend the night together. At this moment Zola identifies "the immense force of [Nana's] sexuality"—that is, "her need for power and pleasure"—with "her urge to possess everything in order to destroy everything" (305).

Nana's destructiveness has to be contained. The only lesbians to whom we are introduced in Zola's Paris are prostitutes, and the only prostitutes punished in Zola's Paris are those who become lesbians, those whose nature has been so thoroughly corrupted by artifice that they pursue pleasure beyond the reach of gold. The novel concludes with a series of fatalities beginning with the death of Satin, mysteriously sickened by "the messy life she had been living" (404). The last time we see Nana alive, she is going off to the hospital "dressed as if for a ball, to give Satin a last kiss" (409). With the prospect of Satin's last kiss, Nana vanishes from Paris. She returns to the city only once, to discover her neglected son dying of smallpox, and then to die most painfully of his infection herself. The sequence implies that Nana perishes from some combination of lesbianism and her failure as a mother, the two most drastic consequences of her prostitution. Her fatal illness seems to have actually been communicated by the kiss of her female lover. Zola ends his novel by describing her dead body in gruesome, punitive detail.

Nana's death also seems to release Paris into history. In the Second Empire city at Nana's feet, time stands still. The speculators in her vicinity see their fortunes rise and fall and rise and fall again with changing economic conditions; the same anxious assessments of Prussian chancellor Otto von Bismarck's strength and military intentions in relation to France are repeated in identical conversations throughout the novel. But as her body lies at the center of the city in the Grand Hotel, crowds outside surge up and down the boulevards shouting, "On to Berlin!" (425). Her death coincides with the beginning of the Franco-Prussian War of 1870, as if her end has ended the Second Empire as well and set history back into motion.

THE VICTIMS OF CAPITAL

From Balzac to Zola, the exchange of gold for pleasure undermined social divisions. As Balzac proposes, "In Paris, extremes meet by way of the passions. Vice indissolubly welds the rich to the poor, the great to the small."[26] Zola's *Nana* brings the threat of the city's underworld to its rulers, as if a

FINISHING THE FRUIT IN A KISS . . .

"Finishing the Fruit in a Kiss . . ." from Émile Zola, *Nana,* trans. Charles Duff, illustrations from the 1st edition (1870; repr., London: Heinemann, 1956).

"fly which had taken off from the cesspit of the slums with its germs capable of putrefying society had poisoned these men merely by settling on them. It was fair, justice had been done, she'd avenged her world, the world of beggars and the under-privileged" (409). At the same time, pleasure and gold were the ruling terms of a radically divided city.

The fictions of Balzac and Zola, as well as the scientific studies, memoirs, exposés, and paintings in which lesbians were represented in Paris—all contributed to an international literature on the divided city that flourished throughout the nineteenth century. That literature included newspapers, government reports, and judicial decrees. These materials repetitively portrayed, to each rapidly developing city's striving citizens, that city's "underworld" as the essence of its urbanity and the site of all of the city's secrets.[27] These underworlds would become the settings in which scientists', memoirists', painters', poets', and novelists' accounts of city dwellers' pursuit of pleasure and gold, and the cities' mixture of nature and artifice, would be worked out. They would also be the grounds on which understandings of the place of the nineteenth-century city in history would be fought over.

Not only could lesbians be located at the junctures of pleasure and gold, nature and artifice, secrets and knowledge, the key terms that dominated developing understandings of the city; they were also particularly useful denizens of the urban underworld for the purposes of debates about the city in history. They represented two versions of the nineteenth-century city, one of the city as an ahistorical place, the other of the city as a product of specific historical changes.

Journalism and fiction about urban underworlds were particularly profitable for their writers.[28] Eugène Sue's *Mysteries of Paris* (1842–1843) "became a literary sensation, arguably the first French best-seller."[29] A combination of sensational fiction and journalism, with a prostitute heroine, Fleur de Marie, it was first published serially as a newspaper feuilleton and then repeatedly dramatized as well as offered in book form. Sue's example prompted such works as G. W. M. Reynolds's *Mysteries of London* (four series, all about "the lazar house, the prison, the brothel, and the dark alley . . . rife with all kinds of enormity") and George Foster's *New York by Gaslight* (1850) and its sequels.[30] "What a task we have undertaken!" Foster announces, as if speaking for them all. "To penetrate beneath the thick veil of night and lay bare the fearful mysteries of darkness in the metropolis—the festivities of prostitution, the orgies of pauperism, the haunts of theft and murder, the scenes of drunkenness and beastly debauch . . . the under-ground story of life in New York!" Foster claimed he was relaying "real facts" and "actual conditions" for the social good, "so that Philanthropy and Justice may plant their blows aright."[31]

The nascent field of political economy added to this literature its somewhat less fevered delineations of the miseries of the new industrial working class and a more substantial commitment to reform. England, industrializing at the greatest rate, was a particular focus of such reports. After "[w]alking in the streets of London and other large cities," Eugène Buret testified in his analysis *De la misère des classes laborieuses en Angleterre et en France,* in 1840, that "[i]n the very heart of the busiest centers of industry and trade you see thousands of human beings reduced to a state of barbarism . . . outside society, outside the law."[32] Friedrich Engels, himself the son of a German factory owner, denounced such circumstances in *The Condition of the Working Class in England,* in 1845. Later in the century, reformers such as Henry Mayhew and Charles Booth would weigh in with their catalogs of the London poor.

All of these works were responses to and (explicitly or implicitly) attempts to illuminate not just individual cities and individual urban experiences but also the city itself, in what English clergyman Robert Vaughan declared, in 1842, "pre-eminently the age of great cities." "Babylon and Thebes, Carthage and Rome, were great cities," Vaughan conceded, "but the world has never been so covered with cities as at the present time, and society generally has never been so leavened with the spirit natural to cities."[33]

Vaughan's invocation of the ancient world was not inappropriate. The only city comparable in size to nineteenth-century Paris and London was imperial Rome. But it was not simply the size of these newly great cities but also the rate of their growth that was unprecedented.[34] This growth was the product not simply of an urban population explosion but of an extraordinary acceleration in the rate of urbanization, an unprecedented shifting of population from rural to urban settings. Though London and Paris, among nineteenth-century cities, achieved the greatest size and provincial cities grew significantly in France, the population shift overall was greatest in England. In "1801 nearly a tenth of the population of England and Wales were living in cities of over 100,000 or larger. The proportion doubled in forty years and doubled again in another sixty years."[35] Dramatic as was the growth of the historic capitals, the new industrial cities of the north of

England were likewise exploding: "London between 1821 and 1841 grew by twenty per cent; Manchester, Birmingham, Leeds and Sheffield by more than forty per cent; Bradford by sixty-five per cent."[36]

The experience of upheaval in the capitals, in both Paris and London, was exacerbated by major projects of urban reconstruction. In mid-nineteenth-century London "the railway and street clearance schemes, continually unsettled the city, displacing whole sections of the town and adding to its desperate congestion."[37] Baron Haussmann's "modernization" of Paris in the 1850s and 1860s—his destruction of the medieval city in the cause of nineteenth-century boulevards, vistas, and political order—had the same drastic effects there.[38] As Baudelaire declared, in "The Swan," "*Old* Paris is gone (no human heart / changes half so fast as a city's face)."[39]

But the pressures on the human heart were intense. In the capitals, as in the new industrial cities, new industrial processes were creating new structures for work and life. Or rather, this was a central point of contention in mid-nineteenth-century accounts of the city. To what extent was Europe witnessing the development of genuinely new urban forms? Was George Saintsbury, for example, correct when he described Manchester's growth, from 1831 to 1841, as producing "strange and to a certain extent unnatural conditions of life, not paralleled in any former state of history"?[40] Or could these urban upheavals be assimilated to existing conceptions of the city? That is, how were these rapidly growing cities to be understood in relation to the history of the city? The ruling terms of the debates that emerged about this question of the nineteenth-century city's relation to history would be Balzac's "pleasure" and "gold," transmuted, in nonliterary settings, into "vice" and "capital."

The association of urbanity with moral corruption had been fundamental to earlier conceptions of the city. Contrasts between city vice and rural virtue can be traced through Western culture back to ancient Greek and Latin literatures. According to Raymond Williams, "[I]t was especially in relation to Rome that the contrast crystallised, at the point where the city could be seen as an independent organism." He cites Juvenal: "What can I do in Rome? I never learnt how / To lie."[41] Given that framework—a historic distinction between city and country based on the contrast of vice and virtue—it is hardly surprising that the urban underworld, defined by its vices, would be presented as definitive of the modern city in its first, most dramatic forms. To lament, in 1840, that "[i]t is in the great cities that vice has spread her temptations, and pleasure her seductions, and folly her allurements; that guilt is encouraged by the hope of impunity, and idleness fostered by the frequency of example" was to ring changes on familiar themes.[42]

In mid-nineteenth-century accounts of the city, much depended, however, on focus—on the older capitals or new industrial centers, on London and Paris or on Manchester. Paris might have been, in Walter Benjamin's frequently invoked twentieth-century retrospect, "the capital of the nineteenth century," but Manchester was, to use historian Asa Briggs's term, the "shock city" of the age.[43] The choice, by contemporary urban commentators, of London/Paris or Manchester as their subject raised in turn another basic question: Could understandings of the city any longer be separated from the fact of industry?[44]

As a literature emerged on the conditions of life in modern cities that was focused on urban underworlds, the debate about the relation of the city to history—about the "modernity" of nineteenth-century cities—became a debate about the causes of contemporary urban conditions, especially the conditions of the urban underworlds. Should the grim conditions in these rapidly changing cities—which is to say, the conditions of the masses of the people—be understood as a product of vice or as a product of capital? In *The Condition of the Working Class in England,* Engels denounces "[t]he writers of the English bourgeoisie," who focused on urban vice, "crying murder at the demoralizing tendency of the great cities," because of their "massing together of the population." "[T]hey sing dirges," he observed, "over . . . the growth of the cities" because "it is extremely convenient for the ruling class to ascribe all the evil to this apparently unavoidable source" and thus to ensure that "the inference that manufacture and the middle class which profits from it alone have created the cities . . . [remains] remote."[45] The predominant challenge to the emphasis on urban vice came from those focused on industrial development.

The broadest political interests at stake in the debates over vice or capital as the explanation of urban conditions were obvious. If urban conditions were the inevitable effect of a natural propensity to vice on the part of the lower classes, then little intervention could legitimately be demanded of governing and economic elites. If urban conditions were the product of capital, then a systemic political response might be required—and widespread revolt feared.

Underlying the decision to see London/Paris or Manchester as representative, and the corollary debate over vice or capital as the source of urban conditions, were assumptions about "nature" in the city. The opposition between "nature" and "artifice" in the novels of the day becomes that between "nature" and "history" in the political tracts. Vice was associated with nature, whereas capital was associated with history. Those focused on a moral analysis of urban conditions assumed an ahistorical perspective, emphasizing the natural spread of vice in urban crowds, in cities that had always harbored grave dangers now heightened by metropolitan growth. They adhered to the historically potent city/country, vice/virtue distinction as if it were an ahistorical truth. By contrast, those who emphasized capital were largely committed to viewing the state of the cities in the mid-nineteenth century as something new and strange: a historical development, not a natural one.

Women "unsexed" by industry. "Lancashire Pit-Brow Women," from the *Illustrated London News,* May 28, 1887. Engraving by English school (19th century). Copyright Private Collection/The Bridgeman Art Library.

In political debate, however—as in the fiction of Balzac and Zola—vice and capital, nature and history could rarely be tidily separated. Even Engels credited those who emphasized the immorality of the working classes if they understood the workers' propensity to vice as an effect of the temptation produced by overcrowding and "the contagious nature of bad example." "It is the peculiar misfortune of the poor in great cities," he quotes one of his contemporaries, "that they cannot fly from these irresistible temptations." He invokes nature himself when he explains that "the great cities really only secure a more rapid and certain development for evils already existing in the germ" (147).

Women, and especially lesbians, were at the center of this complex of understandings of cities—whether the terms of discussion were vice and capital or nature and history—because of the ways in which dominant cultural understandings of gender and sexuality allowed for the entangling of these terms. Women could so easily be transformed into prostitutes, after all. It was "the development of the female character," Engels warned, which was particularly at stake, and "not favor[ed]" by urban/industrial circumstances. "The moral consequences of the employment of women in factories" are dire, he observes, citing one local reporter who insisted "that most of the prostitutes of . . . [Leicester] had their employment in the mills to thank for their present situation" (170). From this angle, factories are analogous to cities, both spreading vice. As Engels explains, "The collecting of persons of both sexes and all ages in a single work-room, the inevitable contact, the crowding into a small space of people, to whom neither mental nor moral education has been given . . . is the same process upon a small scale which we have already witnessed upon a large one in the great cities. The heaping together of population has the same influence upon the same persons, whether it affects them in a great city or a small factory" (169–70).

At the same time, gender norms were threatened by the industrial employment of women and by the new industrialists' preferences for hiring women, who could be paid less than their male counterparts. Engels denounces the "crowding out of adult males," from which "follows of necessity that inversion of the existing social order which . . . has the most ruinous consequences for the workers" (165). "The employment of women," he continues, "at once breaks up the family." Either no one tends the children, "when the wife spends twelve or thirteen hours every day in the mill, and the husband works the same length of time there or elsewhere," or "the family is . . . turned upside down. The wife supports the family, the husband sits at home, tends the children, sweeps the room and cooks" (165–67). This process finally "unsexes the man and takes from the woman all woman-liness" (168).

Prostitutes, as we have seen, could be presented as living at the nexus of pleasure and gold, nature and artifice. As Gustave Flaubert wrote, in 1853, to his mistress Louise Colet, "There is, in this idea of prostitution, a point of intersection so complex—lust, bitterness, the void of human relations, the frenzy of muscles and the sound of gold—that looking deeply into it makes you dizzy; and you learn so many things!"[46] But prostitutes could also be found to join vice and capital, nature and history.[47] "Women" could become "lesbians" after passing through the intersection of pleasure and gold or of vice and capital. Lesbianism could be presented as the vice of whores, in historic capitals. But lesbianism might also be an extreme effect of industrialization, in the newest urban centers, because of industrialization's fostering of prostitution and its disruption of gender norms.

As I have already argued, in the fictions of the modern city, lesbians could represent the city's threat and allow for the reassuring erasure of that threat. As figures in whom vice and capital, and therefore nature and history, could be joined as the causes of urban conditions, lesbians as subjects could also help defuse the problem of the city's relation to history by blurring the distinction between industry and the city, and so between industrial centers like Manchester and historic capitals like London and Paris.

Cesare Lombroso and Guglielmo Ferrero, representing the new "science" of criminology in the later decades of the nineteenth century, cite Balzac, Zola, and other novelists, as well as Parent-Duchâtelet and more contemporary sexual scientists such as Albert Moll, to confirm with confidence that "lesbianism . . . is widespread among women," and especially prostitutes.[48] They offer three different explanations of lesbianism. To begin with, they assume "the basic immorality latent in all women," leaving all women subject to corruption (199). Prostitutes in particular, however, become lesbians, they argue, because of the sheer contiguity of women in brothels and in jails. In fact, "the gathering of many women" in any setting could be a "cause of lesbianism . . . especially if the group includes prostitutes or lascivious women, provok[ing] imitative behavior, intensifying the vices of each individual and increasing collective vice" (177). But prostitutes are lesbians, or produce lesbianism, not only because of their sexual behavior but also

"Lesbian couple in prison," from Cesare Lombroso and Guglielmo Ferrero, *La Donna delinquente*, 1893. Reprinted in Cesare Lombroso and Guglielmo Ferrero, *Criminal Woman, the Prostitute, and the Normal Woman*, trans. Nicole Hahn Rafter and Mary Gibson (Durham, N.C.: Duke University Press, 2004).

because, by their example, they challenge gender norms. "The majority of lesbians are not born lesbians," they explain, "but . . . borrow the virile traits of the criminal and the prostitute" (181).

As the subject of lesbianism became less likely to invoke state censorship, there was a series of reports in France and England of factories producing not just prostitution but specifically lesbianism, giving a new emphasis to Engels's identification of factories with cities as sites in which people were crowded temptingly together. In 1889 journalist Ali Coffignon, in *Paris vivant: La Corruption á Paris,* warned of "sapphism, now widespread among all classes of society." He explains that, "[w]ith working girls, the nervous tensions resulting from working in a sitting position for too long causes the thighs to rub together with the disastrous consequences that doctors know only too well."[49]

The new sexual science concurred, explicitly joining same-sex sexual behavior to "unsexing," echoing the gender inversion Engels deplored in industrial settings. English sexologist Havelock Ellis, in his *Sexual Inversion* (1897), cites the moral endangerment of "seamstresses, lace-makers, etc. confined for hours in close contact with one another in heated rooms." He then goes on in more detail to offer different cases illustrating "the conditions prevailing in factories" and workshops in England and especially in Rome and in Spain, where the industrial employment of women had been "more thoroughly studied."[50] His instances include a case in Seville of a violent attack by one woman worker "of masculine air, tall and thin, with an expression of firm determination on her wrinkled face" on a "plump . . . good-looking and . . . pleasing" younger woman, motivated by jealousy of the younger woman's friendship with the forewoman of her workroom. In Ellis's view, "the abnormal sexuality stimulated by such association in work" is clear.[51]

THE HEROINES OF MODERNISM

The images of lesbianism and the identification of lesbians with Paris that were produced by Balzac, Zola, and Baudelaire would be transmitted around the globe during the next 150 years. In the United States in 1892, the *Memphis Public Ledger,* reporting on the murder of a young local woman by her female beloved, could proclaim the case "a tragedy equal to the most morbid imaginings of modern French romances." The doctors and lawyers involved in the case cited Balzac and Zola.[52] Nearly one hundred years later and worlds away, the British urban sociologist Elizabeth Wilson could confidently begin a history of lesbianism with the assertion that "[t]he lesbian is an inhabitant of the great cities, first glimpsed by Baudelaire in Paris, 'capital of the nineteenth century.'"[53]

The images of cities offered by Balzac, Zola, and Baudelaire would also travel and would also persist. "Capital of the nineteenth century," as a description of Paris, is perhaps the most famous phrase of the German critic Walter Benjamin, who in the 1920s and 1930s would make Baudelaire's writings central to his own exploration of nineteenth-century Paris as the epitome of modernity. On the basis of his essays and the fragments of his unfinished *Arcades Project,* Benjamin became, posthumously, one of the later twentieth century's most celebrated commentators on Baudelaire and, through his meditations on Baudelaire, on the great city itself.

As I have already noted, Balzac's and Zola's urban fictions are cited as sources of fact by early twenty-first-century authorities on the modern city, such as David Harvey in his recent *Paris, Capital of Modernity* (2003). The writings of Baudelaire and Benjamin—separately and, especially, together— became touchstones for urban advocates in the last decades of the twentieth century. As Elizabeth Wilson observes in a 1997 discussion of the role of nostalgia in contemporary accounts of "the city," both "[f]rom a more conservative perspective, Leon Krier and Prince Charles," and "from a more left position, Richard Sennett, Ken Worpole and others," in urban studies in the 1980s and 1990s, the ideal invoked was "the good city." She identifies this "good city," about which everyone "wrote lovingly," as "the pedestrian city, the city of many villages, the city of spectacle," a "nineteenth-century metropolis such as had been described and explored by Baudelaire and Benjamin." It is a city, that is to say, "very unlike Victorian industrial cities," as well as a dramatic alternative to the late twentieth-century "nightmare city of crime, anomie and danger."[54]

All of these persistences demonstrate the ongoing cultural usefulness of the Paris proffered by Balzac, Zola, and Baudelaire (especially as elaborated by Benjamin), a Paris constructed in part out of their images of lesbianism. Because their lesbians were figures in whom pleasure/vice and gold/capital, as the causes of urban conditions, and nature and artifice, as urban qualities, could all be joined, these fantasy women helped these writers in their efforts to represent the modern city, to shape understandings of the relationship of the city to history, and so to shape their own relationships as artists, intellectuals, and middle-class men to the city. The city's relation to history mattered because it shaped political as well as artistic responses to urban conditions. That relation also mattered to these men because of its implications for the effects on elite men such as themselves of the social and political shifts in motion in the modern city.

Benjamin highlights Baudelaire's representations of lesbianism as the heart of the poet's cultural project, "the task imposed upon him as his very own; to give shape to modernity."[55] He emphasizes that "Baudelaire for a long time had the title *Les Lesbiennes* in mind" for his major poetic work. For Baudelaire, he insists, "[t]he lesbian is the heroine of modernism" (90).

But why Baudelaire was so interested in lesbians is a question that has long seemed to require explanation. Various commentators have proffered personal reasons. Baudelaire's contemporary and friend the photographer Nadar proposed that the poet's longtime mistress, Jeanne Duval, commonly identified as biracial (a "mulatto"), was also bisexual.[56] Marcel Proust, who was as committed as Benjamin to emphasizing Baudelaire's interest in *les lesbiennes,* suggested that the poet himself was homosexual and his lesbians a projection of his own same-sex desires. (This was, however, apparently a complex projection of Proust's own.)[57] Most recently, literary critic Joan DeJean has argued that Baudelaire's *lesbiennes* were a marketing ploy, a means of making gold out of cultural capital. She connects his invocation of lesbianism with the lesbian references, in the period 1845–1850, of his friends and peers Arsene Houssaye and Philoxene Boyer. Both produced Sapphic *drames* just as Baudelaire was announcing that his forthcoming collection would be titled "Les Lesbiennes." DeJean describes all of these young men as "attempt[ing] to capitalize on the sensationalism of 'amours lesbiennes' to promote their literary efforts." "They concluded," and correctly, she writes, "that 'Sappho' was a brand name with the potential to commercialize texts." They then took up Sappho's brand to "commercialize themselves as men of letters on the strength of Sapphic, and sapphic, notoriety."[58]

Lesbianism was also a subject through which Baudelaire, and Benjamin in turn, plotted the city's relation to history. In the process they elaborated a relationship to the rapidly changing city for themselves that would come to be seen by subsequent generations of readers and critics as the characteristically modern relationship of the urban commentator to the modern city.

"HISTORY" IS THE bedrock of Benjamin's explanation of the primacy Baudelaire gave his *lesbiennes*. It would be hard to miss Baudelaire's interest in the ancient world, given the poems' focus:

> Lesbos! where the kisses, languid or rapt,
> cool as melons, burning as the sun,
> adorn the dark and gild the shining days
> given to Latin games and Greek delights.[59]

According to Benjamin, in order to be Baudelaire's heroines of modernism, lesbians had first to be ancient heroines. He explains that "the lesbian" represents for Baudelaire "a historical ideal, that of greatness in the ancient world"; "Greece supplied [Baudelaire] with the image of the heroine which seemed to him worthy and capable of being carried over into modern times" (90).

Conveniently, lesbians could not only be "carried over" into the modern world, they could represent "modern times." They could be seen as the characteristic product of modernity—if modern times were identified with industrialization and lesbians were identified as masculine women. That modernity was industrial and lesbians masculine were both assumptions that would be more explicitly articulated, as I have suggested, in the decades between Baudelaire's *Les Fleurs du mal* and Benjamin's commentaries on Baudelaire's work. Benjamin could then take these propositions as self-evident. "The nineteenth century began to use women without reservation in the production process outside the home," he explains, "primarily . . . by putting them into factories. Consequently . . . masculine traits were bound to manifest themselves in these women." These masculine traits "were caused particularly by disfiguring factory work," yet apparently "political struggle"—another, if subsidiary, aspect of modern times—also took women "outside the home" and likewise "promote[d] masculine features" in women (93–94). Finally, according to Benjamin, what "makes the [central] position of the lesbian in the *Fleurs du Mal* unmistakable" is that she can represent the ancient and the modern and, at the same time, Baudelaire's "erotic ideal . . . the woman who bespeaks hardness and mannishness" (90).

What is most telling here is Benjamin's insistence on Baudelaire's erotic engagement with his subjects. There are, after all, no traces of "modern

times"—of industry, politics, or masculinity—just as there are no city streets, in Baudelaire's "lesbian" poems. But Benjamin circumvents what might seem a flaw in his analysis by explaining Baudelaire's poetic focus on the erotic as a cover for his interest in the industrial (and the political), vice as a cover for capital. Benjamin explains that the passionate embraces of Baudelaire's *lesbiennes* are a blind, just as Engels argued that the proponents of vice as the source of the grimmest modern urban conditions were attempting to obscure the responsibility of industry. "At the same time" that his imagination was engaged by modernity, Benjamin argues, Baudelaire "sought to free [himself] from economic bondage. Thus he reached the point where he gave a purely sexual accent to this development" (93–94).

Benjamin offers us Baudelaire's *lesbiennes* allowing not just for the obscuring of capital by vice (economics by moral analyses) nor for the merging of capital with vice (economic with moral analyses) but for the sinking of capital into vice. Baudelaire, according to Benjamin, set the stage for the rhetorical exchange of an industrial, political modernity for a sexual modernity, of gold for pleasure, capital for vice, an industrial, political city for a sexualized city.

Moreover, the particular sexuality Baudelaire invoked—lesbianism—by joining the antique to the contemporary, could simultaneously signal the modern and moderate modernity.[60] Greece and modern times are both highlighted and fused to produce a metropolis both ancient and new. In this sense, Baudelaire's *lesbiennes* join not only vice and capital but also nature and history, cascades and couches, ahistorical and historical understandings of the city.[61]

LESBIANISM IS, THUS, pivotal to Benjamin's construction of Baudelaire's (and, by extension, his own) relation to modernity. He proposes that Baudelaire's representations of lesbianism capture a fundamental ambivalence in his engagement with modernity. The "deterioration of the 'realistic' element which is evident in Baudelaire's attitude towards lesbians" is "characteristic," he argues, of a broader refusal of realism. Benjamin bolsters this assertion with Jules Lemaitre's 1895 criticism of the "contradictions" in Baudelaire's commitment to modernity: "He curses 'progress,' he loathes the industry of the century, and yet he enjoys the special flavour which this industry has given today's life" (94).[62]

At the same time, as lesbians offer Baudelaire and Benjamin a means of reframing, even retreating from, a contemporary reality of industry and politics into a sexual fantasy with classical authority, they also allow these writers to focus on the margins of the modern city and thereby to position themselves at those margins. Baudelaire argued that if modernity was to be captured, attention had to be redirected from the "public and official subjects" of art, from "our victories and our political heroism," to "private subjects which are very much more heroic than these": the "pageant of fashionable life and the thousands of floating existences—criminals and kept women—which drift about in the underworld of a great city."[63] The rapidity of his slide here from the spectacle of "fashionable life" to that of "floating existences" suggests that he was interested not simply in the private rather than the public, or the quotidian rather than the grand. Rather, the urban underworld, the realm of vice, is offered as representative of the modern city, as it was overall in the nineteenth-century literature of the divided city. And again lesbians are representative of these social margins. Benjamin insists that the marginality of Baudelaire's *lesbiennes* was crucial to their value: "To him, social ostracism was inseparable from the heroic nature of this passion" (93).[64]

By taking up ostracized subjects in his pursuit of urban modernity, Baudelaire, and Benjamin on his behalf, helped establish those on the margin of the city as the quintessential modern urban subjects. Benjamin insists that the poet's interest in the "irregular" was central to his contribution to the literature of modernity. The modern poets, of whom Baudelaire is Benjamin's chief representative, come to "find the refuse of society on their street and derive their heroic subject from this very refuse" (79). At the same time, the poet's focus on marginal subjects like lesbians allows Baudelaire and, by extension, Benjamin to identify themselves as marginal to the world on which they are reporting. In that process they both contribute to establishing the view from the margin as the characteristic modern/urban pose.

Baudelaire's *lesbiennes* had a male counterpart—variously labeled the dandy and the flaneur—who came to embody both Baudelaire's and Benjamin's projections of the view from the margins characteristic of modern urban life. Balzac had offered an early version of this type in *The Girl with the Golden Eyes*, identifying "the cheerful, easy-going species of loiterers, [as] the only really happy people in Paris, which from hour to hour, from one quarter to another, offers them its poetry to savour."[65] The flaneur would become the typical inhabitant of the "good city" that Wilson claims late twentieth-century urbanists celebrated.

Baudelaire helped construct, and Benjamin celebrated, the flaneur's identification with the city. For Baudelaire the flaneur is, like the lesbian, a figure of "heroism" and "antiquity," as he writes in "The Painter of Modern Life" (28, 26).[66] Both are ambiguously gendered: the first, masculinized by her industrial and political life "outside the home"; the second, the famously passive flaneur (his passage through the city always a wandering one), a "passionate spectator" whose feminizing goal is to "set up house in the heart of the multitude" (9). Also like the lesbian, the flaneur is a sexualized figure. His project is not only domestic but also erotic. If "[t]he crowd is his element," according to Baudelaire, "[h]is passion and his profession are to become one flesh with the crowd" (9). He is identified by Benjamin with the prostitutes of the city, "abandoned in the crowd . . . shar[ing] the situation of the commodity . . . the intoxication of the commodity."[67]

At the crux of Baudelaire's and Benjamin's accounts of the flaneur and of the lesbian is a pair of complementary contradictions. Both appear to be marginal figures, yet neither is what she or he seems. Never actually marginal, they both can always be returned to their different places at the cultural center.

The flaneur is, by definition, an outsider, according to Benjamin: "[H]is city is—even if, like Baudelaire, he happened to be born there—no longer native ground. It represents for him a theatrical display, an arena."[68] But as Baudelaire had already insisted, the flaneur is never a real outsider. Instead, "[this] spectator is a *prince* who everywhere rejoices in his incognito."[69] However happy he is incognito, that is, this spectator happily remains a prince. The unreality of the flaneur's marginality is key to his status as the representative modern urbanite.

Baudelaire and Benjamin invest their lesbian with a similar duplicity. She is a social *because* she is a sexual outcast. Her claim to be sexually independent of men is understood politically as a refusal of the second-class status of women. Rejecting the traditional female sexual role, she also claims the power to engage in a public life. But, just as the passively wandering flaneur is actually a prince and so potentially the heir to all he surveys, this lesbian is always actually a woman, and thus lacks any independence or power at all.

BENJAMIN GOES so far as to read Baudelaire through Proust to present the heterosexual flaneur's love as perpetually thwarted in the city and lesbian love as a potential of all *Parisiennes*. He repeatedly returns to "A une passante," "one of [Baudelaire's] most perfect love poems."[70] The narrator/poet desires a woman he passes but cannot reach, or reach out to, in the crowd. "Lovely fugitive / whose glance has brought me back to life!" Baudelaire writes. "Of me you know nothing, I nothing of you—you / whom I might have loved and who knew that too!"[71] Benjamin insists that Baudelaire's poem "reveals the stigmata which life in a metropolis inflicts upon love," offering Proust as his evidence. "Proust read the sonnet in this light," he argues. He then quotes one of Proust's descriptions of his novel's narrator, Marcel's, beloved Albertine, "resembl[ing] the type of the fiery and yet pale Parisian woman, the woman who is not used to fresh air and has been affected by living among masses and possibly in an atmosphere of vice, the kind that can be recognized by a certain glance which seems unsteady if there is no rouge on her cheeks."[72] In this passage the masses of the city are identified with vice; and the representative *Parisienne,* the "unsteady"

Henri de Toulouse-Lautrec (1864–1901), *Two Friends,* 1895. Pastel. Copyright Private Collection/Peter Willi/The Bridgeman Art Library.

Albertine, who has abandoned nature ("fresh air") and turned to artifice ("rouge on her cheeks"), with both the masses and vice.

"This is the look," Benjamin goes on to explain, "of the object of a love which only a city dweller experiences . . . of which one might not infrequently say that it was spared, rather than denied, fulfillment."[73] That is, the *Parisienne*'s likely "vice" is such that her observer is lucky to be unable to pursue his desire. Benjamin chose to elucidate one of the best-known heterosexual poems of *Les Fleurs du mal* through the prism of a novel most often understood as a portrait of homosexuals hidden behind heterosexual masks: Proust's unlucky Marcel is famously obsessed with the fear that Albertine is "really" a lesbian; critics have most often read Albertine as a young man and Proust's beloved.[74] Consequently, when Benjamin concludes his discussions of "A une passante" by declaring "love itself" to be "stigmatized by the big city," he implies both that "love"—heterosexuality—is stigmatized in the city and that the representative love of the city is a stigmatized love—such as lesbianism.[75]

But if lesbianism were the love of the city, then heterosexuality might not have been stigmatized, or defeated, at all. The basic condition of Benjamin's urban love is that the women of the city are unavailable to the male poet/flaneur. The city either sweeps them away in an urban crowd before contact can be made or corrupts them, making them vicious and not worth desiring anyway. Nevertheless, the women of the city are infinitely available in fantasy. Although it might seem that when the object of the poet's gaze is identified as a lesbian she becomes less available, the lesbians in this literature are, after all, only figures of (male) fantasy.

Baudelaire was happy, in Benjamin's phrase, to "abandon" lesbians "to their doom"; he needed them to remain outcasts if they were to model his own marginality.[76] Focusing on marginal subjects and simultaneously claiming a marginal position and perspective would become standard moves in the work of elite men writing about the modern city. By claiming allegiance to the margins, such men could sidestep the prospect of their own eclipse by modernity, the threat to their gender and class status contained in the potential empowerment of women of all classes and the urban "masses."

Eroticizing the modern city through their vision of lesbianism in particular, however, was a way for elite men to reassert their control. At the trial of *Les Fleurs du mal,* the stumbling block for Baudelaire's defense was the charge of realism. But Benjamin acknowledges that Baudelaire's *lesbiennes* are not "real." As he notes, "Baudelaire's readers are men. It is men who have made him famous; it is them he has redeemed."[77] Baudelaire's fantasy lesbians—like the lesbians of Balzac and Zola—are ultimately defined neither by the objects of their desires nor by their purported masculinity but rather by the poet's belief that they cannot satisfy one another. Their insatiable desire makes them fit representatives of Balzac's, Zola's, and Baudelaire's Paris, "the city [that] sings, and laughs, and screams, / mad in pursuit of pleasure."[78] Likewise, it confirms women's dependence on men. Baudelaire's "Lesbos" is, after all, organized around the lesbians' loss of Sappho, "the lover and the poet" who "broke her vow / and died apostate to her own command" as a result of her passion for the boatman Phaon.[79] Lesbianism could be represented as, and so could represent, a repudiation of male authority that is no repudiation after all. In this way, Baudelaire's and Benjamin's *lesbiennes* were, for elite men, ideal heroines of the modern city: hypothetically masculinized women who yet were never really threats, because they were never able to replace men sexually; apparently uninterested in men but nevertheless not only inferior to them but inevitably available to them. Moreover, in a sexualized city such as the city these writers created around their lesbians, the sexual is a sufficient realm for the reassertion of proper status, and more than just proper sexual status.

In the modern city there might be no more princes to go flaneuring incognito. Taking up the possibility laid out by Balzac in *The Girl with the Golden Eyes*, Baudelaire and then Benjamin used their *lesbiennes* to place the city in history to their own advantage, as a defense against modernity. In an all-too-historical modern city, they reasserted the fantasy of an ahistorical male authority in an ahistorical city, through their fantasy lesbians.

Napoleon Sarony (1821–1896), *Oscar Wilde*, 1882. Adoc-photos/
Art Resource, New York.

2
Oscar Wilde in Los Angeles

READING LESSONS

In the early 1880s, in the midst of Oscar Wilde's fabulously successful North American tour, the magnates of the Southern Pacific Railroad, having laid the groundwork for Los Angeles's economic future with their new rail lines, begged him to visit their fledgling city. They even offered "a special train and private car" to transport him in a manner appropriate to a figure of such style.[1] Wilde's presence, they hoped, would draw attention to their achievements, and so would advance Los Angeles toward the great future they envisioned.

A century later, Italian architect and urban theorist Aldo Rossi framed the first American edition of his landmark study of urban memory, *The Architecture of the City*, with a reference to Wilde's contemporary Henry James, and in particular James's 1896 story "The Figure in the Carpet." "The Figure in the Carpet" is a tale about the difficulty of reading. James's protagonist, a young literary critic, struggles to see, but is ultimately unable to discern, the pattern that the novelist he admires above all other men insists is clearly visible throughout his fiction—"the clue" to which, the novelist claims, is in "every page and line and letter."[2] "Perhaps . . . this is the meaning of the architecture of the city," Rossi proposes. "[L]ike [James's] figure in the carpet, the figure is clear but everyone reads it in a different way."[3]

These are glancing moments in the densely interwoven modern histories of homosexuality and of cities. Within this web, as in James's story and in Rossi's city, there are patterns at once "lucid" and elusive. Baudelaire's *lesbiennes* lead to one such pattern; Wilde and James lead to another.

Yet these moments, when Wilde and James suddenly come into alignment with the histories of cities, are of very different kinds. One is a matter of social and economic calculation, the other a textual allusion. One is
a matter of soliciting a person, the other of soliciting a paradigm.

We are accustomed to thinking of the histories of homosexuals in cities
as a matter of the soliciting of persons. That is the connection most easily
traceable: from the literary, journalistic (even scientific) emphasis on lesbianism as the vice of whores in nineteenth-century Paris I described in the
preceding chapter to the focus on cruising for sex in the battles between
different groups of gay men over the lineaments of gay male culture in late
twentieth-century New York, which I will consider in my afterword. Men
had been finding each other in public places for sex in Paris since the beginning of the eighteenth century, women since at least the last decades of the
nineteenth century.[4] The history of New York City offers abundant evidence
of similar patterns.[5]

Persons matter. But if the city is a collection of ideas as well as bodies, or,
as early twentieth-century sociologist Robert Park put it, "a state of mind"
as much as a physical entity, then the soliciting of paradigms is inseparable
from the soliciting of persons.[6] And Oscar Wilde was always a peculiarly
paradigmatic person. As he himself declared, "I was a man who stood in
symbolic relations to the art and culture of my age. . . . I awoke the imagination of my century so that it created myth and legend around me."[7]

The moments I have cited, when Wilde and James suddenly come into
alignment with the histories of cities, are quite ambiguous, given these
writers' complex personal histories and the complexities of the history of
sexuality to which they both contributed. Wilde was not yet publicly homosexual when he toured North America, between January and October 1882.
He might not even have begun his private homosexual life: his most recent
biographers and critics seem to agree that though his fascination with young
men was already apparent, his same-sex encounters did not begin until years
after he had returned to England, when he took up with Robbie Ross in
1886.[8] He would not begin his fateful involvement with Lord Alfred Douglas
until the early 1890s. But a decade earlier, Wilde had already established the
distinctive public persona intrinsic to his effort to bring art to America and
himself to the attention of his age. That persona already manifested those
qualities—"the entire, vaguely disconcerting nexus of effeminacy, leisure,
idleness, immorality, luxury, insouciance, decadence and aestheticism"—

which, as literary critic Alan Sinfield and others have argued, were forged into the most widely recognized type of the modern homosexual by the drama of his 1895 trial on charges of "acts of gross indecency" between men.[9] And that persona, apparently even before it was identified as a homosexual archetype, already matched the understanding of an urban ideal of Los Angeles' developers.

James was much more discreet than Wilde, despite his stories of the obsessions of literary men with one another, and despite the romantic epistles he sent late in his life to a series of younger men: Jocelyn Persse, Hugh Walpole, Hendrik Andersen. (James's feeling for Persse is described by his official biographer, Leon Edel, as "love at first sight").[10] In fact, James vehemently distanced himself from Wilde—again, even before Wilde's public identification as homosexual—insisting to a friend that "'Hosscar' Wilde is a fatuous fool," a "tenth-rate cad," and "an unclean beast" after a meeting when both were visiting Washington, D.C., in 1882.[11] Publicity—or a fear of publicity—was at the center of James's later response to Wilde's trial, which he described in letters to sympathetic friends as "the Oscar Wilde horrors," "[o]ur earthquake . . . social, human, sexual (if that be the word when it's all one sex)," and a spectacle "over which the ghoulish public hangs and gloats."[12]

Nevertheless, because of, rather than despite, James's discretion, his writings as well as his life could a century later be discussed alongside Wilde's as paradigmatically queer. "The Figure in the Carpet," in particular, demonstrates the workings of an "open secret"—a pattern of truths simultaneously known and unknown, visible but unseen, either illegible or unacknowledged. This concept of the open secret, of "the closet," as it has been developed by literary critic Eve Kosofsky Sedgwick and others, partly from readings of James's fiction, has become central to an understanding of the closet as the defining feature of modern homosexual experience, and so has become a key term in late twentieth-century lesbian/gay/queer analysis of social life and cultural presence.[13] As Baudelaire and Benjamin served late twentieth-century urbanists as extraordinarily productive points of reference, so Wilde and James have served contemporary queer theorists.

Neither the image of Wilde nor the interpretive paradigm that James's writing offers represents the broad range of the actual social or literary options available to gay men and lesbians during the later decades of the nineteenth century or over the course of the twentieth century. But then

Baudelaire's *lesbiennes*, likewise, were not "real." Baudelaire was not interested in the lives of nineteenth-century Parisian women who desired other women. He, and Benjamin in his commentary on Baudelaire's *lesbiennes*, was engaged in constructing what would become mainstream understandings of modern urbanity. What Wilde and James represent, in lieu of options for living or writing (and represent most fully) are the social and literary models most immediately legible as homosexual to the cultural mainstream and to those on its margins over the past hundred years. That prominence is what makes them useful for my project.

What has been most persistently legible in modern accounts of homosexuality, from the sexual science of the late nineteenth century to contemporary LGBT politics, has been concern for the legibility of homosexuals. Wilde and James are paired in recent discussions in lesbian/gay/queer studies as representatives of the two extremes of the social experience of homosexuality before the advent of gay liberation: a homosexuality understood sometimes in terms of flamboyance, sometimes of discretion, but always

Anonymous, *Henry James*, ca. 1890. Adoc-photos/ Art Resource, New York.

in terms of the management of appearances and their interpretation, that is, of legibility itself. Although "visibility" is often said to be what is being managed, the term "legibility" evokes to a greater degree the crucial relation between person or text and interpreter. The railroad executives wanted Wilde to make L.A. not only visible but also legible as a prospective "great" city. Legibility is the subject of "The Figure in the Carpet": the author within the story insists that the motif of his writing, which the critic is unable to decipher, is clearly apparent.

As homosexuals, Wilde and James shared in this problem of legibility. In the moments I highlight here, they bring this problem of legibility to the city. That convergence is not accidental. The presence of Wilde and James in urban history reflects the concern about legibility central to that history. Wilde and James, as homosexuals, share *with "the city"* the problem of legibility. This shared problem of legibility is the strand of the web linking homosexualities and cities that I will follow in this chapter of my study.

Paradoxically, the subject of legibility brings into focus the two different—though not always distinct—dimensions of the combinations of persons and paradigms underlying connections between homosexuality and urbanity. Homosexuals can most clearly, and most early, be seen as model citizens of the modern city, and as a type of, or figure for, the city itself, when legibility is a central concern of urban citizens and urban studies.

THE TERM "LEGIBILITY" has, of course, literary connotations, and both of the moments I have cited here have a literary aspect. The railroad executives thought a literary man would dignify their as-yet-undignified Los Angeles. Aldo Rossi turned not only to a literary figure but also to a story about literary interpretation for his model of urban analysis. In that sense, both moments model not just the presence of homosexuality in our discourse of the city but the presence of literature in our discourses of the city and of homosexuality alike.

These moments, then, complement the lesson of the history of Baudelaire's poetry, of the influence of literary works on the development of understandings of the city, including the use that Benjamin made of Baudelaire's writing in his reconstruction of nineteenth-century Paris. Few have matched the complexity of Benjamin's transformation of Baudelaire's poetry and critical essays into urban history. Yet a remarkable number of pioneering commentators on the modern city either had significant literary histories

themselves or drew very heavily on literary sources. In Britain, for example, Henry Mayhew was a journalist and an editor, and wrote plays and
a series of novels (in collaboration with his brother)[14] before embarking
on his monumental study of London, *London Labour and the London Poor*
(which appeared in successive volumes from 1852 to 1865). More than a
century later, Marxist critic Raymond Williams, in *The Country and the
City* (1973), could map a history of English urban and rural life based almost
entirely on the literary record, from the ancients to contemporary fiction.
Williams argues, in fact, that Charles Dickens was pivotal to the creation of
modern urban consciousness through the form as well as the perspectives
he developed in his "new kind of novels," novels that encompass "the random and the systematic, the visible and the obscured"—the "double condition," with its potential for the production and maintenance of secrets,
that is the most significant aspect of the modern city as a social form.[15]

In the United States, Lewis Mumford produced influential work on
American architecture in *Sticks and Stones* (1924) and equally important
studies on Emerson, Thoreau, Melville, Hawthorne, and Whitman in *The
Brown Decades* (1931), all in the same early phase of his work, before going
on to write *The Culture of Cities* (1938) and to his subsequent career as a
preeminent urban critic. The chief alternative to Mumford's urban vision
in the United States for much of the twentieth century was that of the Chicago School of sociology. The Chicago School's founder, W. I. Thomas, was
originally trained in Romance languages and literature. Robert Park, whom
Thomas brought to the University of Chicago and who would become the
school's defining voice, was a devotee of Whitman. Park freely admitted
that "[w]e are mainly indebted to writers of fiction for our more intimate
knowledge of contemporary urban life."[16] As Elizabeth Wilson's observations about the roles of Baudelaire and Benjamin indicate, later twentieth-
century urban scholars such as Richard Sennett, Marshall Berman, Thomas
Bender, David Harvey, and others, in the United States and internationally,
have followed up with great faith on Park's admission, drawing freely on
poets and novelists (from Baudelaire to Dostoyevsky, Whitman to Dreiser)
in their accounts of the conditions of modern urban life.

Pioneering sexologists and gay advocates were every bit as committed
to literature as the urbanists of their generations. Havelock Ellis wrote on
Shakespeare, Whitman, Ibsen, and Tolstoy, among others, before he began
his multivolume *Studies in the Psychology of Sex* with a volume titled *Sexual*

Inversion (1897). Among early gay advocates, John Addington Symonds wrote poetry and literary criticism (also on Whitman) before his collaboration with Ellis on *Sexual Inversion*. Symonds's most complete independent writings on same-sex desire—his privately published *A Problem in Greek Ethics* (1883) and *A Problem in Modern Ethics* (1891)—extraordinarily affirming for their moment, were both based in literary study. And socialist and gay advocate Edward Carpenter wrote poetry (in the style of none other than Whitman) and literary essays as well as a defense, *The Intermediate Sex* (1906), and other similar works.

Moreover, like the urbanists, the sexologists and gay advocates drew very heavily on literature as a source of evidence. Ellis, for example, was particularly free with literary works in his discussion of female homosexuality.[17] Many of the comparatively rare mid-twentieth-century statements in support of homosexual life or explorations of LGBT cultures and history were produced by writers or based on literary study. (The protest of poet Robert Duncan, "The Homosexual in Society" [1944], and the literary history of Jeannette Foster, *Sex Variant Women in Literature* [1956], are indicative here.)[18] And when lesbian and gay studies emerged in the universities (and outside of them) in the wake of the gay liberation movement and the lesbian feminist politics of the late 1960s and early 1970s, just as when "queer theory" developed as an interpretive mode in the early 1990s, both intellectual/political projects were heavily indebted to literary sources.

It could be said that literary works have been so central to the modern study of cities and homosexuality because of the cultural authority of literature in the modern period. Still, the reliance on literary evidence everywhere manifest in the study of cities and in the study of homosexuality is remarkable. Given literature's loss of cultural authority in the late twentieth century, it is especially significant that literary sources have remained so salient in these fields.

In practice, understandings of homosexualities and cities have been bound together by their shared dependence on the literary. This is true, however, not only because literary works have been such significant sources of accounts of cities, of lesbian/gay/queer experience, and of homosexuals in cities; the connections exist because the question of legibility, of appearances and their interpretation, is a problem of both cities and homosexuals (not to mention, obviously, of literature). Literature, it might be said, has taught us how to read—that is, how to interpret—homosexuals and cities. And in large part, literature has taught us to read both as deeply enmeshed in the making of meanings.

Certain understandings of cities and homosexuals have persisted because of the role of literature in the study of cities and of homosexuality. In 1990 Eve Sedgwick could note that "the array of analytic tools available today to anyone thinking about issues of homo/heterosexual definition is remarkably little enriched from that available to, say, Proust."[19] Proust, writing in the 1920s, was himself a product of the later nineteenth-century world of Wilde and James. Wilde—"the poet one day fêted in every drawing-room and applauded in every theatre in London, and the next driven from every lodging, unable to find a pillow on which to lay his head"—was, in his disgrace, Proust's emblematic homosexual.[20] It is still possible to argue, in fact, that despite the tectonic shifts in social and intellectual possibilities initiated by gay liberation and feminist politics in the late 1960s, there has been a remarkable consistency in cultural conceptions of homosexuality in the West, from the era of Wilde and James to the present.

The same could also be said of our analyses of urban life. Conventions for the representation of cities that developed in response to the shock of nineteenth-century urbanization have been presented and re-presented across the twentieth century as sources of sociological fact. However dubious their truth value, these conventions have accrued profound ideological weight. Writings about the culture of cities over the past century have consistently relied upon a core set of assumptions and concerns that have been extended but not superseded in self-consciously postmodern urban debates. Wilde and James give us access to the juncture at which homosexuality and the city meet—through literature—on the grounds of legibility.

THE LEGIBLE CITY

If Wilde both was and was not yet "Oscar Wilde" when he was invited to visit Los Angeles in 1882, Los Angeles in that year was hardly the city it has since become: not only a great city but a "global" city, a center of the "new" global economy. By the 1990s, Los Angeles could be presented as the future of urbanity—if not the future itself—by urban commentators such as Mike Davis, Edward Soja, and others.

Nevertheless, there is a certain continuity between Los Angeles then and now. The developers' invitation to Wilde suggests that Los Angeles then was already ruled by economic interests and already preoccupied with flash and publicity, artifice and appearances. Los Angeles now, it is said, is the apotheosis of an alienated urban fakery that otherwise runs along an axis, via the Walt Disney Company, from Celebration, Florida, to Times Square, New York. It is an icon of postmodern simulation, a city of appearances best viewed through the windscreen of a car or on a video screen, a city of surfaces waiting to be read.[21]

After invoking Henry James's figure in the carpet, Aldo Rossi himself, in *The Architecture of the City,* proposes "a type of reading for urban structures," asking, "[F]rom what points of view is it possible to read the city; how many ways are there for understanding its structure?"[22] "Reading" the structure of the city has become a common concern in urban studies in recent decades, from the work of urban planners such as Kevin Lynch to

Gustave Doré (1832–1883), "Dudley Street, Seven Dials," from *London: A Pilgrimage,* 1872. Engraving. Copyright Bibliothèque des Arts Decoratifs, Paris, France/Archives Charmet/The Bridgeman Art Library.

literary critics such as Steven Marcus, who took up Lynch's model. In 1960 Lynch proposed the legible city as an ideal. This legible city would be one "whose districts or landmarks or pathways are easily identifiable and are easily grouped into an over-all pattern," he explained, "[j]ust as [a] printed page, if it is legible, can be visually grasped as a related pattern of recognizable symbols."[23] Taking the idea of the legible city back to the birth of the modern city, and identifying one with the other, Marcus argued in 1974 that the process of reading the city was begun by Engels in his account of the new industrial city of Manchester in the 1840s, where Engels "demonstrated that one had to read . . . shops, commercial buildings, pubs, warehouses and factories" in order to navigate the city, all of which "function" both economically and "as appearances, symbols or symptoms" of social structures that they simultaneously conceal and reveal.[24]

Despite such mid-nineteenth-century antecedents, the interest in making the city legible that is epitomized in Lynch's 1960s work and in Marcus's reprise of Engels in the 1970s, and that reached fruition in accounts of Los Angeles from the 1990s, is inseparable from late twentieth-century anxieties about the increasing replacement of "authentic" city spaces with false fronts, facades, and artificial structures—representations of urbanity. Those recent anxieties can be traced through discussions of the new urbanism, of the city as theme park and of the electronic "city of bits."[25] Nevertheless, anxieties about the legibility of buildings and streetscapes, about being able to interpret the cities and versions of cities that we see, however appropriate to the postmodern, postindustrial city, are also an extension of the anxiety about legibility that was fundamental to accounts of the nineteenth-century city. That anxiety can be traced in literary works (in the concern with Parisian physiognomies, the sea of faces Balzac describes as "masks" at the beginning of *The Girl with the Golden Eyes*) as well as in the urban commentaries of Engels and his contemporaries. It is an anxiety about the "facades" of individuals rather than of buildings, about the artifice of urban life undermining the legibility of persons in the city. Postmodern anxieties about the reading of urban structures echo the anxieties of the denizens of great cities about the reading of persons.

Given the geographical mobility that fed the explosive urbanization of the nineteenth century, it was perhaps inevitable that the experience of arriving in the city would shape modern urban life. Concern about reading persons in the city was surely fed by the shock of encountering urban crowds after beginning life in a village or "small community"—which was the experience of more and more people as the decades of the nineteenth century passed. But that concern about legibility was also in part produced by the repeated presentation of the contrast between the village and the city, which formed the foundation of so much of the discussion of cities. The repetition of the village/city dichotomy and its corollary, a cultural focus on the experience of young men from the provinces, helps keep the village/city dichotomy alive in accounts of the modern city from the mid-nineteenth century onward and reinforces the identification of the city with the problem of knowing. The village or small town is repeatedly described as a "knowable" community; the city, by contrast, is the place of not knowing.[26] The representative urban experience becomes not knowing; the representative urban person becomes the stranger, the person not known; and the representative urban problem becomes the problem of knowing and being known.

"[P]erception of the new qualities of the modern city had been associated, from the beginning," Raymond Williams insists, "with a man walking, as if alone, in its streets."[27] Here we have Baudelaire's flaneur. Yet the other representative urban experience, as Engels observed in London in the 1840s, was that of encountering the sheer numbers of persons on the streets, "[t]he hundreds and thousands of all classes and ranks crowding past each other." According to Engels, these numbers in themselves helped isolate urban individuals, encouraging withdrawal into the self, "the dissolution of mankind into monads, of which each one has a separate essence, and a separate purpose." "[T]he world of atoms," he insists, "is here carried out to its utmost extreme." At the same time, he writes (from his own perspective as a reporter on the conditions of English workers), a distinction between the ranks and classes, between observers and observed, is always present. "What is true of London, is true of Manchester, Birmingham, Leeds, is true of all the great towns," he declares. "Everywhere barbarous indifference, hard egotism on the one hand, and nameless misery, on the other."[28] Every urban person, then, is not equally isolated. There is a fundamental cleavage between those in "nameless misery" and those egotistically indifferent to that misery.

What emerged as the century progressed were two paradigms for observations of the city, both contained in embryo in Engels's account: one focused on the isolation of the individual in the city; the other emphasized the hierarchical structure of classes or ranks fundamental to urban life, the radically divided city of Balzac and Zola. Both of these paradigms emphasized the problem of legibility in the city.

The typical nineteenth-century urban commentator, an upper-middle-class professional man—whether sensationalist journalist or principled reformer—hardly relieved concern about legibility when he offered to explicate a radically divided and hierarchical city by looking from his own position at the urban underworld. The mystery of that world, as well as its vice or misery, was the subject of these commentators, such as Blanchard Jerrold and Gustave Doré in *London: A Pilgrimage* (1872), Andrew Mearns in *Bitter Cry of Outcast London* (1883), and George Sims in *How the Poor Live* (1889).[29] Such urban guides could be commercial or political projects. As commercial efforts, they depended on the illegibility of persons, insofar as that illegibility was the source of the guides' value. As the work of reformers, the guides were premised on the force of the revelation they promised of a depth, a degradation, previously unknown to the reader. The obscurity of their subjects was a rhetorical precondition of all of these

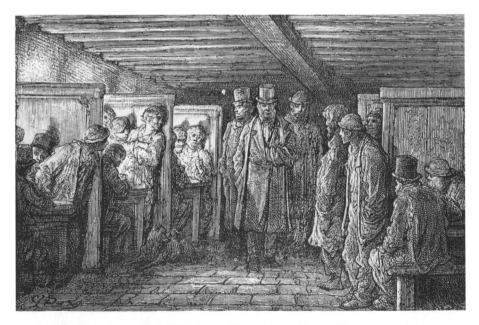

Gustave Doré (1832–1883), "The Shelter." London. Private Collection. Snark/ Art Resource, New York.

projects of urban explanation, implying the respectability of writer and reader, as well as providing a rationale for their efforts. After all, we are told, the writer in every case is a person who has ventured forth into streets beyond the familiar limits to study a world that would otherwise be opaque even to him. And his readers are far too genteel to be able to find and interpret that underworld for themselves.

Prospects for urban legibility were not improved when the city was presented as a field of atomized individuals rather than in terms of class and hierarchy. Pioneering German sociologist Georg Simmel, writing at the turn of the twentieth century and drawing on his own experience of Berlin, echoed Engels's vision of the city as a site for "the dissolution of mankind into monads" in "The Metropolis and Mental Life." Simmel focused on the city as the setting for individualization. The freedom of individuals to develop distinct selves, he proposed, was the achievement of modern life. "[T]he metropolis conduces to the urge for the most individual personal existence," he declared, "individual independence and the elaboration of individuality itself."[30] Not only personal but also economic development was at issue. According to Simmel, the size of the modern city not only allows for but requires economic individualization. "In order to find a source of income that is not yet exhausted, and to find a function which cannot readily be displaced," he explains, "it is necessary to specialize in one's services." This economic specialization affects the worker her- or himself and also "promotes differentiation, refinement, and the enrichment of the public's needs, which obviously must lead to growing personal differences within the public."[31]

Simmel's city produces economic/material individualization and also "the individualization of mental and psychic traits."[32] The city fosters differentiation among its inhabitants in their psychic as well as their work lives, in their consumption as well as their productive activities. The size of the modern city, according to Simmel, ensures that urban experience is the experience of an infinite proliferation of stimuli. That proliferation of stimuli, he argues, produces in reaction a characteristic "reserve" in the urban person. Psychic distance and distinction become necessary to the preservation of an individual self, in the absence of physical distance and distinction. Each citizen in practice and by design necessarily makes her- or himself less legible to his or her peers.

In order to achieve such reserve, the city requires that everyone take refuge behind a false front, a "blasé attitude." But at the same time, according to

Simmel, in order to maintain any individuality amid the excess of stimuli in the city, the urbanite must display as well as defend her- or himself. Paradoxically, then, this situation produces a "mental attitude" of reserve among "metropolitans" and a commitment to extravagant self-advertisement.[33] Urban citizens take up "the strangest eccentricities . . . specifically metropolitan extravagances . . . of caprice, of fastidiousness . . . [as] a form of being 'different,'" in a desperate attempt to make themselves "noticeable."[34] The goal, Simmel insists, is not simply to make oneself stand out among the urban crowds; metropolitan man "has to exaggerate this personal element in order to remain audible even to himself."[35]

This individualized urbanite—opaque not because she or he inhabits a social depth but precisely because of the effort to preserve her or his individuality, and not only because she or he is hiding an authentic self but also because she or he is displaying an artificial self—only heightens the problem of legibility in the city. In other words, urbanites acquiesce in and engage with the process of being turned into texts. Simmel is as defensive about as he is insistent on these metropolitan "extravagances." He reassures his readers that "the meaning of these extravagances does not at all lie in the content of such behavior, but rather in its form of 'being different,' of standing out in a striking manner and thereby attracting attention."[36] Metropolitan extravangances, that is, signify nothing more than residence in the metropolis. They tell us nothing about the person who displays them. We might wonder what it is that metropolitan extravagances *would* signify, if "such behavior" ever had significance in itself.

Neither as members of opposing classes nor as individuals, then, can city dwellers be easily interpreted. Their urban lives have brought them all, in practice, to the position of Wilde and James.

The Genius of Criminals

Writing in 1895 of "L'Affaire Oscar Wilde," André Raffalovich, a French journalist and himself homosexual, observed, "Partout . . . Sodome existe, vénale et menaçante, la ville invisible."[37] But as he himself was well aware, Wilde was not the first literary representative of the not-so-invisible city of Sodom within the great cities of the nineteenth century.

In London, in 1888, six years after his return from America and two years after the beginning of his affair with Robbie Ross, Wilde wrote an essay celebrating deception, "The Decay of Lying," in which he "discovered his own genius."[38] He used Balzac's fiction as the foundation for this, his first fully developed aesthetic statement, which was above all a celebration of false appearances. "What is really interesting about people in good society ... is the mask that each one of them wears, not the reality behind the mask," he argues.[39] "Life imitates Art far more than Art imitates Life," because art makes life legible. "To look at a thing is very different from seeing a thing," he proposes. Artists teach us to see.[40] To illustrate his assertions about the authority of art, he announces that "[t]he nineteenth century as we know it, is largely an invention of Balzac. Our Luciens de Rubempré, our Rastignacs, and de Marsays made their first appearance on the stage of the *Comedie Humaine.*" We, the people, are "merely carrying out, with footnotes and unnecessary additions, the whim or fancy or creative vision of a great novelist," but the characters entirely created by the great novelists thrive.[41] Wilde even cites Baudelaire's insistence that "[a]ll Balzac's characters ... are gifted with the ... ardour of life," to support his own assertion that those characters "dominate us, and defy scepticism."[42]

He then goes on to declare, "One of the greatest tragedies of my life is the death of Lucien de Rubempré. It is a grief from which I have never been able to completely rid myself. It haunts me in my moments of pleasure. I remember it when I laugh."[43] This statement might seem to be merely, if extravagantly, a testimony to the literary by a literary man. But Wilde's claim here is not so simple. It is hardly surprising that he found this young man's death so memorable, especially in his "moments of pleasure." After all, in *A Harlot High and Low,* one of Balzac's greatest novels of "Parisian life," Lucien commits suicide when his entanglement with an older man leads them both to prison.

Lucien de Rubempré is a quintessential example of a nineteenth-century literary type, "the young man from the provinces" who sets out for the capital to make his fortune and becomes central to the great city. Like Lucien, who imagines himself a poet, such young men often have literary aspirations. But their artistic ambitions are largely indistinguishable from their social desires, and their social desires largely indistinguishable from their sexual prospects. Like Lucien, the young man from the provinces is archetypically favored with "good looks" as well as youth.[44] These good looks are, in fact, often his chief capital. They allow him to manipulate, for his own profit, his legibility in the city—to make different aspects of himself visible and invisible. As Balzac explains in *A Harlot High and Low,* good looks can render a "pleasant young fellow" gripped by "poverty's iron hand" indistinguishable from "the best-bred son of a duke and peer" (18). They can also obscure the drive and the calculations that fuel his attempts to rise above his station, "hid[ing] deep abysses in his nature and life" (19). Good looks are their own—and, in these cases, a crucial—mask for negotiating city life. And in Balzac's Paris, the good looks of young men from the provinces attract the useful patronage of powerful women and men.

In "The Decay of Lying," Wilde cites, as representative of the nineteenth century, not only Lucien de Rubempré but also de Marsay and Rastignac, the three most famous characters among Balzac's young men. These three all become entangled in same-sex desires in the city. As we have seen in *The Girl with the Golden Eyes,* de Marsay pursues a woman already the lover of another woman. Rastignac and, most fatefully, Lucien are pursued by

"*Old* Paris is gone." Charles Marville (1816–1879), "Building of Avenue de l'Opéra, butte des Moulins, rue Saint-Roch, Paris, 1858–78." Photograph. Copyright Musée de la Ville de Paris, Musée Carnavalet, Paris, France/Lauros/Giraudon/ The Bridgeman Art Library.

the same man. Wilde does not mention that man, Vautrin—the homosexual criminal genius who presides over Balzac's Paris—but Vautrin hovers just behind Wilde's lament for Lucien's death. He is as emblematic in his own way, in nineteenth-century accounts of the city, as the young men from the provinces whom he favors.

By taking the great tragedy of Vautrin's life—the death of Lucien—as his own, Wilde identifies himself with Vautrin. Balzac's portrait of Vautrin, with its emphasis on same-sex relations at the heart of urban life, allowed Wilde to situate himself within the nineteenth century and the city. But Vautrin offered to Wilde, as he did to the nineteenth century, not only a model for the pursuit of same-sex desires in the city but also a model for the experience—and the representation—of urban life as a project of concealment and display.

Vautrin first appears in the Paris boardinghouse at the center of *Père Goriot*, in hiding from the police. Feminized by a wig and dyed whiskers, he claims to be "a retired merchant" but is actually primarily occupied in the pursuit of Eugéne Rastignac.[45] He reappears at the conclusion of *Lost Illusions*, at the side of Lucien de Rubempré, disguised as a Spanish cleric traveling through the provinces. There he forestalls Lucien's first attempt at suicide (prompted by the various failures of his first endeavor at life in Paris) and promptly carries the younger man back to the capital. In *A Harlot High and Low*, still posing as a Spanish cleric, Vautrin directs Lucien's second attempt to ascend through Paris society, the second phase of his life as a young man from the provinces. He bankrolls Lucien's ambitions. He manages the younger man's unproductive interest in the beautiful and devoted "harlot" Esther Gobseck, and he harnesses her passion for Lucien to an elaborate scheme for advancing him toward the social pinnacle he most desires.

In fact, Vautrin's entire path through Balzac's *Comedie humaine* is determined by the needs of the young men whose interests he adopts. According to the police, his first imprisonment (which we never see) was the result of his "agree[ing] to take the responsibility for another man's crime . . . a forgery committed by a very fine young man whom he had taken a fancy to" (*Père Goriot*, 186). After pursuing Rastignac in *Père Goriot*, and Lucien in *Lost Illusions* and *A Harlot High and Low*, he resumes responsibility for Theodore Calvi, "his queen" (*Harlot High and Low*, 455), his chain-mate and "partner" from a previous jail term, when they are reunited in prison after Lucien's death. In the last part of *A Harlot High and Low*, Vautrin transforms himself most completely, through a dizzying series of narrative twists and turns, becoming chief of the Paris police so as to save Calvi from execution.

But homosexuality itself is not—at least nominally—what makes Vautrin a criminal, what Vautrin is making illegible through his many disguises. Homosexuals had been freed from legal restraint in France by the Revolution. That 1791 decree was confirmed by the Napoleonic Code, though this legal freedom did not mean that same-sex desires went unpunished in literature or in life.[46] In *The Girl with the Golden Eyes,* de Marsay professes "perfect indifference with regard to all kinds of moral deviation. . . . [H]e took no umbrage at vice."[47] But his technical neutrality does not forestall Paquita's grisly end and the frustration of her mistress. As already noted, Zola represents Nana's death with peculiar relish. As the history of Baudelaire's poems further indicates, writers representing lesbianism could be prosecuted. Men pursuing same-sex encounters in the "public" spaces of Paris were routinely arrested, even entrapped, at different moments in different locations around the city, throughout the nineteenth century.[48]

"I live only for sentiments," Vautrin declares. "I have turned life inside out, only one real sentiment exists—friendship between man and man" (*Père Goriot,* 182–83). The problem for Vautrin (and for Balzac) is not how to conceal but how to make legible his sentiments. Balzac has Vautrin offer a plethora of explanations for his desire and offers a range of explanations himself, as narrator. Vautrin tries identification: "The handsome young man is myself," he declares.[49] Satan is frequently invoked: Balzac describes the relationship between Lucien and Vautrin as a "pact between a human being and a demon, a child and a diplomat" (*Lost Illusions,* 650), and Vautrin appears as "the Devil, in his dealings with" a Lucien described as a "man half woman" (*Harlot High and Low,* 94). Alternatively, Vautrin declares his godlike possession of Lucien: "I've . . . brought you back to life, and you belong to me as a creature belongs to its creator . . . the body to the soul! . . . I shall live in you!" (*Lost Illusions,* 650). As he works to establish a connection with Lucien, Vautrin tries to explain his interest to the younger man through a series of hierarchical paradigms from public and private life in which they are each alternately represented as masculine and feminine: "You want to be a soldier? I will be your commanding officer. Obey me as a wife obeys her husband, as a child obeys its mother" (*Lost Illusions,* 649); "my son—I'm going to adopt you and make you my heir" (*Lost Illusions,*

650). Vautrin elaborates heterosexual parallels, comparing his devotion to that of a woman, and so implying the sexual aspect of his interest. In *Père Goriot* he declares, about Rastignac, "He is a man worth loving. If I were a woman I would die (no, nothing so stupid), live for him" (205). In *A Harlot High and Low*, he even identifies with the harlot of the novel's title, proposing to Lucien's mistress, Esther, that when the young man makes the great marriage that the older has schemed to arrange and becomes "son-in-law of the Duc de Grandlieu, if you then feel like jumping into the Seine . . . we'll join hands and jump in together" (206–7).

Vautrin finally proposes to Lucien that he is "the author," Lucien "the play" (*Harlot High and Low*, 93). Demonstrating Wilde's contention that artists make reality legible to us, Vautrin most consistently uses literary allusion to explain his own attachments. Just as many would later cite Wilde, and just as Wilde cites Balzac (and, obliquely, Vautrin), Vautrin cites the seventeenth-century English playwright Thomas Otway. In *Père Goriot*, he tells Rastignac, "Pierre and Jaffir, such a bond as theirs is what I care for most. I know *Venice Preserved* by heart" (183); and in *Lost Illusions*, he asks Lucien, "Have you pondered Otway's *Venice Preserved*? Have you understood the deep friendship between man and man which binds Pierre to Jaffir, makes them indifferent about women and alters all social relationships for them? . . . I'm putting that question to the poet in you" (654; ellipsis in original).

The two sets of terms in which Balzac frames Vautrin's homosexual and urban careers—that is, his experiences of the problem of legibility—are the criminal and the literary. The two kinds of texts he chiefly invokes are police files and novels. Throughout the *Comedie humaine*, Vautrin works to conceal his criminal status and to make his desires legible. But the setting in which those desires are most legible is the criminal. In Balzac's Paris, prostitution is always female and crime male. Men have their all-male prisons, just as prostitutes have their all-female brothels; lesbianism is the vice of whores, love between men is the vice of criminals. The connection between homosexuality and criminality is confirmed by the structure of the Palais de Justice itself, the court and prison complex at the center of Paris and of *A Harlot High and Low*. This prison includes a particular building identified by "[t]he governor . . . with an expression of disgust" as "the *queens'* quarters." When asked to explain, he elaborates, "That's the third sex" (454; emphasis in original). In addition to a physical structure, there is also, within this prison, a social structure for the devotion of one man to another. Male couples like Vautrin and Calvi are identified as "chain-mates" long after the particular imprisonment during which they were first "united." Stories of male couples in prison were, in fact, "major attractions in vaudeville and boulevard comedies" in Restoration France.[50] Meanwhile, Balzac's identification of male homosexuality with criminality—even when homosexual behavior was not a crime—linked desire between men to the problem of legibility, by way of the need for secrecy that rules criminal lives.

In addition, Balzac identifies both homosexuality and the problem of legibility with the city, through his insistence on the connection between the city and crime. Balzac's Paris is a city of police and criminals, dominated by the Palais de Justice. "What Parisian, foreigner or provincial is there," Balzac asks us, "though he may have spent a mere two days in Paris,

Cruising in the passages of modern Paris. "Galerie d'Orléans at the Palais Royal," from *Paris et ses environs*. Engraved by Auguste Bry; published ca. 1850–60s (lithograph) by Jean Jacottet (1806–ca. 1843). Copyright Private Collection/ The Stapleton Collection/The Bridgeman Art Library.

who has not noticed [its] black walls . . . ?" (*Harlot High and Low*, 309). The Palais, where the authorities and the criminals come together, is not only the center of Paris, however; it stands on the site of the city's origin. Balzac describes in careful detail the prison's stone staircases and mazes of corridors, the relationship of cells to offices and passages to courtrooms, and the facilities for execution, all constructed atop what was "the whole of the original city" (310). The Palais is "still . . . the most monumental among so many monuments," "the cradle of Paris" (311).[51] Both inside and outside of this complex of prison and court, criminals swarm, depending on the city to make them illegible: "The department of the Seine and its fifteen hundred thousand inhabitants . . . [are] the only point in France where these unfortunates can hide" (444).

Logically, given the problem of legibility, Balzac's Paris is a literary city, waiting to be read. The emphasis on urban masking with which he begins *The Girl with the Golden Eyes* is reiterated when he opens *A Harlot High and Low* with "an Opera fancy-dress ball." "[T]o country cousins, inexperienced young men and foreigners," this event is "no more comprehensible than the stock exchange to a peasant." Nonetheless, it is here where, despite their masks, "the various circles of which Paris society is composed meet, recognize and observe each other" (17). In fact, Balzac notes, for "the initiated, the seemingly unintelligible black book of conflicting interests is so precisely notated that they read [the ball] as though it were a novel" (18). Divided between those proper urbanites—the initiated—who can and those who cannot interpret its social signs—the not properly urban/Parisian, the country cousins, the foreigners, the inexperienced young men—the city is a literary form.

The most committed readers of the city are the police, who make elaborate efforts to ensure the legibility of Parisians by keeping "files . . . on all families and individuals whose way of life is suspect, whose acts are considered reprehensible." No one eludes their notice: "However highly placed a family may be, it cannot avoid this social provision." But many avoid prosecution: "[T]he law never punishes half of the outrages and criminal acts committed annually." The police are not, after all, committed to revealing their knowledge. Instead, the information in their files illuminates the figure in the carpet of the city, in language strikingly like Henry James's: "These are the threads which show on the reverse side of the tapestry of crime, the materials, otherwise unseen, out of which the pattern was made."

Although this information is used discreetly, it is not made public: the files "contain the truth condemned to stay underground, as the truth is everywhere and always" (330). Master criminals can become policemen, because the police are as invested as the criminals in the manipulation of information, especially in "the truth condemned to stay underground."

Sex, and especially sexual deviation, is of the essence of criminality in this city, and so too of the police's investigations. "Passion is almost always . . . the original reason" for crime, Balzac explains (446). Although his master criminal is motivated by his feelings for other men, more ordinary criminals are motivated by "the excessive love which draws them, *constitutionally*, say the doctors, towards women" (446; emphasis in original). "[A]ll" the police "do is listen to the paroxysmal words of passion, hear what information is laid, take notes and keep them" (331). Balzac warns specifically, "No abnormality goes unrecorded" (330).

Vautrin is the supreme negotiator of the city as both a literary universe and a police state, a novel as well as a set of criminal records. He turns his own and others' lives into art, just as he advises Lucien to treat his public life as a performance: "Make a display of your beauty, grace, wit, poetic talent . . . in the great theatre which we call the world" (*Lost Illusions*, 647). His skill at the manipulation of information renders him one of the "men of genius" in his own métier. "In the sphere of crime," Balzac rhapsodizes, "this prodigious man's instinct for the truth was as sure as Molière's in dramatic poetry, like Cuvier's among the relics of a vanished world" (338).

Vautrin is nevertheless subject to the rule of the novelist (to Balzac's manipulation), as we all are, according to Wilde. Although this master criminal's "law of laws" is "secretiveness!" (*Lost Illusions*, 648), Balzac lets us know that Vautrin is known by the police. "Let me tell you a secret," a detective confides in *Père Goriot*, "he doesn't like women" (189). No abnormality goes unrecorded in a city in which Balzac also controls the police. Nevertheless, claiming the authority of a novelist himself (the authority Balzac himself claimed), Vautrin confidently declares, "I know everyone in Paris" (*Lost Illusions*, 640).[52] He knows more than the police, then, but why? He knows everyone in Paris because he knows that the distinction between normal and abnormal (or moral and immoral) is not so clear, that "we are all at the beck and call of something, perhaps a vice, perhaps a need" (648). His career is a commentary on legibility itself, as well as on the relation of the outcast to the secure and the improper to the proper. From behind his masks, Vautrin knows that the abnormal is everyone, or at least everyone in the city.[53] Such knowledge, on the part of Balzac's leading man committed to sentiment between men, is the reason Balzac's was the century in which Wilde understood himself to be living.

ERNEST IN TOWN

The Oscar Wilde who was invited to relieve Los Angeles of its provincial obscurity and who went on to feel so deeply the death of Lucien de Rubempré had himself been a young man from the provinces. He arrived in London from Ireland, by way of Oxford, in style and with privilege, as well as family, at his back. But he had, nevertheless, to make a place for himself in the London of the 1880s and 1890s. He would become the artist Lucien was never to be: a critic, a writer of fiction, occasionally a poet, and finally, most appropriately as well as most successfully, a dramatist with a secret.

But, perhaps because "life is terribly deficient in [artistic] form," as Wilde observed, he would come to play out aspects of the role of Vautrin as well as Lucien in his own story.[54] He would develop a double life. He would become a criminal in a country in which sex between men was a crime. And, because of his inability or unwillingness to keep his criminal behavior secret, because of his commitment to display as well as concealment— to Simmel's "metropolitan extravagance"—he would go to prison for his (social) sins. Ultimately, he would be absorbed into the scientific study of sexuality, as well as into first the informal and then the formal histories of (modern) queer culture that were already developing as he entertained stableboys at London's Savoy Hotel. Despite his fate, in 1898 he could still in retrospect commend his first male lover, Robbie Ross, humorously, for his "extraordinary power . . . in supplying temptations to others . . . in the solitude of great cities."[55]

Wilde's life and his essays, fiction, and plays, with their insistent focus on legibility, especially the legibility of moral failures, demonstrate the degree to which legibility is as much a concern of the cultural history of homosexuality as of the cultural history of cities. Wilde obsessively and publicly rehearsed the possibility that we all, like Vautrin's Parisians, have hidden sinful or criminal selves. I have already cited his celebration of social masks and deception in "The Decay of Lying." In a companion piece, "Pen Pencil and Poison" (1891), he celebrated the early nineteenth-century writer and poisoner Thomas Griffiths Wainewright. "His crimes seem to have had an important effect upon his art," Wilde announces. "They gave a strong personality to his style. . . . One can fancy an intense personality being created out of sin."[56] Through the personality that crime allows the artist to develop, the crime, the artist, and his art become one. By the late 1880s, these essays indicate, Wilde was madly flirting with self-destruction in his writings as well as in his life. Displaying his interest in concealment, he also displayed, by implication, his own criminal sexual self.

The Picture of Dorian Gray (1891), Wilde's only novel, is a prototypical account of the modern homosexuality Wilde would come to represent: modern homosexuality as an amalgam of art and interpretation, of art and the problem of knowing. The painter Basil Hallward's admiration for the young aristocrat Dorian Gray ("I worshipped you too much. I am punished for it") intimates same-sex desires. So do Wilde's innumerable references to Dorian's unnameable sins, especially when those sins are somehow connected with other men. "Why is your friendship so fatal to young men?" Basil asks Dorian.[57] These moments in the novel are particularly suggestive because they link the feelings of one man for another to punishment or fatality in a social context in which sex between men is a crime. Like Balzac's Lucien, Dorian comes under the influence of a hypnotic older man, the endlessly epigrammatic Lord Henry Wotton, who steals the beautiful young man away from his artist friend and according to Dorian, corrupts him. As I have suggested, when *The Picture of Dorian Gray* was written, it was already part of a lineage of writings about desire between men, a lineage of which Wilde was perfectly conscious.

Nevertheless, the key to the novel's emblematic force as a homosexual text, as it is the key in Balzac's *A Harlot High and Low,* is its obsession with legibility. Written just as sexual scientists in Germany, France, and Britain were becoming increasingly confident in and increasingly known for their efforts at categorizing sexual deviations, *The Picture of Dorian Gray* plays out an obsession with the legibility of sin in art as well as the legibility of sin on the body, through Wilde's use of art as a subject as well as through the structure of his narrative. In this grim, fantastical story of a divided self, Wilde simultaneously denies and insists upon the legibility of sin—in art and on the body—in a world convinced, as Hallward declares, that "[s]in is a thing that writes itself across a man's face. It cannot be concealed. People talk sometimes of secret vices. There are no such things. If a wretched man

"Society's Hopes and Fears," *Society,* January 18, 1882. Reprinted from H. Montgomery Hyde, *The Annotated Oscar Wilde* (New York: Clarkson Potter, 1982).

has a vice it shows itself in the lines of his mouth, the droop of his eyelids, the moulding of his hands" (165).

Hallward expresses his feelings for Dorian in terms of his, Hallward's, art. "[H]is personality has suggested to me an entirely new manner in art, an entirely new mode of style," he rhapsodizes. "I can now recreate life in a way that was hidden from me before. . . . [H]e defines for me the lines of a fresh school" (13). In fact, he insists, Dorian's influence on his work is greatest when Dorian himself is not the subject. "[H]e is much more to me than a model or a sitter" (13), he claims, citing as his best evidence of Dorian's influence an empty landscape painted while the young man was present beside him. The painter is, however, afraid of the legibility of his feelings for Dorian in his work. These feelings might be traceable, the novel implies, even when the beloved is not the object of the artist's study. Hallward certainly does not want his portrait of Dorian exhibited, although he understands it to be the finest work he has ever done. He is sure that, "without intending it," he has "put into it some expression of all this curious artistic idolatry." "I will not bare my soul," he declares (14).[58] The artist, apparently, cannot control the reflection of his feelings in his work, but can only try to control the work's fate.

Hallward's portrait of Dorian is, in fact, given an uncanny capacity to represent feelings, but they are the feelings of its subject rather than its painter. The work of art becomes hyperlegible, recording every one of Dorian's sins, which, because they appear only in the picture, remain otherwise invisible. By taking the burden of representing his sins from Dorian's body in this fashion, the picture perversely demonstrates the accuracy of the social belief that sin is always visible. Protected from the social consequences of his immoral actions by his unmarked face, which perpetually offers a false image of innocence, Dorian moves freely between the West End entertainments of the elite and the riverside dives of London. But his sins are always visible somewhere, even if not on his person. His painted image grows persistently more foul.

The Picture of Dorian Gray both thwarts and fulfills the social expectation of the legibility of vice to which Hallward testifies, just as Dorian's portrait both reveals and obscures his vices. But in the end Wilde enforces social norms. The story concludes when Dorian kills himself as he is attempting to destroy the picture—the evidence of his sins—by tearing at the canvas with a knife. When he is discovered, his dead body bears the marks of his corruption, and the figure in the picture has been restored to its young and shining original. Dorian cannot remove from the world—nor, finally, from his own body—the physical evidence of his sins. Legibility is, ultimately, inescapable.

But the ending of *The Picture of Dorian Gray* was only a moment, not an ending at all, in the overall trajectory of Wilde's career. Because a playwright can put actors onstage to enact his fictions before audiences, drama provided a particularly appropriate form for Wilde's obsession with the interpretation of social appearances. Like some of his most resonant essays, and like *The Picture of Dorian Gray,* Wilde's plays are all about secrets revealed. They repeatedly turn on the difference between appearances and actuality, between propriety and impropriety, between morality and immorality—and on the difficulty of distinguishing between these qualities. The secrets at issue are most often sexual secrets: adultery in *Lady Windermere's Fan* (1892); seduction, betrayal, and illegitimacy in *A Woman of No Importance* (1893). Even when the moral failing to be revealed is financial or political, as in *An Ideal Husband* (1895), the playing out of the moral quandary generates suspicions of sexual misconduct.

Wilde had two plays running in London's West End as his trial unfolded, *An Ideal Husband* and *The Importance of Being Earnest* (1895). In *An Ideal Husband,* the mysterious corrupter of the apparently virtuous husband and politician Sir Robert Chiltern is a German, Baron Arnheim, who knows "men and cities well, like the old Greek" but is "without the dreadful disadvantage of having a Penelope waiting at home for him."[59] With his "wonderfully fascinating quiet voice" and "a strange smile on his pale, curved lips," he persuades Wilde's hero to the deceit that will enrich them both during a tour of his "wonderful picture gallery . . . his tapestries, his enamels, his jewels, his carved ivories." The Baron's connoisseurship, "the strange loveliness of the luxury in which he lived," echoes that of Dorian Gray, just as his influence over Chiltern echoes Lord Henry's influence over Gray.[60]

The relationship between public and private life is the subject of *An Ideal Husband.* In contrast to *The Picture of Dorian Gray* however, this play endorses Chiltern's assertion that "public and private life are different things" and "have different laws, and move on different lines," against his wife's conviction that there should be no such distinction.[61] Chiltern suffers privately for his moral failings, but briefly and not irrevocably, and in the end loses neither his wife nor his political career. The secret of the illegal financial speculation on which his fortune is based is revealed but also contained within the frame of his private life. Public scandal is evaded. He does not have to leave London or his parliamentary career. Indeed, he is elevated to a seat in the Cabinet, as if rewarded for his defiance of the threat of exposure. For someone in Wilde's position, the lesson is reassuring.

The outcome of Wilde's final and best-known theatrical work, *The Importance of Being Earnest,* is similarly benign. By the time he wrote this play, Wilde had turned into farce his exploration of reserve and display in life and in art, as well as the moral crises of revelation with which he was preoccupied. His hero is that type of nineteenth-century English fiction, an orphan child whose origins no one knows. But that young man is not, it turns out, the tragically illegitimate scion of a ruined family. He is merely an artistic accident, his nurse, Miss Prism, having absent-mindedly checked the baby in lieu of her own novel manuscript at Victoria Station many years before. The subject of the play is, nonetheless, still knowing and being known, a problem of which one part is secrecy and the other naming.

Organized around a conventional urban/rural contrast, *The Importance of Being Earnest* offers us an irresistible picture of the possibilities for manipulating self-presentation that are enabled by city life. Wilde's hero, a quintessential child of the metropolis, emerging fully formed from the cloakroom at Victoria Station, has reached adulthood with two lives and two names, "Jack in the country" and "Ernest in town."[62] Like Dorian Gray, he is a divided figure. Being countrified, Jack is, of course, morally upstanding, whereas Ernest is an urban scapegrace, a roué. Ernest has, in fact, been created by Jack precisely for the purpose of escaping the "very high moral tone on all subjects" that he feels it is his "duty" to maintain with his family in the country, and escaping the country itself. For a "high moral tone" does not, it becomes clear, "conduce very much to either one's health or one's happiness."[63] The desirability of the city is also affirmed by the lesson that corruption might be not just urban but ubiquitous. As Lady Bracknell announces protectively, "A girl with a simple, unspoiled nature, like Gwendolen, could hardly be expected to reside in the country."[64] So it is Ernest—a city dweller—that he must finally become, in order to marry Gwendolen, his lady love.

In *The Importance of Being Earnest,* in fact, the false and immoral urban self is desirable, even necessary, to health and happiness. What is more, in

"Trial of Oscar Wilde," *Illustrated Police News,* May 4, 1895. Reprinted from
H. Montgomery Hyde, *The Annotated Oscar Wilde.*

the end that self turns out to be the true one, when Jack, the opposite of earnest, turns out to have been named Ernest all along. Secrets are common and attractive: "How secretive of him! He grows more interesting hourly," Gwendolen declares. Truth, on the contrary, is rare and resisted: Jack, admitting his deception, declares, "[I]t is very painful for me to be forced to speak the truth. It is the first time in my life that I have ever been reduced to such a painful position." And appearance is everything: "In matters of grave importance, style, not sincerity, is the vital thing," Gwendolen announces, reprising "The Decay of Lying" in what would become one of Wilde's most famous lines.[65]

WILDE'S INSISTENT FLIRTATION with the display of his desires, with those metropolitan extravagances that draw attention, was not illegible in his own time. *The Picture of Dorian Gray* was immediately read as being about homosexuality by at least some of Wilde's contemporaries. The reviewer for the *Scots Observer* (Edinburgh), in July 1890, complaining that the book's "interest is medico-legal," referred to "unnatural iniquity" and to a recent London homosexual scandal, the Cleveland Street Affair of September 1889, as he denounced the novel as written for "outlawed noblemen and perverted telegraph boys."[66] The novel was even tendered as evidence against Wilde during his trials. According to the newspaper reports of the day, the lawyers read at length from the text before demanding of its author, "Is 'Dorian Gray' open to certain interpretations?" and, "Do you consider the feeling there described as a proper or improper feeling[?] . . . You think that is a moral kind of feeling for one man to have toward another?" Wilde defended himself by accusing his adversaries of being bad readers: "Only . . . brutes and illiterates . . . [and] the Philistine" would see in his work those "certain interpretations." He also tried to take refuge in his art—as does Hallward in the novel—sidestepping the question of propriety and morality by declaring that the sentiments he was describing were "the feeling of an artist toward a beautiful personality."[67]

One of Havelock Ellis's informants in *Sexual Inversion* reported finding a Dorian Gray in an unspecified American city, in those "cafés, where inverts are accustomed to foregather." There the "boy-prostitutes" bore "fanciful names, some of well-known actresses, others of heroes in fiction"— all, that is, from art. The name itself, in fact, seems to have been popular: "Rivals, [Dorian] complained, had assumed the same appellation," Ellis's informant reports, "but he was the original Dorian."⁶⁸ Moreover, Wilde's trial, and its attendant worldwide publicity—prompted initially and ironically by his own rejection of the charge that he was "posing" as a sodomite— not only produced Wilde himself as the model of the modern homosexual but also broadcast far and wide the lesson that homosexuality was revealed by "style," by appearances. So another of Ellis's cases, "H.C., American, aged 28, of independent means," describes "purchas[ing]" and "scrutinizing," with "an effeminate fellow-student," "photographs of Oscar Wilde" in response to the trials.⁶⁹

Addressing "the opinion of some, [that] English homosexuality has become much more conspicuous in recent years" at the end of the introductory chapter of *Sexual Inversion,* Ellis offers two possible explanations for this view. The first is Wilde. Although insisting that "it can scarcely have sufficed to increase the number of inverts," Ellis is willing to grant that "the celebrity of Oscar Wilde and the universal publicity given to the facts of the case by the newspapers may have brought conviction of their perversion to many inverts who were before only vaguely conscious of their abnormality, and, paradoxical though it may seem, have imparted greater courage to others." Because of Wilde, Ellis suggests, homosexuality became more legible to homosexuals and, emboldened by Wilde's public spectacle, they made their sexuality more legible to others. Ellis's preferred explanation for the increasing conspicuousness of homosexuals, however, is the changing city itself: "[T]he development of urban life renders easier the exhibition and satisfaction of this as of all other forms of perversion."⁷⁰ Wilde and the city are joined here, both identified with either the increasing numbers or, as Ellis prefers, the increasing legibility of homosexuals in the late nineteenth century. But the alternatives need not be Wilde *or* the city; rather, perhaps, Wilde *and* the city.

After all, Wilde embodied the urban type in his person, even in his own sense of the mistakes or vulnerabilities that led to his criminal conviction. Writing from his prison cell, he records, as a source of regret, "amus[ing]" himself "with being a *flâneur,* a dandy, a man of fashion." But he does not regret the city. When he tries to help himself through his ordeal by imagining his future, the "much [that] is waiting for me outside that is very delightful," the city remains. He looks forward to experiencing again both the natural world, "what St. Francis of Assisi calls 'my brother the wind, and my sister the rain,' lovely things both of them," and "the shop-windows and sunsets of great cities."[71] Wilde's trial, completing the impulse projected by Balzac through his recurring portraits of Vautrin, definitively joined the flaneur, the dandy, and the man of fashion to the criminal and, in all of these forms, the urban type to the type of the homosexual.

SOCIALISM AND INTERPRETATION

Wilde's crime was understood, from the moment he was charged, as political as well as moral. "A nation . . . goes swiftly to wreck and decay by precisely that brilliant corruption of which we have just had the exposure," London's *Daily Telegraph* announced in the midst of his trials. Wilde's threat to the nation lay in his art, "[t]he superfine 'Art' which admits no moral duty and laughs at the established phrases of right and wrong." That art, the newspaper declared, "is the visible enemy of those ties and bonds of society—the natural affections, the domestic joys, the sanctity and sweetness of the home."[72] It is the enemy of a nation that rests on the "natural affections" of the heterosexual family—"the domestic joys"—properly ensconced in what is clearly by implication a properly middle-class home. The newspapers, that is, could use "art" to talk about sexuality as adeptly as Wilde himself.

Wilde's trials also confirmed (also always in contrast to the sweetness of the family in its sanctified home) a developing cultural identification of sex between men with a politically threatening violation of class divisions. The prosecuting attorney articulated the suspicious nature of Wilde's relationships by emphasizing the social status of the younger men in question. "[I]n not one of these cases were the parties upon an equality with Wilde in any way," he insisted. "They were not educated . . . not his equal in years . . . out of employment, and of their antecedents Wilde professed to know nothing." As critic Ed Cohen has argued, because "Wilde had transgressed those boundaries . . . that delimited the realm of 'natural association' for the Victorian middle class . . . his relationships could 'logically' be perceived to signify 'something unnatural.'"[73] That logic would be one basis for the popular identification of homosexuality with political radicalism throughout the next century.

But Wilde had also already asserted himself as a political actor. He began describing himself as a socialist in the early 1880s.[74] In 1888, the year he declared his grief for Lucien de Rubempré, he published his politics in

"The Soul of Man under Socialism." Political radicalism in itself was by then firmly identified with cities, and the politics of cities already identified with bonds between men.

In the 1840s Engels had defined "the great cities" as "the birthplace of labour movements." It is in the great cities, he argued, that "the workers first begin to reflect on their own condition, and to struggle against it; in them the opposition between proletariat and bourgeoisie first made itself manifest; from them proceeded the trade unions, Chartism, and Socialism." Moreover, in his account great cities are catalysts for political struggle because they make social conditions as well as their potential solutions legible: "The great cities have transformed the disease of the social body, which appears in chronic form in the country, into an acute one, and so made manifest its real nature and the means of curing it."[75]

Balzac had also deftly joined the sexual deviations as well as the crimes of his great city to politics. His always sexually deviant criminals are, by definition, "in revolt against society" (*Harlot High and Low,* 445). But it is the man committed to bonds between men who personifies his city's political threat.[76] At the conclusion of *Père Goriot,* the novelist explains that Rastignac "had seen society in its three great aspects: Obedience, Struggle and Revolt; or, in other words, the Family, the World and Vautrin" (271). It is Vautrin, Balzac's incarnation of revolt, who most masterfully navigates the city, manipulating urban elites and urban authorities alike.

Whitman would fuse the city, politics, and male relationships most literally, as in his vision in "For You O Democracy" (1860) of "inseparable cities with their arms about each other's necks," made "By the love of comrades, / By the manly love of comrades."[77] In "I Dream'd in a Dream," also from 1860, he proposed a city constructed entirely of such bonds between men, which was therefore "invincible to the attacks of the whole of the rest of the earth." This place was "the new city of Friends": "Nothing was greater there than the quality of robust love, it led the rest, / It was seen in every hour in the actions of the men of that city, / And in all their looks and words."[78]

Even as Wilde was going to trial, his contemporary Edward Carpenter, a socialist as well as an explicit advocate for the public recognition of what he called "the intermediate sex," cited Whitman as his authority as he argued in favor of the "social function of 'intense and loving comradeship, the personal and passionate attachment of man to man'" as "a moving force in the body politic." Homosexuals' interest in cross-class relationships, he argued, should be considered as a benefit to the entire society, "in these days when social questions loom so large upon us."[79] "Eros is a great leveller," Carpenter insisted. "It is hardly needful . . . to emphasise the importance of a bond which by the most passionate and lasting compulsion may draw members of the different classes together. . . . A moment's consideration must convince us that such a comradeship may, as Whitman says, have 'deepest relations to general politics.'"[80]

Wilde's "Soul of Man under Socialism" was preceded, by only two years, by Henry James's great novel of political London, *The Princess Casamassima* (1886), a consummate distillation of the nineteenth-century literature of great cities as well as of its own urban moment. In fact, James and Wilde converge, through their shared focus on radical politics in these writings of the late 1880s, on the problem of legibility and the possibilities of cities.

The two diverged, however, in the detail of their accounts of socialism and their responses to it. Wilde elaborated his own very particular beliefs; James described a vaguely defined nexus of shadowy groups. All that is clear

Crowding past each other. James Valentine (1815–1880), *Bridge in London*, ca. 1890. Adoc-photos/Art Resource, New York.

in *The Princess Casamassima* is that James's radicals are opposed to the inequities of the class system made manifest in the great city. Wilde embraced socialism as he understood it, whereas for James the world of radical politics remained a potentially threatening subject of curiosity.

Their political divergence reflected their different responses to the late nineteenth-century crystallization of homosexual/heterosexual distinctions that Wilde's trials would advance, and so reflected their very different commitments to legibility. Those differences resulted in their imagination of quite different cities. In contrast to James's summation of the urbanity of their moment, Wilde can be seen to have projected a politics, and a city, of the future.

PRESENTING HIMSELF AS a quintessential observer of the great city, James explains that *The Princess Casamassima* "proceeded quite directly" from his own flaneuring, "the habit and the interest of walking the streets."[81] "[H]aunt[ing] the great city," he implies that the knowledge he is seeking is sexual: "to penetrate [the city], imaginatively, in as many places as possible—*that* was to be informed" (48; emphasis in original). As in the many urban exposés that preceded this one, in *The Princess Casamassima* the knowledge the city offers the elite observer is knowledge of how much is not known. "The value I wished most to render and the effect I wished most to produce" in the novel, James proposed, "were precisely those of our not knowing, of society's not knowing, but only guessing and suspecting and trying to ignore, what 'goes on' irreconcilably, subversively, beneath the vast smug surface" (48). And the sexual is inseparable from the political. In *The Princess Casamassima*, the subjects of all this "not knowing" are the relationships among his central characters as well as both the conditions of life for the mass of the city's inhabitants, its poorest citizens, and the revolutionary groups that have arisen in response.

James's heroine, Princess Casamassima, who sees herself as pursuing the "modern" (259), is, like her author, a member of the elite who find the city illegible. But she is determined to discover its secret "truth." She is an unself-conscious model of the nineteenth-century urban commentator as social investigator, as well as a model of the avid consumer of such commentator's works. "I want to know London; it interests me more than I can say—the huge, swarming, smoky, human city," she declares, "real London, the people and all their sufferings and passions; not Park Lane and

Bond St." (201). Suffering and passion are joined in her imagining of urban "reality." She is sure that the city's truth is to be found in its grimmest depths, among its most miserable citizens and the revolutionaries who champion their cause.

James complements his portrait of this elite seeker after urban truths with an ambiguously situated hero, Hyacinth Robinson. Hyacinth both does and does not fulfill the task of representing "the people" assigned him by the princess—and by the conventions of the literature of the city already in place. His life is, above all, a matter of secrets, which is all to the good in terms of his representative value. But those secrets are essentially personal and sexual, the crimes of passion that produced him and his indeterminate class and nationality. (Hyacinth's mother, a French maid, was consigned to prison for murdering his father, the English gentleman who first seduced and then abandoned her.) Like Balzac's Paris, James's London is founded in crime and centered on a prison. *The Princess Casamassima* begins with the boy being taken to London's Milbank Prison to be seen by his mother—by then fatally ill—for the first and the last time.

The young Hyacinth is not told who this woman is to him. As he grows up, he gradually discovers his origins. James evokes the emphasis on masking in Balzac's Paris and strikingly prefigures the gradual emergence into sexual self-awareness of the protagonists of twentieth-century lesbian and gay novels. The more Hyacinth learns, the more he becomes convinced that he must "cover . . . up" what he thinks of as "[h]is own character . . . as carefully as possible: . . . to go through life in a mask, in a borrowed mantle: . . . to be, every day and every hour, an actor" (109). His life, like those of Balzac's Vautrin and the protagonists of later lesbian and gay novels, becomes a matter of managing his secrets, of his own often inadvertent revelation of those secrets, and the responses of others to his masked and his revealed selves. As Hyacinth's story develops, the mysteries of his passionate and violent origins and ambiguous status are joined to a political secret: his commitment to revolutionary violence. The political secret he acquires can be seamlessly grafted onto his history.

All would-be readers of the secrets of the city, in James's novel, are in retreat from heterosexuality and the family. The princess has taken up London and revolution as an alternative to her husband and his relatives, whom she has most happily left behind in Italy. (The princess's husband comes to London repeatedly, over the course of the novel, to reclaim her, and she just as repeatedly rejects him.) Hyacinth, a product of heterosexual betrayal and violence, is raised by his mother's friend, an elderly seamstress—herself completely without relations of blood or marriage. Though he dallies with Millicent, a young woman of the city, and is dazzled by the princess, who takes him up in her quest for urban guides, Hyacinth's heterosexual impulses are weak. The novel's pivotal human connection, between the patroness of revolutions and the young revolutionary, never becomes a romance.

The novel's seekers after and embodiments of urban truths all find themselves in same-sex pairings. The princess's most developed personal enthusiasm is for another woman, a fellow aristocrat and fellow traveler in the urban depths, Lady Aurora, who is well aware that her own urban exploits are a means of escaping her family. The princess turns from Hyacinth—because he is both too much and not enough "of" the people—to Lady Aurora for guidance: "'I must get *you* to tell me the truth,' she murmured. 'I want so much to know London—the real London. It seems so difficult!'" (411; emphasis in original). Lady Aurora's response to the princess is wholehearted. "If I were a man," she explains to Hyacinth, "I should be in love with her" (429). Being instead a woman, she expresses her emotions through the hope that she and the princess "might work together" in the city (429). Hyacinth, meanwhile, is most closely attached to another political young man, Paul Muniment, who directs him toward his ultimately fatal commitment to the revolution.

Hyacinth himself embodies the practice of reading the city. James introduces him as a child standing in the street reading the first pages of stories in the papers posted in shop windows. He grows up to become a bookbinder. But, despite his having roamed "through the great city since he was an urchin" (106), Hyacinth, like the princess, sees London as illegible, a source of secrets. Also like the princess, he declares the secret of the city to be urban misery and its political emanations. "It is more strange than I can say," he tells her, confirming all of her assumptions. "Nothing of it appears above the surface; but there is an immense underworld, peopled with a thousand forms of revolutionary passion and devotion. . . . And on top of it all, society lives! People go and come, and buy and sell, and drink and dance, and make money and make love, and seem to know nothing . . . and iniquities flourish" while "[i]n silence, and darkness, but under the feet of each one of us, the revolution lives and works" (330).

Here is the conflict in James's novel, and in his city. Despite the knowledge Hyacinth shares with the princess, his origin suggests that the real secrets of the city are individual rather than collective. Moreover, his interactions with the princess, opening up to him a previously unknown world of aesthetic pleasures, only heighten his individuality, an individuality thereby allied with the aesthetic. But the requirements of both individuality and aesthetics are in conflict with the political demands, as Hyacinth understands them, of James's class-divided city. Hyacinth must choose between the cultural riches the Princess Casamassima has revealed to him and the revolutionary act to which Paul has led him to commit himself. He can pursue his individual interest or the cause of the suffering masses, but not both. The sexual potential of Hyacinth's opposite-sex relations is not fulfilled, but neither is the political potential of his same-sex connection. What James produces is a deadlock. Because the bind in which he finds himself is produced by the different values of his cross-sex and same-sex relations (individuality and aesthetics versus politics), Hyacinth's suicide—with which James ends his novel and his account of urban life—seems as much the result of a conflict between cross-sex and same-sex loyalties as between the different values those loyalties represent.

In *The Princess Casamassima,* James accedes to the developing cultural association of same-sex bonds and radical politics, an association that would soon be reinforced not only by Carpenter and Wilde but also, tellingly, by Havelock Ellis, also a socialist. Even after Wilde's trial, Ellis would praise his politics in *Sexual Inversion,* commending him for "essential judgement[s] on life and literature [that] were unusually sound and reasonable" and describing "The Soul of Man under Socialism" as "witness[ing] to his large and enlightened conception of life."[82]

James's ambivalence about politics might be read as an ambivalence about both same-sex loyalties and sexual classifications—that is, the loss of individuality threatened by homosexual legibility. Hyacinth's conflict is possible only in the city, where he can be taken up by both the princess and Paul. And it is the city, in the end, that supplies James with a means of finessing his novel's, if not Hyacinth's, conflicts between same-sex and opposite-sex relations and between politics and individuality/aesthetics. The most potent force in *The Princess Casamassima* is desire for London itself, that place which James describes as the "richest expression of the life of man" (480). Sexual desire is not so much suspended as displaced onto the plenitude of the city through which his characters, in many different pairings as well as alone, continually take the longest walks. And there sexual desires can merge with political and aesthetic desires. Even though James's socialists are pledged to bring down the city in its current form, the great city serves as the template for their utopia. Hyacinth's first political mentor, M. Poupin, a Frenchman exiled to London, "believed that the day was to come when all the nations of the earth would abolish their frontiers and armies and custom-houses, and embrace on both cheeks, and cover the globe with boulevards, radiating from Paris, where the human family would sit, in groups, at little tables, according to affinities, drinking coffee . . . and listening to the music of the spheres" (116).

IF FOR JAMES socialism and same-sex desires stood in opposition to individualism, for Wilde they led to it. Wilde's socialism was inseparable from his homosexuality. He flirted with concealing and displaying his desires even as he declared his politics. "Socialism itself will be of value because it will lead to Individualism," he proposed at the beginning of "The Soul of Man under Socialism," and at the end concluded, "The new Individualism is the new Hellenism."[83] In England during the second half of the nineteenth century, as Linda Dowling has explained, Victorian liberals promoted a "Hellenism" that represented "all of the dimensions of human experience denied under the Calvinist dispensation of religious fundamentalism or starved under the materialist regime of industrial modernity." At the same time, this Victorian Hellenism offered advocates of homosexuality such as Wilde's contemporary John Addington Symonds, as well as Wilde himself, a culturally celebrated discourse that contained within it "the possibility of legitimating male love."[84]

In contrast to James, socialism and homosexuality were joined in Wilde's thinking by individualism, and individualism brought his politics back again to urbanity. Individualism was the quality Georg Simmel would describe a decade later, in "The Metropolis and Mental Life," as most distinctive of the modern city. In Wilde's "Soul of Man under Socialism," as in the city Simmel anatomizes, the pursuit of individualism is inseparable from the problem of legibility.

In "The Soul of Man under Socialism," Wilde locates his socialism not in relation to an underworld of revolutionaries but to a city-based project of social amelioration. He establishes his analysis as antithetical to that of

the English settlement houses, where "educated men who live in the East
End" among London's poor work to alleviate their miseries (258). The resonance of Wilde's socialism with contemporary urban concerns does not
lie in a discussion of the conditions of modern cities and their possible
remedies (which he does not offer). Rather, that resonance lies in the ways
in which, unlike James, Wilde unites politics and individualism. He joins
the class-based urban analyses of Engels and his peers and followers to the
focus on the individual of Simmel's early urban sociology. James wrote
about the city, and the city of the nineteenth century, whereas Wilde wrote
about the condition of urbanity and the city as it would develop in the
twentieth century.

Wilde's advocacy of individualism had antecedents in the history of
socialism as well as in the history of the city. Forty years before "The Soul
of Man under Socialism," Engels wrote to Marx about the "egoism of the

MOB IN ST. JAMES'S-STREET, OPPOSITE THE NEW UNIVERSITY CLUB.

"Riots in the West End of London: Mob in St. James Street, Opposite the New
University Club," from the *Illustrated London News*, February 13, 1886. Engraving
by English school (19th century). Copyright Private Collection/The Bridgeman
Art Library.

heart" that was necessary for their political projects: "[W]e have to make a cause our own before we are prepared to work for it. . . . [A]part from any hope of material gain, we are communists out of egoism. . . . If we take the living individual being as the basis, the starting point for our image of . . . humanity . . . our egoism of the heart—will be the ground of our love of humanity and give it sound roots."[85] Wilde puts it differently. Imagining the reconstruction of the social order, he declares, "Under Socialism . . . [t]here will be no people living in fetid dens and fetid rags, and bringing up unhealthy, hunger-pinched children in the midst of impossible and absolutely repulsive surroundings" (258). What his socialism promises everyone, as an alternative to urban misery, is self-realization: "Individualism . . . is what through Socialism we are to attain" (267).

Wilde repudiates not only James's opposition of individualism and politics but also James's opposition of aesthetics and politics. In Wilde's socialism, art is to be one of the key means by which individuals achieve the self-realization he promises. "Art is individualism," Wilde declares (277). Like socialism and like the city, art is "a disturbing and disintegrating force," threatening to the "monotony of type, slavery of custom, tyranny of habit, and the reduction of men to the level of a machine" (273). Moreover, art joins socialism, through individualism, to the problem of legibility.

One of Wilde's chief claims is that socialism will lift the burden of false (because they are hostile) interpretations from works of art, from the individual artist, and ultimately from us all. Like Simmel's city, Wilde's socialism centers on the possibility of claiming a private life. For both Simmel and Wilde, the private life at issue is not a family life. Wilde advocates the abolition of private property, because, he claims without explanation, that abolition alone will make private life possible by leading to the abolition of marriage "in its present form" (266). "Socialism," Wilde declares, "annihilates family life" (266). The demise of marriage, which will "make the love of man and woman more wonderful, more beautiful, more ennobling," will also create "a form of freedom that will help the full development of personality" (266).

Even in the absence of private property, marriage, and the family, individuals will have to struggle to claim a properly private life, to control what is known about themselves—which is also, of course, a definitive experience of life in Simmel's modern city. The problem of "Public Opinion" remains: "[T]he public have an insatiable curiosity to know everything"

(277). "The private lives of men and women should not be told," Wilde pre-
sciently insists. "The public have nothing to do with them at all" (277).[86]
Not only individuals but also works of art, he argues, need to be defended
against the public. Through his defense of the privacy of fully realized individuals who will therefore be artists, his advocacy of socialism becomes a
critique of public responses to the art of the day.

The public's leading complaint about works of art it does not approve is
that they are "unintelligible," Wilde tells us. Public opinion, that is, demands
that both individuals and works of art be legible. The public complaint that
art and artists are unintelligible, according to Wilde, is routinely followed
by charges of "immorality," "exoticism," "unhealthiness," and "morbidity."
(These are all terms that would become fundamental to the vocabularies
of antiurban and antigay sentiment.) Wilde, however, attempts to reclaim
those hostile terms. First, he accuses public opinion of its own obfusca-
tions: "[O]ne of the results of the extraordinary tyranny of authority is
that words are absolutely distorted from their proper and simple meaning,
and are used to express the obverse of their right signification" (284). Next,
he offers his own exegesis of the public's criticisms of art: "When they say
a work is grossly unintelligible, they mean that this artist has said or made
a beautiful thing that is new; when they describe a work as immoral, they
mean that that artist has said or made a beautiful thing that is true" (273).
Finally, he goes on to daily life. "What is true about Art is true about Life,"
he explains. "A man is called affected nowadays, if he dresses as he likes
to dress ... [o]r ... selfish if he lives in the manner that seems to him most
suitable for the full realization of his own personality." On the contrary,
Wilde proposes, "[a]ffectation ... consists in dressing according to the
views of one's neighbour," and "[s]elfishness is not living as one wishes to
live, it is asking others to live as one wishes to live" (284).

For James, divorcing aesthetics from politics, the city could become a
text to be read; and the problem of knowledge that the great city offers, an
inexhaustible subject. Same-sex desires need not be endorsed. Politics, as
he understood it, need not be, ultimately, his concern. Wilde, joining aesthetics and politics, proposed that the process of reading—that is, legibility itself—might be political. Flirting as always with self-revelation, in "The
Soul of Man under Socialism" he advocates rebellion. "It is through disobedience that progress has been made, through disobedience and through
rebellion," he declares (260). At a historical moment when homosexuality

might be both crime and sin, his "rebellion" explicitly encompasses both: "A man . . . may break the law, and yet be fine . . . may commit a sin against society, and yet realize through that sin his true perfection" (266). Wilde identifies the individualism he advocates with love and with social difference: the new individual he imagines "will love [others] because they will be different" (264). He justifies the individualism he promises in terms of "joy" and "pleasure" as well as "nature": "Pleasure is Nature's test, her sign of approval" (288).

"[S]ecrets are always smaller than their manifestations," Wilde observed from prison.[87] On the basis of what he understood to be his own narrow secrets, he constructed a broad vision. In a gesture consistent with all of his flirtation with discovery, Wilde advocates transparency in art and life, as well as privacy. In "The Soul of Man under Socialism," he imagines a socialist future in which we "will know the meanings of words, and realize them in . . . free, beautiful lives" (285), in which we will be both better readers and free. In fact, Wilde imagines and even attempts to inhabit a space in which homosexuals might live legible yet still private lives—a possibility that would become available only gradually, in the city, over the next century.

JAMES AND WILDE both loved London. "[F]or the real London-lover," James wrote, "the mere immensity of the place is a large part of its savour. . . . [I]ts immeasurable circumference . . . gives him the sense of a social, an intellectual margin. There is a luxury in the knowledge that he may come and go without being noticed, even when his comings and goings have no nefarious end." Not only does London offer James as an individual a welcome "margin" of illegibility, it offers that margin to every possible group as well. "The great city spreads her mantle over innumerable races and creeds," he continues, "and I believe there is scarcely a known form of worship that has not some temple there . . . or any communion of men that has not some club or guild."[88] Wilde could be more succinct and, on occasion, more insistent on the literary. "Town life nourishes and perfects all the civilized elements in man," he observes. "Shakespeare wrote nothing but doggerel verse before he came to London, and never penned a line after he left."[89]

Like Balzac's, James's writings, especially *The Princess Casamassima*, have provided fodder for late twentieth-century commentators who have sought to conjure nineteenth-century great cities. Because James was committed to the problem of knowledge rather than the revelation of secrets—to the figure in the carpet but not its explication—his work was useful, a century later, to an architect and theorist like Aldo Rossi. Rossi could take James's metaphor to signify not only the necessity of reading the city but also the inevitable multiplicity and indeterminacy of the readings the city occasions. Wilde, drawing on his experience of desire for other men in the great cities of the nineteenth century, projected the homosexuality as well as the urbanity of the future.

Wilde was just becoming Wilde and Los Angeles just becoming Los Angeles in the 1880s, when his presence there was solicited. A century later, Los Angeles would be not only the quintessential city of images—a place where the great city dissolved into the interpretive condition of urbanity—but also the site of the world's first "gay" municipality, West Hollywood. In the 1880s, however, the nascent metropolis was not a substantial enough spot to command Wilde's attention. He did not accept the railroad magnates' offers.[90] Nevertheless, theirs seems, in retrospect, to have been a prescient invitation. If anyone could have hastened the process of turning Los Angeles into itself, it would have been Wilde.

PART II

Claiming Residence

GROUPES DE GRÉVISTES PARCOURANT LES RUES

"Strikers Demonstrating on the Streets of Chicago during the Pullman Riots of 1894," ca. 1895. Engraving by French school (19th century). Copyright Private Collection/Archives Charmet/The Bridgeman Art Library.

3

Perverts in Groups

In 1921, a young Chicago woman in Floyd Dell's novel *The Briary-Bush* explains, "We're all a little . . . queer" here. Moreover, she continues, Chicago "is beginning to realize that it needs us. Chicago wants to be a metropolis. And all the stock-yards in the world won't make a metropolis. Enough of us, given a free-hand—can. And Chicago knows it."[1] During the decades between Oscar Wilde's prosecution, in the 1890s, and the publication of Dell's novel, in the 1920s, Chicago became the "shock city" of the age, just as Manchester had been half a century before: the model, the magnet, and the prism for contemporary battles over urban development. Recovering with renewed energy from the great fire of 1871, the city surged ahead on a tide of immigration and industrialization unprecedented in U.S. history. By 1890, the metropolis on Lake Michigan was the second-largest city in the country. People came from the American Midwest, from the American South, and from eastern and southern Europe. The German and Irish immigrants of the 1850s and the Swedes who arrived in the 1860s were joined, in the 1890s, by Czechs, Poles, Italians, and Russian Jews.[2] The city became a manufacturing giant, described in Carl Sandburg's poem "Chicago" (1916) as the "Hog Butcher for the World, / Tool Maker, Stacker of Wheat" and, quintessentially, the "City of Big Shoulders." Sandburg's poem became the constantly repeated point of reference in subsequent portraits of the city.[3] But, not unlike Manchester a half century before, at its manufacturing heart Chicago was a chaos of unregulated neighborhood growth, densely crowded housing, unpaved streets, and uncollected garbage, all under a constant rain of soot. It was presided over by a city government and business elite jointly committed to minimal governance and devoted to supporting industry rather than addressing its infrastructural crises or providing services for its poorer citizens.

Chicago would be shaped and reshaped by broad demographic, social, and political shifts: continuing urbanization in western Europe and the United States; waves of immigration from eastern and southern Europe to other American cities, especially New York, as well as directly to midwestern farm towns; and the Great Migration of African Americans within the United States, "not only toward the North and the Central Midwest, but city-ward and to the great centers of industry," as Alain Locke described it. Locke characterized this migration, in *The New Negro* (1925), as "a mass movement toward the larger and the more democratic chance . . . a deliberate flight not only from countryside to city, but from medieval America to modern."[4] Economic upheavals in Chicago were matched by upheavals in labor nationwide. Lincoln Steffens's *The Shame of the Cities* (1904) signaled the spreading call for the reform of city government across the country. Changes in the status of women, especially in the United States, were marked by battles over suffrage, the increasing access of middle-class and elite women to higher education and professional employment, the struggles of women workers to unionize and improve conditions and wages, and the struggles of women workers and professional women for roles in urban life and development. Those changes would also have their impact on the city. So would the changing sexual attitudes that accompanied the rise of the "new woman," including the decline, in dominant cultural discourse from the 1890s to the 1920s, of assumptions about women's asexuality.

During these decades, the association of homosexuals with cities, both in Europe and in North America, became increasingly explicit as new accounts of homosexuality emerged into public view and as the "crisis" represented by the modern city became a settled conviction. In Germany, defenses of same-sex sexuality initiated in the mid-nineteenth century by Karl Ulrichs became campaigns for legal reform in the later decades of the century. The new sexual science pioneered by Richard von Krafft-Ebing in Germany and Havelock Ellis in England was centrally preoccupied with same-sex sexuality. At the same time, the developing field of sociology became the setting for an increasingly formalized study of the city, especially in the United States. Literary sources, earlier studies of prostitution, the new fields of anthropology and criminology, and the new medical discourses of psychology and psychiatry would all be treated as sources of evidence in the scientific study of sexuality (which would become known as sexology), and in the newly formalized study of the city. Perpetuating the assumption that the definitive urban experience was that of the socially marginalized, of the urban underworlds, this new study of the city often focused on sexualized communities. At the same time that same-sex desires were gradually made more public by gay advocates and in the discourse of the developing sexual and social sciences, freedom for explicit discussion of homosexuality in both literary and journalistic settings was also gradually increasing. (By the 1920s a "gay press" had emerged in Germany.)[5]

Nevertheless, from the 1890s through the 1920s, gay advocates, sexual scientists, and literary writers were all still subject to formal censorship, and their work was shaped by the prospect of censorship. From the initial publication of Krafft-Ebing's *Psychopathia Sexualis,* in 1886, through successive editions that appeared over the next twenty years, both German and translated versions rendered the supposedly salacious phrases in Latin. "A scientific title has been chosen, and technical terms are used throughout the book in order to exclude the lay reader," Krafft-Ebing explained in his preface to the first edition. These precautions were all part of his direction of the entire work toward a legitimate professional audience of doctors and lawyers whose job it might be to adjudicate the fortunes of the unfortunates he described.[6] Less cautiously presented, Havelock Ellis's *Sexual Inversion* was banned in Britain when it first appeared, in 1897. Ellis shifted the publication of the successive volumes of his *Studies in the Psychology of Sex* to the United States. But the often-updated editions of his work were still directed toward the authorities by his U.S. publishers, until copyright was transferred to a mainstream press, Random House, in the 1930s.[7]

The concerns of nineteenth-century debates about the urban persisted. The city's relation to history; the roles of vice and of capital, of nature and of artifice, in determining its forms; and the possibilities for legibility within its boundaries remained open questions. These concerns continued to be pursued through discussions of prostitution, art and artists, crime and criminals, and the disruption of gender norms and the family. But it was the idea of community, of a group existence, within urban life—as a lost hope, a threat, or a goal—that became central to representations of cities and of homosexuality in the first decades of the twentieth century, because homosexuality could be explained as a product of both the breakdown of (proper) social relations and the intensification of (improper) social relations, that is, the simultaneous failure and flourishing of "combination," in the city. All of these questions and concerns can be traced in *The Social Evil in Chicago*, one early official acknowledgment of homosexuality in that city.

THIS 1911 STUDY of prostitution by the city's Vice Commission focused on women, but it also offered a brief report on "sex perversion." The idea that there must be a particular, even causal connection between urbanity and homosexuality hovers behind the commission's repeated assertion that "the practice of sexual perversion . . . was . . . very prevalent and growing in Chicago."[8] Social as much as sexual relations were the subject of the Vice Commission's concern. Although its investigators acknowledged the presence of homosexual men in all classes, from "the very well-to-do" to "the lowest stratum of society," as well as the "much more occasional cases among women," they focused on the presence of "whole groups and colonies of these men who are sex perverts." They were particularly concerned about the absence of legibility among these groups of men, "who do not fall into the hands of the police on account of their practices, and who are not known in their true character to any extent by physicians because of the fact that their habits do not, as a rule, produce bodily disease" (296). The commission, in fact, foregrounded the possibility of community as if that were inseparable from (il)legibility, as if the difficulty of "know[ing]" these men were intrinsic to their formation of groups and colonies, or at least intrinsic to the threat to the social order that such groups and colonies represented.

The investigators were interested not so much in the relationships within these groups or colonies as in the groups' relationship to the city as a whole, and especially to those who might not "know" these men "in their true character." To protect the "innocent," the commission offered signs of homosexual difference. Consequently, even as they insisted that homosexuals were illegible, they wrote that "there is a large number of men . . . who mostly affect the carriage, mannerisms, and speech of women . . . lean[ing] to the fantastic in dress and other modes of expression" (297).

These groups of simultaneously illegible and legible sex perverts not only embody homosexuality as an interpretive problem of the sort to which Wilde obsessively returned, they also embody their investigators' anxiety about homosexuals as producers of an interpretively problematic culture of

Charles Demuth (1883–1935), *Vaudeville Musicians,* 1917. The Museum of
Modern Art, New York, New York, U.S.A. Digital image copyright
The Museum of Modern Art. Licensed by SCALA/Art Resource, New York.

the type Wilde came to represent.[9] Culture is, in fact, the medium of their threat. "They have a vocabulary and signs of recognition of their own," the Chicago report insists, but they produce literature, photographs, songs, and music-hall performances available to all: "The cult has produced some literature, much of which is uncomprehensible to one who cannot read between the lines," as well as "pernicious photographs." "[I]n one of the large music halls recently," the commission complained, "a much applauded act was that of a man who by facial expression and bodily contortion represented sex perversion, a most disgusting performance. It was evidently not understood by many of the audience, but others wildly applauded." Similarly, "one of the songs recently ruled off the stage by the police department was inoffensive to innocent ears, but was really written by a member of the cult, and replete with suggestiveness to those who understood the language of this group" (297). The authorities, ironically, must, and apparently did, understand "the language" of "the cult" in order to protect the "innocent."

The threat of a culture corrupted by such a cult cannot be separated from its members' sexual threat. If the uninitiated cannot tell the difference between culture produced by homosexuals and proper culture, they also apparently cannot tell the difference between homosexuals and proper women. If these Chicago men successfully "impersonate women," making themselves legible to the authorities as sex perverts, they are nevertheless still illegible to the innocent. "[T]heir disguise is so perfect, they are enabled to . . . solicit for drinks the same as prostitutes" in local saloons, the commissioners lament (297).[10] And if they are soliciting, they are surely not soliciting only for drinks.

The Social Evil in Chicago links the past and the future of urban study as well as urban study and homosexuality. The Chicago Vice Commission's report carried on the tradition of combining urban study and the study of sexuality, social margins and policing, that had been represented almost a century earlier by Alexandre Parent-Duchâtelet's *La Prostitution a Paris au XIXe siecle* (1836). Yet the commission included faculty members from the first generation of the University of Chicago School of Sociology, one of the first centers and, in the first half of the twentieth century, the most influential department of sociology in the United States, known for its self-conscious promotion of urban study as a modern scientific project.

Even the Vice Commission could be threatened with censorship. Despite its official connections, its commitment to social control, and what were seen by at least one commission member, the Chicago School's W. I. Thomas, as its "tame and conservative" conclusions, "[t]he post office declared the report obscene literature, and the members of the commission were technically liable to a penitentiary sentence."[11] None of the writers of *The Social Evil in Chicago* went to jail, but Thomas, who was known for his "advanced" views about sex, would in 1918 be caught up in a highly publicized heterosexual sex scandal and dismissed from his faculty position, in part as a result of a growing conservatism in the university administration traceable in the subsequent development of the Chicago School.[12]

For Chicago School sociologists, Chicago represented the "outstanding fact of modern society . . . the growth of great cities."[13] Nevertheless, they differed among themselves in the degree to which they saw the great city as a product of industrialization, as had earlier generations of urban observers. E. W. Burgess insisted that "[n]owhere else have the enormous changes which the machine industry has made in our social life registered themselves with such obviousness as in the cities," whereas Louis Wirth warned against "the danger of confusing urbanism with industrialism and modern capitalism." "The rise of cities in the modern world," Wirth claimed, "is undoubtedly not independent of the emergence of modern power-driven machine technology, mass production, and capitalistic enterprise; but different as the cities of earlier epochs may have been by virtue of their development in a preindustrial and precapitalistic order from the great cities of today, they were also cities."[14]

The Chicago School was particularly committed to "pursu[ing] with . . . vigor and profit . . . [a] constant search for systematic knowledge concerning human frailties—juvenile delinquency, vice, poverty, family life, and mental disorder." This was the underworld of the city—its subject, if not its methods—dating from a century before.[15] At the same time, Chicago sociologists can be seen as developing empirically the theoretical work of later nineteenth-century European social thinkers, especially Georg Simmel. Robert Park, who would become the dominating figure among the second generation of Chicago School scholars, in the 1920s, attended Simmel's lectures at Humboldt University in Berlin in 1899–1900 and later acknowledged, "It was from Simmel that I finally gained a point of view for the study of . . . society."[16] Wirth, Park's student and then colleague, would, in 1925, describe Simmel's "The Metropolis and Mental Life" as "[t]he most important single article on the city from the sociological standpoint."[17]

ALL IT TAKES to be "a little . . . queer" in Floyd Dell's Chicago of the 1920s is to not "want to make a million dollars."[18] But the thoroughgoing "queer" who prompts his novel's discussion of queers and the metropolis is Paul, a "shrill" fellow, a theatrical set designer who speaks with a "mincing accent" in an "unnatural and 'prissy' voice," and has "graceful . . . and beautifully manicured" hands he "wave[s] . . . helplessly." He lives in a room with "tattered Persian rugs" on the walls, "bronze figures" on the shelves, and books on the floor.[19] What is particularly telling, though, is that Paul sounds as if he has come to Chicago from London, although he is actually in flight from Arkansas.

Quite specific messages are conveyed about queers as well as about cities when anyone declares all of the citizens of a city a little queer or proposes that queers might "make a metropolis." If everyone in the city is a little queer, then some degree of queerness is necessary to urban life. If queers "make a metropolis," then queers produce urban life. If "Chicago wants to be a metropolis[, a]nd all the stock-yards in the world won't make a metropolis" but "[e]nough" queers can, then the metropolitan status that queers confer is understood as an alternative to the specificity of any particular place. Queers generalize the city, producing or at least signifying an urban space that exceeds local and even national limits. They signify great cities. Hence the London accent of Paul from Arkansas, living in Chicago.

We know that in practice the queer cultures developing in Chicago in the first half of the twentieth century were a crossroads at which many different experiences were explored. It was in Chicago, in 1924, that Henry Gerber, a young German immigrant, decided to pursue the model of gay rights organizing he had observed at home. With five peers he founded the earliest documented gay advocacy organization in the United States, the Society for Human Rights, which he chartered with the State of Illinois. The society even began a paper, *Friendship and Freedom*, "'to promote and protect the interests' of people who, because of 'mental and physical abnormalities,' were hindered in the 'pursuit of happiness,'" and to "combat . . . public prejudices" by conveying "scientific" facts, although it was able to publish only two issues before society members were arrested, prosecuted, and fined.[20]

By the early 1930s, European and American novels from the 1920s and 1930s with lesbian and gay themes—such as Andre Tellier's *Twilight Men*, Anna Elisabet Weirauch's *The Scorpion*, Blair Niles's *Strange Brother*, and

Radclyffe Hall's *The Well of Loneliness*—were circulating rapidly through Chicago communities. Although "upscale retailers . . . refused to carry them because of their suggestive titles," they were so popular that they were continuously on loan from the commercial lending libraries, both those run by downtown department stores and those in white working-class neighborhoods around the city.[21] A young working-class white man might read such a novel and, setting out to find the "fairies" it described, discover them in the center of town, congregating on the Michigan Avenue Bridge. He might then leave his family to establish a new gay life of cruising and office work with his new gay friends, in a different part of town from that in which he had grown up.[22]

By 1935, Alfred Finnie was holding his first drag balls, "in rented rooms or halls adjoining taverns and clubs on the city's predominantly black, poor South Side."[23] Welcoming black and white performers and spectators for the next four decades, Finnie's balls would become a local institution, "the city's most prominent . . . [drag] event," prominently reported in the city's black press. A young working-class black man might perform in drag for pay in clubs for straight audiences, as well as at these balls, and help to support his family through the Depression by doing so.[24]

But "public prejudices" about homosexuality, often scarcely distinguished from "scientific" facts, were more influential than the complexities of individual lives. Queers can generalize a city because they are relentlessly generalized. Even though Chicago School sociologists sent their students to gather information from the deviant groups of the city—and left archives that contemporary historians now mine—the faculty did not often write explicitly or at length about homosexuals. Nevertheless, those sociologists' accounts of city life drew on late nineteenth-century understandings of urbanity, on the social implications of same-sex desires, and on the conjunction of the two. They fostered the development of generalizations about queers and cities throughout the twentieth century.

MODERN NERVOUSNESS

In "The Metropolis and Mental Life" (1903), Georg Simmel had described modern cities as, quintessentially, sites of overstimulation—of an unprecedented "*intensification of nervous stimulation* which results from the swift and uninterrupted change of outer and inner stimuli." This "intensification of nervous stimulation" was the "psychological basis of the metropolitan type of individuality," Simmel argued, so it led to all of the other qualities of urban experience.[25] That belief would persist in the analyses of the Chicago School. Thus, Ernest Burgess, in his "The Growth of the City" (1925), assumed, in his account of the "mobility of city life," an "increase in the number and intensity of stimulations." Burgess went on to argue that the intensity of these stimulations "tends inevitably to confuse and to demoralize the person. . . . Where mobility is the greatest, and where in consequence primary controls break down completely, as in the zone of deterioration in the modern city, there develop areas of demoralization, of promiscuity, and of vice."[26] Sociologists' understanding of the city as a site of excessive nervous stimulation and their belief that such stimulation would produce sexual excess were widely shared.

That the modern city represented not just a material but also a mental crisis, and not just a mental but also a sexual crisis, and not just a sexual crisis but also sexual illness, became a popular truism in the 1880s. The "mental life," the psyche, that Simmel took as his subject was the focus of a late nineteenth-century convergence of understandings of the city and of sexuality, especially of homosexuality, as urban life was increasingly seen as affecting the psyche and homosexuality was seen as a psychic effect. "Nervousness" and its frequent consort "degeneration" were the two concepts that provided a framework, across academic specialties and in the popular press, for debating urbanity and homosexuality and the relationship between the two.

In his *American Nervousness* (1881), Dr. George Beard "coined the word 'neurasthenia' to describe the malady of the noisy and crowded streets," that is, the malady of urban life—or urban life as a malady.[27] The assumption that this "modern disorder" was "a new nervous disease which had developed specifically in America" was "of course erroneous," according to European doctors who nevertheless adopted and advanced Beard's diagnosis. They understood his confusion as to the American origin of this illness of urbanity to be logical, however, because of their own association of America with a "modern way of life" characterized by "unbridled lust" and "haste for gold and possessions."[28] This despite the fact that these very qualities had characterized Balzac's Paris half a century before.

Beard presented himself as the representative and popularizer of a medicine that encompassed, and self-consciously joined, psychology and sociology, mental and material conditions. His writings were internationally influential in the latter decades of the nineteenth century.[29] He was committed to explaining the modern, and thus the modern city, as a complete break with a past that was for him best represented by the ancient world. In contrast to Baudelaire's linking of Greece and the present in the interest of an ahistorical city, Beard illustrated the distinctiveness of modernity with discussions of "life in Ancient Athens and New York Contrasted—Greece *vs.* America."[30] "[M]odern civilization," he insisted, "is distinguished from the ancient by these five characteristics: steam-power, the periodical press, the telegraph, the sciences, and the mental activity of women"—that is, technical and industrial development, new forms of communication, and challenges to gender norms.[31] Moreover, according to Beard, in *American Nervousness* and in *Sexual Neurasthenia* (which was first published in 1880 and had gone through five editions by 1898), modern civilization and "sexual perversion" were clearly linked.

Queer costume ball in Berlin. Still from *Anders als die Anderen* [Different from the Others], Richard Oswald, director, 1919. Copyright Kino International, Kino/Photofest.

Some two decades before *The Social Evil in Chicago*, Beard warns in *Sexual Neurasthenia* that "cases of sexual perversion are very much more frequent than is supposed" and bemoans the "class of people" who often "do not consult scientific men" because they "do not wish to get well." "[T]here are . . . great numbers of such cases in the city of New York," he observes.[32] This concentration of "perverts" can be explained only in terms of his conceptions of sexuality and of the city. At base, those conceptions are inextricable. "[T]he hysterical, the sensitive, the nervous—those who live in-doors and use mind much and muscle very little," as do "the delicate, finely organized lads of our cities," are "tormented with sexual desire," he contends, in ways and to degrees never experienced by "[t]he strong, the phlegmatic, the healthy . . . who live out-doors and work with the muscle more than the mind."[33] He likewise distinguishes between those "like . . . the cases described by [gay advocate Karl] Ulrichs, whose sexual instincts are perverted"—that is, "those who inherit this tendency"—and "those who acquire this condition as one of the symptoms of sexual debility."[34] But these types cannot be absolutely separated, when the latter acquire their perversion as a result of the sexual excess that accompanies urban life. According to "the psychology of perversion," Beard explains, "excess in a normal way tends to make us hate the partners in our excess." As a result, "the sex" of those who indulge in sexual excess becomes "perverted; they hate the opposite sex, and love their own; men become women, and women men, in their tastes, conduct, character, feelings, and behavior." Moreover, "when the sexual debility becomes organized in families, then children may be born with this tendency," he warns, producing "the congenital cases of sexual perversion" he previously distinguished.[35] If the modern city is the site of sexual excess, the modern city can then be held responsible for both acquired and inherited forms of homosexuality, irrevocably corrupting families across generations.

Although Beard was extraordinarily influential, much of his work consisted of recycling a few basic suppositions. Krafft-Ebing, who had produced fourteen editions of *Psychopathia Sexualis* by 1903, gathered hundreds of case studies (from his own practice, from literary and other cultural sources, and from the flood of personal statements sent to him by individuals who saw their own experience reflected in his pages) and fit them into a multipart system of sexual and gender categorization. His analysis, nevertheless, begins with an emphasis on "the higher and more stringent demands which circumstances make upon the nervous system" in modern life. Like

Beard, he insists that "[e]xaggerated tension of the nervous system stimulates sexuality, leads the individual as well as the masses to excesses, and undermines the very foundations of society, and the morality and purity of family life." He concludes, with reference to "the mysteries of modern metropolitan life," that "[l]arge cities are hotbeds in which neuroses and low morality are bred."[36] He complains largely about the culture of the modern city, with its "horror plays, adultery comedies, trapeze artists, nerve-shattering music, loud color patterns, strong wines, cigars, liqueurs, gambling dens, [and] exciting press reports on crimes and accidents." To all of these—manifestations of "the commotion of the modern metropolis, marked by its pursuit of money and enjoyment and its unleashing of savage passions," and the consequent abandonment of "physical and mental rest, sleep, family life and bliss"—he opposed a rural world identified with the heterosexual family and "the peace and quiet of . . . rustic family life."[37] Lest there be any doubt of the necessity of his own work, he explained in *Psychopathia Sexualis* that "[c]areful observation among the ladies of large cities soon convinces one that homosexuality is by no means a rarity," and cites a February 1884 Berlin newspaper report of a "Woman-haters Ball," "to show something of the life and customs" of his homosexual subjects.[38]

Like Beard, Krafft-Ebing distinguished between inborn and what would later be called "situational" homosexuality, a distinction that again made plausible the view that homosexuality might be produced by cities. His terms were "perversity" and "perversion." Under one rubric, that of "immoral perversity," homosexual acts are the result of circumstance, lack an emotional element, and have no bearing on the actor's underlying character. Under the other rubric, "sickly perversion," the reverse is true: there is profound emotional investment, and the subject's homosexual acts are indicative of his or her character overall. The best indicator of perversion, in Krafft-Ebing's scheme, is gender nonconformity. So the city, long identified with gender confusion, might foster perversity, yet it is clearly identified with perversion as well.

Beard and Krafft-Ebing seem to have shared in the conviction that political radicalism, like sexual perversion, resulted from the mental strain of urban life. Beard was explicit about the role of new freedoms for women, as well as "civil and religious liberty" and even democracy itself, in producing American nervousness.[39] Seen as a political as well as sexual hotbed, the city, he believed, fosters the social circumstance that figures most

prominently in these complexes of social and political anxieties: the blurring or crossing of social divisions. Not only were gender divisions challenged: Krafft-Ebing deplores "effeminacy," explaining that "episodes of
moral decay always coincide with the progression of effeminacy, lewdness
and luxuriance of the nations."[40] Threats to class and racial distinctions
were also frequently invoked.[41] Beginning "in the 1880s . . . [among] medical authorities on both sides of the Atlantic Ocean," there arose the conviction that American cities were being overrun by homosexuals because
cities were such "remarkable sites of ruptured traditions, licentious consumption, and cultural 'miscegenation.'"[42] A Dr. Charles Hughes observed
with horror, in 1907, that "[m]ale negroes masquerading in women's garb
and carousing and dancing with white men is the latest St. Louis record of
neurotic and psychopathic sexual perversion." "These perverted creatures,"
he explained, "appear to be features of million-peopled cities."[43]

As the idea that homosexuals belonged in cities rapidly became a staple
of the new sexual science and of late nineteenth-century medical literature
more broadly, Havelock Ellis noted the apparently increased presence of
homosexuals in Britain and confidently quoted "a well-informed American
correspondent," who argued that "[t]he great prevalence of sexual inversion
in American cities is shown by the wide knowledge of its existence. Ninety-
nine normal men out of a hundred have been accosted on the streets by
inverts, or have among their acquaintances men who they know to be inverted."[44] (Rather than invoke nervousness, Ellis, as already noted, emphasizes the possibility of legibility in the city: "[T]he development of urban
life renders easier the exhibition and satisfaction of [homosexuality] as of
all other forms of perversion.")[45]

Even Freud, in the early 1900s, highlighted "the connection between the
'increasing nervousness' of the present day and modern civilized life." "The
physician is frequently given matter for thought," he notes, "by observing
that neurosis attacks precisely those whose forefathers, after living in simple,
healthy, country conditions, offshoots of rude but vigorous stocks, came to
the great cities where they were successful and were able in a short space of
time to raise their children to a high level of cultural attainment."[46] While
others thought that the problem of urban life was sexual excess or, even
more emphatically, the city's production of sexual excess, Freud thought
sexual disorders were created by the city's (that is, "civilization's") sup-
pression of sexuality, its "disturbance" of "the development of the sexual

impulse." But according to either assertion about urban life—that the city incites sexuality or that the city suppresses sexuality—the city produces sexual deviants, especially, Freud notes, homosexuals, "in whom . . . the sexual aim has been deflected from the opposite sex" by the demands of civilized life in the modern city.[47]

Beyond the medical and scientific literature—so often directed, after all, to specialists—such views of the city were most broadly disseminated in the work of cultural commentators such as Max Nordau, who was for three decades, beginning in the early 1880s, regarded by the "literate public in Germany, France, Austria, England, and Eastern Europe . . . as a preeminent journalist, literary critic, and iconoclast," according to historian George Mosse. His widely translated, best-selling critique of modern culture, *Degeneration* (1892), Mosse argues, was "one of the most important documents" of the last decades of the nineteenth century.[48] ("Degencration"

A modern romantic triangle. Still from *Pandora's Box,* Georg Pabst, director, 1929. Photofest.

was a concept that Krafft-Ebing, for example, drew on.) In *Degeneration*, Nordau cites the extraordinary nervous strain of city life in order to link "the rank growth of large towns" with "degeneracy"—homosexuality in particular—and with literature.[49] "Parallel with the growth of large towns," he explains, "is the increase in the number of degenerates of all kinds—criminals, lunatics, and the 'higher degenerates' . . . [who] natural[ly] . . . play an ever more prominent part in endeavoring to introduce an ever greater element of insanity into art and literature."[50] His key argument, Mosse writes, is that "degenerates are not always criminals, prostitutes, anarchists, and pronounced lunatics; they are often authors and artists."[51] Among those he names are Baudelaire, Zola, and Wilde. Wilde was also surely one of those he had in mind when he complained of "[t]he degenerates of to-day [who] chatter of Socialism."[52]

In "The Soul of Man under Socialism," Wilde describes attacks on individualism and social difference masquerading as critiques of works of art. Nordau illustrates Wilde's analysis by attacking homosexuality under the guise of literary criticism. The insanity introduced into literature by degenerate authors, he argues, can be traced to their commitment to homosexual subjects and, as Wilde had predicted, to unintelligibility. "Mere sensuality passes as commonplace, and only finds admission when disguised as something unnatural and degenerate," Nordau laments. "Books treating of relations between the sexes, with no matter how little reserve, seem too dully moral. Elegant titillation only begins where normal sexual relations leave off. . . . Vice looks to Sodom and Lesbos . . . for its embodiments." At the same time, "[t]he book that would be fashionable must, above all, be obscure. The intelligible is cheap goods for the million only."[53] For Nordau, as for the Chicago Vice Commission, the illegibility of homosexuals offers no protection to the social order but, rather, is intrinsic to their threat. And the purported unintelligibility of homosexual texts mirrors the threat of illegibility in the city itself.

La Ville invisible

From the last decade of the nineteenth century through the first three decades of the twentieth, a fundamental shift occurred: homosexuals themselves increasingly represented their lives in the city—whether they themselves were legibly gay, like the German sexual scientist and gay advocate

Magnus Hirschfeld and the English novelist Radclyffe Hall, or not, like the French novelist Marcel Proust and the American social activist Jane Addams. The different responses of each of these influential figures to the identification of homosexuality with the city—and consequently with modern nervousness—can be traced through their accounts of homosexuals' social experience.

Magnus Hirschfeld, who was both gay advocate and sexologist, offered the first study of urban homosexual life, *Berlins drittes Geschlecht* (Berlin's Third Sex), in 1905.[54] His work was part of a series of urban studies, "Documents of Life in the Big City," offered by his publisher. All of the books in the series were focused, in the pattern we have already seen unfold, on urban underworlds, "bohemians, dance halls, and the like," according to Mosse. Berlin is "presented as the home of all those living on the fringes or outside respectable society." Although Hirschfeld himself wanted "to testify to . . . [the] respectable behavior" of his subjects, he nevertheless listed "the clubs, restaurants, hotels, and bathhouses frequented by Berlin homosexuals."[55] He faced contradictory pressures: the publisher's interest in homosexuality as a part of the urban underworld (and, as such, a subject that would sell books), and his own commitment to homosexual rights, in particular to the repeal of paragraph 175 of the German penal code, and hence his interest in a broader picture of gay life.

Writing in 1925, the Chicago School's Louis Wirth listed Hirschfeld's "study of the homosexuals of Berlin as a sample of the grouping of population in the large city."[56] In late nineteenth- and early twentieth-century accounts of the city, that is, the group life of homosexuals was seen as representative of group life in the city. But understandings of the collective life of homosexuals were routinely subject not only to contradictory economic and political pressures but also to contradictory assumptions about the relations of gay persons to each other and to the heterosexual world. As the Chicago Vice Commission report indicates, there existed a broad cultural fear of the secretly powerful group life of homosexuals, a cultural fantasy, as Hirschfeld would later write, "that they form a large secret society among themselves, with all kinds of signs and defensive and offensive strategies."[57] Nevertheless, as he recorded in his masterwork, *The Homosexuality of Men and Women* (1913), there also existed broad public skepticism about whether homosexuals could form social groups at all, given the focus on sex in conventional conceptions of homosexuality. Some apparently wondered whether homosexuals could have any relationships among themselves other than the sexual. Hirschfeld found himself having to explain "that besides erotic needs, homosexuals have a natural desire for expression and understanding, which they find most easily with their own kind of people" (776).

Gay advocates such as Magnus Hirschfeld (often drawing on the work of the English socialist Edward Carpenter), likewise had to argue that homosexuals could contribute to "society" as a whole, that "the love from which no new beings at all are born is also productive" (726). They had to counter what was often presented as homosexuals' primary sin, their failure to reproduce, which was routinely interpreted as a failure (or refusal) to fulfill their social responsibilities. They also had to struggle against the different but equally threatening implications of each of the contradictory assumptions cited earlier: If homosexuals constituted a tightly bonded secret society, they might successfully conspire against social norms, on the one hand. On the other, if they were perpetually isolated, their inability to form connections among themselves could be seen as both prefiguring and producing a broader breakdown of social order, especially given the breakdown of gender norms and of the family that homosexuality was routinely taken to signal, and especially in the cities, where homosexuals were known to congregate.

THESE CONTRADICTORY IDEAS were so pervasive that they—and their social implications—can be traced in the homosexually affirmative work of scientist Hirschfeld and in the deeply ambivalent pages of his contemporary the novelist Marcel Proust. These men dealt very differently with their own homosexuality. Hirschfeld established himself as a public figure committed to scientific study and advocacy. Proust, by contrast, avoided any acknowledgment of his sexuality, although it was known in his circle. He even challenged to duels people who dared to hint at his deviance.[58] Yet, in a combination of reserve and display echoing Wilde's, he made homosexuality a fundamental subject of his writing. Moreover, Hirschfeld's *The Homosexuality of Men and Women* and Proust's *Remembrance of Things Past* (especially in the fourth volume, *Cities of the Plain*) converge in their reporting of the fundamental terms of gay and urban life in the late nineteenth and early twentieth centuries.

At the center of the contradictory ideas surrounding the possibility of perverts in groups is the figure of the homosexual as a social pariah who simultaneously embodies and acts out the disorder of urban life. "[T]he majority of homosexuals live in voluntary isolation," Hirschfeld insists (779). These are people shut out of intimate relations by the necessity of keeping their shameful desires secret—and/or the impossibility of fulfilling those desires—Proust proposes: they are "sons without a mother"; "friends without friendship"; and "lovers who are almost precluded from the possibility of . . . love . . . since they are enamored of precisely the type of man who has nothing feminine about him, who is not an invert and consequently cannot love them in return."[59]

This isolated figure stands at the center of discussions of same-sex activity in the city. Hirschfeld acknowledges the public settings of much homosexual sex—"to a much greater extent than normal people, [homosexuals] have to rely on places outside their homes for sexual gratification"—and goes on to explain this public presence in terms of stigma. "[I]n contrast to heterosexuals," he argues, "Urnings want to keep their residences as devoid as possible of sexual activity, . . . to preserve the secret of their names, and . . . to keep themselves free from the suspicion of neighbors with regard to their orientation" (794). While documenting bathhouses and cafés as sites for sexual activity, he focuses on the street. "[I]t is the street," he explains, "where homosexuals make contacts for fleeting relationships (some of which also often develop into lasting ones). This is the place where people can feel relatively safe, and . . . it is universally accessible" (759). The homosexual city has its own distinct geography: "Just as in normal intercourse, in homosexual relations there are also certain streets and areas of the city that are chosen as gathering spots. There are Urnings who own a series of city maps on which the streets preferred by homosexuals are marked with blue or red lines" (798). It is also an implicitly masculine city. The relative safety and universal accessibility of the streets he describes are more routinely available to men, particularly middle- and upper-class white men. The city allows for the meeting of otherwise isolated homosexuals in bathhouses and cafés and on the streets, and they in turn give the city their own order, represented by the streets they favor and the alternative maps they devise.

But as Proust and Hirschfeld pursue the subject of homosexuals' social relations to each other, contradictions begin to emerge in accounts that emphasize simultaneously homosexuals' disinterest in joining forces and the wide range and intensity of the groups they construct. Hirschfeld insists that, "apart from small assemblies, [homosexuals] almost completely lack

Proust's model dandy. Giovanni Boldini (1845–1931), *The Count Robert de Montesquieu,* 1897. Musée d'Orsay, Paris, France. Erich Lessing/Art Resource, New York.

the spirit of solidarity. . . . [T]here is hardly any other class of people which [has] understood to such a small degree how to organize themselves to protect their common rights and interests" (777). He cites a range of causes for such isolation, including fear of guilt by association, shame, self-hatred manifested as antipathy toward other members of the group, and competitiveness. Proust concurs emphatically, describing homosexuals as "shunning one another" and as "excluded even . . . from the sympathy—at times from the society—of their fellows, in whom they inspire only disgust at seeing themselves as they are" (638–39).

Yet at the same time, Hirschfeld describes a plethora of groups, gatherings, and gathering places, both private and public—clubs, lodges, associations, bars, teas, restaurants, bathhouses, balls, theater balconies, private socials, dances, musical evenings, "picnics, community outings and summer festivals"—where homosexuals converge (780). In fact, he observes, "[e]ven if the majority of homosexuals lives in voluntary isolation, and nowhere is as visible as populous urban centers, and even if homosexuals exclusively devote themselves to one single person, nevertheless, the number of those who look for social contact and expression with other homosexual people is really quite large" (779). The urban centers he cites include Berlin, "Dusseldorf, Munich, Hamburg, and other German cities, . . . Amsterdam, London, Paris, Rome, [and] Constantinople" (780).

Proust is even more lyrical on the subject of the group life of homosexuals than he is on the subject of their misery and isolation. He describes his miserable isolates, who a moment earlier he explained shunned one another, not only "finding a relief in frequenting the society of their kind, and even some support in their existence . . . [but also] forming a freemasonry far more extensive, more effective and less suspected than that of the Lodges, for it rests upon an identity of tastes, needs, habits, dangers, apprenticeship, knowledge, traffic, [and] vocabulary" (639). Not only are the bonds within this group more intense than those of the normal world, he insists, but they also cannot be evaded: "[E]ven members who do not wish to know one another recognise one another immediately by natural or conventional, involuntary or deliberate signs which indicate one of his kind to the beggar in the person of the nobleman whose carriage door he is shutting, to the father in the person of his daughter's suitor, to the man who has sought healing, absolution or legal defence in the doctor, the priest or the barrister to whom he has had recourse" (639–40). Thus, in the opening of *Cities of the Plain,* Proust confirms the dominant cultural fantasy of a secret but powerful homosexual underworld.

The contradiction between homosexual isolation and intensive group life that is laid out in Hirschfeld's and Proust's very different works sustains itself. It is homosexuals' status as pariahs, the stigma they bear, that not only produces their isolation but also secures their connections, as when Proust explains that they are "all of them obliged to protect their own secret but sharing with the others a secret which the rest of humanity does not suspect" (640). But this contradiction is also sustained by "the city." It is the "populous urban centers" themselves that mediate between the isolation Proust and Hirschfeld (and others) emphasize and the group life that they (and others) describe: the city where "more practical, busier men" do not merely keep their secret or reveal it but instead "have formed two societies of which the second is composed exclusively of persons similar to themselves" (640–41).

In the model of the city developing from Balzac to Simmel, the urban person must work to control his or her legibility. Proust's Charlus embodies the problem of legibility. He represents all of those "acquaintance[s] whom for long years," the narrator explains, are "never suspected until the day when, upon the smooth surface of an individual indistinguishable from everyone else, there suddenly appear, traced in an ink hitherto invisible, the characters that compose the word dear to the ancient Greeks" (636). Not only is the homosexual body a page, in Proust's account, but the homosexual person is a sentence. "Now [that] the abstraction had become materialised, [and] the creature at last discerned had lost its power of remaining invisible," he explains, "everything that hitherto had seemed . . . incoherent, became intelligible, appeared self-evident, just as a sentence which presents no meaning so long as it remains broken up in letters arranged at random expresses, if these letters be rearranged in the proper order, a thought which one can never afterwards forget" (637). This is a particularly powerful sentence: once read, never forgotten.

Proust's other representative homosexuals—already representative city dwellers from Balzac to Simmel—are those familiar figures, young men from the provinces. Proust's young men "speedily discover" *la ville invisible,* "other young men who are drawn to them by the same special inclination . . . [and] meet . . . at gatherings to which no outsider is admitted" (641). Their "reserve" is such that they can even meet as a group in public, in such a quintessentially urban space as a café: "No one . . . in the café where they have their table knows what the gathering is, whether it is that of an angling club, of an editorial staff . . . so correct is their attire, so cold and reserved their manner" (641). Proust even goes so far as to explain that different homosexuals negotiate the line between reserve and display in different ways, comparing their groups to political or cultural organizations of different degrees of radicalism or aesthetic purity: "the 'Union of the Left' . . . [or] the 'Socialist Federation' . . . some Mendelssohnian musical club . . . [or] the Schola Cantorum." "[O]n certain evenings, at another table," then, at the same café where the most reserved gather discreetly, there may be "extremists who allow a bracelet to slip down from beneath a cuff, or sometimes a necklace to gleam in the gap of a collar," and who engage in "persistent stares . . . cooings . . . laughter . . . [and] mutual caresses," to signify their difference from those around them (641).

Where those appalled by the possibility of same-sex sexuality in the nineteenth century cast lesbians as victims of capital, lesbians and gay men would increasingly, over the course of the twentieth century, be described as the children of capital, as capital's products or beneficiaries. Gold was fundamental to Balzac's urban pleasures. Simmel proposed that "[i]ndividual freedom and the expansion of commercial enterprise are interdependent," and that freedom and commerce both—the functioning of the modern city—depend on the supposed neutrality, the impersonality, of purely financial exchanges (which foster fractured interactions, and so both reserve and display).[60] Proust's young men in groups can negotiate reserve and display in the city, even in the most public spaces, in part because of this rule of money, so frequently denounced as a quality of urban life in conjunction with critiques of sexual excess. Even the group displaying themselves in the café are "served with . . . civility" despite the "indignation" of their "waiter who . . . would have the greatest pleasure in summoning the police did he not find profit in pocketing their gratuities" (642). Proust describes the city at its most commercial as essential to the most isolated homosexuals, who "benefit from those facilities by which commerce and big business have transformed the lives of individuals by bringing within their reach commodities hitherto too costly to acquire and indeed hard to find." In the city ruled by money, even the pariahs—even the immediately legible—have access to "a plethora" of opportunities that "by themselves they had never succeeded in discovering among the densest crowds" (643).

Dominant understandings of urban life sustained not only contradictory conceptions of homosexuals' relations to one another; the city also provided a framework for similarly contradictory accounts of homosexuals' roles in the larger, heterosexual social world. Proust and Hirschfeld both insist on the ubiquity of homosexuals. Proust describes the "adherents" of homosexuality as "everywhere, among the people, in the army, in the church, in prison, on the throne; living . . . in an affectionate and perilous intimacy with the men of the other race," that is, heterosexuals (640). In fact, Proust describes his homosexuals—again paradoxically—as pursuing this perilous intimacy, "seeking out those who are most directly their opposite, who do not want their company, forgiving their rebuffs, enraptured by their condescension" (638–39). Hirschfeld similarly explains that the problem "of how to find a place for homosexuals in society" was "resolved long ago." He asks rhetorically, "[I]n Berlin, just show me a friend of the arts who has not taken joy in the art of a [homosexual] dramatist" or singer (731). He then suggests that his presumably heterosexual and elite readers think again about their cooks, dressmakers, and flower merchants, as well

Paris by night. Brassaï (Gyula Halász, 1899–1984), *Un costume pour deux, au bal des invertis du "Magic-City,"* ca. 1931. Private Collection. Copyright Estate Brassaï–RMN, Réunion des Musées Nationaux/Art Resource, New York.

as the writers, heroes, and thinkers they admire; their "best friend[s] . . . sisters and brothers"; and, finally, their children (731). But the ubiquity and intimacy Proust and Hirschfeld claim are both predicated on the illegibility of homosexuals, and so on the enabling conditions of city life.

Although homosexuals might be ubiquitous, they do not obey the rules of the dominant heterosexual world—not just sexually, but also in their propensity for crossing social boundaries and linking otherwise divided groups. As Proust explains, "[T]he ambassador is a bosom friend of the felon, the prince . . . on leaving the duchess's party goes off to confer with the ruffian" (640). According to Hirschfeld, "[S]ame-sex love balances out many differences between classes, castes, races, and national origins"; defeats age barriers, "build[ing] a bridge between . . . younger and older people— the adult woman and the maturing girl, the adolescent boy and the mature man"; and even allows homosexuals to help to bring men and women together (728). If homosexuals are seen as people in whom masculine and feminine are mixed, as in English gay advocate Edward Carpenter's model of the "intermediate sex," Hirschfeld can argue that "their nature enables them . . . to give equal understanding to both sexes; it predestines them to . . . ease the battle that from time immemorial has existed between both sexes" (728). Such dissolution of proper social divisions was also, as we have seen, thought to be an effect of the modern city itself.

Contrary to conventional understandings that such disruptions and the forging of links between otherwise divided social sorts were a threat, Hirschfeld sees them as a valuable contribution by homosexuals to the culture. That contribution is augmented, in his view, by the many homosexuals who contribute, through political and cultural institutions, to the nonsexual aspects of public life that flourish in cities. Hirschfeld insists that "by nature homosexuals are eminent[ly] social beings, striving hard to grow and to be productive while making efforts to participate in the advancement and development of the whole by working together with others" (725).

Hirschfeld explains the particularly intense engagement of homosexuals in public life as resulting from the absence of family ties and, consequently, domestic obligations in their lives. In this argument he draws on and reinforces Carpenter's analyses in *The Intermediate Sex*. This absence of family and domestic life could be viewed either as a source of time and energy to devote to cultural and political tasks, or as a lack to be compensated for by engagement in cultural and political tasks. Carpenter had declared, "It is difficult to believe that anything can supply the force and liberate the ener-gies required for social and mental activities of the most necessary kind so well as a comrade-union which yet leaves the two lovers free from the responsibilities and impediments of family life."[61] In contrast, Hirschfeld proposes an "unconscious striving to create an equivalent to the family life they lack" as the motivating force for queer contributions to public life, despite his previous insistence on homosexuals' status as brothers, sis-ters, and children (737). (The possibility of homosexuals' having significant connections within their own subculture—groups of their own that might command their time and energy or offer an equivalent to family ties—is elided in such arguments.) The subject of homosexuals in public life brings us back, then, to the figure of the homosexual as simultaneously—and in-extricably—a social outcast and a weaver of social webs; but the groups they are now supporting are not their own.

Such arguments mark a mutually reinforcing convergence between a vision of urban life as lacking family or domestic ties and a similar vision of homosexual life, a vision of urban life focused on the public and a vision of homosexual life with the same focus. This convergence would help to cement such visions of homosexual and city life throughout the twentieth century.

ASSUMPTIONS ABOUT THE gender of the homosexuals under discussion are threaded through all accounts of homosexuals on city streets. Assumptions about gender norms, as well as homosexuals' violations of those norms—that male homosexuals are fundamentally feminine and lesbians fundamen-tally masculine—are similarly threaded through the broader discussion of homosexuals in public life. Gay men are routinely assigned an implicitly feminine "culture" as their arena of social engagement, and lesbians a not-always-implicitly-masculine politics. Hirschfeld makes these conjunctions of sexuality, gender, and social service explicit. "A special endowment of talents in literature and art may . . . be the reason for joining relevant clubs" on the part of gay men, he explains. Meanwhile, although "male homosex-uals participate less in political life than the normal man . . . virile [lesbians] are . . . fully and completely equal to any man in political club life" (737). Similar assertions can be found from the work of Edward Carpenter to the new field of psychoanalysis that was being developed by Sigmund Freud in the late nineteenth century and the early decades of the twentieth.

Freud described homosexuals' commitment to "the social" as a truism: "It is well known that a good number of homosexual persons are distinguished by a special development of the social instincts and by a devotion to the interests of the community."[62] When talking about men, he proposes that "[t]he constitution of those suffering from inversion—the homosexuals—is indeed often distinguished by the sexual impulse lending itself to 'cultural' sublimation in a special degree."[63] But when Freud identifies lesbians with the social, he emphasizes their supposed masculinity and politics. In his "Psychogenesis of a Case of Homosexuality in a Woman" (1920), he even offers political beliefs as evidence that his patient had "a strongly marked 'masculinity complex,'" that she was "not at all prepared to be second to her slightly older brother," and that "[s]he was in fact a feminist, she felt it unjust that girls should not enjoy the same freedom as boys, and rebelled against the lot of women in general."[64]

When gay men are identified with cultural pursuits and lesbians with the political, especially with the women's movement, by advocates such as Carpenter and Hirschfeld, both the cultural and the political are seen as significant avenues for social contribution. Gay men and lesbians are commended as public actors, and their work is seen as a source of social strength and as an argument for the social acceptance of same-sex desires. But for heterosexual commentators of the period, from Ellis to Freud, lesbians were understood very differently in social contexts. The contributions of lesbians to public life were seen as intrinsically vexed, because of the masculinity that these men ascribed to lesbians interested in political engagement, whether in the women's movement or for other causes. Such potentially divergent views of gay men and lesbians' engagement in public life echoes and reinforces the different relationship of gay men and lesbians to the public spaces of the city, including city streets.

In practice, of course, gay men acted in political as well as cultural arenas, as the works of Carpenter and Hirschfeld demonstrate. Likewise, lesbians pursued political causes (including the cause of the city itself) and also produced culture (with the city as a crucial setting), as the very public careers of Jane Addams and Radclyffe Hall illustrate. For both Addams and Hall, as I will discuss in the following chapters, as for their male contemporaries, questions about the roles of homosexuals in domestic and in public life were key. Their understandings of the meaning of group life in the city were pivotal to both women's responses to those questions.

"Jane Addams holding a book," 1913. Photograph by American photographer (20th century). Copyright Schlesinger Library, Radcliffe Institute, Harvard University/The Bridgeman Art Library.

4

City of Women

THE SOCIAL CLAIM AND THE INDUSTRIAL CITY

American cities should have been sites of particular anxiety on the part of Americans and others about the psychic and social consequences of modern urban life. After all, one American city, Boston, had given its name to the long-term partnerships of women associated with the politics—women's education, woman suffrage, and urban reform—as well as the literature through which educated white women in particular were attempting to gain a role in public life. "Boston marriages" were identified with a cultural "type" as much as with the realities of the lives of the intellectual and reforming women of New England. They exemplified the conjunction of lesbianism and politics emphasized by gay advocates and sexual scientists alike.[1]

The preeminent literary representation of this fusion of a city, female partnership, and politics is Henry James's *The Bostonians* (1886). James's protagonist, the educated and wealthy Back Bay "spinster" Olive Chancellor, pursues her passions for other women through the political causes of urban poverty and woman suffrage. Taken with "the romance of the people," Olive has "an immense desire to know intimately some *very* poor girl."[2] It is therefore "her dream to establish" an "evening club for her fatigued, underpaid sisters" (62). She actually takes up, though, with Verena Tarrant. Miss Tarrant is not a "pale shop-maiden" (62), though she is neither wealthy nor noticeably educated; her ambiguous class status originates in a family history mingling abolition, spiritualism, and fraud. Olive hopes to further the cause of woman suffrage by uniting her own knowledge and financial

111

resources with Verena's beauty and oratorical skills—to support, live, and work with the younger woman as she becomes a preeminently effective speaker for women's political rights.

James proposed to his publisher that "[t]he relation of the two girls should be a study of one of those friendships between women which are so common in New England. The whole thing as local, as American, as possible, as full of Boston."[3] The "relation" of Olive and Verena is identified as a "friendship," the sexual implications of "marriage" being neutralized by the political valence of "Boston." The city the novel represents, a jumble of intellectual and commercial values, of past reform commitments and present publicity hounds, stands in contrast to a more purely commercial New York. But, as we have seen, cities did not usually neutralize sexual suspicions, especially not sexual suspicions of women.

That Olive's passions are sexual as well as political is manifest in her repeated struggles against heterosexual men and their claims on the women who embody her causes. The poor girls she engages in conversation "always ended by being odiously mixed up with Charlie . . . a young man in a white overcoat and a paper collar . . . [for whom] in the last analysis . . . they. . . . cared more . . . than about the ballot"—or about Olive (62). James's entire novel is organized around these alternatives writ large in the contest between Olive and her cousin Basil Ransom over whether Verena should stay with her "friend" and devote herself to the political advance of women or marry and be summarily removed from public life altogether.

JAMES'S LINKING OF women's relationships to their engagement in public life and to the city, and his opposing of the whole to a heterosexual fulfillment combining marriage, family, and private life, had already, as we have seen, become a common cultural pattern by the 1880s. The cause of woman suffrage, so dear to his heroines, was in practice only one of the ways through which American women sought to enter public life. Olive's interest in poor young women underscores another way in which women in Boston marriages could work not only in public but in the city, and not only work in the city but work on the structure and politics of the city: through the settlement house.

Oscar Wilde invoked the settlement house movement when he distanced himself from the "educated men who live in the East End," at the beginning of "The Soul of Man under Socialism."[4] The premise of this movement, which began in London in the 1880s with Toynbee Hall, was that university-educated, upper-class men and women should reside in the industrial centers of great cities. They were to unite the nation by building new cross-class communities, while studying and working to ameliorate local conditions in the process. The significant differences between middle-class men's and women's education and access to public life in Britain and the United States shaped the different histories of the settlement movement for women and men in the great cities of each country, making a mode of urban political engagement that was peripheral for Wilde but crucial to certain contemporary American women.

The focus on building community in British settlements was based on establishing individual relationships across class lines, between "settlers" and the workers they settled among. This fantasy clearly draws on Edward Carpenter's model of social change advanced by cross-class bonds between men.[5] It was supported in part by the fact that much of the still-rapidly-growing urban population in England was native-born. But middle-class values remained the premise and their dispersal the goal of these projects. Although women were involved, in practice settlement houses in Britain became paths for elite young men into existing civil service jobs or the ministry.[6]

Conditions in the United States were different in two significant respects. Because urban growth in the United States in the later nineteenth century was propelled by foreign as much as internal immigration, American cities were a welter of different national as well as class groupings. This made the prospect of social salvation through personal bonds seem remote to middle- and upper-class native-born settlers. At the same time, there were many more newly educated middle-class women in the United States than in Britain, where the battles over women's education were more bitter and prolonged. Yet in the United States there was less space for such women to put their education to use in existing socialist movements. With personal relationships between settlers and their subjects less a focus, as well as a pool of women eager to invest in public causes, settlement houses in the United States were, much more than in Britain, dominated by women. Women settlement house workers fought for improved city services and for state legislation to correct the grim conditions they identified, as well as to create city and state structures to monitor such services and the application of the new legislation. They then struggled to gain access to positions in those civic structures. This was the generation of women who invented "social work."

The settlement movement expanded in the United States with extraordinary rapidity. According to historian Kathryn Kish Sklar, "In Chicago and other cities in the 1890s social settlements stepped into the breach created by rapid urbanization on the one hand and traditions of limited government on the other. Settlements grew in number from six in 1891 to seventy-four in 1897, over one hundred in 1900, and four hundred by 1910."[7] They included houses affiliated with Protestant religious groups and with colleges and universities, some single-sex and others coed. But "[b]y 1905 American women settlers outnumbered men by about four to one. Between 1886 and 1911 more than three-fourths of American settlement heads were women."[8] Settlement houses in the United States became homosocial sites for the exploration of relationships between middle-class women, Sklar concludes, "free[ing] women to love other women, as sisters, as comrades, and as sexual partners," as well as a means for newly educated late nineteenth-century women to influence the shape of urban development.[9]

Among the founders of Boston's Denison House in the 1890s, for example, were "several" women who "eventually engaged in Boston marriages, including Vida Scudder and Florence Converse, and Katherine Coman and Katherine Lee Bates."[10] Converse wrote about such couples in her 1897 novel *Diana Victrix*. Fulfilling Olive Chancellor's fantasy, she describes a woman rejecting a male suitor for her female friend and her "work" simultaneously. "[T]he woman and I understand each other, sympathize with each other, are necessary to each other," the character explains to her would-be husband. "I am not domestic the way some women are. I shouldn't like to keep house and sew. . . . It would bore me. I should hate it! Sylvia and I share the responsibility here, and the maid works faithfully. There are only a few rooms. We have time for our real work, but a wife wouldn't have. And, oh, I couldn't be just a wife."[11]

The allusion of Converse's character to the "maid" makes the class basis of such relationships clear. Cross-class relationships seem to have been the exception in American settlement houses, just as they were the exception among Boston marriages. In one cross-class female relationship in the settlement movement, that of Frances Kellor and Mary Dreier, together from 1904 to 1952, both women were socially mobile. Kellor was a working-class woman who gained a law degree from Cornell and then studied sociology at the University of Chicago, and Dreier was a New York "socialite with a social conscience."[12] Both ended up working in first private and then public social service agencies at the city, state, and national levels. Both violated class expectations. Through an education sponsored in part by a series of women mentors and possibly lovers, Kellor worked herself into the middle class, whereas Dreier took on a career of social engagement rare for a woman of her position.

The settlement movement in the United States freed educated middle-class and upper-class women from domestic expectations. It enabled both same-sex partnerships and engagement with the public world, the possibility of collective living and living in the city, through a focus on the government of the city. The most influential of the settlements and the leaders of the U.S. movement were to be found in Chicago at Jane Addams's Hull-House.

HER "OLD-TIME school friend," Ellen Gates Starr, was the first person to whom, in April 1888, Jane Addams confided her plan for the founding of an American settlement house in Chicago, after visiting Toynbee Hall in London: "[T]o rent a house in a part of the city where many primitive and actual needs are found, in which young women who had been given over too exclusively to study, might restore a balance of activity along traditional lines and learn of life from life itself." It was, moreover, "the comfort of Miss Starr's companionship, the vigor and enthusiasm which she brought to bear on it, [that] told both in the growth of the plan and upon the sense of its validity," she recorded in *Twenty Years at Hull-House* (1910).[13] Although she was willing, in public and in retrospect, to use the language of tradition, Addams had, in fact, no interest in restoring "a balance of activity along [the] traditional lines" of marriage and motherhood. In private, in January 1889, Addams wrote to Starr, "Let's love each other through thick and thin and work out a salvation."[14] Here, she expressed the merger of love and work that actually characterized their project, the radical possibilities of settlement house life for American women, and her future relation to the city. The two young women—with Miss Mary Keyser to do housework, Addams notes carefully in retrospect—would, in September of that year, be the first residents of Chicago's Hull-House settlement.

Starr provided initial support, but it would be Mary Rozet Smith who would become Addams's lifelong companion. She entered Addams's life

Norah Hamilton (1873–1945), "Polk St., Opposite Hull-House," from *Twenty Years at Hull-House, with Autobiographical Notes,* by Jane Addams (New York: Macmillan, 1910).

when she appeared at the settlement house in its first year as another young woman seeking a goal. After Addams had expended much of her own inheritance, Smith used her private fortune to help fund the venture, donated a building, and became a Hull-House trustee.[15] Smith's financial support helped to enable Addams's and Hull-House's independence from other political, religious, and institutional interests in their city, and so enabled their leading roles in the movement nationally and internationally.[16]

Jane Addams lived the model life of lesbian social and political engagement that came to be described with praise by Carpenter and Hirschfeld and with suspicion by Ellis and Freud. For Addams, the path to "individual salvation" was through "social . . . salvation" (87). She described herself as having saved herself from a life of aimlessness and isolation by responding to the "social claim" of "the industrial city." In doing so, she used both the realities of contemporary urban life and contemporary cultural understandings of the modern city as a basis for negotiating her own emotional and work lives. In order to free herself (and the women who joined her) from the demands of family life, she invoked a social claim that would legitimate their engagement in the public realm. If this social claim was to justify their public life, the city from which it arose had to be "industrial"— in a dire state, in crisis, in desperate need of intervention. The industrial city, with its grim conditions and the fears of social upheaval that those grim conditions evoked in the members of her own class, contained Addams's salvation. This salvation had two dimensions: socially acceptable access to love and work, and socially acceptable access to combination with others to work for broad social purposes. Through "the city," she was able to exchange family life for collective life.

If Addams's city had to be industrial, the industrial areas of that city had particularly to be central to her vision of the city. Addams's focus on industrialization is expressed in her conception of the city as a place of uncontrolled growth. She presents Chicago as distinct among American cities in the rate of its expansion and, in the 1890s following the Haymarket riots, in the vehemence of its public debate about urban conditions and remedies. "Chicago has been foremost in the effort to connect the unregulated overgrowth of the huge centers of population, with the astonishingly rapid development of industrial enterprises," she proposes, "quite as Chicago was foremost to carry on the preliminary discussion through which a basis was laid for like-mindedness and the coördination of divers wills" (129–30). But

she also offers Chicago as representative of "American cities," cities "awakening to self-consciousness, [and] . . . slowly perceiv[ing] the civic significance of . . . industrial conditions" (129).[17] If Chicago contains the potential
for "like-mindedness and the coördination of divers wills," so then might
all those other American cities.

Although Addams needed her city grimly industrial, not merely "nervous" or disordered, she argued for the promise of that city's collective life,
a life she was, after all, herself pursuing. That promise was manifest most
concretely in the cause of labor. "The discovery of the power to combine
was the distinguishing discovery of our time," she declares.[18] The manufacturers were combining and, therefore, so must the workers. She insisted
that she was not "technically" a socialist because she could not adopt "the
creed," yet Hull-House provided space and other support for labor organizing, including that by socialists. Hull-House residents fought for legislation to protect workers, and Addams affirmed the "socialism" that Wilde,
Carpenter, and others drew from Whitman, a recognition "that no personal
comfort nor individual development can compensate a man for the misery
of his neighbors . . . [and] that social arrangements can be transformed
through man's conscious and deliberate effort" (124).

The labor movement in the cities, she argued, was at the center of American life. Because the classes were interdependent, it was "a general social
movement concerning all members of society and not merely a class struggle" (142). The social interactions of the settlement house setting were to
demonstrate class interdependence: "Hull-House was soberly opened on
the theory that the dependence of classes on each other is reciprocal; and
that as the social relation is essentially a reciprocal relation, it gives a form
of expression that has peculiar value" (64). "[W]ithout the advance and
improvement of the whole," she insists, "no man can hope for any lasting
improvement in his own moral or material individual condition" (87).

Addams highlights the joining of the personal and the political in her
vision of "combination." She presented her project simultaneously as a
deeply personal enterprise and as a release from the personal into "the larger
life . . . which surrounds and completes the individual and family life," a
life which she understood as "her duty to share . . . and her highest privilege to extend."[19] She could, thus, tell her own life story as the history of her
settlement in *Twenty Years at Hull-House*. She presents herself as easily
"renounc[ing] 'the luxury of personal preference'" (100). But Hull-House

was explicitly an endeavor of feeling. "The social claim," she explains, "is a demand upon the emotions as well as upon the intellect."[20] The emotions she avows, however, are for the industrial city, the city's inhabitants, and the prospect of social change. A "genuine preference for residence in an industrial quarter to any other part of the city" was required of her settlers (76). "A Settlement is above all a place for enthusiasms . . . [for] those who have a passion for the equalization of human joys and opportunities," she declares (123).

Addams makes it clear that the settlement house—and by extension the city itself—was a refuge as much for its residents as its clients, insisting on what she calls the "subjective necessity" for settlement house work. "[T]he residents in the early Settlements," she explains, "were in many cases young persons, who had sought relief from the consciousness of social malad-justment in the 'anodyne of work' afforded by philanthropic and civic activities" (119). Whether the "social maladjustment" at issue was that of the world or the young persons remains unclear. But at least one quality of this refuge is articulated: at the settlement house, the residents could identify (or be identified) so completely with their work that they became invisible, or perhaps illegible. "[W]hat we wanted," she asserts, was "to disappear into the bulk of the people . . . [and] something of the sort does take place after years of identification with an industrial community" (201).

Following from her commitment to combination, Addams does not con-trast urban isolation with rural community. She acknowledges the poten-tial isolation of city dwellers, whether newcomers or longtime residents, individuals alone or within families, but she assumes that real isolation is found in rural life. Urbanites, she points out, can "lead a life as lonely and untouched by the city about them as if they were in remote country dis-tricts" (232).[21] Everywhere she emphasizes "the very real danger to the indi-vidual who fails to establish some sort of genuine relation with the people who surround him" (232).

Nor does she contrast family disruption in the city with family cohesion in the country. Family life, on the contrary, is neither opposed to nor de-stroyed by urban conditions, whether for settlement women or for those they were working with. Addams acknowledged, however, that settlement women could not take up their work in the city without dealing with the social assumption that a woman should have "no motive larger than a desire to serve her family." Seen as "solely an inspiration and refinement to the family itself . . . her delicacy and polish but outward symbols of her father's protection and prosperity," a daughter was thought to be without "duties outside of the family, to the state and to society in the larger sense."[22] Consequently she argues, in *Democracy and Social Ethics* (1902), for the necessity of an "adjustment between the family and the social claim."[23] This adjustment might take one of two forms: either the family must acknowledge a woman's larger responsibilities or the family must be integrated into the larger social world.

Addams was willing to enlist gender norms in her argument that the family must acknowledge women's larger responsibilities. She invoked the training in femininity of the elite and middle-class daughters of her generation. "[F]rom babyhood the altruistic tendencies of these daughters are persistently cultivated," she observes. "They are taught to be self-forgetting and self-sacrificing, to consider the good of the whole before the good of the ego" (82–83). That model of female service was simply being adapted at Hull-House, she argued, to the greater good. "The modern woman finds herself educated . . . to act her part as a citizen of the world," she explains.

When she talks about the families of the settlement's neighbors, Addams speaks as often of mothers as of daughters. She describes "[t]he maternal instinct and family affection [as] woman's most holy attribute." But if a mother "enters industrial life, that is not enough," Addams argued. "She must supplement her family conscience by a social and industrial conscience . . . [and] must widen her family affection to embrace the children of the community." The willingness of mothers to work for any wages, however low, in the sewing trades, for example, "to keep [their own] children clothed and fed" helped keep the entire industry depressed.[24] Such mothers had to be organized to see the benefit to all the children of the community of struggling together to raise wages.

Addams was more than willing to call into question the very survival of the family as it currently existed to drive home her arguments. She warns elite families that "only that child can fulfill the family claim in its sweetness and strength who also fulfills the larger claim."[25] At the same time, no working-class children will be adequately clothed and fed, she argues, without the combination of their families' efforts.

But she was equally insistent that "[t]he family in its entirety must be carried out into the larger life."[26] For example, the immigrant families she encountered need not be pulled apart by city life, she argued, if they would engage with the city. The family that would be carried into the larger world must, however, adapt: mothers could be "of . . . use to these normal city working girls," if only they would "develop a sense of companionship with the changing experiences of their daughters . . . modify ill-fitting social conventions into rules of conduct which are of actual service to their children in their daily lives of factory work and city amusements . . . [and] substitute keen present interests and activity for solemn warnings and restraint." Such mothers not only would help their children individually negotiate an alien environment but also could create a "vigorous family life [that] allies itself by a dozen bonds to the educational, the industrial and the recreational organization of the modern city."[27]

In such ways Addams not only attempted to reconceive the family but also used "the family" as a lens through which to reconceive the industrial city and the social claims she sought to advance. The family, for the purposes of her project, had a dual aspect, typified by good and bad fathers. The former included Addams's own father, whom she identifies with no less a figure than Abraham Lincoln.[28] He (who had died before she decided to move with her friend to the industrial center of Chicago) appears in her writing as her chief model for the civic action that became her life. Bad fathers were typified by Shakespeare's King Lear, on the one hand, and Chicago's notorious industrialist George M. Pullman, on the other. Through an analysis of these bad fathers, Addams could read urban/industrial conflict—exemplified by Chicago's famous Pullman strike of 1894—in terms of family relations, and family relations in terms of urban/industrial conflict. Both Lear and Pullman were apparently generous men—Lear giving over his kingdom to his children, Pullman building a model town for his employees. But each, Addams argued, was so focused on his own beneficence to those children or workers that he could not credit the possibility of their independence. Each responded harshly to any sign of individuality on their part or any commitment other than to him. To receive these fathers' generosity, their children or workers had to be and to remain subordinate.

"Patriarchal authority" was not, in Addams's view, class-bound and was to be questioned in the families of workers as well as among the elite. She extols the sacrifices that immigrant parents—often fathers—made for the education of their children, but she warns that "immigrant parents who, eager for money and accustomed to the patriarchal authority of peasant households, hold their children in a stern bondage which requires a surrender of all their wages and concedes no time or money for pleasures" can lose those children completely (163). A bad father might appear to be good, to have his children's needs at heart, but families fail—especially, repeatedly, fathers fail—in her narratives if they fail to credit the difference and the rights of children.

Addams could carry the family into the city as a template for understanding urban/industrial relations, whereas Pullman's failure was not only that he would not accept the independence of his workers but also that he would not distinguish between family life and public—that is, city—life. A bad father fails to recognize not only the limits of his own authority but also the limits of the family. Pullman, Addams argues, wanted to substitute family for industrial relations, the personal for the community. He "desired that his employees should possess the individual and family virtues, but did nothing to cherish in them those social virtues which his own age demanded. He rather substituted for that sense of responsibility to the community, a

Norah Hamilton (1873–1945), "Chicago River at Halsted St.," from *Twenty Years at Hull-House, with Autobiographical Notes,* by Jane Addams.

feeling of gratitude to himself, who had provided them with public buildings, and had laid out for them a simulacrum of public life."[29] However far the family might be carried into the city, there was a space beyond the family where larger responsibilities were to be found and combination prevailed.

Addams was obviously negotiating her own role in the city through her accounts of the family. It is telling that the stories of Lear and Pullman, to which she repeatedly returned, are accounts of space and place as well as family and power relations, given her own turning from family relations to space and place as sites for her engagement with power. Lear offers a kingdom, Pullman a model town. Addams did not want the kingdom—the social status and freedom from engagement with the world—that she inherited from her father. Nor did she want to be a parent in the city, to set herself up as a provider of a model urbanity for passive workers. For her, to live in the city was to escape the family. The public city life that is not genuinely collective, she proposed, is only a simulacrum of "the public" and of "the city."

ADDAMS BEGAN HER settlement work and her writing about that work just after James published *The Bostonians* and just as the sexologists in Germany, Britain, and to a lesser extent France and the United States were beginning their elaboration of sexual disorders. The most visible literature that imagined lesbianism until that point had imagined lesbianism in the city and even identified lesbianism with the city. But that lesbianism was the vice of whores, or of the victims of capital, or of whores who were victims of capital—evidence of the depths of capitalism's depredations. Even in the city, a woman of Addams's class was not legible as a lesbian. Nevertheless, although she highlighted her friendship with Ellen Starr and their joint interest in Hull-House, she barely mentioned Mary Rozet Smith in her autobiography. Addams apparently thought of herself and Smith as, in effect, a married couple: in 1902 she wrote to Mary, then traveling abroad, "You must know, dear, how I long for you all the time. . . . There is reason in the habit of married folk keeping together."[30] Close friends and Hull-House residents acknowledged Smith as Addams's "dearly beloved" partner, but Addams was mindful of the need to maintain her respectability.[31] As she wrote in 1902, in *Democracy and Social Ethics*, about "the bulk of contented society"— that is, the majority "who have not felt the 'social compunction'"—they "demand that the radical, the reformer, shall be without stain or question in his personal and family relations, and judge most harshly any deviation from the established standards."[32]

In *Twenty Years at Hull-House,* in what seem preemptive moves, she describes others' views of the settlement as both "unnatural" and "strange." The young women settlers were told they were engaged in "one of those unnatural attempts to understand life through coöperative living" (63). "I remember one man," she notes, "who used to shake his head and say it was 'the strangest thing he had met in his experience'" (75). She then counters both charges, insisting that her choices were "normal" and "natural." She responds to the critique of "collective living" by insisting "that the very companionship, the give and take of colleagues, is what tends to keep the Settlement normal and in touch with 'the world of things as they are'" (63). As to the charge that the residence of these elite women at the center of the industrial city was "strange," she insists, "[I]t was 'not strange but natural.' . . . If it is natural to feed the hungry and care for the sick, it is certainly natural to give pleasure to the young, comfort to the aged, and to minister to the deep-seated craving for social intercourse that all men feel" (75). She deflects the charges of both unnaturalness and strangeness by asserting the value of community, of "the social claim."

The social claim, however, would not justify Addams indefinitely. It would not be until after World War I that new ideas about women's sexuality and new levels of speech about sex were popularized in the United States—and that "Freudian theories as to dangers of repression were seized upon by agencies of publicity, by half-baked lecturers and by writers on the new psychology," she wrote angrily.[33] But by the 1920s, hitherto respectable Boston marriages, even single women living alone, had become suspect. In 1912 Addams could argue, echoing Carpenter and Hirschfeld, that "the sexual instinct" is "not only . . . essential to the continuance of the race, but also, when it is transmuted to the highest ends . . . a fundamental factor in social progress."[34] But in 1930, she was citing a letter from her friend Emily Greene Balch, the economist and pacifist, to explain how "strange" it was for the unmarried educated women of their generation "to read interpretations of life, in novels, plays, and psychological treatises that represent sex as practically the whole content of life; family feeling, religion and art, as mere camouflaged libido, and everything that is not concerned with the play of desire between men and women as without adventure, almost without interest."[35] The possibility of "transmuting" and/or obscuring sexuality in social claims had been fatally undermined by the newly popularized "scientific" theories of sexuality and by the dissolution of the social claim in the new emphasis on sexual freedoms.

In *The Second Twenty Years at Hull-House* (1930), Addams relies on Balch to claim a space between active female heterosexuality and "abnormality." "Is it compatible with the modern theories about sex that two generations of professionally trained women lived . . . completely celibate lives with no sense of its being difficult or misunderstood?" she quotes Balch asking rhetorically. What those lives were misunderstood to be is left unclear. Balch answers her own question first by conceding that "it has been a serious loss . . . to have missed what is universally regarded as the highest forms of woman's experience." But she goes on to defend her peers by insisting that "there is no evidence that they themselves or those who know them best find in them the abnormality that the Freudian psychoanalysts of life would have one look for."[36] By citing Balch, Addams avoids having to make any claim of celibacy, any admission of loss, or any assertion of normality on her own behalf.

But Addams's belief in combination, which allowed her to transmute her own sexuality into the pursuit of the social claim of the industrial city, was being publicly eclipsed by a new emphasis on the personal as well as the sexual. The social claim was dissolving in the 1920s as political concern shifted from the group to the individual and from the economic to the sexual. It is "obvious" to young people, Addams writes, "that the previous generation was too exclusively concerned for the masses, too intent upon the removal of what seemed unfair restrictions for the man at the bottom of society." Now, "self-expression and self-development and the determination to secure a new freedom in sex relations seems at moments to absorb the entire reforming energy of the young."[37] Addams's own choices were being reversed. It would be another four decades before an analysis of the politics of personal life- -including sexual life—would be developed by the gay and women's liberation movements, thus allowing for combination in pursuit of interests she could see only as individual.

AT HOME ON HALSTED STREET

Henry James began *The Bostonians* with a detailed description of Olive Chancellor's Back Bay, Boston, drawing room. The "very provincial" visiting

southerner Basil Ransom, whose provinciality is demonstrated by his preferring women to "be private and passive," "not to think too much [and]
not to feel any responsibility for the government of the world" (41–42), is
particularly struck by his cousin Olive's domestic New England setting. He
"had never seen an interior that was so much an interior . . . had never felt
himself in the presence of so much organized privacy or of so many objects
that spoke of habits and tastes. . . . The general character of the place struck
him as Bostonian. . . . He had always heard Boston was a city of culture, and
now there was culture in Miss Chancellor's tables and sofas, in the books
that were everywhere" (45–46). What pains Olive most in her quest for reform (before she has to struggle with Ransom for Verena Tarrant's affections) is the ugliness of the rooms in which her fellow reformers gather.
The most expressive sign of the abandonment of personal life by the novel's
most thoroughgoing reformer, Miss Birdseye, is that her drawing room is a
grimly bare meeting hall. Nevertheless, the detail and the security of Olive's
own home are themselves a harbinger of social movement. James eventually explains her rare wealth and independence by reference to a pair of
brothers killed in Civil War engagements. But that Olive possesses such a
home, into which she might welcome another woman, confirms not only
the material base but also the social promise of Boston marriages.

In *Twenty Years at Hull-House,* Jane Addams describes herself and Ellen
Starr in 1890, furnishing their settlement "as we would have furnished it
were it in another part of the city, with the photographs and other imped-
imenta we had collected in Europe . . . a few bits of family mahogany . . .
[and] new furniture . . . in character with the fine old residence. Probably
no young matron ever placed her own things in her own house with more
pleasure" (66). It is intrinsic to their particular commitment to reform that
they furnished Hull-House in their own style—as if for the part of the city
they are expected to occupy and within a framework of family and tradition. The new furniture would suit the old building, the photographs from
Europe evoke an even more distant past. At the same time, their young
matronly pleasure signifies their setting up a home, a home that would be
the setting for their adult lives.

As James implies, even in his choice of the title for his novel, "the city" is
deeply entangled, for all of these reforming women, in the shifting between
public and private entailed in their political goals. But a house was key.
To have established residence was fundamental to Addams's relation to her

Norah Hamilton (1873–1945), "A Hull-House Interior," from *Twenty Years at Hull-House, with Autobiographical Notes*, by Jane Addams.

city, which offered her not just work and a way of life but also a place to live. As historian Sarah Deutsch proposes, "The settlement house used a domestic form to create a public, urban institution. It did not so much mediate between public and private for its female residents . . . as eradicate the bounds between public and private—eradicate the notion of home as refuge from the world outside it and of women as limited in their proper sphere to the space within four walls. Living in the house was itself a public action. The settlement house was both part of a city reconceived and a vehicle for reconceiving the city."[38] That Addams established a home in the city is the factor from which any analysis of her role in the history of the great city must proceed. I am interested in the complex changes she rang on earlier understandings of the life of the city, as well as her interactions with the theories of Chicago School sociology that were developing as Hull-House flourished.

BENJAMIN PROPOSED THAT Baudelaire's mid-nineteenth-century Parisian *lesbiennes* were a way of dealing with his own response to industrialization, the economics and politics of modernity. Addams reversed this pattern in the last decade of the nineteenth century and the first decades of the twentieth in Chicago. For her, as I have suggested, the industrial—the economics and the politics of the city—became a means for negotiating her own lesbianism. The distinctiveness of Addams's city was a result of her interest in "the public," from which followed her emphasis on combination, on urban community rather than isolation, and on new urban family forms rather than the urban destruction of rural family cohesion. But Addams's role in the history of the great city turned on her complication of already conventional conceptions of the relation between observer and observed, subject and object, in urban settings. Her decision to live in the great city was central to that complication, because that decision crystallized the ambiguity of her own status as observer and observed, subject and object.

Jane Addams was white in a country divided by race, and well-off in a country divided by class. But she was also a woman in a country divided by gender, and a woman romantically interested in other women, in a country where and at a historical moment when such desires were barely alluded to in public, and then always with condemnation. To set up a home as she did was to enact her gender and class, when the domestic was, in nineteenth-century America, the province of genteel women. Yet, insofar as she set up her home with other women and in the industrial center of the city, she flouted gender and class conventions. Like Olive Chancellor, she had escaped family control. Addams's father, who figures largely at the beginning of her autobiography, established an early male authority in her life, but he died when she was only twenty-one. Hull-House began admitting male residents in 1893, but they remained a minority who lived in a separate building.[39]

Because of the ambiguities of her own status, Addams occupied neither of the opposed positions from which, by the late nineteenth century, urban analyses routinely proceeded. She was neither an elite male observer nor a denizen of an urban underworld—most often, when female, either a sex worker or a sexualized worker. That she occupied neither of these positions was made clearest by her setting up house. Yet she might have occupied both of these positions. That possibility was also made manifest in her house.

Addams's actions highlight the artificiality of the conventional frame of urban study. In addition, her house makes visible the absence of houses—of domestic spaces—as well as of women who are neither whores nor victims of capital in earlier urban discourses, where female households are most likely either the luxurious apartments of courtesans or brothels. But if Addams had been known to be a woman sexually and emotionally engaged with other women, her household could have been incorporated into that rhetoric of vice.

Baudelaire's flaneur sets up house in the street yet remains perpetually, if languidly, in motion. He yearns to become one with the crowd, apparently through some form of osmosis (or sexual encounter). Addams pursued literally the path that the flaneur pursues metaphorically. Her house, if not in the street with the crowd, was on one of the most crowded streets in the heart of Chicago. Like the flaneur, she sought to be absorbed by the city. But as a woman of her class, she could not have wandered the streets observing the crowd and engaging in random exchanges. Instead she planted herself in the midst of the city to facilitate a complex of ongoing relations between largely middle-class and native-born settlement house workers and their working-class and often foreign-born neighbors.

Baudelaire's flaneur remains, always, a prince incognito. By setting up house in the city, Addams and her fellow settlement house workers refused the flaneur's incognito. Addams and the women who joined her could do the work they sought to do in the industrial city only by drawing on the status, the educations, and the incomes given them by their class position. To bring the family mahogany to "the slum" was an acknowledgment of that fact as well as a commitment to a level of engagement that could not be sustained if premised on a false front. At the same time, setting up house in the city together allowed these women to take advantage of the masking possibilities of the city that had been laid out by Balzac and enjoyed by Baudelaire's flaneur, among many others. Addams and those of her female peers who also loved other women were able to live together and to pursue their desires without publicity. They remained deviants incognito.

Addams had to live in the industrial heart of the industrial city; this location was, as I have already noted, necessary to legitimate the liberating social claim she found in urban life. As a consequence, her focus on the city, like that of Baudelaire and Engels, was on an urban underworld. Her underworld, like Engels's, was the world of the people who served the industrial structure upon which the city rested, not the sexual and artistic underworlds that fascinated Baudelaire. Like them both, however, she presented this aspect of the city as representative of the whole. In fact, Addams's account of the city can be seen as contributing to the broader historical tendency to present urban extremity as the essence of the city and the city, in turn, as the site of an essential authenticity. As Addams explained when she framed her project, the industrial city was the locus of "real needs"; the city was where middle- and upper-class settlement workers could learn of life from "life itself."

As Addams worked directly in the reform tradition of urban engagement, her goal was to foster social change by gaining knowledge as well as providing services. She wrote copiously. In her settlement's early years, she and her colleagues produced *Hull-House Maps and Papers* (1895), a collection of essays that included analyses of the local immigrant groups, especially Jews, Bohemians, and Italians; discussions of their economic and social situations (wages, working conditions, child labor, family and political structures, and the social agencies in place to work with these groups); explanations of and arguments for the settlement house project in relation to the labor question; and maps of the immediate neighborhood indicating national groups, wages, occupations, and housing conditions. The Hull-House women who worked on this book drew on European models, including Engels's 1845 account of Manchester (recently translated into English by Florence Kelley, who became a Hull House resident in 1891 and was a central contributor to *Hull-House Maps and Papers*), and the two-volume edition of Charles Booth's *Life and Labour of the People in London,* published in 1891, which itself followed the path marked out by Engels.[40]

The complex connections between Addams's sexuality and earlier urban studies, like a reflection in a mirror, offer us a reversed view of the sexual framework of Engels's observations of Manchester. Although Engels never alluded to the fact, it was a working-class woman, Mary Burns, with whom he lived, who guided him through that city and helped to make it legible to him.[41] In both cases, sexual practices were recast as a form of urban engagement. But Addams's sexuality was facilitated by, rather than directed at, the urban world. At the same time, her experience was a variation on the growing public identification of homosexuality with cross-class relationships. Addams's homosexuality facilitated cross-class relations, although those relations themselves were not sexual. In fact, relations across class lines obscured intraclass homosexuality within the settlement house movement.

The sexuality embodied in Baudelaire's and, subsequently, Zola's prostitutes and highlighted in Engels's explanations for the vice created by urban conditions also appeared in Addams's work on the temptations of the city in *The Spirit of Youth and the City Streets* (1909) and on prostitution in *A New Conscience and an Ancient Evil* (1912).[42] But, unlike her predecessors, Addams focuses on economic pressures and extols the potential for virtue in urban conditions, instead of debating the naturalness (or otherwise) of urban vice. "Life in the Settlement," she explains in *Twenty Years at Hull-House,* "discovers above all what has been called 'the extraordinary pliability of human nature,' and it seems impossible to set any bounds to the moral capabilities which might unfold under ideal civic and educational conditions" (289). This proposition underscored the respectability of settlement residents as well as clients.

In building a house in the city for herself and her peers, Addams recognized early in her Hull-House days that the problem of housing for women in the city was hardly confined to women of her own class who wished to work in the world. Her own urban residence, like those of all unmarried women of the time, was, after all, framed by an elaborate public rhetoric that swelled from the 1880s to the 1930s, lamenting the new population of "women adrift" in American cities. In Chicago alone, "the female labor force" increased "by over 1,000 percent" in this period. Working- and middle-class women seeking jobs in the city, "black [and] white, single, widowed,

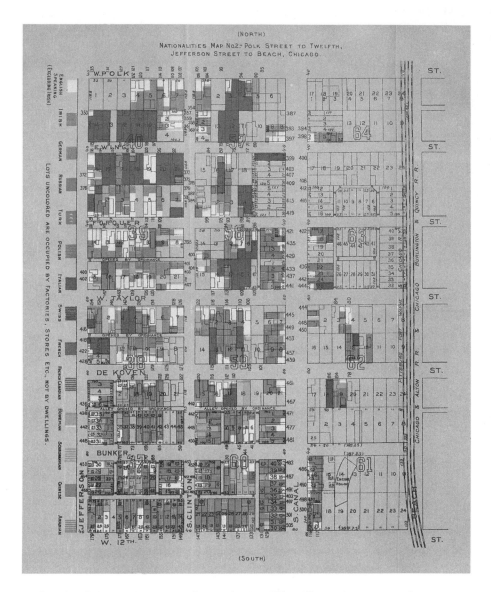

"Nationalities Map No. 2—Polk Street to Twelfth, Jefferson Street to Beach, Chicago," *Hull-House Maps and Papers,* by residents of Hull-House (New York: Crowell, 1895). Reprinted by the Chicago Neighborhood History Project, supported by the National Endowment for the Humanities.

separated or divorced," were berated and preached at for their temerity in leaving their families behind.[43] In actuality these women faced dire choices in the rooming house districts of cities such as Chicago, where they were rarely paid enough at their jobs in stores and factories to afford adequate housing. By June 1892, Hull-House was contributing initial rent and furnishings to help set up a cooperative residence for working women, known as the Jane Club. By 1897, the Jane Club housed about thirty women, a population it maintained into the 1920s. The residents shared costs, housework, and decisions. Some lived there for more than a decade.[44]

ADDAMS'S CONCEPTIONS OF the city and Hull-House's work there were framed by earlier literary and social studies, whether she was drawing on or challenging their premises, in public or in private. But her conceptions of the city and her settlement there were also deeply and practically interwoven with the first decades of the Chicago School's American sociology. The settlement predated the founding of the University of Chicago by three years. Addams observed in *Twenty Years at Hull-House* that when "[t]he University of Chicago . . . the first great institution of learning to institute a department of sociology," opened its doors, in 1892, "the new social science was not yet a science at all but merely a name under cover of which we might discuss the perplexing problems of the industrial situation" (122). Such discussions had already been going on at Hull-House, among neighborhood residents from many nations and political persuasions as well as between neighbors and a stream of visiting lecturers. The Working People's Social Science Club, which met weekly for seven years, drawing between forty and a hundred people to each gathering, had been organized in 1890 by an English worker (120).

There were many exchanges between Hull-House and the new program. Men and women from the university visited and lectured at the settlement house. Jane Addams and Florence Kelley taught briefly at the university.[45] Addams worked particularly closely on various reform efforts in Chicago with her friends George Herbert Mead and W. I. Thomas, early Chicago faculty members whose theories of "symbolic interaction" explored the interdependence of individuals and their social circumstances. With Mead, Addams saw individuals as shaped by their group settings. With Thomas, Addams saw the disruption of traditional patterns by the city as a source of potentially valuable new social forms.[46] *Hull-House Maps and Papers* served

as a model for the empirical studies of local neighborhoods and their institutions that would become the hallmark of Chicago sociology.

But, again, the fact of Addams's home looms large. The complex relations
between Hull-House and the Chicago School turned first on the development of sociology as a science and what that meant for the relationship of
settlement house workers to their city neighbors. In her work as well as
in her personal life, "science" would become a source of vexing challenges
for Addams. She was willing to present Hull-House as "an experimental
effort to aid in the solution of the social and industrial problems which are
engendered by the modern conditions of life in a great city" (86). In fact,
the settlement's charter declared it committed "to investigate" as well as
"improve the conditions in the industrial districts of Chicago" (77). But the
language of "science" was a source of ambivalence for Addams. She could
explain that the settlement "should demand of its residents a scientific
patience in the accumulation of facts and the steady holding of their sympathies as one of the best instruments for that accumulation" (87), but what
was the relation to be, in the end, between facts and sympathies? Did that
"steady holding" mean holding on to their sympathies or holding them in
abeyance?

The settlements were first conceived as laboratories early in the 1890s by
Robert Woods, an early leader in the American movement.[47] But Addams
insisted, "I have always objected to the phrase 'sociological laboratory'
applied to us, because Settlements should be something much more human
and spontaneous than such a phrase connotes, and yet it is inevitable that
the residents should know their own neighborhoods more thoroughly than
any other" (201). Residence inevitably produces knowledge, but residence
should also produce the friendship and identification to shape that knowledge. As she writes about a hypothetical resident, "The depth and strength
of his relationship to the neighborhood must depend very largely upon
himself and upon the genuine friendships he has been able to make" (289).

Although Addams could see the settlement house residents as "pledged
to devote themselves to the duties of good citizenship," such citizenship was
inevitably personal and partisan, based on identification as well as committed to reform. The Chicago School of sociology, like the university as a
whole, in contrast, responded to late nineteenth-century political crises in
Chicago and the pressure of its industrialist backers by steadily withdraw-
ing from explicit reform commitments. Science had been pursued in the

service of urban reform by faculty such as Mead, yet increasingly from 1910, and especially in the 1920s and 1930s, as the professionalization of the social sciences proceeded, "science" was presented as an alternative to sympathy and partisanship.[48]

Robert Park, who would come to represent Chicago sociology in its most professional mode, was brought in at the climax of this process (his appointment was confirmed in 1918), and he himself helped to shape a narrative about the development of the Chicago School's urban studies. In that narrative, sentimentalism was ascribed to the settlement house impulse; settlement houses and early Chicago sociology became mere precursors to the scientific project he and his peers and students represented. Knowledge became *the* goal, and "social disorganization" the subject. "[T]here is growing up in the universities and elsewhere," Park promised, "a body of knowledge about human nature and society which will presently enable us to . . . gain a deeper insight into the social conditions and social processes under which . . . forms of personal and social disorganization occur."[49] Park opposed the promise of "individualization" offered by city life and championed by his colleague W. I. Thomas (though it had been advanced by Simmel decades before), to the threat of "social disorganization."[50]

Chicago School sociologists continued to produce studies of communities of the kind Hull-House had begun, but the focus of their studies was more and more explicitly "[t]he subtle changes in our social life . . . [the] problems that alarm and bewilder us, [such] as divorce, delinquency, and social unrest, [that] are to be found in their most acute forms in our largest American cities."[51] The conditions of labor, wages, and housing that concerned Addams were superseded as social problems by women, youth, and politically radical foreigners. Such an interpretation of these terms is supported by the Chicago School's developing sense of the typical demographic of the city. As E. W. Burgess explained in 1925, there were "certain distinctive characteristics of urban as compared with rural populations. The larger proportion of women to men in the cities than in the open country, the greater percentage of youth and middle-aged, the higher ratio of the foreign-born [sic]." All of these, alongside "the increased heterogeneity of occupation" in urban settings, "increase[d] with the growth of the city and profoundly alter[ed] its social structure."[52] In this rendering, the city could come to be characterized as insufficiently occupied or controlled by older, native-born white men.

Addams's vision of the city, defined by its industrial center, became a city scientifically mapped, by Burgess, into a series of concentric circles. On this map, Addams's industrial neighborhood made up one ring, "encircling the central business section" and buffering that economic center from more and more distant and comfortable rings of housing. This area, where "are always to be found the so-called 'slums' and 'bad lands,' with their submerged regions of poverty, degradation, and disease, and their underworlds of crime and vice," was reconceived as the "zone of deterioration." This zone remained the site of distinctive social groupings within the city. "Within a deteriorating area are rooming-house districts, the purgatory of 'lost souls,'" Burgess explained. "Near by is the Latin Quarter, where creative and rebellious spirits resort. The slums are also crowded to over-flowing with immigrant colonies—the Ghetto, Little Sicily, Greek-town, China-town—fascinatingly combining old world heritages and American adaptations. Wedging out from here is the Black Belt, with its free and disorderly life." The zone of deterioration is thus contrasted with the other circles of the city, which are imagined as congeries of businesses or (intact) families. Addams's neighborhood remains the source of the city's energy: "The area of deterioration, while essentially one of decay, of stationary or declining population, is also one of regeneration, as witness the mission, the settlement, the artists' colony, radical centers—all obsessed with the vision of a new and better world."[53] But it is not clear that this energy is desirable. Though the city mapped as a series of circles might have been expected to offer more settings for investigation, the zone of deterioration as the site of urban problems—mobility, "juvenile delinquency, boy's gangs, crime, poverty, wife desertion, divorce, abandoned infants, vice"—remained the focus of sociological concern.[54]

Addams's interest in combination as a social goal was superseded as a source of urban understanding by Robert Park's interest in "association" as a social problem. "The thing of which we still know least," Park repeated, "is the business of carrying on an associated existence."[55] Addams, as we have seen, worked to reframe "the family" in order to gain access to urban life for herself and her peers. She identified urban life as productive of social combination, not just social disruption. For Park, by contrast, the relationships between individuals and their families were comparatively seamless and unproblematic compared to the difficulties of associative life in larger groups. The "community . . . with its less immediate purposes and its more deliberate aims, is always more or less outside of, and alien to, us," he wrote, "much more so than the family . . . or any other congenial group." The community, as he threateningly described it, "surrounds us, incloses us, and compels us to conform."[56]

The differences between Addams and Park are apparent in their divergent understandings of the city as "organic." Addams assumed an organic city. As she wrote of the settlement house residents at home, in *Twenty Years at Hull-House*, in 1910, "They are bound to regard the entire life of their city as organic." What follows from this understanding of the city was, for her, "an effort to unify it, and to protest against its over-differentiation" (87). Addams's understanding of the city as organic was the basis of her effort to strengthen connections and emphasize the whole—hardly surprising, given her interest in combination. Known for their theory of "the organic city," Chicago School sociologists presented the organic nature of the city as the source of an inevitable "differentiation into natural economic and cultural groupings [that] gives form and character to the city."[57] That differentiation was understood as integral to "natural" cycles of conflict and competition in the city, because "[t]he processes of competition, invasion, succession, and segregation described in elaborate detail for plant and animal communities seem to be strikingly similar to the operation of those same processes in the human community."[58]

Addams's vision of the organic city, manifest in her belief in the interdependence of classes, was her proof of the responsibility of each person to work to improve the conditions of all others. In her organic city she could claim that it was natural to minister to others, and consequently natural— that is, justifiable—for her to be at home. By contrast, understanding the organic city as naturally divided helped Park and the second generation of Chicago School sociologists he led to justify their move away from direct social engagement and toward "science."

Although Park, as we shall see, believed that the potential for vice was inherent in some individuals, he rejected what he referred to as "the well-known doctrine of the 'natural depravity of man'" overall.[59] That was the doctrine Engels had begun to battle, in an urban context, in the mid-nineteenth century, a doctrine that had led many to believe that the harsh conditions of modern cities were simply an expression of the weaknesses of urban populations and could not be ameliorated. But, for Park, "the natural depravity of man" was replaced by an alternative but still "natural" explanation for the crises of urban life. Such crises were evidence of "how utterly unfitted *by nature* man is for life in society," especially certain men.[60] In discussions of the social disorganization produced by urbanization in the 1920s, Park singled out and aligned "Negroes" moving north, "immigrants from Europe," and "the younger generation of women who are just now entering in such large numbers into the newer occupations and the freer life which the great cities offer them" as populations peculiarly unfit for urban life.[61] If city development was still organized "naturally" in these early twentieth-century terms, then reform efforts would always encounter "natural" limits.

Park "demanded of his students 'the same objectivity and detachment with which the zoologist dissects a potato bug.'"[62] Such a demand echoes Walter Benjamin's description of Baudelaire's flaneur "botanizing on the asphalt." The observer could hardly have been made more clearly distinct from the observed. Chicago faculty and students returned to the traditional model of urban analysis, that of elite male observers of subjects situated safely in their subordinate places.

A modern marriage—Radclyffe Hall and Una Troubridge. *Radclyffe Hall,* 1927. Fox Photos/Hulton Archive/Getty Images.

5

Radclyffe Hall at the
Chicago School

THE CRIMINAL, THE DEFECTIVE, AND THE GENIUS

No one goes to Chicago in *The Well of Loneliness,* although New York, London, and particularly Paris all make their contributions to Radclyffe Hall's 1928 novel of lesbian life, which the fury of government censors in Britain and the United States helped ensure would become the twentieth century's most widely read account of female homosexuality. Despite Chicago's queer potential, until the 1920s at least, the United States still derived most of its impressions of lesbianism from European literature, a source eventually leavened by European scientific authorities. In Paris, the end of the century was marked by the cultural phenomenon labeled at the time "Sappho 1900." Following the pattern established by Baudelaire and his peers, male writers continued to exploit lesbian images, especially references to Sappho. Pierre Louÿs's *Chansons de Bilitis* (1894) and Remy de Gourmont's *Le Songe d'une femme* (1899) were among the most notable of their works.[1] Sensationalist journalists remained committed to denouncing lesbianism in their profitable excoriations of the vices of Paris. French lesbian and bisexual women were also increasingly visible, in culture and social life, and not only in the cabarets and the brothel paintings of Toulouse-Lautrec. The novelist Colette, for example, with her Claudine series (beginning with *Claudine à l'ecole,* in 1900) and her notoriously scandalous stage performance (*Rêve dé Egypte,* with her then lover, Missy, the Marquise de Belbeuf, in 1907), drew popular as well as police attention.[2]

"Sappho 1900" also drew on the presence, and the writings, of expatriate American and English women in Paris, such as Natalie Clifford Barney and Renée Vivien. Barney began her long romantic career by successfully courting the notorious Paris courtesan Liane de Pougy, in 1899. Vivien was writing hothouse prose and poetry and courting Barney, among others, by 1900.[3] Barney and Vivien's presence in Paris was supplemented by two generations of middle-class and elite lesbians, women a generation and more younger than Jane Addams, mostly from North America, who took up residence on the Left Bank from the 1900s through the 1930s. This group, including Gertrude Stein, Alice B. Toklas, Romaine Brooks, Berenice Abbott, Janet Flanner, Djuna Barnes, Sylvia Beach, H. D., Bryher, Margaret Anderson, and Jane Heap, lived on various combinations of inherited income, the gifts of patrons, and paid work as writers, painters, photographers, journalists, editors, publishers, and booksellers. These women, in the interwar years, helped to shape modern art and literature, as well as the myth of Americans in Paris. In addition, they cemented, in the minds of Europeans and Anglo-Americans, the association of lesbianism with that historic capital.

These women sought the city. Gertrude Stein, for example, one of the older members of this group and more nearly Addams's contemporary, chose Paris, art, and lesbianism over politics, the professions, and status as a "new woman" in the United States when she abandoned her medical training at Johns Hopkins University in the first years of the new century. In *The Autobiography of Alice B. Toklas* (1932), she repeated what she claimed had been her response to a feminist friend who protested her decision to fail out of medical school: "Marion Walker pleaded with her. . . . Gertrude, Gertrude remember the cause of women, and Gertrude Stein said, you don't know what it is to be bored."[4] Stein does not mention, in that work, the emotional complications of her life in Baltimore that had resulted from her unrequited interest in another young woman. *Q.E.D.*, the novel she wrote about that relationship, appeared only after her death. But in the opening pages of *The Making of Americans* (written 1906–1908, though not published until 1925), she justifies her flight to Paris in terms that would become familiar. In the United States, she explains, "we have not made enough . . . yet" of "singularity that is neither crazy, sporty, faddish, or a fashion. . . . It takes time to make queer people, and to have others who can know it, time and a certainty of place and means." Echoing Oscar Wilde's paean to individualism, she addresses herself to her "Brother Singulars." "We flee," she explains, "before the disapproval of our cousins, the courageous condescension of our friends who gallantly sometimes agree to walk the streets with us, from all them who never any way can understand why such ways and not the others are so dear to us, we fly to the kindly comfort of an older world accustomed to take all manner of strange forms into its bosom."[5]

By the 1920s, Paris could be presented as the definitive setting of lesbian life in Hall's definitive lesbian novel. Although the differences between Addams and Hall were many, including their different generations and nations, they both produced culturally resonant accounts of the modern city that reflect the convergence of homosexuality and urbanity I am tracing. Addams's and Hall's examples of this convergence encompass both types of the great city: the new industrial center that was Addams's Chicago and the ancient capital transformed by modernity that was Hall's Paris. They also represent the two different patterns that would develop within LGBT cultures over the course of the twentieth century: in regard to Addams, a radical tendency prefigured by Wilde, self-consciously modern, political, and urban, with a broad commitment to social combination; in regard to Hall, a conservative tendency, ambivalent about modernity, politics, and the city, and holding to a narrow understanding of social combination. As I will demonstrate, Hall's model of homosexuality fit the ambivalence about, and even hostility toward, the city, dominating urban analyses in the United States from the 1920s through the 1950s even as LGBT communities gained strength in American cities. The political breakthrough made by the gay liberation movement in the 1960s constituted a resurgence of the values Addams claimed, as well as her embrace of the city.

The pivotal points of divergence between Addams and Hall in their representations of the city were their different responses to science (the new science of sexuality in particular) and their different responses to the prospect of group life, of combination. In contrast to Addams's hostility to science, Hall embraced the developing scientific codification of same-sex desire and used that scientific discourse to support her plea for social tolerance. She accepted the model of homosexual as sexual deviant. Her novel epitomizes the post–World War I turn to sex as a focus of social reform that made Addams so uneasy. Moreover, in contrast to Addams's faith in combination, Hall conveyed ambivalence even about the group—homosexuals—whose interests she was advocating. Hall's demand for the social acceptance of homosexuality may have been radical, yet her underlying conceptions of gender and of such social institutions as the family were deeply conservative. In contrast to the conventional linking of same-sex sexuality and political radicalism (and to the tradition in which they were joined), Hall had no broader political concerns. In that sense, her work testifies to the abandonment of the "social claim" Addams feared. Whereas Addams determinedly and very publicly campaigned for pacifism before, during, and after World War I, Hall represented that war unquestioningly in her novel as a setting in which lesbians and gay men demonstrated their social value to a skeptical world through their eager and unquestioning service to the nation.

As the increasingly conservative second generation of Chicago School sociology, with Robert Park's elaboration of Georg Simmel's work at its core, drew away from Addams, it came to fit very precisely the vision of urban and homosexual life Hall was offering. What becomes apparent when Hall's novel is read in the context of later Chicago School urban studies are the striking congruities between Hall's and the Chicago School's accounts of homosexuality and the city. The Chicago School and Hall share an investment in the "difference" of cities and homosexuals, which frames their accounts of the city and the invert; in fact, Hall's invert emerges as a model citizen of the Chicago School's great city. This emphasis on difference plays out in their respective accounts of "communal life." For both, the negotiation of "communal life" stands as the definitive dilemma of urban citizens and homosexuals alike. Both Hall's fiction and Chicago School analyses likewise turn on the same two subjects: cities and deviance. Deviance emerges as a category within urban study just as the newly categorized homosexual emerges to take up the mantle of deviance in urban life. Homosexuals are obviously not the only deviant individuals who find their way to great cities, but some deviants exemplify the urban better than others. As I will demonstrate, homosexuals exemplify the urban best of all.

TO BEGIN WITH, Hall and the Chicago School shared a faith in the representative example. They shared an interest in the paradigmatic, whether cities or queers. Chicago sociologists asserted that American cities were uniquely representative. As Ernest W. Burgess wrote, "All the manifestations of modern life which are peculiarly urban—the skyscraper, the subway, the departmental store, the daily newspaper, and social work—are characteristically American."[6] As their work developed, these sociologists came more and more explicitly to study the city before them for what could be learned about "great cities" as a form: "While the city of Chicago is used as a labo-ratory . . . it is assumed that the processes of urban life in one community are . . . typical of city life throughout the United States."[7]

Hall shares this impulse, sending her lesbian to Paris in *The Well of Lone-liness* even though she herself stayed in London. Throughout her novel "this very city" is also "every city": the invert is isolated in Paris "as in all the great cities of the world," and the homosexual society of Paris is "the stream that flows . . . through all great cities."[8] In fact, Hall presents Paris as a representative city whenever she invokes it as a setting for lesbian life. For her, as for Floyd Dell, the city that the queer inhabits is a generalized metropolis, a great city.

The claims of the main character in Dell's novel *The Briary-Bush* concern-ing queers and cities (see chapter 3) are, of course, a novelist's invention. As we have seen, however, literary works are key sources of, vehicles for, and even engines of the interdependent development of modern understand-ings of homosexuality and the city. Chicago School sociologists shared with Hall a faith in fiction, whether about cities or homosexualities, as a source of information. Robert Park, a devotee of Whitman, acknowl-edged prominently that "[w]e are mainly indebted to writers of fiction for our more intimate knowledge of contemporary urban life," citing Zola in particular.[9] Park's colleague Louis Wirth observed, "The city is remaking human nature and . . . [the] influences of city life are of prime interest to the sociologist." He went on, however, to point out that "[t]he materials bearing on this question are not primarily those collected by the scien-tist, but by the artist. It requires insight and imagination to perceive and to describe these deep-seated changes."[10] Hall herself, in *The Well of Lone-liness,* not only makes her protagonist, Stephen Gordon, a novelist, but places squarely in her hands the "duty" of explaining the invert to the rest of the world, the duty of awakening the understanding of the "thought-less . . . happy people" who persecute homosexuals without knowing what they are doing (389).

As the Chicago School became increasingly committed to its scientific claims, the researchers' emphasis on the literary highlighted a tension between literary and "scientific" sources. Park followed his commendation of literature with the caveat that the new science would supersede literary authority, because "the life of our cities demands a more searching and dis-interested study" (93). Similar tensions are also apparent in Hall's fiction.

Even though Stephen accepts that written words might dispel the hostility of the heterosexual majority, she points to existing scientific studies as the proper source of information. The ignorant "can read," she insists, "there are many books." But, she is told, the scientific studies that already exist are inadequate because they are inaccessible ("they [the ignorant] will not read medical books") as well as biased ("[W]hat doctor can know the entire truth? Many times they meet only the neurasthenics, those for whom life has proved too bitter" [390]). As a "normal invert" as well as a novelist, Stephen could do better, she is told, because "the whole truth is known only to the normal invert" (390).

Nevertheless, Hall believed, and Chicago School sociologists concurred, that although literature was true, science alone would give their analyses credibility. Park, for example, wanted to claim for urban study the "patient methods of observation" and the legitimacy granted "anthropologists like Boas and Lowie" (92); he wanted to "make of the city a laboratory or clinic in which human nature and social processes may be conveniently and profitably studied" (130). Hall asked sexologist Havelock Ellis to comment on her work and then prefaced *The Well of Loneliness* with his scientific guarantee of its "notable psychological and sociological significance."[11] In the course of the novel, first Sir Philip Gordon, the heroine's father, and then Stephen herself come to understand her sexuality by reading Richard von Krafft-Ebing. Stephen's father, she discovers after his death, has locked away in his library a collection of "battered old book[s]" in which he has turned his daughter into another "case": their margins are covered by "notes in her father's small, scholarly hand and . . . her own name appeared in those notes" (204). The reader is thus repeatedly invited to see Stephen in scientific terms.

But in order to secure the justification of scientific authority, both the Chicago School and Hall had to claim for their subjects a distinction that would justify scientific study. That is, they had to differentiate the city and the homosexual from their surroundings—other kinds of places, other kinds of persons. What distinguished the Chicago School's city was the difference of the city's homosexual inhabitants; what distinguished Hall's homosexuals were the cities they inhabited.

Robert Park claimed the status of anthropologist by asserting an analogy between Franz Boas and Robert Lowie's "study of the life and manners of the North American Indian" and his and his colleagues' "investigation of . . .

Little Italy on the lower North Side in Chicago, or . . . the more sophisticated folkways of the inhabitants of Greenwich Village . . . New York"
(92–93). Moreover, "Every large city tends to have its Greenwich Village."[12]
When Burgess developed his map of the city, it became clear that ethnic
groups and perverts occupied the zone of deterioration together, as in
practice the Italians and the homosexuals did in Greenwich Village.[13] But
the "distorted forms of sex behavior" of the Greenwich Villagers were of
much more use than ethnic enclaves in the Chicago School's pursuit of scientific credibility. Like a laboratory, the "great city," Park believed, "spread
out and lay bare to the public view . . . all the human characters and traits."
This the city could do "[b]ecause of the opportunity it offers . . . to the
exceptional and abnormal types of man" (130). The "exceptional" and the
"abnormal" turned the city into a laboratory or clinic; together they became
the pivotal subjects of Chicago School readings of the city.

Hall made a parallel move. The distinction of life in the city gave structure and substance to the portrait of homosexual difference that justified
her scientific claims. If gender inversion and same-sex desire stand as the
origins of homosexuality in Hall's novel, a homosexual life is built out of the
lesbian's inevitable journey from a family identified with the countryside
to the others of her kind whom she will find in the city. Stephen Gordon's
growth from uncomprehending boyish girl to self-consciously inverted
masculine woman is inextricable from her exile from a home county dedicated to the heterosexuality of the Anglo-Saxon aristocracy and her arrival
in a foreign city where Jews and Negroes as well as inverts gather.

Lest there be any doubt about the significance of the city in Stephen's history, her exile first to London and then to Paris is prompted by her romantic passion for Angela Crossby. Angela, though she initially seems just a
country neighbor, has already been tainted by a sojourn in New York. An
immigrant from genteel poverty in the American South herself, she hated
"that great hideous city! . . . the long angular streets, miles and miles of
streets; miles and miles of faces all strange and unfriendly—faces like masks.
Then the intimate faces of would-be employers, too intimate when they
peered into her own—faces that had suddenly thrown off their masks" (178–
79). Angela's urban experience tells us that the secret behind the masks of
the city is a sexual threat. Her city life explains her initial willingness to re-
spond to Stephen as well as her eventual cruelty, when she betrays Stephen
and so shuts her out of her family and the countryside forever.

The lesson of *The Well of Loneliness*, that the city is the proper site of a homosexual life, is reinforced by the fact that the city is the focus of all the homosexual lives in the novel. Every lesbian and gay character introduced has come to the city from elsewhere. The painter Wanda perpetually recalls the small town in Poland, "with its churches, its bells that were always chiming" (373), that imbued her with the fervent religiosity that drives her to drown her self-loathing in alcohol. She is exiled from her home, Hall implies, by her brothers, "men of stone and iron . . . seeing only the straight and narrow path" (374). Jamie and Barbara, whose respective deaths in Paris from tuberculosis and suicide epitomize lesbian suffering in the novel, expire there together largely because of their exile from the small Scottish Highland village where they grew up together and from where they were driven by the hostility of the village's "good people" to their love (359). By contrast, the American Valerie Seymour's supreme comfort with her own lesbianism is mirrored in her apparent lack of any particular life before her arrival in the city and her complete identification with Paris once there.

That Hall sends everyone, in the end, to Paris rather than London underlines her investment in the difference of homosexuality and of the city. London could not represent the difference of the city for a character of Stephen Gordon's class background. Her visits to that city with her mother and, later, her shopping at the Bond Street jewelers where her father had bought a wedding ring—all before she leaves home—reflect a historical continuity between the county and the city, the countryside and London, for the English gentry. She can meet a gay man of her own class—the playwright Jonathan Brockett—in London, but Paris is the city Brockett talks about "with ardour, as a lover might talk of a mistress" (238). London cannot be Stephen's queer city because it is culturally too close to home.

For the Chicago School sociologists as much as for Hall, as for urban commentators from Balzac to Simmel, the great city was a city of newcomers, specifically—to emphasize the difference of the city—newcomers who had come from afar psychologically and/or geographically. The intensity of stimulation in the city, the full force of its disorganizing effects, was felt only by such immigrants. Consequently, the Chicago sociologists and Hall were all interested in emphasizing the contrast, for urban immigrants, between the places they had left and the places to which they had traveled. Park, following Simmel, rests his analysis of the city on a reading of "smaller communities" as places where "intimate and permanent associations" (126) are built at the cost of surveillance and repression. In smaller communities, "no individual is so obscure that his private affairs escape observation and discussion" (124), and because of this proliferation of observation, "exceptional and abnormal . . . human characters and traits . . . are ordinarily obscured and suppressed" (130). In case we are in any doubt, Park makes it clear that smaller communities are the home of the "normal man," the place where "the normal man, the man without eccentricity or genius . . . seems most likely to succeed" (130).

In *The Well of Loneliness,* Hall heightens the distinction of the great cities in which the adult Stephen will take refuge by emphasizing the idealized country setting of her childhood and adolescence, the great houses set in lush parks, and parks set in turn among rolling green hills punctuated by picturesque villages. The surveillance and the hostility to difference that Park ascribes to "smaller communities" are everywhere to be found in Hall's countryside, where Stephen is subjected to years of suspicious observation by the local worthies before she is driven away. She is scorned for her ease when riding astride with the local hunt as a child and for her clumsiness in evening dresses and with the small talk of dinners and dances as a young woman. Only when her neighbors briefly assume she will marry her friend Martin Hallam do they "at once" become "friendly and welcoming" (108). But when Martin vanishes, their hostility is even greater than before. "[T]hey feared her," Hall tells the reader, "they instinctively sensed an outlaw, and theirs was the task of policing nature" (110). They protect the "natural" world by scrutinizing and then excising her.

But Hall's invert is more than just one of the multitude of newcomers to the Chicago School's great city. In Robert Park's schema, the paradigmatic urban newcomer is the person with the most to gain from the city, one of those least favored in the country, the not normal, "the criminal, the defective . . . [and] the genius" (126). These least favored figures are paradigmatic because "the small community often tolerates eccentricity," he observes, but "[t]he city . . . rewards it" (126). Such rewarding of the deviant is, in fact, key to the difference that defines this city. As one among the criminal, the defective, and the genius—or, from different perspectives, all three— Hall's queer urban immigrant Stephen Gordon lives at the center of Park's great city.

Stephen is representative of the Chicago School's urban newcomer in part because abnormality is rewarded by the city but also because hers is

Paris by night. Brassaï (Gyula Halász, 1899–1984), *Fat Claude and Her Girlfriend at Le Monocle*, ca. 1932. Musée National d'Art Moderne, Centre Georges Pompidou, Paris, France. Copyright Estate Brassaï–RMN. CNAC/MNAM. Distributed by Réunion des Musées Nationaux/Art Resource, New York.

the quintessential abnormality rewarded there. Following the path of modern anxiety about the city's disruption of family life, the Chicago School distinguished between smaller communities and great cities not only in terms of their levels of social scrutiny and their different treatment of the normal and abnormal, but also in explicitly sexual terms. Park's small communities are the sites of heterosexuality and reproduction, which are, in turn, actively threatened by the city. Echoing claims made over the course of the nineteenth century in very different contexts, from Engels in the 1840s to Nordau in the 1890s, Park warns that "metropolitan life inhibit[s] and suppress[es] . . . natural impulses and instincts": "[I]n the country" marriage occurs earlier and children "are counted as an asset," whereas "in the city" children are "a liability" and "[m]arriage takes place later." Sometimes, in fact, it "doesn't take place at all" (129). Louis Wirth, in his classic essay "Urbanism as a Way of Life" (1938), continues this line of argument, citing "low and declining urban reproduction rates" as evidence that "the city is not conducive to the traditional type of family life, including the rearing of children and the maintenance of the home as the locus of a whole round of vital activities."[14]

Hall's opening description of the Gordon family in *The Well of Loneliness* begins to make much the same argument. An ideally manly man, Sir Philip Gordon, marries an ideally womanly woman, Lady Anna, amid the natural beauties of the surrounding landscape: the countryside is firmly identified with heterosexual love and reproduction. By contrast, Hall acknowledges the city as not only a sexualized space but a homosexual space, even as she resists the narrative logic whereby her heroine should find sex there. Although Stephen neither meets a lover nor begins her sexual life in Paris, the city is sexualized from the moment she arrives: Jonathan Brockett insists to Stephen, "[Y]ou've got to have an affair with Paris!" (238). Stephen recognizes that the city offers sexual permission, particularly to people like her: "There was many another exactly like her in this very city, in every city; and they did not all . . . deny . . . their bodies . . . [and] becom[e] the victims of their own frustrations" (299). Her happiest adult years are those she spends with her lover, Mary Llewellyn, at home in Paris. At the novel's conclusion, when Mary finally flees our heroine, lesbianism, and Paris simultaneously, for the wide-open arms of Martin Hallam, she is also fleeing to the wide-open spaces of his Canadian prairie, where he will undoubtedly give her the babies Stephen cannot provide.

Not only does Hall's invert fit neatly within the Chicago School's analysis of the relationship between the great city and the smaller communities they describe as its alternative, but the Chicago School sociologists' and Hall's stories of the city and of the invert, focused as they all are on newcomers, also share the same central preoccupation, a preoccupation with becoming—whether the "becoming" in question is becoming urban or becoming gay. Underlying this preoccupation is the question of how much of a process this "becoming" might be. Are urban persons, or homosexuals, made or born? Insofar as they answer "born," these commentators are all concerned with the degree to which their subjects are "natural."

Balzac's city as a sea of masks and Baudelaire's *lesbiennes* occupying a landscape of cascades and couches are emblematic of the collision of the natural and the artificial in modern conceptions of cities and of homosexuals. Cities had been, and through the twentieth century continued to be, represented as unnatural, artificial spaces, in part because the city was taken to be the home of such clearly unnatural (or artificial) persons as homosexuals.

The Chicago School sociologists and Radclyffe Hall, however, were equally invested in the "naturalness" of their subjects. As I have already noted in my discussion of Jane Addams, Park and his colleagues viewed the great city as "organic," as "a living entity" (93), "a product of nature, and particularly of human nature" (91). Although Hall's opening identification of heterosexuality with the natural world of the countryside in *The Well of Loneliness* implies a corollary identification of homosexuality with the unnatural, by the end of the novel the one subject on which her opposed avatars of modern homosexuality, Stephen Gordon and Valerie Seymour, agree, is that homosexuality is a natural phenomenon. Protesting "the preposterous statement that inversion [is] not a part of nature"—"since it exist[s] what else could it be?"—Stephen declares the invert "God's . . . creation" (405). Valerie describes "Nature" as a feminine life force "trying to do her bit." "Inverts," she argues, are "being born in increasing numbers" (406).

Park's theory of the organic city depends on two interdependent propositions: first, the city's population naturally divides and segregates itself; and, second, although the city might reward abnormal persons, it does not produce their abnormality but merely fosters the "innate dispositions" they bring with them from the smaller rural communities they are fleeing. These propositions come together at the characteristic site of naturally occurring social organization within Park's account of the segregated city, the "moral region." According to Park, individuals naturally, and therefore inevitably, segregate themselves into moral regions based on shared interests or passions. The quintessential form of his moral region is the "vice district," a "detached milieu . . . in which vagrant and suppressed impulses, passions, and ideals emancipate themselves from the dominant moral order" (128). For Park, "the forces which in every large city tend to develop these detached milieus," if they are natural, must be a product of the "latent impulses of men" (128). In his analysis, then, to "become" urban might be "to develop," but only to develop a possibility already present in the self, one already produced by nature. The "reward" the city offers to Park's criminals, defectives, and geniuses is "the . . . opportunity to develop [their] innate disposition[s]" (126).

Consequently, the city's relation to nature depends, for Park, on the relation to nature of the city's emblematic "abnormal" residents, people such as the city's queers. They must have an innate disposition to their deviance for the city to develop. The right relation to nature of the invert, then, guarantees the city's right relation to nature. The question of the "naturalness" of cities merges with the question of the "naturalness" of homosexuality. Park's argument for a natural city is in this sense supported by Hall's natural-born homosexual. However, Park's organic city is flexible. It is "rooted in the habits and customs of the people who inhabit" it, those habits and customs both shaped by and shaping even the material conditions of urban life (93). "[T]he city possesses a moral as well as a physical organization," he observes, "and these two mutually interact in characteristic ways to mold and modify one another" (93). For Hall, in contrast, to be natural is to be fixed. Stephen's and Valerie's natural homosexuality is "born"; it simply "exists." By all rights, the fixity of Hall's invert ought to make her an alien creature in Park's organic city. Nevertheless, not only do Park and Hall discuss similar subjects similarly, but in the end Hall's portrait of the natural invert, Stephen Gordon, is a description of precisely the kind of urban citizen Park needs. It is, paradoxically, precisely because of her fixity that Hall's natural homosexual not only belongs in Park's organic city but is required by it, for Park's vision of a flexible, living city is based on his belief in a fundamentally fixed human nature—a belief in "latent impulses" and "innate dispositions."

At the same time, Park's vision of a natural city supports Hall's portrait of the natural homosexual. As I have noted, she focused on the French capital rather than London as the ultimate setting for her representative lesbian because Paris was some distance for her elite Englishwoman to travel. But there is at least one other reason Stephen Gordon ends up living on the Left Bank rather than by the British Museum. The distinction Hall establishes between the city in which Stephen settles and the other great cities in her novel lies in their relations to nature. She presents New York and London as commercial and/or industrial centers: Angela Crossby tramps the "long, angular streets, miles and miles of streets" (179) of Manhattan in search of employment; Stephen finds "sunshine devoid of all warmth," and "tall factory chimneys" belching soot over the river, and "disheartened" trees in London (209). But no one works for a living in Hall's Paris (except Stephen's servants, in what seems to be a semifeudal arrangement). No industrial processes impose themselves upon the landscape. Without commerce or workplaces, Paris serves as the focus of Hall's presentation of the queer "great city" as a natural city, where the urban homosexual world that Stephen and Mary join can be described as a "stream that flows silent and deep" (356).

In the end, in both Park's and Hall's accounts, the city becomes its own peculiarly natural world, with inverts as its natural denizens—a natural world *because* of the inverts who are its denizens. In this they echo Balzac from eighty years earlier, naturalizing Paris by describing the city as a jungle or a forest filled with criminal hunters and hunted. Park concludes that "[w]e must . . . accept these . . . more or less eccentric and exceptional people . . . as part of the natural, if not the normal, life of a city" (130). This is also Hall's lesson: the city, "every city," becomes the space in which Stephen Gordon and "many another exactly like her" can live "natural lives—lives that to them [are] perfectly natural" (299).

Finally, however, despite Park's commitment to a city that merely fosters innate differences and Hall's insistence that homosexuals are born and not made, neither could sustain the commitment to fixity against the pressure of the urban life each had invoked. Neither Park nor Hall could ignore the possibility that the organic city might itself produce deviants. As Park admitted, "Great cities have always been . . . melting pots. . . . Out of the vivid and subtle interactions of which . . . have come . . . the newer social types," and "not merely vocational, but temperamental types" (125). What, then, we might ask, is the relation of these newer, "temperamental" types to the "innate dispositions" of urban immigrants? This question arises also in *The Well of Loneliness,* in the characters of those lesbians in Hall's great city whose nature is unaccounted for. We have Stephen Gordon's history, for example, but not Valerie Seymour's.

These "newer . . . temperamental types" were prefigured in late nineteenth-century catalogs of the effects of modern nervousness. But which are new: the types or the typologies? Simmel observed that the multiplicities of urban life required a new social and scientific exactitude. Wirth, building on the arguments of Simmel and Park, highlighted the increase in categorization, and the greater susceptibility of individuals to categorization, in the city. The city, he explained, put a "premium upon eccentricity, novelty, efficient performance, and inventiveness." But "[i]ndividuality . . . must be replaced by categories" when "the economic basis of the city," the "fullest exploitation of the possibilities of the division of labor and mass production," required the "standardization of processes and products."[15] This is to say that although the great city might incite new individualities, it certainly required that older as well as newer behaviors be newly organized.

Communal Lives

The underlying subject of the Chicago School's arguments about naturally occurring segregation and the moral regions such segregation produced— the subject that Park's Chicago School urban studies set out to address— was the problem of the organization of the city, that is to say, the problem of association, of communal life. This problem, in their view, had two dimensions: the isolation experienced by individuals in the city and the connections the city offered. We have already seen, in the writings of Hirschfeld and Proust, that organization was also a vexing subject in contemporary analyses of homosexual life, especially given the heterosexual culture's persistent belief in a vast homosexual conspiracy and persistent skepticism about the possibility of organized homosexuality. "Communal life" was also the central dilemma of the invert's life in Hall's novel and has, for her invert, the same two dimensions it has for the Chicago School: isolation and connection. In no case do the opportunities for connection offered by the city ease isolation.

As I noted earlier, according to Park, "[W]hat . . . makes the city what it is" is the "absence" of the "amazing amount of personal information afloat among the individuals" within "small communities" (124). That absence of information means inevitably the absence of "the more intimate and permanent associations of the smaller community" (126). The individual in Park's great city is not known and consequently is not intimately or securely connected to others, any more than Engels's atomized monads are. Park consciously follows Simmel (and other early sociologists, such as Émile Durkheim) in emphasizing the urban exchange of personal for instrumental relationships. As Wirth would subsequently elaborate, "Frequent close physical contact, coupled with great social distance, accentuates the reserve of unattached individuals toward one another and, unless compensated by other opportunities for response, gives rise to loneliness."[16] "Here, as in all the great cities of the world," Stephen declares bitterly of Paris, inverts are "isolated until they . . . [go] under" (406).

In lieu of intimacy and personal connection, according to Park, in the great city "the individual's status is determined to a considerable degree by conventional signs—by fashion and 'front'—and the art of life is largely reduced to a skating on thin surfaces and a scrupulous study of style and manners" (126).[17] In Wirth's analysis this emphasis on the visual underscores the urban person's dependence on categories, and clarifies what is implicit in Park's emphasis on style and front—an increasing dependence on artifice: "We see the uniform which denotes the role of the functionaries, and are oblivious to the personal eccentricities hidden behind the uniform. We tend to acquire and develop a sensitivity to a world of artifacts, and become progressively farther removed from the world of nature."[18]

For the invert, the very relationship Park posits between personal information and intimacy, on the one hand, and permanent associations, on the other, is, as it were, inverted. Stephen is isolated and judged before she reaches the great city. As a member of Park's class of "the exceptional and abnormal," she is deprived from the outset of access to the "intimate and permanent associations" that smaller communities provide to the normal. That deprivation is apparent in Stephen's relation to her family as well as to the broader social world in which she grows up. Although her family and neighbors have information about Stephen, only her father translates that information into knowledge, and he does not tell anyone—including his daughter—what he knows. When her mother gains this knowledge, she explicitly denies her daughter intimacy and permanent association by banishing her from her family, home, and neighborhood. Like the city, the invert undoes the family; Stephen's parents are estranged from each other as well as from Stephen because of her difference.

In *The Well of Loneliness,* the world of the invert is always dominated by appearances. From Stephen's childhood on, she is subject to her own as well as others' obsessive interpretations of her "signs" and "style and manners." At war with the feminine clothing appropriate for her gender and class—"soft and very expensive dresses" (73), accompanied by "large hats trimmed with ribbons or roses or daisies, and supposed to be softening to the features" (72)—as a despairing young woman she examines her own body in a mirror for signs of her stigma. She comes to see that body as "a monstrous fetter imposed on her spirit" (187) and to describe herself as "Cain whom God marked" (205).

American lovers in Paris—I. Berenice Abbott (1898–1991), *Janet Flanner.* Copyright Berenice Abbott/Commerce Graphics, NYC.

But Hall's insistence that homosexuals convey their abnormality through their distinctive style and manners converges with peculiar force with the urban focus on style and manners that Park and others describe. In the city, Stephen is constantly subject to the visual scrutiny and judgment of others. In London, "[p]eople stared at the masculine-looking girl. . . . And someone, a man, laughed and nudged his companion: 'Look at that! What is it?' 'My God! What indeed?'" (165). In Paris, in restaurants, and on the streets, "people . . . stare at the tall, scarred woman in her well-tailored clothes and black slouch hat. They would stare first at her and then at her companion. . . . There would be a few smiles" (326). Those assessing Stephen in the public places of the city are confident of their ability and their right to define her by reading her appearance. Even in the queer social world Stephen eventually finds in Paris, people look at her "curiously; her height, her clothes, the scar on her face . . . rivet their attention" (348). And after all, these people's confidence and curiosity are justified, for the narrator herself catalogs the lesbians of Paris largely in terms of their looks: "the build of an ankle, the texture of a hand, a movement, a gesture" (352). Her admission that "the grades [of difference] were so numerous and so fine that they often defied the most careful observation" (352) only underlines her commitment to the visual sign. The smiles of those who observe Stephen and Mary on the streets of Paris confirm the implication of the Londoner's question, "What is it?" Even in the city, Stephen is read as abnormal. But that is how both the Chicago School and Hall needed her to be read.

The city is nonetheless the only place of community, according to Chicago School sociologists and Hall, for the abnormal and exceptional. As Park explains, "[E]very individual"—even those who would be dismissed in a small town as "impracticable and queer" (127)—"finds somewhere among the varied manifestations of city life the sort of environment in which he expands and feels at ease . . . the moral climate in which his peculiar nature obtains the stimulations that bring his innate dispositions to full and free expression" (126). Hall's Paris exemplifies Park's "spontaneously" divided city in which "the population tends to segregate itself, not merely in accordance with its interests, but in accordance with its tastes or its temperaments" (128). When Valerie Seymour declares that "nearly all streets in Paris lead sooner or later to Valerie Seymour" (298), she is asserting the centrality of her lesbian self to Paris. But as even Valerie concedes, there are some streets that do not lead to her. As Park observes, "[T]he segregation of the urban population . . . establishes moral distances which make the city a mosaic of little worlds which touch but do not interpenetrate" (126).

Hall dramatizes the segregation of the great city by offering many different versions of Paris in *The Well of Loneliness*. The first is the "tourist Paris" to which the flamboyantly gay Jonathan Brockett initially introduces Stephen, leading her "through the galleries of the Luxembourg and the Louvre; up the Eiffel Tower . . . down the Rue de la Paix" (241). The last is the heterosexual Paris to which "the thoroughly normal" Martin Hallam introduces Stephen and Mary, a city of fashionable restaurants where "neat, well-tailored men . . . [and] pretty, smartly dressed women . . . laughed and talked, very conscious of sex and its vast importance" (417). But the novel's city centers on the gay social world that Brockett has brought Stephen to Paris to join. Stephen insists that homosexuals isolated in the great city have only one option: "in their ignorance and resentment, they turn . . . to the only communal life a world bent upon their destruction had left them; . . . to the worst elements of their kind, to those who haunted the bars" (406).

Despite Stephen's grim conviction that bars are the only form of gay communal life, however, so "great" a city is Paris that Hall offers an alternative in Valerie Seymour's salon. In this regard, Hall complicates Park's picture of "detached milieus . . . emancipate[d] . . . from the dominant moral order" (128) by acknowledging the workings of class and gender distinctions. In her novel, the bars are public, commercial, and presided over by men who are heterosexuals and/or drug dealers. In the bars, people "[o]f all ages, all degrees of despondency, all grades of mental and physical ill-being . . . laugh shrilly . . . [and] dance together" (387). Theirs is the democracy of misery. But Valerie's salon, private rather than either public or commercial and presided over by a woman who is also a lesbian, is a genteel haven for the elite. There is neither alcohol nor dancing at Valerie's. Lesbian and gay "writers, painters, musicians and scholars" (349) mingle with tolerant heterosexuals, while "Valerie, placid and self-assured, create[s] an atmosphere of courage" (352).[19]

Nevertheless, the emphasis on difference that guides Hall's work weights her novel toward the bars, just as Park weights his analysis of the city toward the criminal, the defective, and the genius. Valerie, a "charming and cultured woman," creates a setting in which "everyone [feels] very normal" (352). This pseudonormality is available to Stephen because of her class and her gender, but neither of these characteristics protects her from identification with the misery of the bars. It is at the grimmest of these bars, Alec's, that Stephen must most fully confront her own abnormality when she is confronted with the community of the abnormal: challenged by a "youth" with "a grey, drug-marred face" who addresses her as "Ma soeur," she acknowledges their connection when she responds, "Mon frère" (388).

DESPITE ALL THIS, a fundamental contradiction between their emphases on isolation and community afflicts both Park's and Hall's works. How can urban experience simultaneously ensure isolation and produce community? Why do the great city's isolated individuals not simply take up appropriate communal lives? For Park, the criminal, the defective, and the genius provide the answer to these questions at the heart of the Chicago School's city, and *The Well of Loneliness* suggests how. As Stephen Gordon's lesbian story illustrates, deviant persons experience both of the dimensions of urban life most intensely. They bring their isolation to the city with them and

American lovers in Paris—II. Berenice Abbott (1898–1991), *Solita Solano.* Copyright Berenice Abbott/Commerce Graphics, NYC.

continue to be isolated, to be marked out as different, even on city streets. At the same time, the city's satisfaction of their need for community is proportional to the degree of their isolation; the reward of the city is peculiarly theirs. But most significantly, they experience the loneliness of the city and its embrace simultaneously because of the experience of deviance as both sociologists like Park and advocates like Hall understood it. The core of that experience is the deviant person's response to categorization.

In *The Well of Loneliness,* as in Park's great city, the reward of Paris is "communal life" (406), but this reward depends on the deviant's acceptance of herself as deviant and of her deviance as defining her self. As Stephen acknowledges reluctantly, and therefore obliquely, "[I]n Paris I might make some sort of a home, I could work here—and then of course there are people . . ." (248; ellipsis in original). "People," which is to say the people of her own sort whom she can find in Paris, make possible Stephen's home and work there; her meeting Valerie Seymour prompts her to stay in the city, and Valerie actually finds her a home. Stephen can and does set up house in the city, although in a space that is as little urban as possible. Hers is a freestanding house, reached through a cobbled courtyard, with its own walled garden attached. Here is a city with domestic space, and Stephen and Mary attempt to lead a domestic life there, even though their attempt is frustrated by Stephen's class (the servants leave Mary with no household tasks to keep her occupied) as well as their sexuality (the absence of babies with which Mary might otherwise busy herself). Unlike for Addams, their home in the city does not represent an engagement with the city. They are never really "at home" in the city. Thus, "people" remain a source of difficulty.

Hall introduces the prospect of community as loss. Stephen's ex-governess Puddle, who first accompanies her to London and Paris, inveighs against "like to like": "No, no. . . . Stephen was honourable and courageous; she was steadfast in friendship and selfless in loving; intolerable to think that her only companions must be men and women like Jonathan Brockett" (242). To take up with such companions—by definition neither honorable nor courageous, neither steadfast nor selfless—is, Puddle implies, to move definitively out of the normal moral world. Park's analysis would only have confirmed her fears. Once "the poor, the vicious, the criminal, and exceptional persons generally" have joined with their own kind, he observes, "social contagion tends to stimulate . . . the[ir] common temperamental differences and to suppress characters which unite them with the normal types about them" (129). It is emphatically a grim moment, in the novel, when Stephen Gordon "turn[s] at last . . . to her own kind" and launches herself and Mary Llewellyn upon "the stream that flows silent and deep through all great cities, gliding on between precipitous borders, away and away into no-man's land—the most desolate country in all creation" (356).

Stephen's profound ambivalence about lesbian/gay/queer communal life is based in her sense of herself. Although Hall's novel invokes sexual science, her protagonist resists categorization. She worries "'that [Valerie] liked me because she thought me—oh, well, because she thought me what I am'" (248). Or as she later explains directly to Valerie, she feared that the other woman's "interest was purely scientific or purely morbid" (408). She does not want to be a spectacle or a case. But in practice, in order to share in the friendship of those "like" herself, Stephen has to acknowledge "what" she is. She has to admit to a stigmatized identity, that is, to admit that that stigmatized identity defines herself. And even if she takes that drastic step, intimacy might still be elusive; she might be "liked" by those "like" herself only for "what" she is. Such a connection would be superficial as well as damning, insofar as she understands herself as having a self that exceeds her deviance.

Hall's and Park's works, perhaps because both were trying to conciliate social hostilities—toward homosexuality, on the one hand, and toward the city, on the other—finally converge on the ground of ambivalence. Hall attempts to create for Stephen a new category, "the normal invert," whose experience might be explained by the doctors but whom, because she is not sick, the doctors never see. (Such "normal inverts" are those who most disturbed George Beard and the authors of *The Social Evil in Chicago*.)[20] She identifies with her own kind—even, as at Alec's, with the most degraded of her own kind—but she also identifies with the "normal" world. Valerie completes the novel's identification of normality with the countryside and the invert with the great city when she proposes to Stephen, "[Y]ou don't belong to the life here in Paris. . . . [Y]ou've the nerves of the abnormal with all that they stand for . . . [but] you've all the respectable county instincts of the man who cultivates children and acres" (407). Apparently Stephen cannot be fully abnormal, which is to say fully urban, given her instincts as a county gentleman, her commitment to proprieties of gender and class. But Stephen, because she is a woman with the instincts of a county gentleman, and so is not fully normal, remains in the city, whether or not she quite belongs. Her ambivalence about the city is most fully reflected in her ambivalence about queer communal life, so she remains both isolated and grouped at once.

It is, ironically, Stephen's ambivalence that completes her fit within Chicago School sociologists' urban analyses, pointing as it does to the final paradox in their work. As they came to understand their subjects, they saw those who remained isolated and grouped at once, who remained at odds with the city, as the most properly urban.

PARK'S CHICAGO SCHOOL initially proposed that the disruption of conventional mores—the "disorganization" experienced by urban immigrants—was merely a prelude to their ultimate "reorganization." That reorganization would be most fully expressed by their moving away from their groups (their immigrant neighborhoods and the zone of deterioration that contained them) to the successively more assimilated settings of the outer rings of the city. Finally, they would meld into the undifferentiated "American" family life of the developing suburbs. In that sense, urban living was presented by the Chicago School as a phase in the journey of entire populations from "folklife" to modernity, just as same-sex desires were presented by Freud (and those popularizers of his work whom Addams deplored) as a phase in the inevitable journey from a polymorphously perverse childhood to the mature heterosexuality of adult life.

Nevertheless, Park came to propose, as the quintessential urbanite, a "marginal man," an immigrant whose attachments to his culture of origin were disrupted but not ruptured. No longer comfortable within his own group, he still remained too much a part of that group to ever be fully integrated into a new world.[21] Whether remaining in a disorganized state or carrying the zone of deterioration with him, Park's marginal man never leaves the city. Stephen Gordon, then, given the ambivalence about her homosexuality that Hall ascribes to her as a "normal invert," remains a model urban citizen. Because she is a "marginal man," she will always be a marginal man.

In the late 1920s, as Hall was publishing *The Well of Loneliness*, Park racialized his marginal man. He cited "the Japanese" as well as "the Negro" in America as prime examples of his type, but he was particularly interested in the "mixed blood, like the Mulatto in the United States or the Eurasian in Asia."[22] Finally, he focused on "the Jew" as "historically and typically the

marginal man" and thus "the first cosmopolite." "Most if not all of the characteristics of the Jews," he asserts, "are the characteristics of the city man."
Still, he is most interested in "the emancipated Jew," whom he describes
as "emerging from the ghetto in which he lived in Europe, [and] seeking
to find a place in the freer, more complex and cosmopolitan life of an
American city."[23]

In *The Well of Loneliness,* Hall aligned her white invert protagonist with
both African Americans and Jews, yet all were nevertheless represented
through racist stereotypes: her black characters were primitive, her Jews
colored. Two "Negro singers," brothers Lincoln and Henry Jones, entertain
Stephen Gordon and her queer community one evening in Paris. Lincoln
has an "intellectual face," but he also has "the patient, questioning expression common to . . . most animals and . . . all slowly evolving races" (362).
Still, the queer group is "spellbound" and "stirred to the depths" by the
singers' performance, which Hall describes as "a challenge to the world on
behalf of themselves and of all the afflicted" (363). The singers ask "[t]he
eternal question, as yet unanswered for those who sat there. . . . 'Didn't my
Lord deliver Daniel, then why not every man?'" (364). The novel's conclusion echoes their song. The Jewish Adolph Blanc (the only non-Anglo-Saxon
in Stephen's circle) is described repeatedly as "quiet," "gentle," "learned," and
"tawny" (389). Nevertheless, Blanc is "the most normal abnormal" (351), who
is described at one point as "actually speaking [Stephen's] thoughts" (390).
He offers her the category of the "normal invert" when he charges her with
the task of explaining their lives so that the hostile world will understand
their suffering.[24] Hall ends her story with Stephen taking up his challenge.

The racism of Hall's contradictory portraits of African Americans and
Jews, all associated with group life, is a further manifestation of the ambivalence about lesbianism, and so about group life, embedded in the novel.
But Chicago School sociology was even ambivalent about the ambivalence
of its typical urban subject. African Americans and Jews would continue
to be presented as representative urbanites for the rest of the century. But
Park could not settle on the racial types he had invoked. He could not settle on the figure of the Jew. In order to stay true to the proposition with
which he began his most influential work, that "the city is a state of mind,"
he had also to invoke the more generalized image of "the stranger." What
first the "abnormal" and then his racialized "marginal man," in particular
the "Jew," offered Park was the possibility of the persistence, in particular

figures, of that urban state of mind. But "the stranger" (whom Simmel had already identified as a type simultaneously marginal and central) offered him the possibility of generalizing that state of mind. Through the figure of the marginal man, he transmuted the abnormal—the criminal, the defective, and the genius—into "the stranger." He then elevated this stranger into his representative urbanite. A stranger might be a person who was ineluctably different or simply someone out of context. Anyone might be a stranger.

Louis Wirth worked out the implications of such generalization in the 1920s. He wrote on "the ghetto" but offered the ghetto as a model for "the origin of segregated areas and the development of local communities in general," representing the Chicago School's zone of deterioration and hence its city overall.[25] "[W]hile the ghetto is, strictly speaking, a Jewish institution," Wirth, himself Jewish, explained, "there are forms of ghettos that contain not merely Jews. Our cities contain Little Sicilies, Little Polands, Chinatowns, and Black Belts. There are Bohemias and Hobohemias, slums and Gold Coasts, vice areas and Rialtos in every metropolitan community."[26]

Wirth's generalization of the ghetto reflects a broader pattern in which he makes explicit much of what is implicit in Park's work. If the abnormal is the fulcrum of Park's urban analyses, Wirth clarifies the ways in which that abnormal is the model urbanite. Evoking not just Hall's elaboration, through the story of Stephen Gordon, of Hirschfeld's and Proust's contradictory queer collective life (the problem of perverts in groups), Wirth even readmits the social claim that Addams used to establish herself in the city.

"All of us," Wirth argues, "on the move and on the make, and . . . transcending the cultural bounds of our narrower society become to some extent marginal men."[27] All urbanites experience isolation when the "[f]requent close physical contact" imposed by city life, "coupled with [its] great social distance . . . gives rise to loneliness."[28] All urbanites experience the failure of the family and the loss of "place" as sources of support and, in response to this failure and loss, create groups of the like-minded. "In view of the ineffectiveness of actual kinship ties, we create fictional kinship groups," Wirth proposes. "In the face of the disappearance of the territorial unit as a basis of social solidarity, we create interest groups."[29] At the same time, "[n]o single group has the undivided allegiance of [any] individual." Everyone leads a divided life. But this divided life is the result of the complexity of city people, not the inadequacy of groups. It is "[b]y virtue of his different interests arising out of different aspects of social life [that] the individual acquires membership in widely divergent groups, each of which functions only with reference to a single segment of his personality."[30]

Similarly, combination is not merely the urbanite's response to isolation, failure, and loss. Some measure of response to Addams's social claim is, Wirth argues, a welcome condition of city life: "If the individual would participate at all in the social, political, and economic life of the city, he must subordinate some of his individuality to the demands of the larger community and in that measure immerse himself in mass movements."[31] Not only was the abnormal the representative urbanite, but by the 1930s all urbanites had taken on the experiences of the abnormal described by Hirschfeld and Proust, Addams and Hall.

PART III

The Fear and Hope of Great American Cities

Flaunting "Homosexuality in America." Bill Eppridge (1938–), *Life*, June 26, 1964.
Photograph copyright Bill Eppridge. All rights reserved.

6

Paris, Harlem,
Hudson Street—1961

ARE CITIES UN-AMERICAN?

By the early 1960s, popular journalists, such as Jess Stearn in his exposé of contemporary lesbian life, *The Grapevine* (1964), were confidently report- ing, with reference to unnamed "sociologists and psychologists," that "two world wars, raising havoc with the personal lives of men and women, have apparently given homosexuality a strong forward thrust."[1] Such reports echo earlier assertions by Krafft-Ebing, Ellis, Nordau, and Beard. There were always, apparently, in the view of anxious heterosexuals, more gay people than there had been before, and those numbers were always rapidly expand- ing. But these reports were also a response to the actual consolidation of gay and lesbian enclaves in urban centers in the United States following World War II. "I thought I was the only girl like myself in the world . . . [u]ntil I met Linda and we came to Chicago," one young woman explained to Donald Webster Cory for his study *The Lesbian in America,* in 1965.[2] Such reports also reflected increasingly common public statements of hostility. "Can [you] think of a person who could be more dangerous to the United States of America than a pervert?" Senator Kenneth Wherry (R-Neb.) had demanded of the U.S. Senate, on April 25, 1950.[3]

Such denunciations, it could be argued, were in fact partly a response to the increasingly legible urban presence of queer persons. But virulent de- nunciations of homosexuals were also a fundamental part of postwar efforts to reorganize a population in which so many lives had been disrupted by depression and war, into a new, consumption-driven economy embedded in conservative political alignments. This reorganization of the population had two intertwined elements: a reorganization of the relations of men and women (under the guise of a relieved return to proper masculinity and femininity), and a reorganization of the relationship between cities and their surroundings (which were to be turned into suburbs as quickly as possible). Heterosexual relations would be reorganized in part through the reorganization of space.

The "nation's metropolitan areas" were "remade" between 1945 and 1961. Across the country new subdivisions, and in effect new towns, were created in a "federally supported home-building boom . . . of such enormous proportions," as urban historian Kenneth Jackson, among others, has argued, that this new suburbia was "a major cause of the decline of central cities."[4] By 1963, Betty Friedan, in one of the first and most influential critiques of postwar American culture, *The Feminine Mystique,* could observe that "the explosive movement to the suburbs" of the preceding decade was intrinsically bound to "a distinguishing feature of these suburbs," that "the great majority" of "the women who live there . . . are full-time housewives." The connection seemed so tight, she continued ironically, that "one might suspect that the very growth and existence of the suburbs causes educated modern American women to become and remain full-time housewives."[5]

Denunciations of homosexuality not only helped to lock postwar American men and women into proper and properly gendered heterosexual relationships. Such denunciations helped to intensify a stew of public hostility to the "un-American" that was identified with cities and thereby confirm the righteousness of proper men and women in properly gendered heterosexual relations in the properly American suburbs. They also point to an underlying cultural campaign of the postwar years.

The denunciation of same-sex attachments was embedded in, even a leading edge of, a broader attack on improper attachments. Homosexuality was clearly, in itself, to be rejected, but it could also represent two other, more general forms of attachment—to social group and to place—which were to become increasingly unpopular. These dubious emotional ties were most often linked, and linked to cities. Cities were places to which attachment had become unacceptable, places that were most often the sites of problematic group attachments in general as well as homosexual attachments in particular. Even though the images of the city, as well as of homosexuals, that were invoked by those inveighing against both were far from specific to the United States, the idea of "America" was central to this campaign.

"Are cities un-American?" William Whyte Jr. asked in the title of his own contribution to the series of studies of contemporary urban life he edited for *Fortune* magazine from September 1957 to April 1958 and then published in book form as *The Exploding Metropolis* (1958).[6] Whyte's collection was the first effort to challenge the postwar reconstruction of the American landscape in favor of suburban living, a harbinger of subsequent "counter movements for urban preservation and environmentally sound urban design" and of "an alternative cultural politics."[7] He argued that cities had become *the* negative point of reference in the postwar reconstruction of "America."[8] "[T]here seems to be a growing alienation," he observed, "between the city and what most people conceive of as the American way of life" (8). This new conception of "the American way of life," he argued, was based on a new emphasis in the 1950s on a "norm" that was unrelentingly familial as well as suburban. "[T]he norm of American aspiration is now in suburbia," he explains. "The happy family of TV commercials, of magazine covers and ads, lives in suburbia; wherever there is an identifiable background it is the land of blue jeans and shopping centers, of bright new schools, of barbecue-pit participation, garden clubs, P.T.A., do-it-yourself, and green lawns." A "home" in the suburbs, the land of happy families, "is becoming a social imperative" (9).

Before *The Exploding Metropolis*, in *The Organization Man* (1956), Whyte had critiqued the role of the corporate world, with its emphasis on conformity, in contemporary American life. He ended that study with a section, comprising almost a third of the book, titled "The New Suburbia: Organization Man at Home." The "organization man at home" occupies a social setting of relentless togetherness, a relentless concern for and desire to fit in with the expectations of his neighbors. Whyte explains: "[N]ot only does suburbia tend to attract . . . [those] who are less 'different'; it speeds up the process in which anyone . . . becomes even less 'different.'"[9] But paradoxically, despite this pressure to fit in, to conform, suburbanites must abandon any group identification. They should not even become attached to their suburb. The expectation was that everyone would pick up and move on to a new location, and a new set of neighbors, without a backward glance, at any moment the corporation, or a rising income, required.

In line with the portrait Whyte painted in *The Organization Man*, the new America he describes in "Are Cities Un-American?" is represented by a white, heterosexual couple "on the way up."[10] "The city," by contrast, "is not for the average now" (25). "More and more," he reiterates, "the city is becoming a place of extremes—a place for the very poor, or the very rich, or the slightly odd" (8). But when "[t]he popular image of the city" is of "a place of decay, crime, of fouled streets, and of people who are poor or foreign or odd" (23), what those leaving leave behind is not only the city but social difference itself, and with that the past, which Whyte identifies with the city, "extremes," and distinct social groupings. "[T]here are still islands of middle-class stability" in the city, he explains, "but . . . those are neighborhoods of the past . . . the last stand of an ethnic group, and the people in them are getting old" (8).

"The city" could so easily be constructed as a foil for postwar surburbanization and as a place ripe for "renewal" not because it actually was "the past" but because of its past. Postwar American attacks on the city drew on an American tradition of antiurbanism that can be traced back to Thomas Jefferson as well as understandings of urbanity familiar from the mid-nineteenth century onward in western Europe.[11] That the city could be seen in the United States in the 1940s and 1950s as a setting of extremes, for example, is a continuation of the preceding century of bifurcated studies of urban misery by elite observers. That pattern had been extended by Chicago School sociologists' interest in social groupings and their "zone of deterioration" as emblematic of urban life. By the 1950s, that zone had apparently become "the city" in its entirety, from a popular as well as a sociological point of view. Park made the abnormal the fulcrum of Chicago School analyses in the 1920s, and Wirth argued in the 1930s that all city dwellers shared qualities and experiences usually identified with the abnormal. Two decades later it was an article of faith that only the abnormal live in the city.

THE QUESTION WHYTE offered as his title, "Are cities un-American?" linked his interpretation of postwar urban/suburban development to the political crusade of the preceding decade, when to be un-American was to be a communist or a queer. Cities and communism "were often conflated in anti-communist rhetoric," as historian Elaine Tyler May has observed: "[C]osmopolitan urban culture represented a decline in the self-reliant entrepreneurial spirit, posing a threat to the national security that was perceived as akin to the danger of communism itself."[12] In fact, before Joseph McCarthy—who would give his name to the cause of challenging "un-American" activities—began denouncing "communists and queers" in government in 1950, he gained attention in the United States Senate as the vice chairman and controlling force on the postwar Joint Committee Study and Investigation of Housing.

McCarthy, in league with powerful real estate interests, had proposed this committee to investigate the housing shortage that had built through the war years and that reached a new level of crisis as the soldiers returned home. His actual goal seems to have been to challenge the New Deal "commitment to a comprehensive federal housing policy" and to "undermine the credibility of . . . [the] broadly based New Deal labor-reform coalition" supporting that plan.[13] He attacked "proponents of public housing and planned towns as socialists and communists"[14] and succeeded in limiting public housing to "low income groups" and achieving "lighter corporation taxes, and land grants to builders who entered the middle-income field."[15] William Levitt, who became famous as the builder of the definitive postwar American suburb, Long Island's Levittown, was a McCarthy supporter who in 1948 praised his man as "typical of the type of leadership that you might expect in Washington from now on."[16] Levitt would go on to justify his own success by declaring, in 1950, that "[n]o man who has a house and lot can be a Communist. . . . He has too much to do."[17]

When McCarthy turned from housing to an unmediated focus on "communists and queers," he drew on persecutions already under way, as well as on fermenting conservative resentment of New Deal programs.[18] Communists and queers could be lumped together because, as McCarthy explained in the February 1950 speech that began his campaign, "the great difference between our Western Christian world and the atheistic Communist world is not political . . . it is moral."[19] What is more, queers could be cast as a political as well as a moral threat. A December 1950 Senate report, *Employment of Homosexuals and Other Sex Perverts in Government,* identified homosexuals as a threat to the nation because of their vulnerability to political subversives. Their susceptibility to blackmail (they could, after all, lose their livelihoods, housing, families, and so on, if their deviation was revealed) as well as the moral weakness that had led to their perverse sexual practices in the first place would lead them to betray their country.[20]

Beyond this, homosexuals and communists shared the same threatening qualities.[21] They were all considered sick. In 1952, when the American Psychiatric Association produced its first *Diagnostic and Statistical Manual of Mental Disorders* categorizing mental illness, homosexuality was included among the "sociopathic personality disorders."[22] Meanwhile, McCarthy declared that "practically every active Communist is twisted mentally or physically in some way," and his views had widespread popular support.[23] In addition, homosexuality and communism were both regarded as contagious. According to the 1950 Senate report on homosexuals, "One homosexual can pollute a Government office."[24] Also in 1950, the attorney general described communism as "like a plague. . . . [E]ach party member 'carries in himself the germ of death for our society.'"[25]

The qualities ascribed to homosexuals and to communists were not only consistently the same but were also the qualities ascribed to urban persons. Long before the 1950s, city people were understood to be peculiarly subject to mental illness (nervousness) and vulnerable to contagion. In the 1950s, homosexuals and communists were above all identified with improper social relationships and problems of legibility, long understood as key aspects of urban life, as we have seen.

Communists, homosexuals, and cities alike disrupt proper relationships. All are hostile to the family. "The first thing Communists would do would be to destroy the family as a unit, because by destroying the family they destroy the basis of a free life," a leading U.S. executive warned in 1950. An FBI agent noted that "opposition to marriage was 'one of the tenets of the Communist Party.'"[26] By the 1950s in the United States, homosexuality had also become a definitive sign of family failure, "an outcome of exposure to highly pathologic parent-child relationships and early life situations."[27] Alternatively, homosexuality was an attack on the family: homosexuals were homosexual because they were rejecting family obligations.[28] That cities disrupt families had been the refrain of commentators from Balzac to Engels, from the mid-nineteenth century onward.

While rejecting family life, homosexuals, like communists, pursued improper connections, and cities, as we have seen, were the place for such pursuits. That homosexuals formed sexual and romantic relationships with members of the same sex seemed at times the least of their potential wrongdoings. Homosexuals' and communists' pursuit of improper social relationships took two other, particularly dire, linked forms in the popular imagination, both dependent on an urban setting. First, they crossed proper social boundaries of class and of race, and second, they formed groups. These behaviors were associated with the city because cities not only contained people of different classes and races but were understood to foster the blurring of class and racial boundaries in the promiscuous intermingling inevitable in urban crowds. Yet at the same time, those who lived in cities belonged to groups.

The association of homosexuality with cross-class relations, as we have seen, was an essential part of the history of the identification of homosexuality with radical politics. That homosexuals crossed racial barriers had been seen as a threat in American cities at least since the turn of the twentieth century. Journalists Jack Lait and Lee Mortimer, who specialized, in the years immediately after World War II, in guides to the urban underground that mirrored such mid-nineteenth-century models as Eugène Sue's *Mysteries of Paris* (1842–1843) and George Foster's *New York by Gaslight* (1850), declared in *Washington Confidential* (1951), "There is free crossing of racial lines among fairies and lesbians." They claimed to have attended "a party in Black Town, an inter-racial, inter-middle-sex mélange, with long-haired, made-up Negro and white boys simpering while females of both races mingled in unmistakable exaltation."[29]

J. Edgar Hoover's view that the Communist Party was "the cause of much of the racial trouble in the United States at the present time" was shared by many conservatives because of the party's efforts, for example, in support of the Scottsboro boys in the 1930s, or its postwar work with northern black communities.[30] As Lait and Mortimer declared, again in *Washington Confidential,* "The Reds and bleeding hearts play up their 'love' for Negroes at every opportunity."[31] In *New York: Confidential!* (1951), they helpfully explain that "[m]any avowed Communists all but push themselves on the Negroes and it is a tenet of the party line in New York City that white women must go out of their way to mingle with their colored comrades."[32]

Homosexuals and communists were understood to form shadowy groups, in a context in which groups were presented as the essential urban social form. McCarthy, talking about homosexuals, "referred not to individuals but to a collective, variously termed 'these gentlemen,' these 'types,' and 'this group.'"[33] Lait and Mortimer described communist "nests" and homosexuals "cling[ing] together in a tight union of interests and behavior."[34] These groups were popularly characterized as much by their members' excessive loyalty to their own as by their excessive hostility to the larger social world.

The improper relationships of communists and queers, whether in crossing social boundaries or in forming groups, were thought to be facilitated

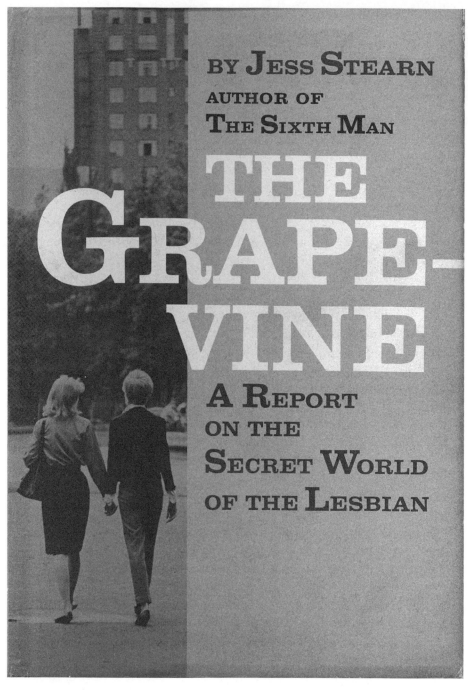

Cover of *The Grapevine,* by Jess Stearn (New York: Doubleday, 1964).

by their potential illegibility to "normal" persons and their invariable legibility to each other. In this sense we are back in the cities of Balzac, of the
Chicago Vice Commission, and of Hirschfeld and Proust. Arthur Schlesinger Jr. could even explain the (il)legibility of communists in terms of the
(il)legibility of homosexuals, by reference to Proust's *Remembrance of Things
Past*. In *The Vital Center* (1949), he explained that communists "identif[ied]
each other (and [could] be identified by their enemies) on casual meetings
by the use of certain phrases, the names of certain friends, by certain enthusiasms and certain silences," behaviors "reminiscent of nothing so much as
the famous scene in Proust where the Baron de Charlus and the tailor Jupien
suddenly recognize their common corruption." He cites Proust describing "both parties speaking the same language, even though they have never
seen one another before."[35] Schlesinger made these matters clear for the
elite; Lait and Mortimer warned the masses that even though "[s]ome are
deceptive to the uninitiated," the fairies "all know one another." Not only do
they "recognize each other by a fifth sense immediately" but "all queers are
in rapport with all others."[36]

HAVING EVOKED ALL of these associations of communists, queers, and cities
with his title, "Are Cities Un-American?" William Whyte offers his readers
the poor, the foreign, and the odd—that is, the black, the ethnic/political,
and the queer—as typical urbanites. The American city had apparently not
been properly "white" for a "long" time. "The once dominant white Protestant majority has long since dispersed," Whyte explained. In postwar
America, even "among the Catholics and the Jews who have been the heart
of the city's middle class, the younger people are leaving as fast as they are
able" (8–9). In another essay in *The Exploding Metropolis,* Daniel Seligman
cites Jacob Riis's writing on "the horrors of the downtown New York slums"
in *How the Other Half Lives* (1890). "One may find for the asking an Italian,
a German, a French, African, Spanish, Bohemian, Russian, Scandinavian,
Jewish, and Chinese colony," Riis explained. "Even the Arab . . . has his exclusive preserves at the lower end of Washington Street. The one thing you
shall vainly ask for in the chief city of America is a distinctively American
community."[37] Having let Riis's words present "the chief city of America"
as devoid of Americans sixty years before, Seligman goes on to observe,
"The minorities have changed since Riis's day, but the observation is still
valid." Despite earlier references to Puerto Ricans, Mexicans, "hillbillies,"

and "American Indians" emigrating to and establishing neighborhoods in contemporary cities, "Negroes, of course," he explains, "are the minority principally concerned today."[38]

The racialization of the city had long been a fixed pattern, especially within accounts of the city divided between elites and slums. Paquita, the cynosure of urban desire in Balzac's *Girl with the Golden Eyes,* is not properly white as well as not properly heterosexual. Balzac describes the city as a forest and a jungle, with a "primitive" population, in *A Harlot High and Low* and other novels. London's East End is presented as analogous to "Darkest Africa" in Henry Mayhew's survey *London Labour and the London Poor* and similar works.[39] And when the great city was identified with its grimmest precincts, racialized groups were presented as responsible for that grimness.

Racial difference and immigrant status were often merged in such accounts, so that a racialized "poor" could be conflated with the "foreign." In *The Condition of the Working Class in England,* Engels describes "the Irish" as congregating in the foulest parts of mid-nineteenth-century Manchester because they are the poorest of the new working class. He concedes that their poverty is partly a result of the discrimination they face as a group, but he also blames their state on their being both the most recent immigrants and, of all of the groups within the developing industrial proletariat he is describing, the people inherently least capable of adapting to the city. "Filth and drunkenness," he complains, "they have brought with them. The lack of cleanliness . . . not so injurious in the country, where population is scattered, becomes . . . gravely dangerous through its concentration here in the great cities."[40] Sociologist W. E. B. Du Bois, in his earliest work, *The Philadelphia Negro* (1899), conceded that "[t]he slums . . . are largely the results of the contact of the Negro with city life," and then tried to redeem one part of Philadelphia's black population—and the city itself—by shifting responsibility to the most recent immigrants, "only a portion [of whom] have had the opportunity of being reared amid the advantages of a great city."[41] Robert Park's interest in "the Negro" and "the Jew" as models for his quintessentially urban "marginal man" was of a piece with this pattern.

In *The Exploding Metropolis,* Whyte and Seligman also try to invoke immigration rather than race as the source of urban difficulties. The "problem," Whyte insists, is not middle-class Negroes but "migrants from poor rural areas in the South" (49), who because they are new to the city don't know enough not to throw garbage out of their apartment windows. Seligman, after insisting that "Negro neighborhoods are not necessarily slum neighborhoods" because the Negro middle class is "now manifest somewhere in almost every metropolitan city," explains that "migrants drawn to the slums tend to be semi-literate, low-income, of rural origin, and members of racial minorities" who "simply don't know how to live in cities."[42] Drawn to the slums, they seem to know only where they belong.

Like communists and queers, these poor and foreign people do not form proper families, ensuring their and the city's status as the antithesis of the suburban world of happy families. "Very few students of the subject now believe that the slums create crime and vice and disease," Seligman calmly explains. There are, rather, "problem families" that "the slums simply attract." He quotes a "close student" of New York's slums: "[W]e thought if we could only get our problem families out of those dreadful slums, then papa would stop taking dope, mama would stop chasing around, and Junior would stop carrying a knife. Well, we've got them in a nice new apartment with modern kitchens and a recreation center. And they're the same bunch of bastards they always were."[43]

In *The Exploding Metropolis*, however, what Whyte claims is popularly understood to be wrong with cities is not only that they harbor the un-American, the poor, and the foreign, none of whom form proper families—that is, maintain proper attachments—but also that their populations are *improperly* attached. Cities are the homes of groups, yet belonging to a group is not in itself American. It is instead a peculiar quality of the poor and/or of ethnic or racial others. Such groups are in turn not only a feature of cities but the source of slums. "Where the slum population is not Negro," Seligman writes, "it ordinarily consists of a distinctive nationality group bound to its slum neighborhood, sometimes after three generations, by special ties of language or religion. Identifiable communities of eastern or southern European origin are usually slum or borderline communities. Virtually all the 'Chinatowns' in U.S. cities are blighted areas."[44] To belong to a group is to be subject to "special ties," which include being bound to "a neighborhood." That is, the particular attachments involved in group life depend on a peculiar, not-American attachment to place. Whites who "give up on the city and flee" once they find themselves in any kind of proximity to "Negro slums" are indicating their commitment to "the way up," whereas Seligman's "slum population[s]" are those whose not being "on the way up" is inseparable from the fact that they are too attached to their group or their neighborhood to be "on the way" anywhere.

Then there are the "odd." The degree of one's oddity was apparently marked by one's distance from family life. Those members of the white middle class who remain in the city, according to Whyte, form "atypical households"—a category that begins with heterosexual pairs who fail to reproduce and ends with "the Bohemians," "the sculptors, the artists, the musicians, [and] the actors" (32). But it is a category that depends on the unmarried. "Widows, divorcees, spinsters, and bachelors," Seligman explains, "find the city far more congenial than suburbia" and consequently "will often pay more for a good apartment in the city than their incomes would suggest" (31). That these women and men are not driven from the city by economic factors—that is, are not "on the way up"—only confirms their oddity. Whyte goes on revealingly to praise the city for "the heterogeneity, the contrasts, the mixture of odd people. Even the touch of Sodom and Gomorrah" (40).

In 1948, Alfred Kinsey, in *Sexual Behavior in the Human Male*, tried to argue, unsuccessfully, against what he acknowledged was the still "widespread theory among psychologists and psychiatrists that the homosexual is the product of an effete and over-organized urban civilization. The failure to make heterosexual adjustments is supposed to be consequent on the complexities of life in our modern cities; or it is a product of a neuroticism which the high speed of living in the city imposes upon an increasing number of individuals."[45] Cities do not produce homosexuals, he contended. He proposed instead that cities allowed homosexuals to form groups. The "distinctive thing about homosexuality in the city," he explained, "is the development of a more or less organized group activity which is unknown in any rural area."[46]

In "Are Cities Un-American?" Whyte proposes, finally, that people who live in cities share in the end only their "lik[ing for] cities," an attachment to place which his own work suggests is an improper object choice: "The people who choose the city, in sum, are of many different kinds, but they have one common like: they *like* the city. They like the privacy; they like the specialization, and the hundreds of one-of-a-kind shops; they like the excitement—to some, the sirens at night are music—they like the heterogeneity, the contrasts, the mixture of odd people. Even the touch of Sodom and Gomorrah intrigues them" (40; emphasis in original). But to "like cities," to be attached to place in a context in which groups (even so nebulous a group as the "odd") are identified with place, implies a series of other social choices in postwar America, where to be attached to groups or places was suspect. Moreover, liking cities exposed people to membership in a group based only on a "common lik[ing]" for an improper object. Is it surprising, then, that "the touch of Sodom and Gomorrah" should "intrigue" them?

HISTORY IN THE CITY

The Exploding Metropolis ends with an essay, "Downtown Is for People," by one Jane Jacobs. In 1961, three years after Whyte's collection was published, Jacobs published the book that would become the most influential work in city planning of the second half of the twentieth century. A journalist and editor at *Architectural Forum,* she had become visible in urban affairs because of her role in battling the urban redevelopment schemes of New York City's planning czar, Robert Moses, for her own neighborhood, Greenwich Village. Her book, *The Death and Life of Great American Cities,* was greeted by a storm of response: Was she or was she not too focused on New York? Could New York, or could it not, be seen as representative of any city other than itself? Still, "the public embraced Jacobs and her book."[47] Jacobs was almost immediately credited with changing the way cities were seen. Over the past half century, her work has been described, by both champions and critics, as variously modernist, antimodernist, postmodernist, and traditionalist.[48] In the 1990s, she was even claimed by, and blamed for, "new urbanism," although the vision of the Congress for the New Urbanism embodies exactly the confusion of fantasies of small-town life with urbanity that she most thoroughly opposed.[49]

Whenever journalists or scholars want to make a point about postwar urban development, the sickness or health of any given American city, or some new city planning scheme, they cite Jane Jacobs. In these citations she is most often paired with one of two figures, Lewis Mumford or Robert Moses. Mumford and Moses, both of whom had begun their careers in the 1920s, were still firmly entrenched in 1961. In print, as well as in person, Jacobs opposed Mumford's analyses and Moses's practices. Mumford, who identified modern cities with "failure . . . monstrosity . . . tyranny, [and] a living death," in Jacobs's words, was known as the "anti-urban city planning theorist."[50] A leading figure in the Regional Plan Association, Mumford was primarily committed to "unbuilding," to "decentraliz[ing] cities and their populations," as Jacobs saw him (408, 20).[51] As head of New York City's postwar Title I Slum Clearance Committee, Moses controlled the largest postwar "urban renewal" program in the country, a program that would serve as a model nationally and around the world. Aspiring city planners and administrators came from everywhere to take lessons in razing existing neighborhoods, streets, and parks for mammoth highway construction projects.[52] Both Mumford's arguments for decentralization and Moses's highways furthered the evisceration of American cities in favor of suburbanization in the decades immediately after World War II, and helped determine those suburbs' sprawling form.

Paired with Mumford or Moses, Jacobs represents the opposing view, and the pairings shape public understandings of each figure. Jacobs is often cast as idealistic but inefficient, for example, in contrast to Moses's aggressively efficient brutalism. Her purpose, nevertheless, was to demonstrate the ineffectiveness of the projects Moses produced in accomplishing his own stated goals, whether those were reducing traffic congestion or improving housing options. These pairings often distort her work.

I want here to pursue an alternative pairing, that of Jane Jacobs with James Baldwin, to highlight the resonance of her work with contemporary gay concerns, and the centrality of his conceptions of the city to his understandings of the world. In the past decade, many gay writers—journalists, critics, historians, and geographers—have drawn on Jacobs's work as they developed accounts of gay and urban life.[53] Although these writers might simply be some among the range of commentators who still cite Jacobs, particular aspects of *The Death and Life of Great American Cities* do mesh tellingly with the urban interests of late twentieth-century and early twenty-first century lesbians and gay men. That meshing is already apparent, however, in the connections between her work and that of her queer contemporary James Baldwin. In contrast to the conventional pairings of Jacobs and Mumford or Moses, I consider Jacobs and Baldwin together not in order to highlight their differences but to illuminate their sometimes shared, sometimes contrasting, and often interlocking accounts of the city— and city people—at a moment of definitive change.

I do not know whether Jane Jacobs and James Baldwin ever met. In 1961, Jacobs was a married white woman in her midforties, a journalist, and a mother, who had come to New York City, and ultimately Greenwich Village, in the mid-1930s, from a doctor's family in Scranton, Pennsylvania. Baldwin, almost ten years younger, a black man from a working-class family who had had both female and male lovers but increasingly wrote about and identified with gay men, had himself traveled from Harlem to Greenwich Village, as well as to Paris and back. Both had only high school educations. Neither of them was one of the stock figures—the elite man or vicious woman—of nineteenth-century urban discourse. But, as in the case of Jane Addams before them, their positions in the discourse of the city were ambiguous. Although "Mrs. Jacobs" was dismissed by some because she was a woman, her sexual and class status was secure.[54] Baldwin, as a black gay man, was always vulnerable to being read as a model of vice.

Baldwin's career had begun in 1948 with the publication of "The Harlem Ghetto," an analysis of the neighborhood in which he was born and had grown up, an essay later collected in *Notes of a Native Son* (1955). By 1961, he had published two very highly regarded novels. *Go Tell It on the Mountain*, which appeared in 1953, was shaped by his family's role in the first wave of the Great Migration: Baldwin's mother came to New York City from Maryland, and his stepfather from New Orleans, both in the early 1920s. *Giovanni's Room*, published in 1956, was set in the Paris to which Baldwin had fled in the late 1940s, when he was in his midtwenties. In 1961, he combined the essays he had written since the mid-1950s into a new volume, *Nobody Knows My Name*. In 1962, he would publish his third novel, *Another Country*, in which the main characters travel restlessly from a small town in the American South and the outer boroughs of New York City, up and down Manhattan and to Paris and back. As Jacobs redirected urban debate, Baldwin, in his essays and fiction about nationality, race, sexuality, and gender, prefigured and helped to shape the politics and political analyses of desire for the rest of the century.

By 1961, Jacobs had spent years as a journalist writing about architecture and as a New Yorker working with her neighbors, fighting efforts to classify as a slum the streets in front of her Village windows. Moses wanted to demolish the existing mix of Federal townhouses, tenements, light industry, brownstones, and apartment houses and replace them with ranks of shining new tower blocks in grass or cement plazas. The towers were to be arranged around a proposed Lower Manhattan Expressway, a highway running through Washington Square Park, at the center of the Village and the base of Fifth Avenue, linking the East River bridges and the Hudson

River tunnels, meant to speed commuters across Manhattan between the suburban prospects of Long Island and New Jersey.[55] That plan was eventually defeated, but Baldwin, returning to New York from Paris in the late 1950s, discovered there had been no such successful opposition to urban renewal in his neighborhood. "There is a housing project standing now where the house in which we grew up once stood, and one of those stunted city trees is snarling where our doorway used to be," he wrote. Projects were, in fact, "lumped all over Harlem, colorless, bleak, high, and revolting."[56] Jacobs's Hudson Street fought off the postwar slum designation that Harlem could not escape. And there were certainly other disjunctions between Jacobs's and Baldwin's lives in 1961. Both were concerned with safety in the city, for example, but only Baldwin wrote about the threat of the police.

Nevertheless, in 1961, Jacobs's passion for cities and Baldwin's passion for other men align them. In 1961, both Jacobs and Baldwin were writing their way between the verities of the postwar world and the upheavals already begun by the civil rights movement, upheavals later compounded by the antiwar, women's, and gay liberation movements, as well as the urban riots of the mid- and later 1960s. They spoke in very different registers, but for both Jacobs and Baldwin cities were a matter of life and death. Jacobs's city was, as her book title declares, in great danger; Baldwin's city was the site of both individual and national crisis; as he advised in *Nobody Knows My Name,* "Walk through the streets of Harlem and see what we, this nation, have become."[57]

Jacobs and Baldwin shared an embeddedness in their subject, which was always the world before them. They also shared an understanding of their respective projects as a matter of "seeing" and recording what they saw. Both can be read as working in the tradition of urban observers testifying to the previously unknown. But the heretofore unobserved scenes that Jacobs was committed to making legible to her readers were neither the elite Victorians' distant urban underworld, occupied by a distant urban underclass, nor the early twentieth-century sociologists' scientifically categorized zone of deterioration, populated by social outcasts and temporarily impoverished newcomers determinedly in transition to a better, less urban location and life. Instead she described what would turn out to be her revolutionary undertaking very mildly, as merely a matter of "look[ing] closely, and with as little previous expectation as is possible, at the most ordinary scenes and events, and attempt[ing] to see . . . whether any threads of principle emerge among them" (13). Baldwin explained in 1965 that his mentor and friend the painter Beauford Delany, another black gay man on his own journey, from Tennessee to Greenwich Village to Paris, had taught him to see as they walked New York City streets: "[T]he reality of his seeing caused me to see. . . . The brown leaf on the black asphalt, for example—what colors were these, really? . . . [T]he light fell down from heaven, on everything, on everybody, and . . . was always changing."[58] He called his experience of seeing and recording "witnessing." Like Jacobs, he proposed that his readers actually look at the streets under their feet.

Despite the deceptive mildness of Jacobs's method and the general understatement of her references to herself, her work radiates the passion of her inquiry. She denounces postwar "urban renewal" with a rage that powers her whole book. "This is not the rebuilding of cities. This is the sacking of cities" (4), she declares. Baldwin, by contrast, claims the passion behind his vision as love: "Because you love one human being, you see everyone else very differently than you saw them before. . . . [Y]ou begin to *see*."[59]

Their methods and their passions guaranteed that neither Jacobs nor Baldwin would defer to established authorities. Profoundly skeptical of received opinion, both assumed that "ordinary people" should be consulted and that they could speak with authority about their own experience. Both were, moreover, less interested in abstractions than in particularities, whether of human beings and human relationships, or of what Jacobs called "the peculiarity of great cities."

Jacobs illustrates her argument for the underlying order of city life by describing residents maintaining and improving neighborhoods to which they were profoundly attached, such as Boston's North End, even though these areas had been officially condemned as slums. She centers her analysis of the intricate interweaving of people and tasks and pleasures in urban life on a detailed observation of the "city ballet" of one day on her own Hudson Street. Similarly, Baldwin draws attention to those living the daily life of the city, whether he is writing about New York or Paris.

Nevertheless, Jacobs concludes her work (echoing Parks's Chicago School focus on the criminal, the defective, and the genius) by insisting that urban planners must pay attention to the "unaverage." Though her unaverage might be material (an eye-catching object) or economic (distinctive stores, schools, or cultural venues), she highlights "public characters." The experiences of "residents or users who are financially, vocationally, racially or culturally unaverage" are crucial to an accurate reading of city life, she argues, much disproportionate to their numbers, for their interpretive value, "as analytical means—as clues" (443). Similarly, Baldwin focuses on the stories of homosexuals, often those living at the center of a broad group of writers, musicians, actors, and other artists, at the centers of his cities.

Homosexuals are absent yet present in Jacobs's work. Gay people appear in *The Death and Life of Great American Cities* only as the habitués of one of the four Philadelphia squares that Jacobs discusses to demonstrate why city parks succeed or fail. Washington Square, she explains, "[s]everal decades ago," became that city's "pervert park . . . shunned by office lunchers and . . . an unmanageable vice and crime problem to park workers and police" (93).[60] Nevertheless, two of the four neighborhoods she repeatedly returns to as her models of successful urban areas—Rittenhouse, the one successful Philadelphia square; and the North Beach/Telegraph Hill district

Greenwich Village in the Naked City. Weegee (Arthur Fellig, 1899–1968), *The Gay Deceiver*, 1939. Weegee/International Center of Photography/Getty Images.

of San Francisco—were, by the 1960s, long-standing lesbian and gay neighborhoods.[61] Rittenhouse Square was "the place to go" for gay men, from the
"poorest to Main Line" residents, for cruising and as "a social thing" by
the 1940s, and its gay and lesbian presence only solidified and diversified as
the neighborhood changed in subsequent decades.[62] North Beach "became
San Francisco's first lesbian neighborhood" in the late 1940s. It was even
the subject of a song, about "mak[ing] frantic love to a cute little Jill, / Who
is shacking up with me on Telegraph Hill," for local entertainer Kay Scott.[63]
Georgetown in Washington, D.C., which Jacobs also repeatedly cites approvingly, began to have a gay presence by the late 1940s, when a newcomer to
the city could discover that three out of the four households on his corner
of Thirty-third and Q streets were gay or lesbian.[64]

Finally, Jacobs's own neighborhood, Greenwich Village, on which she relied as a model of successful urban life, was notorious from the first decades
of the century on as the most visible location in the entire country of
homosexuals, artists, and other "refugees from America."[65] As early as the
second decade of the twentieth century, Robert Park cited Greenwich Village as the ideal source of the kind of abnormal subjects that made sociology significant. Caroline F. Ware, in her classic study, *Greenwich Village,
1920–1930* (1935), observed that it was "easily possible for strangers to find
their way" to "the Lesbians" in 1930.[66] Two decades after Ware and a decade
before Jacobs, Lait and Mortimer helpfully explained in their 1951 edition
of *New York: Confidential!* that although "[n]ot all of New York's queer . . .
people live in Greenwich Village" and not everyone in the neighborhood
was queer, "most of those who advertise their oddities, the long-haired
men, the short-haired women, those not sure exactly what they are, gravi-
tate to the Village."[67] Harlem's reputation for "gay" life had been established
by the decade of Baldwin's birth, the 1920s.[68] But in 1940 Baldwin also made
his way to the Village, where he met Beauford Delany, when he was sixteen
years old.[69]

BECAUSE JACOBS AND Baldwin were skeptical of received opinion and committed instead to observing the world before them, they were both at odds
with a culture in which great American cities could be dismissed as a part
of "the past" to be escaped by a national surge toward a suburban life that
could be carried on perpetually in the present. They shared the broader
cultural identification of cities with the past, but they argued that the ways

in which cities dealt with their citizens, and the ways citizens experienced their cities, were intelligible only if read historically. Moreover, that history had to be confronted in the city if the city and the nation were to progress.

Their understandings of history in the city were brought into focus by two different, fundamental, and interrelated assumptions about city life made over the previous hundred years. Those assumptions had been put to work before World War II by the sociologists of the later Chicago School, who opposed "social disorganization" to "individuality" but saw both as key urban qualities. By the 1950s, "social disorganization" and "individuality" were more popularly understood as the threat of urban "disorder" and the promise of urban "freedom." Those convinced of the primacy of disorder thought urban freedom produced disorder, and those committed to the possibility of freedom thought urban disorder allowed freedom. Jacobs rejected the assumption of urban disorder, Baldwin the assumption of urban freedom.

In *The Death and Life of Great American Cities,* Jacobs proposes two kinds of urban order: an order in the history of conceptions of the city that led to the powerful belief in urban disorder, which she is attempting to undermine; and an order in the present, in the uses of city streets, which she wants to make legible. She argues that the reigning conviction—that cities embodied social disorder—among urban planners and others who administered cities (either directly, through city governments, or indirectly, through financial institutions) was a product of assumptions embedded in the history of city planning. Post–World War II urban planners, she contends, drew on Victorian responses to the brutal effects of industrialization in the poorest sections of the great cities of the nineteenth century, cities perceived as chaotic in themselves as well as politically and morally threatening to the established social order. Those Victorian responses were exemplified in urban planning by Englishman Ebenezer Howard's extraordinarily influential 1898 proposals for the dispersal of the London masses into alternative "garden cities." The goal of the Garden City movement, Jacobs argues, was not only the dispersal of people; the orderly separation and distribution of areas for work, for residence, and for organized play would facilitate social control as well.

Jacobs traces the lineage of the urban planning schemes that accompanied the subsequent development of modern great cities through London, Paris, and Chicago, from the Garden City advocates and the contemporary

City Beautiful movement (associated with the architect Daniel Burnham) that first flowered at the Chicago World's Fair of 1893, to the decentrists of the American regional planning movement of the 1920s (most fully identified with the work of Lewis Mumford), and to France and Le Corbusier's proposal in the 1920s for a Radiant City of monumental towers set in empty parks. "[M]oralisms on people's private lives," Jacobs insists, were routinely and "deeply confused with concepts about the workings of cities" (41). Each of these movements and plans, she argues, was founded on a fundamental distaste for "[p]eople gathered in concentrations of big-city size and density," a belief that such gatherings were "an automatic . . . evil." These planners assumed "that human beings are . . . noxious in large numbers" (220), because large numbers contain the possibility of encounters across social boundaries and of moral and political disruption, just as the post–World War II defenders of "America" against its cities feared. The drive of urban planning was, she argues, to "decontaminat[e]" (25). This combination of moralism and political fear produced, according to Jacobs, a commitment to sorting out and containing civic uses and persons, and ultimately to abstracting civic uses and persons from the city street itself.

Postwar "urban renewal" projects were the grim flowering of this history, Jacobs argues. She indicts contemporary planners for their eagerness to demolish entire neighborhoods and replace them with cheap versions of Radiant City tower blocks in empty plazas. According to such schemes, the city could be recreated in an orderly fashion based on the segregation of populations into "price-tagged" groups and a concomitant segregation of uses (shopping, industry, cultural centers, and so on), just as in the new suburbia, intensifying racial as well as class divisions (4). As Baldwin observed in 1965, "Negroes" knew that "when someone says 'urban renewal' some Negroes are going to be thrown out into the streets."[70] Of the tens of thousands of people displaced in New York by Moses's Slum Clearance Committee, a vastly disproportionate number were poor African Americans and Puerto Ricans.[71]

In contrast to the assumptions crystallized in these urban renewal projects, Jacobs argues that only density and "a most intricate and close-grained diversity" of persons and of uses "that give each other constant mutual support, both economically and socially," would support functional cities by producing healthy streets (41). Such diversity must also include a wide range of ages and types of buildings, for a wide range of commercial and residential uses. Although she admits the legal as a boundary—"The greater and more plentiful the range of all legitimate interests (in the strictly legal sense) that city streets and their enterprises can satisfy, the better for the streets and for the safety and civilization of the city" (41)—she explicitly rejects moral explanations for the problems of urban life. She mocks "[r]e-formers [who] have long observed city people loitering on busy corners, hanging around in candy stores and bars and drinking soda pop on stoops, and have passed a judgement, the gist of which is: 'This is deplorable!'" (85). She advocates both bars and churches, and their proximity, as on her own Hudson Street: "There is not only room in cities for such differences and many more in taste, purpose, and interest of occupation; cities also have a need for people with all these differences in taste and proclivity" (41). Unlike so many earlier urban observers, she was not interested in whether social differences are natural or whether cities produce them or simply foster them. Her city, however, *needs* social difference to produce the continuing sequence of users who provide social and economic stability on city streets. On that basis, she traces what she calls the "organized com-plexity" in the patterns of urban life—the daily "ballet" of Hudson Street—rather than either the simple disorder others claim to find or the simple order they want to produce (433).

While Jacobs battled assumptions of urban disorder, Baldwin battled the myth of urban freedom, of the infinite possibilities for the elaboration of individuality bestowed by the city, which had been seen as both the source and the result of urban disorder. In his early fiction, his homosexual char-acters—black and white—all young men from the provinces in their own ways, flee to "the city" (even those who were born in cities), as if the city will make them free. For John, the young black boy at the heart of *Go Tell It on the Mountain,* "the city" is downtown from the Harlem uptown in which he lives. It is only after we are first told of John's "sin," the interest in other boys and men that he barely understands himself, that we first hear of "his decision. He would not be like his father, or his father's fathers [*sic*]. He would have another life."[72] Pausing on a hill in Central Park, in the journey downtown he makes in the middle of the novel's day, he is described as "willing to throw himself headlong into the city that glowed before him" (33). His thinking infused with the religion of the father he is rejecting, he imagines that "he would live in this shining city which his ancestors had seen from far away. For it was his" (33). Similarly, David, the white protagonist of Baldwin's *Giovanni's Room*, goes to Paris to "find him-self" after years spent "in constant motion" fleeing desires "which shamed and frightened" him.[73] In *Another Country*, Eric, growing up white and gay in a small town in the American South, imagines escaping to a North entirely urban ("'New York? or Chicago? or maybe San Francisco?' . . . [or] Hollywood") and, after reaching New York, moves on to Paris.[74]

But Baldwin's city does not offer freedom. Instead, it intensifies what-ever conditions these refugees bring. In Baldwin's writings, people come up against their own history, their least individual experience, in the city: gay men have their homosexuality confirmed in New York or Paris; Afri-can Americans have their second-class status as black men and women in America confirmed in New York; and all Americans have their status as Americans confirmed in Paris. So in *Go Tell It on the Mountain*, John's hopes of the city downtown are immediately chilled by his fear of "the people he had seen in that city, whose eyes held no love for him" (33). Similarly, each of the members of his family, who had moved to New York City in search of greater freedom, found that they could escape there nei-ther their personal histories nor the ongoing history of American racism. David in *Giovanni's Room*, in Paris, finds "the same self from which I had spent so much time in flight" (21).[75] When Eric gets to New York, in *Another Country*, he finds the same racial divisions he grew up among. He endures years of loneliness in Paris before he establishes a relationship with another man, and they are shown in their most idyllic moments together outside of the city.

In his essays, Baldwin often chose Paris as the focus for his explication of Americans' entrapment in history. That city, for Americans after World War II, as for previous generations, he wrote, epitomized "the city's" promise of freedom, that is, sexual freedom and even or especially freedom from America: "Paris [was], according to its legend, the city where every-one loses his head, and his morals . . . and thumbs his nose at the Puri-tans—the city, in brief, where all become drunken on the fine old air of freedom."[76]

In this mythical Paris, Baldwin observed, his compatriots pursued one of two apparently distinct paths. Either they embraced the freedom proffered by the city's legend (which required living in Paris oblivious to the French) or they attempted to become Parisian (which required becom-ing French). Pursuing the freedom of the city in Paris meant abandoning

Greenwich Village in the Naked City. Weegee (Arthur Fellig, 1899–1968), *Girls at the Bar*, 1946. Weegee/International Center of Photography/Getty Images.

any sense of local social obligation, whereas attempting to become French meant abandoning any sense of national obligation. Baldwin described both efforts as quintessentially American. Each was based, he proposed, on "the very nearly unconscious assumption," characteristic of Americans, "that it is possible to consider the person apart from all the forces which have produced him." This "assumption," he argued, was "itself based on nothing less than our history, which is the history of the total, and willing, alienation of entire peoples from their forbears."[77] Nothing reveals the embeddedness of Americans in their own national history, he concluded, so much as their acting out such attempts to abandon their individual histories in the quintessential great city.

The city that could offer Baldwin, as an African American gay man, any measure of those freedoms conventionally ascribed to all great cities had to be in another country. In Paris, he gained mobility: "I was born in New York, but have lived only in pockets of it. In Paris, I lived in all parts of the city . . . and know all kinds of people."[78] There he also gained privacy. "Paris . . . by leaving me completely alone," he wrote, offered "total indifference [which] came as a great relief and, even, as a mark of respect."[79]

But he still could not disregard the history and present particularity of Paris, even though that city was in another country. Baldwin would write later in his life, "I had never . . . been even remotely romantic about Paris. . . . I knew too much about the French Revolution for that. I had read too much Balzac for that."[80] He was insistent about the necessity of paying attention to "the life of Paris itself . . . the lives, that is, of the natives," as well as to the experiences of other immigrants and to contemporary French politics, especially the struggle over Algeria and its impact on the Arabs and Africans in the city.[81] Baldwin was acutely aware that his mobility and privacy in Paris were based not only on the structure of Paris as a city and his distance there from "home" but also on his status as an American. He described Richard Wright as "fond of referring to Paris as the 'city of refuge'—which it certainly was, God knows, for the likes of us. But it was not a city of refuge to the French, still less for anyone belonging to France; and it would not have been a city of refuge for us if we had not been armed with American passports."[82] He wanted his readers always to be aware that whatever freedom was to be found in the city was entangled with constraint, based on categorical status (one's own or others'), and embedded in the histories of cities and of nations.

Even when Jacobs's and Baldwin's senses of the place of their city in the history of cities diverged, they agreed on the aspect of urban history most salient to their present. Jacobs identified the myth of urban disorder she was battling as a legacy of fears of the horrors of Victorian cities, fears of the great city as it was developing. Baldwin began *The Fire Next Time* (1963) by presenting the persistence of that Victorian city as a measure of African Americans' lack of freedom in the city and the world, when he wrote to his nephew, "[Y]our countrymen, have caused you to be born under conditions not very far removed from those described for us by Charles Dickens in the London of more than a hundred years ago."[83]

CHILDREN AND STRANGERS

Just as in the face of a contemporary "American" rejection of the past Jacobs and Baldwin insisted on the force of history, in the face of a contemporary America relentlessly focused on the family they were both intensely concerned with connections beyond the family—connections which they (along with everyone else) identified with the city. Moreover, that those nonfamilial connections, whether a matter of personal relations or social structures, were founded on interdependence was an article of faith they shared.

In *The Death and Life of Great American Cities,* Jacobs presented interdependence as "the first fundamental of successful city life: People must take a modicum of public responsibility for each other even if they have no ties to each other" (82). Postwar "urban renewal" was so destructive of the fabric of city life (as well as of the lives of the tens of thousands of people who lost their homes, businesses, and jobs), she set out to demonstrate, because of its violation of this "first fundamental."

For Baldwin, interdependence was a matter not only of individual interactions but also of the relationships between social groups and between understandings of social groups, especially sexual and racial groups. In "Preservation of Innocence," in 1949 (along with "The Harlem Ghetto," one of his earliest published essays), Baldwin asserted the interdependence of cultural understandings of homosexuality and heterosexuality, arguing that in the postwar United States, hostility to homosexuality was being intensified to support the version of heterosexuality (based on caricatured gender roles) that was so actively advocated. The homosexual's "present debasement and our obsession with him" he proposed, "corresponds to the debasement of the relationship between the sexes; and . . . his ambiguous and terrible position in our society reflects the ambiguities and terrors which time has deposited on that relationship."[84] In *Nobody Knows My Name,* in 1961, he would argue in a similar vein, about relations between black and white Americans, that "the country's image of the Negro, which hasn't very much to do with the Negro, has never failed to reflect with a kind of frightening accuracy the state of mind of the country."[85] Baldwin also insisted on the consequences of such projections for those doing the projecting—for heterosexuals, for whites, and for "America." He concludes "Fifth Avenue, Uptown," an essay in that 1961 volume, about the relations between black and white embodied, as its title implies, in the contrast between Fifth Avenue uptown and downtown, with these words: "It is a terrible, an inexorable, law that one cannot deny the humanity of another without diminishing one's own: in the face of one's victim, one sees oneself."[86]

This was not a lesson postwar America was eager to learn. As Jacobs recognized, the high-handed postwar schemes for "urban renewal" rested (as did the simultaneous push toward suburbanization) on a culture that acknowledged the family as the only significant social group and saw families as operating fundamentally in isolation. "[T]he supposed feasibility of large-scale relocation of citizens," she observed, depended on planners turning individuals into "statistics" about income and family size: "[T]hese citizens were no longer components of any unit except the family, and could be dealt with intellectually like grains of sand, or electrons or billiard balls" (437). If a family moved intact—whether it was forcibly displaced by "slum clearance," unable to afford city housing any longer, or eager to escape the city for more space and newer appliances in the suburbs—all of its members' human needs and claims could be assumed to have been dealt with. Meanwhile, the tearing apart of communities was rendered invisible.[87]

Jacobs herself sidesteps the family (though she authorizes herself by referring glancingly, perhaps half a dozen times, to her own children or her husband). Her focus is on city relations as relations beyond the family *and* beyond communities of the "like." When she grudgingly admits that a certain social setup works sometimes, but only for very narrowly defined groups of very similar people, she is telling her readers that that social setup does not help at all to sustain urban life.

In opposition to the history of European and American urban planning that she describes as hostile to the street, and in opposition to the contemporary American cultural focus on the family, Jacobs focused her account of the city on the workings of streets, the sites of the interaction of the greatest number of unrelated people. Her account of city streets is organized around two figures, "the child" and "the stranger," both also key figures in Baldwin's early work.

JACOBS SIDESTEPS FAMILIES, yet she makes the children who were central to the family focus of postwar America also a focus of her own demonstration of the order and value of effectively functioning city streets. Children are also the most frequent subjects of her anecdotes illustrating the breakdown of that public life. We hear about a child trapped in the elevator of a high-rise project, to whose cries for help no one responds (66); two Puerto Rican boys rousted from their seats on a bench in Stuyvesant Town and sent outside the fence by a pair of security guards (49); and a white boy growing up in a fenced enclave who is surprised and slightly threatened by the idea that there are some buildings anyone can walk up to (50). That children will be the victims of urban social failure is Jacobs's lesson. But send your children out to play in the streets, she advised the parents of postwar America. Your children will flourish. And those streets, and America, might survive.

The "peculiarity of cities," Jacobs observes, is the presence of strangers on their streets: "Great cities are not like towns, only larger. They are not like suburbs, only denser. They differ from towns and suburbs in basic ways, and one of these is that cities are, by definition, full of strangers" (30). For Jacobs, the stranger, like the child, is not just an urban presence but a test. Functional cities must be able to cope with strangers and allow strangers to cope with each other and with the streets. Lack of safety in the city is not a product of "poor" or "minority" neighborhoods or the presence of "the outcast" (31). Thriving neighborhoods are those constantly in use by "people of every race and background," strangers to one another (33). Such intense use makes these neighborhoods thrive.

By bringing together the child and the stranger, Jacobs directly engages the most basic element of the fear of the city fundamental to the rhetoric of her cultural moment: the assertion that strangers are a threat to children. At the center of her explanation of why city streets are not in fact unsafe, she tells the story of "a suppressed struggle going on between a man

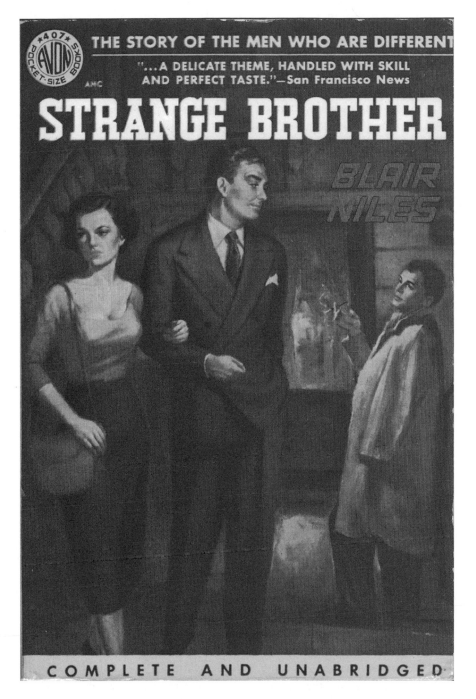

Cover of *Strange Brother,* by Blair Niles (1931; repr., New York: Avon, 1952).

and a little girl of eight or nine years old. The man seemed to be trying to get the girl to go with him" (38). She saw this struggle from her Hudson Street window and considered going down to the street to intervene, she explains, when it became apparent to her that many others—storekeepers, residents, and visitors to the block—were also observing and were poised to prevent "a little girl . . . [from being] dragged off" (39). Children and strangers, separately and especially together, are routinely the subjects of such watchful surveillance, she insists. This child and this stranger turn out to be daughter and father. They are not officially, therefore, though they might have been in practice, strange to one another. They do not need the street's surveillance. But even the family, in public, is subjected to the "eyes on the street," the evidence of interdependence that ensures, on properly functioning blocks, the propriety of strangers and the safety of children.

Jacobs's anecdote attempts to counter an assumed division between the safety of relationships within the family and the danger always potential in relationships outside of the family. That the threat of strangers to children was usually seen as a sexual one is reflected in her pairing of a man and a small girl. The prospect of girls being dragged from the street by strange men is part of the history of the sexualized city. It is also the most extreme manifestation of a broader fear Jacobs locates in the urban planning literature. She identifies this fear as "a fantasy" about the transmission of sexual knowledge whenever a "population of children is condemned to play on the city streets. These pale and rickety children, in their sinister moral environment, are telling each other canards about sex, sniggering evilly and learning new forms of corruption as efficiently as if they were in reform school. This situation is called 'the moral and physical toll taken of [*sic*] our youth by the streets,' sometimes it is called simply 'the gutter'" (74). In this fantasy, sex epitomizes the city's threat to the invariably unhealthy ("pale and rickety") children condemned to its environs.

The quintessential stranger of postwar American culture was understood to be the sexual psychopath, and he (always he) was understood to be especially threatening to children. And the quintessential sexual psychopath of postwar culture was the male homosexual, whatever the gender of the child under attack. Two waves of intense public panic about sexual psychopaths in the United States occurred in the mid-twentieth century, the first from 1937 to 1940 and the second immediately after the war, from 1945 to its peak in 1955. This last panic was whipped up by sensationalized newspaper accounts of attacks on children; magazine articles such as a 1950 *Collier's* series, "Terror in Our Cities"; "scientific" reports; and laws to contain this menace, proposed and passed in state capitals across the country. "[M]en diagnosed as psychopaths were more likely to be accused of pedophilia and homosexuality than of rape or murder," given that homosexuals were repeatedly represented as, by definition, child molesters.[88] As Dr. J. Paul de River, "a crude popularizer of theories of sexual psychopathology," warned in *The Sexual Criminal* (1949), "[T]he homosexual is an inveterate seducer of the young of both sexes ... not content with being degenerate himself: he must have degenerate companions and is ever seeking for younger victims."[89]

In *The Death and Life of Great American Cities,* Jacobs tries to redefine "the stranger," to distinguish between "predatory strangers" and "the many, many peaceable and well-meaning strangers" (36) going about their business on city streets. She does this partly by recasting the relations of strangers and children. In Jacobs's city, to be a stranger is not necessarily to be hostile. It is also not necessarily to be indifferent. The presence of peaceable strangers, she argues, is a sign of safety on the streets. Strangers produce safety for children, for other strangers, and for themselves. They offer material help. They are the unknown people walking by who will intervene if someone is threatening a child or has had an accident. But the presence of strangers also teaches children the nature of safety. Jacobs argues that children should learn that they are part of "a web of public respect and trust" (56), of protective and productive exchanges beyond the family. In this way they will learn about a social compact broader than that based on (hetero)sexual relations, and will gain a more complex understanding of the social world than that provided by the family alone. "[O]nly from the ordinary adults of the city sidewalks," she argues, and "from the experience of having *other people without ties of kinship or close friendship or formal responsibility to you* take a modicum of public responsibility for you" there, can "children learn ... the first fundamental of successful city life: People must take a modicum of public responsibility for each other even if they have no ties to each other" (82; emphasis in original).

Jacobs's reference to the role of "corruption" in her account of the fantasy of "the gutter" suggests, however, that the concern underlying fears about children in the city, about the meetings of children and strangers, is not simply that the city or its strangers will harm children; historian Estelle Freedman has argued that a "major motive of the psychopath laws was to prevent the contagion of homosexuality from spreading from adults to youths."[90] This is one version of the general fear (which is in fact Jacobs's hope), that strangers will teach children that the world beyond the family is not to be feared. In the popular imagination, the city, or the strangers whom the children of America might meet there, could harm them by luring them away from the family and turning them into strangers themselves, which is to say, into (im)proper and permanent denizens of the city.

IN *NOTES OF a Native Son,* Baldwin declares himself a child of America. In *Nobody Knows My Name,* he declares himself a stranger there. Like Jacobs, he uses the experience of children as a measure of the state of the city, and so of the world. He concludes "The Harlem Ghetto," "I can conceive of no Negro native to this country who has not, by the age of puberty, been irreparably scarred by the conditions of his life. All over Harlem, Negro boys and girls are growing into stunted maturity, trying desperately to find a place to stand."[91] In "Fifth Avenue, Uptown," he warns, "[C]hildren do not like ghettos. It takes them nearly no time to discover exactly why they are there."[92] Baldwin wrote a great deal about children (gay children, both black and white) in his early work, especially in his fiction. They invariably experience themselves as strangers in their own families and often in the world of the city as well.

When Baldwin describes, in fiction or in essays, children on the street, for him, as for Jacobs, it is a scene inseparable from surveillance. Of East 131st Street at Lenox Avenue, he writes, "All along the street there are people who watched me grow up, people who grew up with me, people I watched grow up along with my brothers and sisters; and, sometimes in my arms, sometimes underfoot, sometimes at my shoulder—or on it—their children, a riot, a forest of children, who include my nieces and nephews."[93] Like Jacobs, Baldwin describes local adults observing the children's behavior, punishing a child for wrongdoing, and then reporting to the child's parents. Jacobs describes a network that extends beyond the family; it might be the storekeeper across the street who reprimands her son for running into the traffic and then speaks to her husband about the incident. Baldwin describes a network of families sharing responsibility for neighborhood children, one mother dealing with another mother's child.

Although his streets are an extension of the family, Baldwin also makes it clearer than Jacobs that a child him- or herself might be a stranger on the streets, even the streets identified with his or her family. In *Go Tell It on the Mountain,* John feels rejected on the streets of Harlem by children and adults alike:

> [L]ittle girls in pigtails, skipping rope, would establish on the sidewalk a barricade through which he must stumble as best he might. Boys would be throwing ball. . . . [T]hey would look at him and call:
> "Hey, Frog-eyes!"
> Men would be standing on corners . . . watching him pass, girls would be sitting on stoops . . . mocking his walk. Grandmothers would stare out of windows, saying:
> "That sure is a sorry little boy." (216)[94]

Families fail Baldwin's strange children. The adults in the vicinity are rarely connected to one another and often indifferent to their children's needs. Although in *Go Tell It on the Mountain* the protagonist is deeply attached to his mother, the boy is subjected to the bitter hostility of his step-father, a man driven by guilt and the relentlessness of white racism, who favors his own son over his stepson at every turn. John is very precariously anchored in their home. In *Giovanni's Room,* David, having lost his mother before he knew her, is raised by his father and his father's sister, who are chiefly connected by their struggle over the gender and sexual proprieties they feel they must impart to the boy.[95] The aunt insists that the father is no adequate model for his son, because of his drinking and his "women," that "[a] man . . . is not the same thing as a bull" (15). The father can only protest, "[A]ll I want for David is that he grow up to be a man. And when I say a man . . . I don't mean a Sunday school teacher" (15). As David grows older, this father wants only to be his son's buddy rather than his parent, to David's dismay. In *Another Country,* Eric's family fails because of his parents' inadequate commitment to each other as well as to parenting. He is the child of wealthy white southerners who leave him to be raised by their African American cook and handyman. His mother spends all of her time as a "civic leader" in the local women's organizations; his father absents himself in the all-male worlds of "the bank and . . . the golf course . . . hunting lodges, and . . . poker tables" (197).[96]

City streets could be a foil for a black family intent on respectability, as in *Go Tell It on the Mountain.* In order to keep his family safe from the city—that is, still a family—the preacher-stepfather tries to keep all of his children off the streets. John "remembered his father and his mother, and all the arms stretched out to hold him back, to save him from this city where, they said, his soul would find perdition" (33). At the same time, although white America identifies the city with black Americans, John knows that "the city" (downtown) is overwhelmingly white. He understands that "he was a stranger there" too (33).

In the postwar white America of *Giovanni's Room*, the "family" offers a fantasy of refuge to someone like David, in flight from his own strangeness. When other social groupings have been erased and places are interchangeable, the family is all that locates an individual in the world, and having children is the only means of ensuring that one is not a stranger.[97] With the intensity of someone who never had such a family, David imagines that if he demonstrates his fulfillment of proper gender and sexual roles by creating a family, he will find a place for himself in the world. As he insists, "I wanted to be inside again, with the light and safety, with my manhood unquestioned, watching my woman put my children to bed" (104). The all-American girl to whom he becomes engaged shares his belief in a connection between family and being located. "I want to get married," she tells him. "I want to start having kids. I want us to live someplace, I want *you*" (161; emphasis in original). But David cannot repress the desire for other men that exiles him from the family and thus, he fears, from any place in the world.

If Baldwin's children are fundamentally strangers, the childishness that is being protected in his writing is most often that of adults. Americans, Baldwin says in "Preservation of Innocence," seek to remain children, "to shun" the "metamorphosis" whereby the child becomes an adult, because they are afraid to admit the complexity, the strangeness, in themselves or others.[98] As David, in *Giovanni's Room*, observes other white Americans in Paris, "even grandmothers seem to have had no traffic with the flesh," while "the boy he had been shone, somehow, unsoiled, untouched, unchanged, through the eyes of the man of sixty" (89–90). Baldwin's strange children, painfully, become the only real adults in his America. At the same time, to be really adult is to be a stranger in America.

As it is for Jacobs's city, for Baldwin's characters survival depends on being able to cope with strangers. The homosexuality that his characters find in the city is, as the 1950s defenders of "America" feared, a matter of engaging with strangers and strangeness, not only in oneself but also in others. Confirming earlier cultural convictions that homosexuality leads to the breaching of social divisions, in Baldwin's novels desire involves crossing racial as well as sexual boundaries. Contemplating the city he longs to embrace, John struggles in *Go Tell It on the Mountain* to balance his father's experience (that whites must be feared) against his own experience (that he has been helped by white teachers). For John, to be gay is to take up the promise of the city, which means not only leaving his family but entering a white world. In *Another Country*, Eric leaves his family and his southern town for a northern city not only because he desires men but because he desires a black man.[99] Homosexuality not only disrupts racial divisions in the city beyond the family, it undermines sexual divisions as well. Eric discovers in New York an "ignorant army. They were husbands, they were fathers, gangsters, football players, rovers, and they were everywhere. Or they were, in any case, in all of the places he had been assured they could not be found and the need they brought to him was one they scarcely knew they had, which they spent their lives denying" (211).

IN THEIR DEPICTIONS of children and strangers, Jacobs and Baldwin both circle around conceptions of the public, the private, and the relationship between public and private life. For both, the relationship between public and private life is crucial, as it has historically been in the city and for homosexuals. But while postwar "America" denied public lives to white women such as Jacobs, it denied black men like Baldwin (and gay men of any race who did not hide their sexuality) both public *and* private lives. Jacobs saw in the state of the cities a crisis produced by a failure of public life, namely, a failure to separate public and private, the denial of acceptable public identities to some people because of their perceived strangeness. Baldwin also saw a crisis in public life, but the crisis he identified was produced, by contrast, by the failure to join public and private, the result of "an emotional poverty so bottomless, and a terror . . . of human touch, so deep, that virtually no American appears able to achieve any viable, organic connection between his public stance and his private life."[100] Whites invented "the Negro" and heterosexuals "the homosexual," he argued, to represent their own exiled private selves, to embody strangenesses which could then be repudiated by denying to "Negroes" and "homosexuals" private lives and public credit.

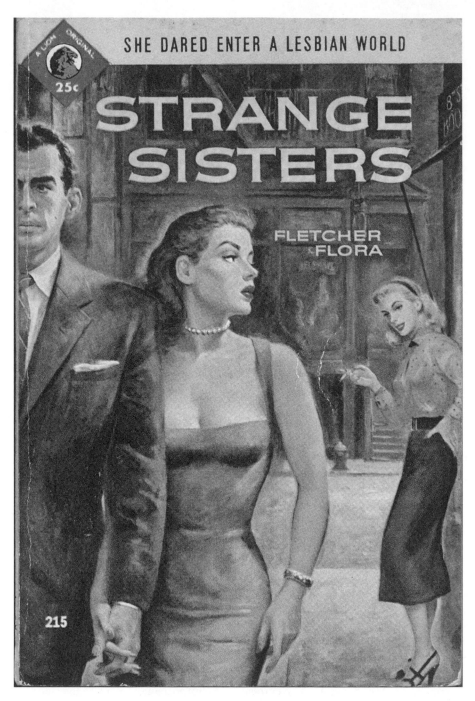

Cover of *Strange Sisters*, by Fletcher Flora (New York: Lion, 1954).

Jacobs's "eyes on the street" are central to a system of surveillance in which strangers protect children and each other by keeping track of what is happening around them. But her model for functional city life depends upon the combination of that system of surveillance with a promise of privacy. She implicitly rejects the ambitions of the flaneur, even as they were modified by Jane Addams. "Nobody can keep open house in a great city," she announces. "Nobody wants to" (55–56). In fact, being able to close one's doors is, she implies, a particular privilege of urban life. Following Simmel and the later Chicago School, but without their counterbalancing anxieties about isolation, she lauds the city for the privacy it offers. "Privacy is precious in cities . . . indispensable," she argues, "a gift of great city life deeply cherished and jealously guarded" (58–59).[101]

An obsession with privacy, Jacobs argued, is disruptive. The projects produced by "urban renewal" were internally dysfunctional as well as antithetical to urban life, whatever the price of the price-tagged populations they contained, she argued, because the new high-rise-tower enclaves were most often turned away from the street—and even actually fenced off—in pursuit of a privacy for their tenants that ruptured the streetscapes of their neighborhoods. The poor are particularly vulnerable to denials of privacy, she knew. She described the ongoing monitoring of residents' incomes, of the number of people living in their apartments, and other such indignities in the public housing being built, making tenants wary even of their neighbors, when the slightest evidence of an economic decline or improvement could lead to their losing their homes. But the desire for privacy, she said, is shared, "one of the attributes of cities that is precious to most city people, whether their incomes are high or their incomes are low, whether they are white or colored, whether they are old inhabitants or new" (58–59).

Jacobs's functional city is a place not only of strangers but of the possibility—even the promise—of being a stranger, of having a public life. That possibility is not simply a matter of default, inevitably produced by the massing of city people that worried earlier commentators. Nor is it ensured simply by the possibility of closing doors. One can be a stranger in the city, Jacobs argues, because one can actively manage information about oneself: "[O]nly those you choose to tell will know much about you" (58).

Valuing the emphasis on "front," the ability to skate on surfaces in urban life that made Simmel and later Park uneasy, Jacobs argues that "a feeling for the public identity of people" creates "a web of public respect and trust" as "a resource in time of personal or neighborhood need" (56). It is crucial to the "informal public life" she advocates that people can and do remain strangers, not only so that they can pass on the street but also so that they can develop neighborhood institutions (57). Such institutions will develop only if "above all, *[they] impl[y] no private commitments*" (56; emphasis in original). City life works because its multitude of daily exchanges can be confined to the public realm. That depends, however, on *everyone's* having access to an acceptable public identity, on there being no populations who need to fear surveillance. Her city cannot afford the naming of some kinds of people as so definitively "strange" that they cannot be understood as peaceable.

But privacy is even harder to find and surveillance much more explicitly threatening for the gay and the black characters, as well as for the interracial couples, that Baldwin focused on in his early fiction than it was for Wilde in the 1880s and 1890s or for the lesbians Hall described in the 1920s. Like Hall's Stephen Gordon, however, Baldwin's characters experience their legibility as being out of their own control. They are always vulnerable to the interpretations of others. In *Another Country*, Eric is unable to hide his sexuality even as a child, when he barely knows that he has a secret to keep and certainly does not know what that secret might be: his "fantasies, however unreadable they were for him . . . [were] inscribed in every one of his gestures . . . betrayed in every inflection of his voice, and lived in his eyes with all the brilliance and beauty and terror of desire" (199). "The trouble with a secret life," Baldwin observes, "is that it is very frequently a secret from the person who lives it and not at all a secret for the people he encounters" (199).

In addition to being watched by the rest of the population, in the city Baldwin's black men are watched by the police. Those police are not interested in distinguishing one black man from another. They drive Richard, John's biological father, to despair and suicide in *Go Tell It on the Mountain* by sweeping him up and brutally beating him because he happens to walk into the vicinity of a crime.

For black men, as for gay men, in Baldwin's world, the problem of their legibility is not confined to the city. Like Hall's Stephen, Baldwin's Eric brings the burden of surveillance from his small town to the city with him. Nevertheless, Baldwin's black and gay characters are particularly closely surveyed—often threateningly—on the street. The adult David, in *Giovanni's*

Room, is obsessed with his own legibility. This obsession is played out in private—the novel begins with him searching his own reflection in a window and ends with him staring at himself in a mirror—as well as in the Paris gay bar he frequents in order to demonstrate that he is not gay. (There he is, of course, avidly watched by everyone waiting for his inevitable "fall.") But his terror is most acute on the streets.[102] He reports finding himself, in Paris, staring at a sailor. When the sailor looks back, David interprets his response as a hostile "I know you" (92). Shaken, "not daring to look back," David considers the exchange: "I wondered what he had seen in me to elicit such instantaneous contempt. I was too old to suppose that it had anything to do with my walk, or the way I held my hands, or my voice—which, anyway, he had not heard. It was something else, and I would never see it. I would never dare to see it. It would be like looking at the naked sun" (92). If David could see his own difference, he implies, he would be blinded.

In *Another Country,* Eric copes by making the problem of his legibility his life's work. As an actor (as so many of the black gay and bisexual men in Baldwin's later fiction are actors or other types of performers), it becomes his job to manage information about himself. He achieves thereby a status fundamental (according to so many commentators) to urban life. To become an actor (or a playwright, as for Wilde, perhaps) is to formalize the experience of surveillance and the commitment to controlling one's legibility that is fundamental to the survival of Baldwin's black and white gay men. But agreeing to be an actor does not in itself produce an acceptable public identity. "[P]art of the price the Negro pays for his position in this society," Baldwin claims, is that "he is almost always acting. A Negro learns to gauge precisely what reaction the alien person facing him desires, and he produces it with disarming artlessness."[103] If the problem of the white gay men whom Baldwin describes in his early fiction is that, however they act, they cannot control their legibility, the legibility of black men as black men, as his early essays suggest, is differently but similarly unmanageable: "One had the choice, either of 'acting just like a nigger' or of *not* acting just like a nigger—and only those who have tried it know how impossible it is to tell the difference."[104]

In *Nobody Knows My Name,* Baldwin writes that "the stigma and danger of being a Negro" rested, in part, on the fact that "[t]here was not, no matter where one turned, any acceptable image of oneself, no proof of one's existence."[105] Black men of any sexuality, as well as gay men of any race, who had to bear the burden of strangeness for the culture had no acceptable public identities, as children or adults. They could not become peaceable strangers. Baldwin anatomizes the concomitant cultural refusal of private life to gays and lesbians in *Another Country*. Writing of Eric, he says, "He knew that he had no honor which the world could recognize. His life, passions, trials, loves, were, at worst, filth, and, at best, disease in the eyes of the world, and crimes in the eyes of his countrymen" (212).

In Jacobs's account of the city, she explains over and over that successful urban life requires that everyone on the street be credited with an acceptable public identity. And without successful urban life, she insists, there will be no successful public life for the nation: "Sidewalk public contact and sidewalk public safety, taken together, bear directly on our country's most serious social problem—segregation and racial discrimination" (71). Baldwin says repeatedly, and more and more clearly, that the country's failure, the failure epitomized by the state of Harlem, is a "failure of private life," which "has always had the most devastating effect on American public conduct, and on black-white relations."[106]

Neighborhoods and Slums

If "children" and "strangers" are the figures Jacobs uses to organize her account of city streets, "neighborhoods" and "slums"—key terms in postwar urban debates—provide the framework for her account of the city as a whole. Neighborhoods and slums were thought to be related in ways similar to strangers and children. Like the distinction between "strangers" and "children," the distinction between "neighborhoods" and "slums" was not so secure. Just as strangers threatened children, slums threatened neighborhoods. The fact that neighborhoods might be—or could become—slums was a more widely admitted possibility than the fact that children might be—or could become—strangers, but it was no less feared. "Slums" might also, according to Jacobs, "unslum." They could become neighborhoods again, with their buildings and their people intact. They did not have to be bulldozed or erased, their populations scattered, everything and everyone replaced with housing and services for wealthier people. But hers was decidedly a minority opinion.

The distinction between neighborhood and slum could be a matter of life and death, for the places and sometimes the people involved. Jacobs begins

The Death and Life of Great American Cities with a description of Boston's North End, a well-maintained and lively neighborhood to which its residents were deeply attached, investing time and energy in their homes and local institutions and drawing visitors from surrounding areas as well as locals to shop and gather there. But Boston's bankers and urban planners, she explains, defined the area as an intractable slum. To designate an area a slum made that area eligible for federally funded "renewal," generating a financial bonanza for the developers, bankers, and planners waiting to move in. Capital was eager to feed on whatever could be declared vicious (and therefore disposable). Attachment was not a factor capital considered.[107]

Behind conventional understandings of the neighborhood, Jacobs argues, lurk assumptions about the family. Fantasies of neighborhood that echo fantasies of family life, however, are "sentimental," she warns, "lead[ing] to attempts at warping city life into imitations of town or suburban life" (112). She is adamant that her readers "drop any idea of neighborhoods as self-contained or introverted units" (114). In fact, in Jacobs's analysis neighborhoods become another site of the particular forms of interdependence that are crucial to functional city life. She talks about neighborhood at three levels: as the street; as a unit for effective urban self-governing; and as an analogue to the whole, "the neighborhood of the entire city" (118). Despite her emphasis on the former (that is, Hudson Street), it is the latter, "the entire city," which allows the "bringing together [of] people with communities of interest" that she describes as "one of [the city's] greatest assets, possibly the greatest" (119).

Behind "the slum," however, waits "the ghetto." Baldwin used the two terms interchangeably. The "neighborhood of the entire city" was not available to all. Midcentury debates about neighborhoods and slums, as we have seen, were always also debates about groups. Although "communities of interest" represented one type of urban grouping, it was with ethnic and racial groups that all debates about neighborhoods and slums in the postwar decades in the United States were completely enmeshed. The subject of groups in the city was, in turn, enmeshed in battles over segregation and mobility, as well as the workings of money and of love.

Because Jacobs and Baldwin shared a belief in social entities beyond the family, they were both skeptical of the geographical mobility touted in postwar America. Both were committed to the value of attachments beyond the family, both to group and to place. But both rejected segregation. For this reason, in the early 1960s, each in a different way simultaneously endorsed and undermined group identifications.

The mobility advocated in postwar American culture is exemplified in Baldwin's early work in *Giovanni's Room,* where David's belief in "the family" as his only possible source of security is underwritten by his own family's perpetual motion. Without loyalty to a group or a place, he cannot imagine an alternative location for himself. "We lived in Brooklyn then," he explains, looking back to his first sexual encounter with another boy. "[W]e had also lived in San Francisco, where I was born, and where my mother lies buried, and we lived for awhile in Seattle, and then in New York—for me, New York is Manhattan. Later on, then, we moved from Brooklyn back to New York and by the time I came to France my father and his new wife had graduated to Connecticut. I had long been on my own by then, of course, and had been living in an apartment in the east sixties" (10). The perpetual motion of David's family mirrors his own flight from his homosexuality.

The mobility of David's family was predicated on their status as white Americans at a historical moment when mobility signified both whiteness and "the way up." As St. Clair Drake and Horace R. Cayton observed in "Bronzeville 1961," an addition to their monumental Chicago study *Black Metropolis: A Study of Negro Life in a Northern City* (first published in 1945), "[W]hite people who were 'getting ahead' . . . symbolized the fact by increasing the physical distance between themselves and Negroes."[108] As Seligman explained in "The Enduring Slums," the only "whites" who would not flee "[o]nce the percentage of Negroes" in any given neighborhood "[got] over a certain point . . . between ten and twenty percent" were "foreign-born and first generation couples."[109] By remaining in the city, such immigrants indicated that they were not really "white."

The subject of neighborhoods and slums brought both Baldwin and Jacobs, in the early 1960s, to the question of whether the experience of black Americans could be understood as parallel to that of other social/ethnic groups, as the term "ghetto" was increasingly being used to frame African American urban experience in particular. Jacobs emphasizes structural similarities in the rhetoric about different social groups. "Nowadays," she observes, "the wholesale desertions by nonslum populations" of once-stable neighborhoods "are sometimes blamed on the proximity of another slum (especially if it is a Negro slum) or on the presence of a few Negro families,

much as in the past slum formation was sometimes blamed on the presence
or proximity of Italian or Jewish or Irish families" (273). She underlines
the perennial nature of the laments of those who "always seem to feel that
there is something inferior about the current crops of slum dwellers themselves, and can point out supposedly dire differences that distinguish them
from previous immigrants" (285–86). She also points to population turnover
within contemporary slums, including black neighborhoods, insisting that
they are less static than they seem. "I see no reason to believe that Negro
slums cannot unslum too," she insists, implying that the situation of black
Americans is not distinct (285).

Baldwin is, not surprisingly, more skeptical. He makes comparisons between African Americans and other groups. He observed, in "The Harlem
Ghetto," in the late 1940s, that hostilities between blacks and Jews were fostered by each group's "precarious position," which created their similar need
to "cover their own vulnerability by a frenzied adoption of the customs of

Walter Daran, *James
Baldwin,* 1965. Walter
Daran/Hulton
Archive/Getty Images.

the country," of which antiblack and anti-Jewish sentiments were prime examples.[110] In the late 1950s, he began "Nobody Knows My Name: A Letter from the South" by comparing a "Negro" who was born and raised in the North going South for the first time, to the child of Italian immigrants going to visit Italy.[111] Yet he also said very clearly, at that moment, "All other slum dwellers, when the bank account permits it, can move out of the slum and vanish altogether from the eye of persecution. No Negro in this country has ever made that much money and it will be a long time before any Negro does." As well as sowing particular chaos in what were understood to be black neighborhoods, the segregated projects of urban renewal did nothing to disrupt this logic. Baldwin acknowledged that people did seem to escape, but added, "The people who have managed to get off this block have only got as far as a more respectable ghetto . . . and it is not . . . in the nature of any ghetto to remain respectable long."[112]

The limited mobility of black Americans reflects their inability to escape identification with and definition through their group as well as identification with and definition through particular places. "[W]hat has happened, unfailingly, whenever a significant body of Negroes move North," Baldwin observed, is that "[t]hey do not escape Jim Crow: they merely encounter another, not-less-deadly variety. They do not move to Chicago, they move to the South Side; they do not move to New York, they move to Harlem."[113] As Elizabeth, John's mother, learns in *Go Tell It on the Mountain*, "There was not, after all, a great difference between the world of the North and that of the South which she had fled; there was only this difference: the North promised more. And this similarity: what it promised it did not give, and what it gave, at length and grudgingly with one hand, it took back with the other" (163).

David's family is not made happier by their ability to move. Because we cannot escape history, Baldwin argues in *Nobody Knows My Name*, we cannot escape either group or place, which remain conceptually entangled. "Even the most incorrigible maverick has to be born somewhere," he insists. "He may leave the group that produced him—he may be forced to—but nothing will efface his origins, the marks of which he carries with him everywhere."[114] Baldwin's own sense of being an American was intensified by his attempt at flight: "I took myself out of the country and went to Paris . . . [and] I found myself, willy-nilly, alchemized into an American the moment I touched French soil."[115] The claims of the group become psychological facts, just as, he proposes, "the social forces which menaced me . . . had become interior."[116]

Whereas mobility promised whites a freedom it could deliver to no one, segregation made it easier to confuse membership in racial and ethnic groups with belonging to the city itself. The groundwork for this assumption was laid by later Chicago School analyses identifying groups, the zone of deterioration, and the city, in the 1920s and 1930s. Jacobs points out that neighborhood continuity had come to be seen as a peculiar result of the presence of ethnic or racial groups by urban commentators who, she sarcastically observes, then concluded "that only hyphenated-Americans are capable of local self-government in big cities" (138). To identify urban neighborhoods as ethnic/racial enclaves in the postwar decades reinforced the message that properly unaffiliated Americans were committed to geographic and economic mobility, the suburbs, and "the way up," as well as giving force to the assumptions that there was something essentially urban about social groups and something inevitable about segregation.

Jacobs argues that segregation—racial, economic, and gender—destroys urban life.[117] The borders of the middle- and upper-income enclaves being rapidly constructed in the 1950s, often on top of poorer neighborhoods demolished for the purpose, were marked by wire fences and patrolled by security forces to keep "the city" out of such pseudosuburban urban islands. The very structure of these enclaves fostered fear of those outside the fences among those within, even as the fences disrupted the flow of people through the area and fostered dull and dangerous vacuums on the enclaves' borders. Meanwhile, segregation in poor neighborhoods, routinely accompanied by financial blacklisting by banks and other lenders, created bitterly trapped populations who lacked the financial resources to better the spaces they inhabited as well as reasons to invest themselves in those spaces. As Baldwin wrote, "The people in Harlem know they are living there because white people do not think they are good enough to live anywhere else."[118]

Neighborhood continuity, group identification, and segregation were far from necessarily linked and were often opposed, Jacobs argued. She cited the disaggregation of these factors in practice, offering specific cases: the many stable neighborhoods, such as Greenwich Village, that were routinely explained as ethnic enclaves but were much more diverse than that label implied; and the many segregated neighborhoods, such as Harlem, that were much less stable than they appeared. At the level of systemic analysis,

Jacobs argued that segregated neighborhoods are condemned to instability because any people who can improve their situation and have any alternative housing option are compelled to leave.

FOR BOTH JACOBS and Baldwin, cities were simultaneously material entities and matters of psychic life. Both describe a city in which capital and vice reemerge as money and love. Money and love make the difference between neighborhoods and slums.

"There are only two ultimate public powers in shaping and running American cities," Jacobs writes, "votes and control of the money," and money seems much the more powerful of the two (131). Baldwin similarly identifies New York in the early 1960s as "a city . . . run entirely . . . for money," with "no sense whatever of the exigencies of human life" (*Another Country*, 316, 230). Money can foster healthy neighborhoods, giving people the resources to maintain their homes. But money is largely, in the postwar city they describe, a destructive force. When whole neighborhoods are redlined (denied financial resources for maintenance and upgrading by banks and public agencies), their deterioration is ensured. Landlords allow properties

Bob Gomel, *Jane Jacobs*, 1963. Bob Gomel/Time & Life Pictures/Getty Images.

to decline when there is no financial incentive to maintain them, or when there are substantial incentives for shoddily subdividing spaces, making it possible to overcrowd and overcharge people without other options. When a neighborhood can be declared a slum, government agencies and private developers move in with what Jacobs called the "cataclysmic money" (293) earmarked for the city's renewal, demolish buildings and social institutions, scatter populations, and make a profit for themselves.

Money destroys the city because it destroys attachment, the crucial countervailing force for both Jacobs and Baldwin. Attachment is inextricable from group identifications and connection to place. Vital urban life, Jacobs argues, requires people who stay put, who can produce the myriad interactions that result from and support a functional city—in which surveillance is required but privacy possible. All of the casual but necessary and even rewarding exchanges that take place on the street between strangers or with people known only in their public capacities—exchanges which Jacobs calls "contact"—are the basis of successful urban life. Contact makes cities work, but attachment, Jacob argues, is what will save them. Both connect people beyond the family, but attachment maintains neighborhoods. Mobility must of course be possible. Neighborhoods will be stable only when people can choose whether or not to stay where they are, when staying does not mean accepting the second-class status that segregation enforces. But neighborhoods are made secure by feeling.

When Baldwin describes New York as a city run by money, in *Another Country,* the city he describes is an arid steel and glass setting reflecting the failure of heterosexuality: women wear "bright clothes like semaphores" but are unable to attract the attention of men striding "purposefully along . . . accoutred with attaché cases" (230); and boys gather in packs, "their very walk . . . a parody of locomotion and of manhood" (231), yet they are terrified of girls and sexuality. There has come to pass a moment when "nearly all of the time's true feeling spitefully and incessantly fermented," hiding "underground" (197). Baldwin's city dwellers all now seem to be "at home with, accustomed to, brutality and indifference" and "terrified of human affection" (231).

In this city there are men who have sex with other men but do not identify themselves as gay. Eric describes the two bars at the end of his New York City block: "The longshoremen never go to the gay bar and the gay boys never go to the longshoremen's bar—but they know where to find each other when the bars close, all up and down this street" (333). Having tried to escape his own history in Paris and come back to New York, Eric however sees admitting to his own deepest attachments, and so to membership in a group, as necessary to having a "life": "[Y]ou've got to be truthful about the life you *have*. Otherwise, there's no possibility of achieving the life you *want* ... [o]r *think* you want" (336; emphasis in original).

Attachment was especially problematic for gay persons. As earlier in the century in Europe and the United States, in the postwar decades a hysterical fear of homosexuals in groups was matched with an equally hysterical insistence by cultural authorities that homosexual life was irredeemably awful because queers were incapable of attachment. As Yves reminds Eric in *Another Country*, "People do not take the relations between boys seriously, you know that. We will never know many people who believe we love each other. They do not believe there can be tears between men. They think we are only playing a game and that we do it to shock them" (223–24). Moreover, to admit to belonging to the group was to accept the stigma of the group.[119] In *Giovanni's Room*, David's fear of his own homosexual desires is most intensely manifest in his fear of the group. He expresses his horror through hostility to an effeminate young man he encounters in the same Paris gay bar in which he meets Giovanni. David finds the man's gender ambiguity so disturbing that he refuses him humanity: "[H]e did not seem real" (39). Yet real feeling between men is not reassuring but terrifying. David declares, as if it is self-evident, that "affection, for the boys I was doomed to look at, was vastly more frightening than lust" (97).[120] Lust might be an effect of circumstances, frustration, even mechanics; affection confirms the seriousness of desire, and so confirms an individual's membership in the stigmatized group of homosexuals and subjection to the stigma of belonging to a group.

Baldwin lays out the dilemma of group identification in terms of nationality in *Giovanni's Room*. David complains, "When Giovanni wanted me to know that he was displeased with me, he said I was a 'vrai américain'; conversely, when delighted, he said that I was not an American at all. . . . And I resented this. . . . [B]eing called an American . . . seemed to make me nothing more than that, whatever that was; and . . . being called *not* an American . . . seemed to make me nothing" (89; emphasis in original). The group is too limited—not to mention out of his control—to represent David's self. But without the group he might disappear entirely. In *Another Country*, Eric realizes that he cannot escape his sexuality, just as he cannot escape being an American. To do so would be to be erased. But he does not want to escape his sexuality, just as the people who maintain cities do not want to escape their neighborhoods. He is bound to his sexuality, as those who stay in the neighborhood are bound, by webs of attachment.

Within the framework of a dominant American culture in which attachment to place and attachment to group are denigrated, Baldwin sees place as well as group as inescapable. In *Another Country,* Eric and Yves make a life together, and from that life a place for themselves: "[F]rom the time of their meeting, his home had been with Yves. . . . [E]ach was, for the other, the dwelling place that each had despaired of finding" (184). But the love that provides a place also needs a "place." Neighborhoods need resources, and so does love: "*Love is expensive,* Yves had once said. . . . *One must put furniture around it, or it goes*" (225–26; emphasis in original).

To accept one's homosexuality is, for Baldwin, like staying in the neighborhood is for Jacobs, a matter of embracing the city. Not only do both decisions signify the acceptance of groups and places as well as attachment itself; both attachments might redeem the city.

The attachments to people and to places that lead people to stay, in Jacobs's city, ensure not only the survival of neighborhoods but also the unslumming of slums: "Unslumming begins with those who make modest gains, and with those to whom personal attachments overshadow their individual achievement" (283). The choice of whether to stay or go, Jacobs argues, "has to do with the most personal content of [the slum dwellers'] lives . . . with [their] personal attachments to other people, with the regard in which they believe they are held in the neighborhood, and with their sense of values as to what is of greater and what is of lesser importance in their lives" (279). The neighborhood and street become objects of affection: "[P]eople who do stay in an unslumming slum, and improve their lot within the neighborhood, often profess an intense attachment to their street neighborhood. It is a big part of their life. They seem to think that their neighborhood is unique and irreplaceable in all the world, and remarkably valuable in spite of its shortcomings" (279).[121]

Baldwin ends *Another Country* with Yves's arrival from Paris to join Eric in New York. Their reunion occupies the space in which a heterosexual marriage would have ended a more conventional story. Baldwin thus gives to his gay couple the force of a novel's happy ending. He also locates their reunion in the city, and presents their attachment to each other as trans-figuring the city he has characterized so grimly throughout the novel. Yves is apprehensive but also excited, and he feels "peace and happiness" when he sees that Eric is waiting for him (433). At that moment, even if only for a moment, Baldwin can describe New York as "that city which the people from heaven had made their home" (436).

Real and theatrical lesbians, the Gateway's club, London. Still from *The Killing of Sister George*, Robert Aldrich, director, 1968. Copyright Cinerama Releasing Corporation, Cinerama Releasing/Photofest.

7

City of Feeling

THE CULTURE OF CITIES

The debates about cities that emerged in the United States from the 1960s into the 1970s, establishing a framework for urban studies until the end of the century, featured two kinds of space: the theater and the ghetto. Jane Jacobs's and James Baldwin's shared interest in legibility, in the management of personal information, reappears in those discussions of urban "theater"; the "ghetto" was at the center of the crises of social relations they wrote about, in a city identified with the idea of the group as well as particular groups. Most subsequent accounts of the theater and the ghetto drew on the emphasis on strangers fundamental to their works. Gays could be identified with both the theater and the ghetto. As I have discussed, homosexuals routinely cast as strangers have had a great stake in the possibilities for controlling legibility that may be found in cities, as well as particularly charged relationships to the idea of the group. Consequently, gay men and lesbians, as strangers within shadowy groups, occupied the junction of debates about the theater and the ghetto in the late twentieth-century literature of the city. At the same time, the theater and the ghetto became central terms in late twentieth-century accounts of lesbians and gays, because reconceptions of the public, and of public/private divisions, to which both Jacobs and Baldwin were committed, became pivotal to urban and lesbian and gay life.

As the 1960s began, the theater was advanced as a model for all social life. However, it almost immediately appeared most applicable to the social life of strangers fostered by cities, and in particular to the strangest of those strangers. In 1959, in *The Presentation of Self in Everyday Life*, sociologist Erving Goffman, the most influential student of the Chicago School, proposed that all social interactions are organized by the necessity of managing information.[1] "[O]rdinary social intercourse is itself put together as a scene is put together, by the exchange of dramatically inflated actions, counteractions, and terminating replies," Goffman observed. "All the world is not, of course, a stage, but the crucial ways in which it isn't are not easy to specify."[2] In *Stigma*, his 1963 study of "spoiled identity," he almost immediately focused his analysis on those for whom the stage is particularly fraught, those who, because of the groups to which they belong, lack acceptable public identities. He observed that it is the social responsibility of stigmatized persons not only to manage information about themselves—whether they were discredited (their stigma being immediately legible) or discreditable (with a stigma that could be obscured)—but also to manage others' reactions to themselves. Consequently, the stranger the individual, in conventional social terms, the more aware that individual must be of the theatricality of social life: "The person with a secret failing . . . must be alive to the social situation as a scanner of possibilities," whereas "normal" people experience the same situation as "a background of unattended matters." Moreover, facing exclusion, the stigmatized are particularly pressed to self-consciously enact conformity: "The more the stigmatized individual deviates from the norm, the more wonderfully he may have to express possession of the standard subjective self if he is to convince others that he possesses it." The stigmatized person, in other words, is most likely to be conscious of the theatricality of her or his self-presentation.[3]

The figure of the stranger propels analyses of the city as a theater in the most widely cited urban studies of the 1970s, such as the work of sociologists Lyn Lofland and Richard Sennett—both of whom mark their moment as one of crisis in the city.[4] In *A World of Strangers: Order and Action in Urban Public Space* (1973), Lofland reiterates the "one respect" in which "the city is not like other kinds of places": its "peculiar social situation" is that it is "a world of strangers, a world populated by persons who are personally unknown to one another."[5] Similarly, Sennett, in *The Fall of Public Man* (1977) and subsequent volumes, identifies the city with its strangers. "There are probably as many different ways of conceiving what a city is as there are cities," he proposes. "A simple definition therefore has its attractions. The simplest is that a city is a human settlement in which strangers are likely to meet."[6]

For both Lofland and Sennett, the presence of strangers produces problems of legibility. Lofland cites the theater as an aid to interpretation, offering
examples from Greek drama, the Elizabethan stage, and nineteenth-century
Boston before settling on "the contemporary theater (along with its technological equivalents, movies and television) [which] continues to provide instructions in 'who looks like what.'"[7] Sennett offers the theater as *the*
model of urban life, citing Balzac among others. "In this milieu of strangers whose lives touch there is a problem of audience akin to the problem
of audience an actor faces in the theater," he argues. "[T]he people who
witness one's actions, declarations, and professions usually have no knowledge of one's history. . . . The arousal of belief therefore depends on how
one behaves—talks, gestures, moves, dresses, listens—within the situation
itself."[8] Both Lofland and Sennett focused on the public life of the city. But
they diverged in their treatment of individuals and groups, and that divergence reflected larger ongoing cultural tensions about the idea of the city
as the setting for group lives, tensions based in ongoing cultural ambivalence about the idea of the group.

Lofland, who accepted the identification of the city with groups, links
urban public life to public identities and recognizes groups as a key source
of public identities. The system she describes, whereby urbanites interpret
each other on the basis of "who looks like what," depends on the "what,"
the group or category, which she sees as fundamental to the mechanism of
urban life. The modern "city created a new kind of human being—the cosmopolitan," she argues, who *did not lose the capacity for knowing others personally. But he gained the capacity for knowing others only categorically . . .
for the surface, fleeting, restricted relationship.*"[9] She embraces and even
intensifies the postwar association of groups and place with urban space
by arguing that the city of strangers is manageable because city people are
identifiable to one another as members of particular groups by their locations even more than by their appearances: "In the preindustrial city, space
was chaotic, appearances were ordered. . . . [A] man was what he wore. In
the modern city, a man is where he stands."[10]

By contrast, Sennett tries to rescue the city from its postwar association
with social groupings. He divides his urban strangers into two types: the
stranger who belongs to a distinct category and the stranger who is an unknown individual. The first, categorical, type of stranger, is bound to a racial,
ethnic, or economic group by family ties, a citizen of "the ethnic city" such

as "New York at the opening of the twentieth century," when people "often migrated as whole families . . . [and] clustered together in ethnic subareas of the city . . . according to the locale or even their village in the old country."[11] The second, clearly superior, type of stranger he identifies was key to the formation of modern London and Paris, "a special sort of stranger [who] played a critical role . . . [who] was alone, cut off from past associations, come to the city from a significant distance."[12] Sennett, that is, accepted the proposition, by then long-standing, that families and cities are inimical to one another. But rather than proposing that cities threaten families, he implies that having a family makes a person less than urban, even if that family is located in a city, because families bind individuals to groups.[13] In fact, the advent in the city of large numbers of these ethnic or racially or economically marked, family-based strangers signals the beginning, for Sennett, of the city's loss of a proper—that is theatrical—urbanity (as if the individual members of the economic, ethnic, and racial groups to which people are attached by family can be fully known by their group affiliations).

In the late 1950s, Goffman included gender among his many examples of behaviors theatrically performed in daily life: "[W]hen we observe a young American middle-class girl playing dumb for the benefit of her boyfriend, we are ready to point to items of guile and contrivance in her behavior," he notes. "But . . . we accept as an unperformed fact that this performer *is* a young American middle-class girl . . . neglect[ing] the greater part of the performance."[14] In fact, the model he proposed for the social performances of "everyday life" was sexual. "To the degree that a performance highlights the common official values of the society in which it occurs, we may look upon it," he writes, as a "reaffirmation of the moral values of the community. Furthermore, insofar as the . . . performance comes to be accepted as reality . . . reality will have some of the characteristics of a celebration. . . . The world, in truth, is a wedding."[15] If the world is a wedding, then the organization of sexuality is central to Goffman's theater of social life.

Sex and gender were also fundamental to Lofland's understanding of the theater of public identities among the strangers in cities. Her first example of the workings of the modern city is gay. An accomplished urbanite knows that "[a] homosexual male is a man in a homosexual bar and not necessarily a man in a pink ruffled shirt," she explains. She goes on to identify a prostitute as "a woman standing alone in the 'Tenderloin,' and not necessarily a woman in a revealing costume"; likewise, the rich are identifiable by where they shop, and the poor by where they live.[16] But sexuality—and deviant sexualities—are, by implication, the first problem of legibility in the city. Certainly that her first illustration of contemporary urban experience should be a man standing in a gay bar suggests both the likelihood of finding homosexuals in cities (not just in gay bars) and the general necessity, in the city, of being able to identify the homosexuals.

Lesbians and gay men—routinely represented as alienated from their families of origin and traveling alone to the city, often from great distances—also seem to be particularly fitting examples of Sennett's ideal stranger. But although he disqualifies people in families from public life because of their group identifications, he insists that sexuality is not a sufficient basis for either a group identity or a public life. Advocates of sexual identities are,

Promenading in the theater district. Still from *Boys in the Band,* William Friedkin, director, 1970. Copyright National General Pictures, National General Pictures/Photofest.

in fact, a threat to the public life of the city, in his view. The Victorians, he explains, understood "eroticism" correctly as a force subject to the self, whereas his contemporaries, he complains, foolishly believe that "sexuality" can define the self, that a person has a "sexual identity."[17] Sennett laments the long decline of urban theatricality, and with it public life, that he proposes reached its nadir in the United States in the 1960s, when the citizenry was seduced by the pursuit of sexual pleasures: "[T]he generation born after World War II . . . has turned inward as it has liberated itself from sexual constraints; it is in this same generation that most of the physical destruction of the public domain has occurred."[18] "[T]oday," he concludes (in 1977), in thrall to a destructive narcissism, "we unendingly and frustratingly go in search of ourselves through the genitals" rather than the polis.[19]

It was, however, during the postwar decades, and especially the 1960s, that the public identification of homosexuals with the theatrical understanding of social life that Sennett wanted to claim for the city was celebrated. The vehicle for this celebration was "camp," an aesthetic and a style that gays developed to express the theatricality and the urbanity of their lives. Novelist Edmund White describes camp, in retrospect, as the dominant homosexual sensibility of the 1950s and 1960s. But when, in the 1960s and 1970s, camp was first publicly discussed, Susan Sontag, camp's original publicist, hailed Wilde as its progenitor. In "Notes on 'Camp'" (1964), she united the theater and the city and joined both with the homosexual. "These notes are for Oscar Wilde," she explained.[20]

Although Sontag's was the definitive literary exposition of camp, Esther Newton, a University of Chicago–trained anthropologist, brought the Chicago School face-to-face with its implicit subjects, introducing Goffman to Wilde in *Mother Camp* (1972), an ethnographic study of female impersonators, the gay world around them, and the camp sensibility that united them all.[21] These key discussions of camp by Sontag and Newton joined literary and social-scientific analyses of homosexuality as they demonstrated the ways in which camp connected homosexuals and cities. They also tied the knot linking homosexuality to the developing social studies of the interactions of strangers and the theatricality of the city represented by Goffman, Lofland, and Sennett.

"Camp," Sontag argues, is a recognition of the theater of social life. "To perceive Camp in objects and persons is to understand Being-as-Playing-a-Role," she writes, "the sensibility . . . of the theatricalization of experience"

(280, 287). The theatricality of camp is manifest in its manipulation of legibility, its practitioners' interest in duplicity, in controlling the relation between public and private, or even multiple publics. One-half of camp's double meaning might be no meaning, "the thing as pure artifice" (281). But camp deals in particular in splitting meanings between different audiences: "[C]amp ... employs flamboyant mannerisms susceptible of a double interpretation: gestures ... with a witty meaning for cognoscenti and another, more impersonal, for outsiders" (281).

Sontag identifies camp with the city and with homosexuality by identifying the theatricality and artificiality of camp with a "city" and a homosexuality that alike are defined as theatrical and artificial. "All Camp objects, and persons, contain a large element of artifice," she proclaims. "Nothing in nature can be campy. . . . [M]ost campy objects are urban" (279). That slide from artifice to the city allows her to present camp itself as the sign of a peculiarly urban identity: "[T]he essence of Camp is its love of the unnatural: of artifice and exaggeration. And Camp is esoteric—something of a private code, a badge of identity even, among small urban cliques" (275).

Camp, then, is the formalization of practices the Chicago Vice Commission feared fifty years before. In fact, the literature on the modern city can be traced throughout Sontag's "Notes on 'Camp.'" "Camp is the modern dandyism," she declares (288), evoking Baudelaire's flaneur. Wilde is her modern dandy. Evoking Simmel's emphasis on urban reserve, on the blasé attitude, she describes "Camp [as] propos[ing] a comic vision of the world," and "comedy [as] an experience . . . of detachment" (288). Her camp, "a vision of the world in terms of style . . . the love of the exaggerated" (279), echoes modern accounts of city life from Simmel to Park's Chicago School.

The modern history of homosexuality also pervades Sontag's observations. Who could those "urban cliques" with the "private code[s]" be? "Camp taste is much more than homosexual taste" (290), she insists defensively. "[O]ne feels that if homosexuals hadn't more or less invented Camp, someone else would" (291). But not only does "one" dedicate "one's" notes to Oscar Wilde, "one" also offers a litany of queer writers and cultural icons—including Christopher Isherwood, Ronald Firbank, Ivy Compton-Burnett, Jean Cocteau, André Gide, Jean Genet, Noel Coward, and Greta Garbo—as points of reference. Garbo allows Sontag to proffer "[t]he androgyne

[as] certainly one of the great images of Camp sensibility" (279). Moreover, she moves immediately from embracing the homosexually identified gender transgression of androgyny to declaring that "Camp taste draws on a mostly unacknowledged truth of taste: the most refined form of sexual attractiveness (as well as the most refined form of sexual pleasure) consists in going against the grain of one's sex" (279).

As Sontag coyly acknowledges, "Obviously, [Camp's] metaphor of life as theater is peculiarly suited as a justification and projection of a certain aspect of the situation of homosexuals" (290). That "certain aspect" is, presumably, the need to hide their sexuality. None of her prevarication can detach camp from the homosexuality that, in true camp practice, she is simultaneously highlighting and obscuring. The "peculiar relation," as she identifies it, "between Camp taste and homosexuality has to be explained" (290). Her explanation depends on an analogy between homosexuality and Jewishness: "Not all liberals are Jews, but Jews have shown a peculiar affinity for liberal and reformist causes. So not all homosexuals have Camp taste. But homosexuals, by and large, constitute the vanguard—and the most articulate audience—of Camp" (290). She grounds her analogy in the city. "The analogy is not frivolously chosen," she explains. "Jews and homosexuals are the outstanding creative minorities in contemporary urban culture. . . . The two pioneering forces of modern sensibility are Jewish moral seriousness and homosexual aestheticism and irony" (290). So, as she identifies homosexuals with camp, she identifies homosexuals, along with Jews, as producers of the modern city.

Such a sense of ownership might be why "[h]omosexuals boast that they can be quickly 'at home' in any city in the world," as Esther Newton notes.[22] She presents the migration to cities by "[p]otential recruits to gay life" as fundamental to the construction of "the core of the homosexual community . . . located almost exclusively in large and medium-sized urban centers" (21). Although these migrants might come to the city alone, they find "special residential areas," and "the homosexual inhabitants of these areas of great concentration generally give the area a name such as 'fairy heights' or 'lesbian row.' In a large city there will be several such concentrations differing in rental prices and social status" (22).

The "culture heroes" of these urban gay worlds of the 1960s were the "drag queens," men who performed as women on stages from small gay bars to larger, "officially" heterosexual nightclubs in small and large cities around the United States. "Drag queens symbolize homosexuality," Newton proposed; although "many homosexuals . . . never go to see professional drag queens . . . never wear drag themselves, and prefer 'masculine' men . . . [drag queens] represent the stigma of the gay world" (3). Camp was the presentational style of the drag queens and of many of the gay men surrounding them when they wanted to perform their homosexuality, because, in Newton's analysis, "[c]amp . . . signifies a *relationship between* things, people, and activities or qualities, and homosexuality" (105; emphasis in original).[23]

"[T]he larger implication of drag/camp" is, however, that "all of life is role and theater—appearance," Newton concludes (108). If anyone, even a man, can successfully "play" a woman, drag queens suggest, then all gender and sexuality might be simply performance. Newton traces around these drag queens a gay world organized around legibility, divided between those who are covert and those who are overt about their sexuality. If all gay persons have to choose, potentially on a moment-by-moment basis, whether to perform heterosexuality or homosexuality, the performances of impersonators echo the theatricality of all gay lives. But the 1960s drag queens demonstrated Goffman's thesis more broadly. "[G]ay people often use the word 'drag,'" Newton observes, "even to include role playing which most people simply take for granted: role playing in school, at the office, at parties, and so on" (108).

Goffman located "shamed groups" in "urban milieux [that,] containing a nucleus of service institutions . . . provide a territorial base for prostitutes, drug addicts, homosexuals, [and] alcoholics."[24] The drag queens Newton wrote about understood themselves as not only quintessentially homosexual but also quintessentially urban. "Female impersonators see themselves as sophisticated urbanites," she explains. "These exotic flowers may have their roots in 'the sticks,' but they bloom in the cities." Moreover, "Their urbanism is more profound than simply a desire for 'bright lights.'" Though "impersonators need the anonymity of cities to exist," controlling their legibility in the city is not their central concern. For one thing, they belong in the city because they are sexualized, and the city is sexualized; like prostitutes, "they sometimes call themselves 'ladies of the night'" (125). But, "more than this, impersonators see themselves as 'unnatural,' and in our culture, the city can accommodate every unnatural thing" (125). Unnatural because homosexual, they are quintessentially urban, when the city is the realm of the artificial. "Impersonators would say of themselves," Newton concludes, "We are city people; we are night people; and we are dishonored people" (125), crystallizing a constellation of identifications of homosexuals and cities that had been developing for the past century and a half.

Both Sontag and Newton read camp in the last moments before the gay and women's liberation movements began to reconstruct homosexuality in America and gay men and lesbians began to reconstruct American cities. These movements would take up the idea that "personal" life might be a matter of social organization, categories, and performances rather than the natural efflorescence of private, authentic selves. They would offer a fundamental challenge to conventional understandings of the public and of public/private divisions. The ground was about to shift under Sontag's "urban cliques" and Newton's "gay world," and not only in the great cities of the United States. Yet the camp culture, and the connections between that culture and the city that Sontag and Newton describe, would persist.

INTO THE STREETS

The definitive image of the birth of gay liberation in histories, novels, and film is a chorus line of black and Latino drag queens high-kicking their defiance of New York City's police, on the evening of Judy Garland's funeral, June 27, 1969, in the narrow streets of Greenwich Village.[25] The Stonewall Inn, the gay bar that the police had expected to shut down that evening, drew a colorful crowd. The status of drag queens as representative homosexuals is confirmed by this picture. Gay liberation is presented as the product of a spontaneous uprising by the fed-up gay "masses." And this image carries forward the association of homosexuals with theatricality and the city into the new gay and lesbian politics.

The Stonewall riots marked the dramatic acceleration of a wave of organizing in cities across the United States and internationally. After beginning their efforts in the later decades of the nineteenth century in Europe, especially in Germany and then England, lesbians and gay men had been trying to organize politically in America at least since Henry Gerber's first efforts in Chicago in the 1920s, and consistently since the end of World War II. The "homophile movement" of the 1950s and 1960s was most successful in the urban centers of the East and West coasts but also established groups in cities across the nation: by the late 1960s, the Mattachine Society had

"Come Out," Gay Liberation Front poster, 1970. Photograph by Peter Hujar. Reprinted from Martin Duberman, *Stonewall* (New York: Dutton, 1993).

chapters in Los Angeles, San Francisco, New York, Boston, Denver, Detroit, Chicago, Washington, D.C., and Philadelphia; the Daughters of Bilitis, in San Francisco, New York, Los Angeles, and Chicago; the Janus Society, in Philadelphia; and SIR (Society for Individual Rights), in San Francisco.[26] We have, by now, complex histories of the rounds of engagement in the United States, in places like San Francisco and Philadelphia, between gay activists and city authorities, including public protests in the years preceding Stonewall, as well as the steady work of gay advocates in the 1960s in Los Angeles and New York.[27] Nevertheless, surely in part because of the roles of New York City and Greenwich Village (and gay theatricality) in the cultural imagination, the movement is familiarly understood to have begun with the riot triggered by the police raid on Christopher Street on that night in 1969.

From its inception gay liberation was framed not only by New York City, and Greenwich Village in particular, but also by those key urban concerns—about legibility and groups—that were the focus of contemporary urbanists' discussions of the theater and the ghetto. Repudiating the second-class status of homosexuals, gay liberation asserted the health rather than the sickness, the pleasure rather than the sufferings, of the homosexual men and women it would publicly redefine as "gay." Arguing that lesbian and gay lives were deformed, and hostile fantasies of homosexuals maintained, by heterosexuals' demand that queers conceal their sex and their emotions, gay liberation's key tactic was "coming out."

In previous decades, to "come out" had meant to come to an understanding of oneself as homosexual and enter into a more or less private, though public, *gay* world. As the 1960s ended, lesbians and gays were suddenly being urged to declare their sexual desires and their emotions not just to their queer peers but also to their families, friends, employers, even strangers on the street—to assert their right to legibility and to claim control over their public identities. It had been, after all, an expressive decade. Modeled on the black power activists' declaration "Black is beautiful," gay liberationists declared, "Gay is good." They wore buttons and T-shirts proclaiming "Gay and proud," "Faggot," "Dyke," and "How dare you presume I'm heterosexual."[28]

Coming out meant, then, declaring group membership. But coming out, it was hoped, would not only defuse the stigma of homosexuality for individuals but also establish the group of homosexuals as one its members would want to publicly embrace. If everyone who was lesbian or gay came out, it would become clear that there were many lesbians and gay men, not just a few; that lesbians and gay men were extraordinarily various, not just cultural stereotypes; that lesbians and gay men could be found in all places and at all levels of society; and that they were socially integrated, even socially vital persons—neither the threatening nor the pitiful outcasts living precariously in the dangerous shadow world of fiction, film, and journalistic exposé.[29]

Gay liberation was a full frontal assault on post–World War II American hostility to attachment and to groups, celebrating attachment and groups simultaneously, and celebrating both by claiming the city to which gays and lesbians had previously been relegated. Not only were the terms of gay liberation's coming out key terms of urban life, but the movement's most immediate impact was on the cities, as "coming out" became a matter of literal as well as figurative movement. "Out of the closets and into the streets," the radicalized exhorted, and although "into the streets" was meant as a call to protest, it also served as a new call to urban settlement.

Psychologist Evelyn Hooker, echoing Magnus Hirschfeld at the beginning of the century, carefully repeated, in 1961, that "a homosexual community . . . exists in every large city in the United States, and indeed, probably in the Western world" and that, moreover, "the community map is fairly standard from one city to another."[30] She cited as community institutions not only bars and "steam baths . . . gay streets, parks, public toilets, beaches, gyms, coffeehouses, and restaurants" but also "[n]ewsstands, bookstores, record shops, clothing stores, barber shops, grocery stores, and launderettes," the latter group of which "may become preferred establishments for service or for a rendezvous," although "they are secondary in importance."[31] These institutions were "not randomly distributed throughout the city," although, she observed, "[t]he concentrated character of these areas is not generally known except in the homosexual community."[32] But after a series of local papers had also weighed in on the phenomenon, *Life* magazine announced to all, in 1964, that although "[h]omosexuality—and the problem it poses—exists all over the United States," homosexuals were "most evident in New York, Chicago, Los Angeles, San Francisco, New Orleans and Miami." Moreover, "the city of San Francisco" already "rates as the [country's] 'gay capital.'"[33] This history had been a premise of Sontag's and Newton's analyses of camp.

Leonard Fink, *Christopher Street Liberation Day Parade*, June 1970.
Lesbian, Gay, Bisexual, and Transgender Community Center National
History Archive, New York.

Gay liberation intensified and made more public the gay urban presence, especially in New York and San Francisco. Journalist Frances Fitzgerald, who went to San Francisco in the late 1970s to observe the state of the nation, wrote in *Cities on a Hill* (1986) that if the "main effect" of gay liberation "was to bring large numbers of homosexuals out of the closet . . . [i]ts secondary effect was to create a great wave of migration into the tolerant cities of the country."[34] From a more personal and a more academic perspective simultaneously, anthropologist Kath Weston, who went to San Francisco in the late 1970s to live and began conducting ethnographic research in the city's lesbian and gay community in the mid 1980s, argued that in the 1970s and 1980s there was a "Great Gay Migration."[35] Implicitly claiming as a point of comparison the Great Migration of African Americans from the rural South to northern cities at the beginning of the century, Weston described lesbians and gay men of all races and classes responding to the liberation movement's promise—as well as to the historic invitation of the city—by coming out and coming to the city to live (at least partially) openly lesbian and gay lives.[36]

BUT OF COURSE the stigma of homosexuality did not immediately dissolve. Legibility and group identification remained burdens for many. The two most visible lesbian and gay novels of the 1970s, Rita Mae Brown's *Rubyfruit Jungle* (1973) and Andrew Holleran's *Dancer from the Dance* (1978), are all about the continuities within queer consciousness, despite gay liberation, that were manifest in the complexities of post-Stonewall gay migrations.[37] Novels were about to become less authoritative as accounts of gay and lesbian life, as they were increasingly supplemented by the flood of memoir, journalism, and political analysis, as well as poetry, theater, and even film unleashed by the gay and women's liberation movements. But for the moment, in the 1970s, novels remained the most broadly available lesbian and gay texts. *Rubyfruit Jungle* was so often reprinted it became the only challenger to *The Well of Loneliness* as the most widely read account of lesbian life in the twentieth century. Holleran's more literary work was also very widely and very well received.

The decisive event in both Brown's and Holleran's novels is the protagonists' move to the city, as was the case for the lesbian and gay protagonists of Radclyffe Hall's and James Baldwin's works in previous decades—though, unlike so many of those others, Brown's Molly Bolt and Holleran's Malone

Leonard Fink, *Christopher Street Liberation Day Parade,* June 1970.
Lesbian, Gay, Bisexual, and Transgender Community Center National
History Archive, New York.

both end up in lower Manhattan, not Paris. Molly hitchhikes from Florida after being thrown out of college and her working-class family when she is found in the arms of another woman. "There are so many queers in New York that one more wouldn't rock the boat," she opines as she sets off for the city.[38] Malone, from an upper-class midwestern family, passes effortlessly through the elite education system—boarding school, Yale University, law school—and into a corporate job for which he travels back and forth between Connecticut and Washington, D.C. Finally, more terrified of his loneliness than his desires, he throws himself out of his exclusive world and into Manhattan and the arms of any man who will catch him.[39]

These novels share the same ambivalence about group life—the anxiety about the implications of "like to like"—that causes both Hall's Stephen Gordon in *The Well of Loneliness* and Baldwin's David in *Giovanni's Room* to be horrified by lesbian and gay gatherings in the cities to which they journey (only to find themselves in the bars nevertheless). Moreover, although the lesbian and gay social worlds Brown and Holleran describe are somewhat more complex than those proffered by Hall and Baldwin (especially Holleran's), they are not dramatically different from the worlds of their predecessors.

In *Rubyfruit Jungle,* Molly is dismissive of lesbian bars, "where secretaries from New Jersey met secretaries from the Bronx and they lived happily ever after" and everyone adheres strictly to butch and femme roles.[40] But she is also scornful of the private parties to which she is invited. These gatherings of professional women—women's college graduates from the 1940s, aging actresses, archaeologists, and stockbrokers—invariably include a few genteel predators eager to set up in style a beautiful young woman like herself and pay her way through school.[41]

Holleran offers a lyrical account of gay partying in the discos and on Fire Island and of sex in the parks and the bathhouses of New York in the 1970s.[42] But, for Malone, this becomes, finally, a wearying and ultimately fatal life. Moreover, Holleran frames his story with a series of disavowals contained in letters between the narrator, a character who is also the "author" of the story, and a gay man who has fled the city for rural peace. No one will be interested in a novel about "fags," the rural correspondent insists. But the novel "is not about fags," according to the narrator: "It is about a few characters who just happen to be gay." He declares, moreover, that he "would LIKE to be a happily married attorney with a house in the suburbs, 2.6 kids, and a station wagon," but unfortunately he happens to be gay himself.[43]

However ambivalent each protagonist and text is, homosexuality in each work is as inextricable from the city as it is in the literature of the preceding 150 years. Brown gives Molly Bolt a "make it here, make it anywhere" commitment to conquering New York: "It's like I'll make my fortune here or something."[44] More subtly, in Holleran's novel, Malone discovers, in the end, a blurring of objects of desire: "[W]hat he was in love with— or any of us, for that matter—was not Rafael, or Jesus, or the man we had been watching on the dance floor . . . [but] only the city."[45] Malone's realization is the completion of a pattern traceable from the Wilde who commended Robbie Ross for his skilled presentation of the temptations of great cities, to the Addams who wanted to be absorbed into the industrial city in which she had chosen to live, to the Baldwin who at the end of *Another Country* reunites his lovers through a vision of New York as a city of angels at home.

BUT ANXIETIES ABOUT ghettoization continue to resonate through novels such as Brown's and Holleran's. They are the same anxieties that produce resistance to self-identification as lesbian or gay for the protagonists of novels from *The Well of Loneliness* through *Giovanni's Room* to these works of the 1970s and beyond. The narrative of gay migration to the city had long been interwoven, through the prospect of group life that the city offered to gays and lesbians, with the idea of the ghetto, where, after all, all other migrations of groups to the city concluded. As the Chicago School's Louis Wirth made clear, in his classic study *The Ghetto* (1928), by the 1920s, "ghetto" and "urban" had become synonymous.

Wirth saw "the voluntary segregation of the Jews in ghettos" as of a piece with "the segregation of Negroes and immigrants in modern cities" and "the development of Bohemian and Hobohemian quarters in the urban community of today." Although "voluntary" residence characterized his ghetto, these spaces, he acknowledged, were always produced by intolerance elsewhere. "The tolerance that strange ways of living need and find in immigrant colonies, in Latin quarters, in vice districts, and in other localities," he argued, "is a powerful factor in the sifting of the population . . . in[to] separate cultural areas where one obtains freedom from hostile criticism and the backing of a group of kindred spirits."[46] Just as "voluntary residence in a ghetto is not entirely voluntary, other experiences of the ghetto Wirth discusses are deeply conflicted. Historically, he claims, the rewards of ghetto life for the Jews were substantial. "The ghetto offered liberation," he explained. "[W]ithin the ghetto [individuals] felt free ... contacts with ... fellow-Jews were warm, spontaneous, and intimate," and group members found "appreciation, sympathy, understanding ... [and] status."[47] But the ghetto also "facilitated social control on the part of the community over its members" and, at the same time, "made the supervision that medieval authorities exercised over all strangers and non-citizens possible."[48] The ghetto not only constrained the individuals and the groups it contained, but also aided the authorities in policing those beyond its boundaries.

Richard C. Wandel, *Gay Pride Parade,* June 27, 1971. Lesbian, Gay, Bisexual, and Transgender Community Center National History Archive, New York.

At the same time, Wirth spoke of the ghetto as Chicago School sociologists as a group spoke of the "zone of deterioration," of which the ghetto was clearly emblematic. Wirth spoke of the ghetto as representative of the city, *and* he spoke in terms that echo Chicago School discussions of the American city as a whole. Like the city, the ghetto is the province of immigrants, in "our American cities . . . the area of first settlement." Like the city, the ghetto is the province of groups: "The ghetto of Western Europe and America . . . shows concretely the actual processes of . . . grouping of our population in urban communities." Like the city, the ghetto is the setting for "strangers" as well as "strange ways of living." Like the city, the ghetto is "not only a physical fact . . . [but] also a state of mind." Like the city, the ghetto is "a laboratory specimen for the sociologist."[49]

The term "ghetto" was taken up in the United States in the postwar decades by anthropologists and sociologists St. Clair Drake and Horace Cayton, in their *Black Metropolis* (1945), to describe northern urban black communities. (Cayton had trained at the University of Chicago with Robert Park.) Subsequently, it was adopted in a series of studies of African American life in New York, Detroit, Cleveland, and other cities. Especially in the 1960s and 1970s, scholars elaborated what was called "the ghetto synthesis—emphasizing the external and internal forces that gave rise to nearly all black communities in Northern cities."[50] Such explanations of black American urban experience cemented the identification of "urban" and "ghetto" as well as "urban" and "black" in the United States. By the 1960s, to be driven to the city was (rhetorically, if not actually) to be ghettoized. For whites, it was also, potentially, to compromise the social status implicit in their whiteness.

For these reasons, in lesbian and gay fictions and other cultural forms, ambivalence about gayness was fed by and expressed as ambivalence about the city. Alternatively, if the gay urban world was explicitly seen as a ghetto, gay urbanity itself could be seen as evidence of gay oppression.[51] That is why Carl Wittman's "Refugees from Amerika: A Gay Manifesto" (1970)—a call to struggle instantly reprinted around the country, becoming "in effect, the bible of gay liberation"[52]—begins with migration and the ghetto. "San Francisco is a refugee camp for homosexuals," Wittman declares. "We have fled here from every part of the nation, and like refugees elsewhere, we came not because it is so great here, but because it was so bad there. By the tens of thousands, we fled small towns where to be ourselves would endanger our jobs and any hope of a decent life; we have fled from black-mailing cops, from families who disowned or 'tolerated' us; we have been drummed out of the armed services, thrown out of schools, fired from jobs, beaten by punks and policemen." But San Francisco has not proved a haven, he insists: "[W]e have formed a ghetto, out of self-protection. It is a ghetto rather than a free territory because it is still theirs. Straight cops patrol us, straight legislators govern us, straight employers keep us in line, straight money exploits us."[53] For Wittman, the gay world as ghetto represents all the constraints that gay liberation would challenge, including the daily masking of the self. "To pretend to be straight sexually, or to pretend to be straight socially, is potentially the most harmful pattern of behavior in the ghetto," he observes.[54] Nevertheless, "[i]n the past year there has been an awakening of gay liberation ideas and energy. . . . And we are revulsed by the quality of our ghetto life."[55]

At the same time, however much fear of a ghettoized urban life fed ambivalence about being gay for some, for others the metropolis promised a group life—release from isolation—that welded lesbian and gay coming-out stories to the narrative of migration and so to the city. This possibility was enhanced after Stonewall, as gay liberation's new defense of the group was articulated.[56] Kath Weston describes the desire to belong to a group as the force that joined the impulse to come out to the conviction that it was possible to be gay only in a city, thus framing the queer adoption of the narrative of migration. "During the Great Gay Migration, countless individuals launched themselves upon a quest for community" when they set out for the city, Weston argues, "[i]n the process . . . interpret[ing] themselves through that attachment" to the idea of community and the process of migration.[57] Even a move from one city to another, from suburb to center, or across town could be understood in terms of this narrative of migration as the journey to the city necessary in a gay life. In other words, "the symbolics of urban/rural relations" are embedded "in the peculiarly 'Western' construction of homosexuality as a sexual identity capable of providing a basis for community."[58] The possibility of migrating to the city, according to Weston, "structures the very subjectivity that allows people to think of themselves or others as gay," as well as what they think it means to be gay.[59] "For many lesbians and gay men in the 1970s San Francisco—or in its stead, the nearest big city—represented a homeland that could elicit the nostalgia of people who had never seen the Golden Gate. In relationship to an urban homeland (and, by inference, rural areas left behind), individuals constructed themselves as 'gay people': sexual subjects in search of others like themselves," she argues.[60] In the narratives Weston describes, the city is a homeland because of those others, the group, the possibility of community.

This gay migration was, however, complicated by gender, racial, and class divisions.[61] Frances Fitzgerald describes gay San Francisco as overwhelmingly white, male, and middle-class.[62] In Marlon Riggs's autobiographical film *Tongues Untied* (1990), Riggs offers graphic images of his own isolation as a black gay man in San Francisco's gay world. The implication is that he then moves on to a world of black gay men in New York City.[63] While Weston interviewed lesbians as well as gay men from a range of racial and class backgrounds for her study of gay migration, "[f]rom its inception," she argues, "the imagined community incarnated in gay neighborhoods has been gendered, racialized, and classed. . . . [T]he 'gay neighborhoods' of the Castro, the Village, and West Hollywood fix the gay subject as wealthy, white and male."[64] Many of Weston's interviewees—including white gay men—were ambivalent or disappointed when they arrived in the city to find they did not fit into the gay world they had imagined. Their ambivalence and/or disappointment became central to her analysis of the great gay migration. As she notes, many people eventually accommodated themselves to the world they found; both the degree of their disappointment and their capacity to accommodate confirmed the strength of lesbian and gay identifications with the city. But why, given the actual variety of men and women making this migration, was the "gay subject" of the "gay neighborhoods" so quickly limited and firmly fixed?

GHETTO GENTRY

Throughout the two decades after Stonewall, the "city" would provide a fundamental conceptual framework—and a point of reference and a physical location—for the arguments of the gay liberation movement in the United States as well as for gay and straight observers of that movement and its outcomes. That framework rested on two terms, "ghetto" and "gentrification," one redolent of the city's preindustrial past and the other of its postindustrial future. As Wittman's 1970 manifesto exemplifies, popular and academic discourses about the ghetto provided a language for rearticulating the experience and the status of lesbians and gay men in America, a crucial aspect of the gay liberation and lesbian feminist projects. As the 1970s progressed into the 1980s, debates about "gentrification" would be woven into that process of rearticulation. The continuing reassessment and rearticulation of lesbian and gay experience in urban terms would not only perpetuate but even reinvigorate the by then historically secure association of homosexuality and urban life. At the same time, "ghetto" and "gentrification" would be terms that shaped discussions of post-Stonewall gay and lesbian life, just as post-Stonewall discussions of gay and lesbian life would shape understandings of American cities in the last decades of the century. The limiting of popular understandings of gay neighborhood residents to wealthy white men would be one outcome of that process.

There were three stages in the use of references to the ghetto. In the late 1960s, gay liberation activists applied the idea of the ghetto to what had been generally referred to as "gay life" or the "gay world," for a series of sometimes conflicting purposes. Over the next decade, lesbians and gays more generally adopted the ghetto designation. Nevertheless, gay commentators such as sociologist Martin Levine, political scientist Dennis Altman, and novelist Edmund White, as well as straight commentators such as journalist Frances Fitzgerald and urbanist Manuel Castells (focusing especially on San Francisco), whether discussing gay culture (as Altman does in *Homosexual: Oppression and Liberation* [1971], Levine in *Gay Macho* [1998], and White in *States of Desire* [1980]) gay urban life in particular (Levine and White), the city (Castells in *The City and the Grassroots* [1983]), or the state of the nation (White, as well as Altman in *The Homosexualization of America* [1982] and Fitzgerald in *Cities on a Hill* [1986]), all found it necessary to worry about whether gay urban enclaves could properly be called ghettos, and at the same time whether gays could properly be credited, or blamed, for the gentrification which they all identified with a contemporary revival of American urban life. Finally, there began to emerge, in the late 1970s and early 1980s, the use of "ghetto" fused with "urban" and "gay," as the basis for differentiating between a radical gay politics derived from gay liberation (then identified with that ghetto) and an emerging gay conservatism committed to improving the status of gays at the expense of the status of the city. This last rhetorical turn, and its accompanying political project, would not be fully developed until the 1990s because of the intervening impact of the HIV/AIDS epidemic on gay life and culture.[65]

"GHETTO" COULD SERVE all of these rhetorical purposes because of the contradictions embedded in the history of the term, laid out by Louis Wirth. Its post-Stonewall use in queer contexts was further complicated, amid ongoing social hostility, by such underlying questions as "Who is lesbian or gay?" and "What does it mean to be lesbian or gay?"

Initially the ghetto, as an idea, provided the advocates of gay liberation with a way of managing their relationship to the group to which they had attached themselves by coming out. "Gay liberation" denounced and also needed to distance itself from the dominant contemporary cultural stereotypes of homosexuals—as people who were sick and/or sinful, effeminate if men and masculine if women, and devoid of meaningful lives. Many of the newly politicized rejected these stereotypes by rejecting existing group life—gay culture and institutions—as "ghetto" life. "Used to play the game of the bars," one San Francisco activist declared six months after Stonewall. "Ghetto-gays soon lose all perspective of reality . . . including the deeper reality of their own existence as Gaypeople."[66]

But even as gay liberation, in some of its rhetoric, rejected the group as it had existed to date, activists advocated two apparently contradictory responses to the oppression of lesbians and gays. One was to reject the homo-/heterosexual distinction itself. Sexual categories, some argued, were arbitrary and oppressive divisions of our desires, social rather than natural in origin, imposed to maintain the power of men over women as well as straight over gay. These categories could be, in fact, rejected as ghettoizing: "Staying in the ghettos, wearing the labels, and limiting our demands to 'gay power' (as opposed to 'people power')," a New York activist declared, meant "copping out of the Sexual Revolution."[67] If sexual categories were not rejected entirely, others warned, all that was being fought for might amount to merely "exchanging one sort of gay ghetto for another."[68]

Simultaneously, however, there was a drive among gay liberationists to re-create the group of "homosexuals." That drive was founded in a desire to give value to previously denigrated people and their lives by "transforming the pseudo-community of secrecy and sexual objectification" of the past "into a genuine community of sister- and brotherhood."[69] The ghetto could then be reconstructed as a "liberated zone."

But by the end of the 1970s, however, "ghetto" had become an ostensibly neutral term, "adopted by gays themselves" to describe the most developed centers of urban gay life.[70] Throughout *States of Desire*, Edmund White's

Cover of *States of Desire: Travels in Gay America,* by Edmund White (New York: Dutton, 1983).

report on his travels around the nation to the cities that in his view constituted "Gay America," White, embracing gay collectivity, distinguishes between urban centers with and without a ghetto. He bases this distinction, benignly, simply on different cities' levels of concentration of gay persons. Thus, Boston has gay "neighborhoods" where "the boutiques and the restored houses . . . attest to a middle-class gay presence," he observes, but no "ghetto." Yet Dupont Circle, in Washington, D.C., is presented without hesitation as the center of a gay ghetto where "Life . . . is dulcet."[71] There are "so many different gay New Yorks that any project to enumerate them would be a pathetic failure," according to White, and each is "so large, thriving and confident that it only dimly suspects the existence of the others." But Greenwich Village remains the "gay ghetto" in that city.[72]

Despite popular use of the term, from the early 1970s into the 1980s, gay and straight commentators alike persistently asked whether gay urban enclaves "should," for the sake of accuracy or political advantage, be seen as ghettos. All were acutely aware that "[c]ontemporary usage," as Martin Levine observed, "has in some instances restricted the concept [of the ghetto] to communities inhabited by racial and ethnic groups, particularly those which are poverty stricken and socially disorganized."[73] These commentators often sought to distance gays from the idea of the ghetto. Sometimes they understood gays as less constrained than ghetto dwellers were thought to be. Or they wanted to register advances in lesbian and gay life since Stonewall. They were sure of the predominance of white men in urban gay communities, or they did not see sexual, racial, and class differences as tidily parallel. For these commentators, the use of the term "ghetto" was tied not only to assessments of the status of gays but also to assessments of gay social difference, based on ideas about who was gay and what it meant to be gay. But status and difference were difficult to disentangle when, in the cultural mainstream, lesbian and gay status remained low partly because it remained an article of popular faith that homosexuals were profoundly different from their heterosexual peers.

Serious assessments of the social difference of gay urban life rested on arguments about what Fitzgerald described in San Francisco as "institutional completeness." To what extent, she and others asked, did urban gays live within a social framework with cultural and emotional as well as sexual content? Still, an institutionally complete group life might or might not connote low status. When Martin Levine proposed that New York City's "clone" culture of the 1970s should be understood as a ghetto culture, he emphasized the group's institutional and residential concentration and its cultural and social isolation—the ways in which the men who occupied the space he delineated belonged to a distinct "community" based on a sexual and social life bypassing the family and the couple for impersonal sex and very personal friendships.[74] That the culture he described was complete seemed to justify his description of the "clones" as ghettoized.

At the same time, assertions that post-Stonewall gay urban life was a matter not just of sex but also of work, friendship, home renovation, and politics could be presented as evidence against a ghetto designation. Dennis Altman, for example, in *The Homosexualization of America,* finds in the "big cities" of the United States—New York, San Francisco, and Los Angeles— "new gay neighborhoods characterized not only as centers of homosexual night life (such areas are common in most large Western cities), but also as places where increasing numbers of gay men . . . live and work."[75]

Most analyses of gay social difference rested on comparisons across lines of sexual identification (homosexual versus heterosexual). But analyses of the status of gays—of degrees of oppression—rested on comparisons across racial and class lines, in part because of the use of the ghetto as a point of reference. Such analyses of status produced analogies that divided sexuality from racial or class differences, thus "whitening" the gay subject (whether the writer's goal was to distance gays from or identify them with the ghetto). Altman and others were clearly uncomfortable claiming that gays were ghettoized, given that ghettos were identified with the economic disadvantage of racial minorities and those persons most legible as gay tended to be economically advantaged, often middle- or upper-class white men. In the early 1970s, for example, Altman cited areas of urban concentration "where homosexual behavior is largely accepted" as areas marked by higher rents, overpriced bars, and inferior spaces and services. But he concluded that "such areas do not suffer from the same constricting socioeconomic features as do ethnic ghettos, and it is poor analysis and bad politics to ignore the difference."[76] The implication was that "gays" were neither ghettoized nor "ethnic." By contrast, Castells took up comparisons across class and racial lines to justify gay ghettos as politically necessary. "[E]ven in a city where they share institutional power, [gays] will need the ghetto," he argued. "[T]erritorial boundaries . . . are required for the same reasons that Jewish people in Europe, black people in America, and oppressed minorities

Stills from *Tongues Untied*, Marlon Riggs, director, 1990. Frameline.

all over the world have always needed them—for survival."[77] Leaving aside Castells's apparent advocacy of ghettos, again gays were represented by implication as not Jewish and not black.

Debates about the status of gays and implicit comparisons across racial and class lines were also played out through discussions of voluntary presence. By the late 1970s, in contrast to Carl Wittman of the gay liberation movement, gay and straight commentators were describing gays as voluntary urbanites living in neighborhoods or liberated zones rather than ghettos. As Altman argues, "Such spaces are as much neighborhoods as they are ghettos, for people move to them voluntarily as places where they can live openly as gay. Their development is an essential part of the growth of a sense of homosexual identity."[78] Castells agrees that calling gay urban enclaves "ghettos" is "misleading," because, "unlike ghettos," "gay territories . . . are deliberately constructed by gay people."[79] Residence in a "real" ghetto is not voluntary, and gays are not like those groups involuntarily confined to their ghettos. Nevertheless, Castells goes on to describe gays as "moral refugees" who endure economic and social sacrifice for a chance to live their "real life" in the city.[80] If in order to be properly gay it is necessary to move to the city, how voluntary can those urban residences be?

Whatever anyone decided, the term "ghetto" remained extraordinarily adhesive. Commentators either rejected the designation in the early 1970s and then had to reject it again in the early 1980s, as did Dennis Altman, or, like Castells, they rejected the term and then continued to use it. Self-consciously taking up gay liberation rhetoric, Castells explicitly describes gay neighborhoods in San Francisco as "liberated zones" rather than ghettos, but goes on nevertheless to discuss "the Castro ghetto."[81] The adhesiveness of the term "ghetto" in itself demonstrates the strength of the identification of gays, groups, and urban life. Given that the term carries with it the stigma from which ghettos originate, its adhesiveness also indicates the persistence of cultural ambivalence about, even hostility toward, both homosexuals and cities.

WHEN DEBATES ABOUT "gentrification" began in the later 1970s, and as they continued through the 1980s, the identification of gays with the city was, if possible, intensified, even though the identification of gays with ghettos was further complicated. Sexual divisions were again opposed to ethnic, racial, and class divisions. If ghettos were historically associated with low social status, gentrification was associated with high status. In the 1980s, any given space that was being gentrified in a U.S. city was, most often, in or adjacent to someone else's ghetto. The identification of gays with gentrification reinforced the idea that gays were white, wealthy, organized, and invulnerable, in contrast to the understanding that ghetto dwellers were not white and were poor, disorganized, and vulnerable. Gays and lesbians who were not white, wealthy, organized, or invulnerable were erased from the picture.

Like "ghetto," "gentrification" seems to have been a peculiarly adhesive term. According to Edmund White, "Without a doubt many gay men are the worker ants of our reviving cities. They deserve credit for having made our inner cities safe and attractive centers once again."[82] Altman rejected the connection: "[I]t is an error to attribute 'gentrification' to gays alone; the trend is a broader middle-class phenomenon in which gay influence varies considerably from area to area," even in different parts of San Francisco. But he could not escape the term: "[T]he very visibility of gays, especially gay men, in the [gentrification] process has made such urban developments a symbol of homosexualization."[83] "[I]t is a fact," Castells observed in 1983, "that gays improved the quality of housing and urban space, mainly through renovation and maintenance."[84] In San Francisco first, but subsequently in cities around the country, he pointed out, gays helped block ongoing urban "renewal" plans by big developers and worked instead to restore the existing urban fabric.

Castells, with a more nuanced understanding of cities than of homosexuality, explored in detail the issues surrounding the idea of gays as gentrifiers. "Are we then in the presence of a typical gentrification?" he asked in his San Francisco study. Were gays separable from a broader "'back to the city' movement by the [white] middle class, part of which happened, in San Francisco, to be gay"?[85] His implicit question was, Were gays dispossessing the poorer and/or nonwhite previous inhabitants of "their" new neighborhoods?

Castells argued both sides of the question: that the neighborhoods gays moved into were in "decline," already abandoned by an ethnic working class that had moved to the suburbs, so that gays displaced no one; *and* that San Francisco was a model of urban vitality because, despite its gentrification, as of the early 1980s the city had retained its "minority" populations. Castells also worked to modify the high-status and potentially pejorative associations of "gentrification" by explaining gay gentrification in terms of the compromised status reflected in gay ghettoization. The gentrification

Stills from *Stonewall*,
Nigel Finch, director,
1995. Strand Releasing/
BBC Films, Arena NY.

of San Francisco, he argued, could stand in contrast to gentrification in other cities because in San Francisco the process had been so specifically gay, and gays came to the city as "moral refugees," building community and simultaneously rebuilding the city "at a financial and social cost that only 'moral refugees' are ready to pay."[86] They might, he argued, have served as "a cultural vanguard" for the middle class back-to-the-city movement, leading the way in their valuation of "personal experience and an active, social street life," but not all gays in San Francisco—not even a majority— were themselves middle-class, wealthy, or professional. Instead, "they orga- nized collective households and were willing to make enormous economic sacrifices to be able to live autonomously and safely as gays" in the city.[87]

White, with a more nuanced understanding of gay life than of cities, saw gentrification as a threat to the cities and the understandings of gays being shaped there. He envisioned the rise of the global city that Saskia Sassen and other urbanists would analyze in the 1980s and 1990s, among "the big old American cities (especially those such as New York, San Francisco, Chicago, Boston, Philadelphia and Washington that are financial centers and of historic interest)." Such cities would be dominated by an economic elite, "the affluent young, the wealthy retired, rich foreigners and middle- class childless couples—and gays," and ringed by "a deeply, structurally poor army of workers . . . already with us . . . illegal immigrants, blacks, Chicanos, Puerto Ricans, and young whites unable to find better employment."[88] Meanwhile, the gay real estate speculators helping to displace poorer and minority populations block by block in San Francisco only confirmed, he argued, public understandings of all gays as privileged, young, white men; of homosexuality as the exclusive province of the privileged; and of homo- sexuals as hostile to all other social claims.[89]

Castells and White, however, together demonstrate that gays could be identified as gentrifiers and ghetto dwellers simultaneously, as "ghetto" and "gentrification" became the dominant lenses through which, both academ- ically and popularly, American cities were viewed in the 1970s and 1980s. Understood as both ghetto dwellers and gentrifiers, gays could represent both of the chief aspects of the American view of cities in the 1970s and 1980s. This pairing of ghettos and gentrification can be seen as the late twentieth-century American version of the class-based, bifurcated vision of "the city" as a world of urban underworlds and elite observers that had shaped accounts of urban life from the mid-nineteenth-century great city onward. Understood as both ghetto dwellers and gentrifiers, and therefore linking those two social positions, gay men in U.S. cities in the late twentieth century embodied the interdependency at the center of this history of dyadic constructions of urban life as well as their own particular version of the dyad, disrupting social boundaries, as homosexuals and cities were expected to do. This identification of gays with both ghettos and gentrification did not advance a nuanced cultural understanding of lesbians and gay men or of cities. Nor did it redound to the credit of lesbians and gays or cities in the popular view.

Introducing what I am describing as the final stage of post-Stonewall uses of the term "ghetto," White concluded his survey of urban gay America by describing the emergence, in the late 1970s, of a division in gay politics, as more conservative lesbians and gay men began to come out and to promote a self-consciously conservative gay politics. This group, paradoxically, identified "urban gay life" with politically radical understandings of homosexuality as the source of broad social difference and the basis for broad political alliances (across racial, class, and gender divisions). They associated all of the above with "the ghetto" and dismissed them altogether. That is to say, formerly the radicals had rejected the gay ghetto as an emblem of gay oppression, whereas now the conservatives rejected the gay ghetto as an emblem of gay radicalism.

White identified these two strains within post–gay liberation gay politics with two different American cities: the more radical strain, in the tradition of gay liberation, he connected with Boston (shades of *The Bostonians*); and the more conservative, with Washington, D.C. He articulated their different understandings of homosexuality through their views of "the ghetto" and through broader cultural understandings of these different cities.[90] This emerging division in LGBT politics—premised on the idea of a ghetto and producing a new, more hostile account of that ghetto—would be both checked and shaped by the HIV/AIDS epidemic, only to reemerge with force in the 1990s.

MAKING URBAN MEANING

As post-Stonewall debates about the ghetto and gentrification demonstrate, in the 1970s and 1980s assessments of lesbian and gay life were inseparable from assessments of the city. Moreover, all of these assessments were woven into contemporary debates about "public life" in the United States. In these debates, public life was identified with city streets, and gay men were presented as the city's past and its future.

The ghetto/gentrification debates were a key site of ongoing struggle among lesbians and gay men themselves over their group's boundaries. Would theirs be a community of all races and classes joined by their shared experiences of sexual difference, or a congress of the wealthy and the white whose only social liability was their sexual deviation? Would their community comprise gay men and lesbians incorporating the gender transgressiveness of their history and working together, or of men repudiating women and the feminine, and women repudiating men and the masculine? These internal struggles were exacerbated by those eager to exploit social hostility to homosexuality for political purposes. It was easy to maintain reservoirs of cultural disdain for cities as well as for homosexuals, if major American cities could be consistently identified with "gays" who were consistently identified as wealthy young white men. It was also easy to hand off responsibility to gay men for all of the displacement and anger produced in urban centers by what were, in the end, broadly middle-class gentrification practices.[91]

As lesbians and gay men were struggling over the meanings of "lesbian" and "gay," battles were also being waged over the meanings of urbanity. Jacobs had begun the project, later taken up by Lofland, Sennett, Castells, and others, of trying to reverse the postwar American rejection of the city. Such a project required, as Jacobs had demonstrated, placing the city in history. Identified as they were with ghettos and with gentrification, not only did gays represent and join the two dominant terms of the postmodern, postindustrial American city emerging in the late twentieth century, but they also represented and joined the medieval city, where ghettos were first established, and the postindustrial city, where "gentrification" was codified as a practice. That is, they attached the newest forms of urban life to the history of the city.

In the mid-nineteenth century and again in the early twentieth century, homosexuality—and especially the ambiguous relationship of homosexuals to "history" (were same-sex desires ancient or modern; the product of an ahistorical nature or historically bound capital?)—was used by urban commentators from Baudelaire to Benjamin to negotiate their own responses to the industrialization and politics of the modern city. By the late twentieth century, detailed histories of same-sex desire were being

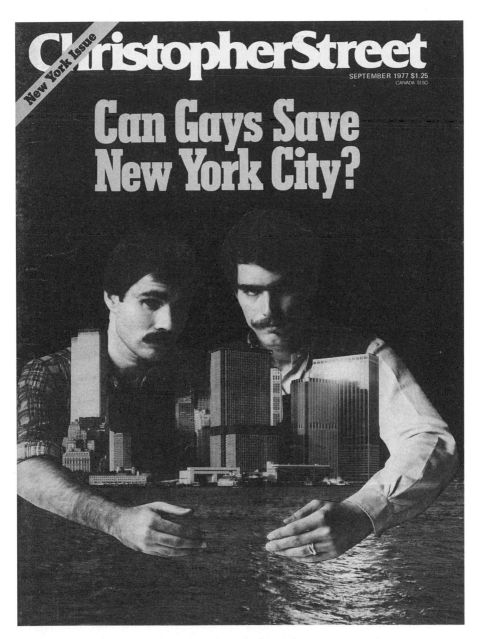

"Can Gays Save New York City?" Cover of *Christopher Street Magazine* 2, no. 3 (September 1977).

constructed by lesbian and gay scholars, as lesbians and gay men were becoming politically organized. But because of their modern identification with the great city—now firmly in place—lesbians and gay men remained supremely useful subjects for urban commentators. Lesbians were the homosexuals most useful in the mid-nineteenth century. As already suggested, gay men took their place in the late twentieth century.

A romance of the gay community would give a new round of commentators a way to address the postindustrial, postmodern city. This romance offered a fantasy of a preindustrial, premodern urbanity to which the emerging postindustrial, postmodern metropolis could be tethered, and by which it might be saved. At the same time, it allowed those commentators to carry forward into the postmodern metropolis a particularly reassuring version of the great city. All of the terms and concepts that fused prior debates about urbanity and homosexuality—not only "history" itself but capital and vice, legibility, the paradox of perverts in groups, the problem of combination, and the possibilities of attachment—would be engaged in this project. The romance of the gay community, as it emerged in the 1970s and 1980s in the United States among urbanists and gays, was founded on a contemporary fusion of same-sex desire, understandings of sexual identity, and expectations of community, with the idea of the city.[92] The promise of community was the force behind this fusion. The community that resulted valued attachment to persons and to places simultaneously.

This romance of the gay community drew simultaneously on the history of associations of homosexuality with pleasure—the pleasures of art and aestheticism as well as sexual pleasure—confirmed as key aspects of queer urbanity by camp. Camp was not only a matter of sex and style but also an emotion, as Susan Sontag explained: "Camp taste is a kind of love, love for human nature"; "a mode of . . . appreciation—not judgement"; "a tender feeling" (291, 292). Attachment, pleasure, art, aestheticism, sex, and emotion had all historically been aspects of private life (most often associated with the elite and the feminine). Straight and gay commentators observing the major cities of the United States in the 1970s and 1980s drew on a combination of these qualities to confer on gay men in particular the promise of a kinder, gentler public life in the city—a life nevertheless properly public because it was male. That promise was confirmed by the concurrent cultural association of homosexuality with theatricality and the commitment to public performance that theatricality implies.

This romance of the gay community depended, however, on a challenge to conventional conceptions of public life and of divisions between public and private set in motion by the struggle for black civil rights begun in the 1950s, the new social movements of the 1960s, and, most emphatically, by the women's and gay liberation movements gaining traction at the end of the 1960s. By coming out, lesbians and gay men epitomized that challenge. The "crisis" of the postwar American city was conventionally understood to be the erosion of public life as people and industry fled. Jane Jacobs and James Baldwin directed attention instead to the damage done by the culture's denial of privacy, especially privacy in public. They highlighted the denial of acceptable public identities to the members of a series of overlapping groups: "the poor, the foreign, the odd," everyone not white, and women who demanded roles in the public realm. ("Lesbian" was, in fact, the hostile charge most often leveled against such women.) Inseparable from these denials, for Baldwin, was a cultural refusal to connect private and public life. As Jacobs and Baldwin together suggested, these denials and refusals were fundamental to the determined postwar rejection of attachment to places and to groups—indeed, to any entity beyond the nuclear family produced by the heterosexual couple.

As a result of social shifts Baldwin helped to initiate, gay men and lesbians in the United States challenged American culture on all of these fronts. They wanted their private lives to be credited, and they wanted acceptable public identities. But insofar as sex was understood as a private matter, acceptable public identities for lesbians and gay men meant breaking down conventional public/private divisions and joining private to public life. The grounds of lesbian and gay declarations of self were, moreover, nothing *but* attachment, both to groups and to places. If, however, the erosion of public life in the postwar American city was a more complicated matter than was commonly stated, gay and lesbian challenges to conventional conceptions of the public and to public/private divisions were also more limited than initially hoped—or feared.

Post-Stonewall, the city could serve as a template for assessments of the past and future of gay politics in terms of public/private divisions. Again White and Castells offer an instructive contrast. The goal of gay liberation, as White explained it, was to "forge links between personal experience and public life, between consciousness and politics."[93] He saw gay gentrification as evidence of the eclipse of those ideals, because of the class, racial, and gender divisions that gentrification fostered among gays and between gays and potential allies, as well as the divisions it fostered between private and public life. Divisions among groups and between public and private were also key to Castells's conclusions, but in gay gentrification in San Francisco he saw the promise of gay liberation made manifest in the ways gays came together and brought others in the city together in the streets. Despite their opposite views of gentrification, both White and Castells saw urban practices as a lens for assessing gay politics, and both represented gays as ideally committed to connecting private and public life.

Post-Stonewall, lesbian and gay politics could also serve as a template for assessments of the past and future of the city in terms of public/private divisions. When Richard Sennett argued that the rise of sexual freedom had proven the fall of public man, the abandonment of urban values, and the decline of city life, he advocated the reassertion of boundaries between public and private.[94] Rather than seeing lesbians and gays committing themselves to the public realm by declaring their right to the kind of public as well as private sexual lives that heterosexuals take for granted, he insisted that sexuality was a private matter and "sexual identity," therefore, a contradiction in terms.[95]

Sennett assumed, as did almost all other urban commentators of the period, that public life—which he identified as city life—was properly masculine. His "good" strangers, those individuals migrating to the city alone and experiencing the full measure of urbanity by doing so, were always male.[96] His argument in *The Fall of Public Man* was not so much an account of the loss of an urban public life, then, as another contribution to the substantial history of anxiety about the modern city's threat to male authority. That history can be traced through the literatures I have discussed, from Baudelaire's mid-nineteenth-century *lesbiennes*, and Benjamin's interest in them as a means of managing anxieties about the status of elite men, onward to late nineteenth-century urban fictions as different as Zola's *Nana* and James's *The Bostonians*. Turn-of-the-century fears of the feminizing of men in cities were expressed by Nordau in *Degeneration* and Beard in *American Nervousness*. The Chicago School lamented the preponderance of women, the nonwhite, and the foreign, at the expense of native-born white men, in the urban centers of the United States in the early decades of the twentieth century. This history suggests the degree to which elite masculinity was never felt to be secure in the great city. Earlier anxieties about male authority in the city were only intensified in the United States in the decades after World War II by the deindustrialization of urban centers.

In *States of Desire*, however, White spoke back to an urbanist as a gay man, explicitly rejecting Sennett's contention that people had been "led . . . to ignore, even despise, the life of the streets." White extolled the pleasures of street life and, at the same time, brought everyone in the city under the rubric of gay urbanity. "What is unique to New York is *cruising*," he asserted. "Everyone—man, woman and child—cruises." Sennett lamented that the city was no longer theatrical, but White claimed that the theater was still a proper model for contemporary urban life, asserting that "the staring" cruising requires "is an acknowledgment that New York life is theatrical . . . a street life does exist, the stage is provided, a sense of being observed is given."[97] Castells agreed, seeing gay theatricality, moreover, as illuminating the intrinsic theater of the city streets, "the intensity of San Francisco's urban culture . . . highlighted by gays' sense of urban theatre."[98]

White's rejection of Sennett and Castells's embrace of San Francisco, in tandem, suggest that in the United States in the 1970s and 1980s, urban commentators had to accept homosexuality in order to appreciate the possibilities for city life. But accepting homosexuality meant accepting the city as a site of insecure masculinity as well as accepting an expanded understanding of "public life." Fulfilling Oscar Wilde's late nineteenth-century vision of a politics in which culture and feeling were joined, and following gay liberation analyses, Castells saw the gay community as "represent[ing] a sexual orientation, a cultural revolt, and a political 'party.'" This gay community was a public entity that joined sex to culture to politics. "[G]ayness," according to Castells, "is more than a sexual preference: it is an alternative way of life, characterized by the domination of expressiveness over instrumentalism and by human contact over impersonal competition." Necessarily, then, this gay community united politics with a "way of life."[99] Gays could, in fact, be declared (as they were by Castells) urban saviors.

BUT GAY AND lesbian challenges to public/private divisions were not as radical as either their advocates or their enemies imagined them to be. And neither was the challenge to gender norms required by visions of the gay community as urban saviors. Although accepting homosexuals as urban saviors in the 1970s and 1980s meant making concessions, in standards of masculinity and public/private divisions, urban commentators were at least able thereby to hold the line at men. Insofar as gays were consistently publicly identified as elite white men, accepting gay men as urban saviors could mean retaining "elite" and "white" as points of reference as well—not straying too far, after all, from the model of the modern urban commentator. There could be no question, in the end, about who the cities were being saved for.

The homosexuals being accepted as urban saviors were men in part because of the cultural, social, and political distances between the most visible lesbians and gay men, as well as the much greater visibility of men in "gay" urban settings in the United States from the 1960s to the 1980s. But gay men were more visible than lesbians partly because of the relatively limited conceptions of the city and of public life that, despite their disagreements, urban observers such as Sennett, White, and Castells all still shared.

As I have already discussed, post-Stonewall debates about gay social difference provoked comparisons across sexual divisions, and debates about the status of gays provoked comparisons across racial and class divisions, all of which reinforced the cultural separation of gay from straight and sexual from racial and class differences. (The latter in particular—the construction of gays as white and middle-class or elite—was particularly useful to the project of casting gays as urban saviors. Given the history of urban studies focused on underworlds, the poor and the nonwhite, the presence of gay people of color and/or poor people in the city would not have been considered news.) Debates about homosexuality and public life in the United States in the late twentieth century provoked comparisons across gender divisions. These debates highlighted the ascription of improper gender to both lesbians and gay men. But they also made especially clear the different social experiences and cultural understandings of lesbians and gay men and thus the different political uses to which lesbians and gay men could be put. Consequently, debates about homosexuality and public life in the 1970s and 1980s highlighted rifts between lesbians and gay men.

The association of lesbians with urban life that originated in the mid-nineteenth century persisted through the twentieth century, the terms of those associations shifting very slowly. As the twentieth century progressed, prostitution gradually ceased to be a focus of city studies, just as it gradually ceased to be routine to identify lesbians and prostitutes.[100] Likewise, by the postwar decades the city and the state were, in theory, providing the social services needed by the industrial working class. Educated women seeking occupations were no longer bound to the provision of such services in the city (although social work would continue to be seen as a woman's occupation). Nevertheless, the heroines of the lesbian novels of the 1950s and 1960s were routinely pictured in public in the city—in bars or at work—their lives routinely contrasted with those of married women immured in the suburbs. When they were not out in public, the lesbians of the 1950s and 1960s were to be found in their own city apartments. Of the three "girls" in Valerie Taylor's *The Girls in 3-B* (1959) who come to the big city to find themselves, the only one to stay does so because she takes up with another woman. As in so many of these works, if the established lesbian is not identifiable by her masculine self-presentation, then she is the woman with the successful career and the apartment into which she can invite another woman to move. (The career and the apartment could also, of course, serve as signs of masculinity).[101] Coming to the city would continue to be a central theme of lesbian novels, as it is in Rita Mae Brown's *Rubyfruit Jungle.*

In the mid-twentieth century, whether or not lesbians and gay men shared social spaces and cultural references depended in part on the city in which they were living. In the 1970s and 1980s, however, as cultural struggles over the meanings of "lesbian" and "gay" continued, and as the nature of homosexual urban life and its visibility shifted, their relative social advantage meant that middle- and upper-class white men, who had been the chief subjects of twentieth-century discussions of same-sex sexuality, came to the fore to a new degree.

Lesbian and gay public cultures developed separately in major U.S. cities in the 1970s and 1980s. That separation was in part the effect of a gap between commercial and noncommercial cultures. In response to the gay and women's liberation movements and in the political tradition of Jane Addams, lesbian activists set up a raft of nonprofit social services (women's centers, rape crisis lines, battered-women's shelters) as well as more or less profitable cultural enterprises (bookstores, coffeehouses, newspapers, art and theater groups, and independent publishers).[102] Gay liberation men established similar institutions, but those were dramatically overshadowed by the rapid expansion of a more visible gay commercial culture dominated by bars and bathhouses, and soon represented in glossy magazines.[103]

Lesbians' relation to the property market was also distinct. As women, they were neither prime wage earners nor prime mortgage candidates. And, needless to say, assumptions about homosexuality and gender transgression did not work to their advantage. Ascribed femininity might make gay men welcome tenants, but ascribed masculinity made lesbians doubly undesirable. Even in San Francisco in the 1970s, "landlords tended to regard homosexual men as favorable tenants because they paid rent on time, took great care of the property, and in general behaved in unobtrusive and discreet ways," but they "were disinclined to rent to [lesbians]—or to women generally." They believed lesbians "were careless about rent payments, poor at housekeeping, contentious about repairs, and disturbingly noisy tenants."[104]

When there were discussions of lesbian ghettos, as in sociologist E. M. Ettore's London study *Lesbians, Women, and Society* (1980), they were small, self-consciously political communities.[105] San Francisco–based journalist Sasha G. Lewis, looking beyond the politically engaged in *Sunday's Women* (1979), described a burgeoning "lesbian underground" increasingly accessible to women across the United States, rather than an urban ghetto. But she acknowledged her own expectation "that the difficulties of . . . coming-out . . . would be lessened for women in cities."[106] In fact, Lewis begins her account of post-Stonewall lesbian life by quoting "Carla," who made her way from Idaho to San Francisco. "I knew that I would find something in San Francisco that was better than where I was. I went there in search of myself, in search of other people, in search of my tribe," Carla explains; when she arrived, "it was as if I had come home."[107] A critique of urban life developed among some politicized lesbians, who saw the city as a source of threat to women, advocated the development of rural utopian communities, and joined the broader back-to-the-land movement. But for every urban critique there was an urban affirmation. As poet Adrienne Rich declared to her woman lover in her coming-out work, *The Dream of a Common Language* (1978), perhaps the most widely read collection, to date, of her celebrated career, "I told you from the first I wanted daily life, / this island of Manhattan was island enough for me."[108]

In practice, lesbians were peripheral to accounts of gay urban life in this period not only because of the distance between gay and lesbian cultures and the related differences in their access to property but also because of assumptions about urbanity as well as gender. Altman noted that "lesbians often live" in or near gay ghettos—in the West Village in New York, or in the vicinity of Valencia Street in San Francisco—but, he added, "women are less likely to cruise the streets."[109] Fitzgerald similarly acknowledged that lesbians lived in the Castro and that there were "small lesbian settlements" nearby, with "women's organizations, theater groups, social-service organizations" and, in Berkeley and North Oakland, "a newspaper, a crafts cooperative, a recording company, and various other enterprises."[110] Again, however, lesbians were described as absent from the street: "[N]owhere did gay women congregate the way gay men did. In the city—feeling themselves vulnerable—they took on protective colorings and melted into the landscape."[111] Castells observed that lesbians, as women, were "[o]n the whole . . . poorer than gay men and have less choice in terms of work and location." He added, however, that lesbians, as women, didn't have "territorial aspirations."[112] So, though lesbians' second-class status as women (less moneyed, less centrally located, and more vulnerable on the street) and assumptions about women's "nature" (women don't cruise, don't congregate, and don't need to mark out their space in/on the streets) explain a great deal, the streets themselves are key. The comparative absence of lesbians

Still from "The Castro," in *Neighborhoods: The Hidden Cities of San Francisco,* 1998. Copyright KQED KQED/Photofest.

from post-Stonewall accounts of gay urban life is an effect of ideas of the city and of public life in the city that favor streets; the public congregation that streets imply; and thus the homosexuals who congregate on the street.

GAY ACTIVISTS AND urban commentators agreed, in fact, that the "public" was defined by the street. Efforts to establish "lesbian" and "gay" as acceptable public identities and to revive the public life of cities could therefore be seamlessly joined. As gay San Francisco city supervisor Harry Britt insisted, "When gays are spatially scattered, they are not gay, because they are invisible."[113] "[M]ost urbanists," according to Castells, "value public life, street activity, and intense social interaction as one of the most distinctive positive dimensions of city life."[114] "Street activity" is here identified with "intense social interaction," and both are presented as interchangeable qualities of "public life." But not all intense social interaction takes place on the street. Street life is, however, the public life of the city as theater.

Street presence led gay commentators like Altman and urbanists like Castells to claim that gays had contributed to American cities in the 1970s and 1980s. According to Altman, gay "neighborhoods remain oases of sidewalk life, with constant movement in and out of shops and bars," because of the street life produced by cruising, "[i]n a way that is rapidly declining elsewhere."[115] Castells found even the street presence of gays' renovated homes in San Francisco impressive. Not only did they produce lovely domestic spaces, but those spaces also added grace to the street. Gay men "occupy a building, and make it distinctive and valuable," he observes. "[I]t has beauty, comfort, and sensuality, and it is saying something to the city while expressing something to its own dwellers."[116] Fitzgerald framed her account of gay San Francisco with a detailed description of a Gay Freedom Day parade. Castells touted an annual sequence of fairs and festivals, from the Castro Street Fair to Halloween parades (as well as the vigils and later the protests in the streets following the 1978 murder of the first gay city supervisor, Harvey Milk), as representative of gay urban life.

Everyone insisted that gay street life had significance beyond the experience of gays themselves. As Altman observed in 1982, "[O]ne of the most important impacts of the changing nature of homosexuality over the past ten years has been on the very appearance and nature of the inner city."[117] The "gay community," Castells wrote, "has shown the city that streets are for people, that urban culture means gathering together to play in public places, and that music, politics and games can intertwine in a revitalizing way, creating a new media for messages and establishing new networks of communication."[118]

Castells's embrace of gay San Francisco was particularly resonant within the framework of arguments about homosexuals and cities that had emerged among historians of sexuality by the early 1980s. Ancient and modern understandings of same-sex desire, and understandings of same-sex desire cross-culturally, it was proposed, should be seen as distinct: modern Western understandings could be explained as a product of the great cities of Europe and the United States. Historians such as John D'Emilio and Jeffrey Weeks, sociologist Henning Bech, and others argued that capitalism, which produced industrialization, was responsible for urbanization and that ultimately capitalism and urbanization together enabled individuals to live independently of the heterosexual family structure, thus creating the conditions necessary for the development of the gay identity manifest in Western urban gay enclaves in the late twentieth century. The gay identity produced by capitalism and urbanization was marked by separation from the family and the creation of alternative communities as a basis for public gay and lesbian social life in the great city.[119]

This argument, first and most succinctly laid out in D'Emilio's frequently cited 1983 essay "Capitalism and Gay Identity," could be seen as a triumphant reversal of the nineteenth-century claim (antiurban in its intentions) that capital produced vice. The "vicious" were finally advocating for themselves and the city alike. Bech described the city as a product of homosexuality and homosexuals as the products of cities. The "moment" a gay man "steps out of the given social world (family, workplace and so on) in order to 'realize himself,'" he proposes, "[h]e comes out in the city." At the same time, "[i]nsofar as they wish to be homosexual," gay men "must get out into 'the city.'"[120]

Castells outlined a next stage for this analysis of the relationship of homosexuals to modernity and capitalism when he offered San Francisco, which transformed itself from a modern industrial to a postmodern, postindustrial city in the 1970s, as a model for the general recovery of American cities from their postwar decline. The combination of economic and noneconomic values that Jane Jacobs had already suggested was crucial for the life of great cities was central, in Castells's argument, to such recovery. Rather than submerging capital in vice, as Benjamin claimed Baudelaire had done, Castells saw economics and feeling united. Deploying contemporary assumptions about sexuality, gender, and the stigma of homosexuality, he framed gay urban life as an ideal merger of economics and attachment. Gay people demonstrated in their own lives and taught everyone else "that a city is not just a combination of capitalist functions and empty streets patrolled by police cars."[121]

For Castells, gay presence on the street and gay home renovation, both forms of gay visibility in San Francisco, were the results of gay men's divergence from dominant masculine ideals. Gay men were not feminine because of their sexuality, he insisted. Instead, their experience of oppression had given them "a special sensitiveness, a desire for communication, a high esteem for solidarity and tenderness that brings them closer to women's culture" while tempering their training in the masculine values of "power, conquest . . . self-affirmation," and "domination." Appreciating "use value" as well as "exchange value," they expressed "this two-fold desire" through "housing renovation," and their beautiful homes were central to the revival of the city.[122]

Castells was convinced that because of their stigmatized status, gays would not be taken in by the economic powerhouses of the city. Even in those economic arenas in which they flourished and fed driving economic forces—small businesses, real estate—they would not succumb entirely to market values. In a social universe in which their stigma made gays "moral refugees," the city had particular meaning for them. "[W]hen a space becomes meaningful, exchange value is no longer the dominant issue," he wrote. "This is perhaps the most important contribution of the gay community to the city: not only housing improvement but urban meaningfulness."[123]

The creation of "urban meaningfulness" seems to have depended on a group, in this case the "gay community," investing the city with other than economic value. Yet public recognition of values other than the economic, in the city, Castells implied, was somehow already an urban quality, perhaps because the noneconomic factor being valued was public life itself. In his analysis, a new version of Addams's social claim emerged as the salvation of gays and cities. Being gay and being committed to the neighborhood were no longer parallel outcomes of the attachment and affection that Jacobs and Baldwin had seen as the city's and the individual's salvation. Instead, being gay and being committed to the neighborhood now merged.

Yet an underlying tension between public and private life remained. Castells presented "housing improvement" as linked to but distinct from "urban meaningfulness." Despite all the talk of home renovation, the domestic was oddly absent from contemporary accounts of gay urbanity. This lack is particularly striking given that, after all the talk about cruising and street festivals, the two terms that had come to dominate discussions of gay urbanity, "ghetto" and "gentrification," both imply residence. When lesbians and gay men migrated to urban centers, long before as well as after Stonewall, they did so, like Jane Addams in reality and Radclyffe Hall's Stephen Gordon in fiction, to live in the city, even to be "at home" there; to share, as Adrienne Rich declared, "daily life."

Drawing on the analyses of the women's liberation movement, gay liberation and lesbian feminism critiqued gender roles, the institution of marriage, and the family structures and expectations of monogamy they produced. Activists in these movements saw all of these entities as sources of social hostility to homosexuals, who were routinely vilified for failing to live up to intertwined gender and sexual norms. But such critiques were also a continuation of decades of elaboration of the possibilities of non-family feelings of attachment and affection within lesbian and gay urban subcultures. After Stonewall, the most self-consciously radical women and men tried communal living. Other lesbians and gay men established social networks that included lovers, ex-lovers, the lovers of ex-lovers, tricks, and "fuck buddies." "Community" would become the focus of discussions of lesbian culture. "Friendship" is the term that recurred especially in post-Stonewall accounts of gay men. As philosopher Michel Foucault proposed in a 1981 interview in the Paris gay paper *Le Gai Pied*, "To be 'gay' . . . is . . . to try to define and develop a way of life," "to arrive at a multiplicity of relationships." But the "development towards which homosexuality tends is . . . friendship."[124] Edmund White proposed that "the city's . . . great offering to gays is friendship."[125]

Nevertheless, the paradoxical structure of conventional understandings of gay social life, of perverts in groups, remained a cultural force. Bech, restating Proust and Hirschfeld in the late 1980s, described gay men as simultaneously "born to loneliness" and "belong[ing] by definition to a group."[126] "The homosexual form of existence is essentially social," he asserted.[127] That is to say, "perverts in groups" both reinforced assumptions of isolation and made elaboration of the details of gay community life unnecessary.

Within some of these accounts of post-Stonewall gay urbanity, there were lingering anxieties about gender. Throughout the twentieth century in the

United States, urban neighborhoods had routinely been seen as the realm of the socially disempowered, including ethnic and racial minorities and, especially, women.[128] Castells cast gay men as urban saviors by feminizing them, describing their "way of life" as "characterized by the domination of expressiveness over instrumentalism and by human contact over impersonal competition."[129] But during the 1970s, many gay men were committed to a very public assertion of gay masculinity. Levine explained the hypervisibility of the gay "clones" he described in New York City as the result of a gay world organized around the (re)assertion of masculinity through looks and social relations, in opposition to a dominant culture in which drag queens could still be seen as representative homosexuals.[130] Bech asserted that it was "[t]he masculinity of the male homosexual" that brought gay men "particularly close to . . . the world of the city, owing to the traditional affinity between masculinity and the public, urban sphere."[131] Thus, assertions of masculinity quickly bring us back to "the traditional . . . public, urban sphere," that is to say, a sphere without women, homes, or complex personal relationships—a very particular street.[132]

BY THE LATE twentieth century, homosexuals could be seen, by heterosexuals, to represent the psychic and sexual history of the city, its unconscious and its underworld simultaneously, as in Frances Fitzgerald's account of gay San Francisco. Fitzgerald described the gay pride parade with which she framed her story as "a municipal dream sequence" in which the city's lesbian and gay citizens appeared as manifestations of "the city's collective unconscious," a possibility in the psychic history of every citizen: "Sigmund Freud, after all, had believed that . . . born bisexual . . . every human being had homosexual desires in some degree. From this perspective it seemed unreasonable that the parade should not include everyone in San Francisco." But Fitzgerald's lesbians and gay men also connect San Francisco to the paradigmatic great cities of the nineteenth century, specifically through sex: "Looking at the costumes . . . I wondered which were new and which had been worn for decades, even centuries, in the undergrounds of Paris or London. Which were the permanent archetypes of desire."[133]

Even though Castells saw gays as the future of San Francisco and of the city generally, engaged "in a process that transforms established cultural values and existing spatial forms," the future offered by the romance of the gay community was inseparable from the urban past it evoked.[134] In his discussion of gay festivals, Castells aligned contemporary gay city life with the history of San Francisco and of urbanity itself. "[G]ays have reinforced the San Francisco tradition of urban life," he explained. "The streets of San Francisco continue to be public places, unlike most American urban streets, partly because of the impact of the gay culture." He went so far back as to compare the San Francisco saved by its gay citizens to "the Renaissance city": "a merchant world and . . . a world of urban freedom . . . of autonomy, exchange, interaction, and cultural experimentation . . . where political freedom, economic exchange, and cultural innovation, as well as open sexuality, developed together in a self-reinforcing process on the basis of a common space won by citizens struggling for their freedom."[135] His repeated references to freedom echo a mantra usually identified with the medieval city, a mantra repeated by urbanists across the century, from Robert Park to Jane Jacobs and onward: "Stadt Luft macht frei" (City air makes men free).[136] If freedom is the essence of urbanity, then gays confirm the urbanity of the city when they are imagined as finding freedom there.

James Baldwin, however, made clear in his essays and novels the radical simplifications of such absolute claims about the freedom of the city. For Robert Park, open markets were the basis of the freedom found in medieval cities: those who reached the city were able to sell their labor there.[137] Castells emphasizes politics and culture, "autonomy," "common space," and "citizens struggling," by implication, together. But economics is the foundation of his account of San Francisco's revival as a whole. That the "Renaissance city" he imagined was a mercantile world allowed him to project the gay city as a realm of economics and feeling, in which capital and vice were merged. "Capital" had not meant industry in the Renaissance city, as it would not mean industry in the postmodern city. The weakness of Castells's vision was his faith that feeling would keep economics in balance.

Despite theoretically new understandings of "the public," of public/private relations, and of gender norms among straight and gay advocates of gay urban life in the late twentieth century, the focus on the street as *the* location of urban public life in their romance of the gay community evoked most powerfully the modern great city. Elizabeth Wilson observed late twentieth-century urbanists' fascination with the mid-nineteenth-century great city of Baudelaire and Benjamin. Marshall Berman, in *All That Is Solid Melts into Air* (1982), declared Baudelaire the "first modernist" and his modernism "even more relevant in our time than . . . in its own." The "distinctive sign of nineteenth century urbanism was the boulevard," he asserted, pairing Baudelaire with Jane Jacobs on the basis of her focus on the street. Baudelaire could thus be linked to 1960s and 1970s battles against the city-destroying forces of "urban renewal."[138]

The romance of the gay community was part of this new, finally unambiguous embrace of the great city, even as that city was being fundamentally transformed. But the great city carried forward by that romance remained a particular, romanticized city, an extension of the space inhabited a century and a half earlier by Baudelaire's *lesbiennes*, in which "vice" became the face of capital, organized around the street and the social margins, yet which somehow still centered on elite men.

The best-known chronicle of gay San Francisco—and one of the most widely distributed sources of the romance of the gay community—the six volumes of novelist Armistead Maupin's *Tales of the City*, reprised the literature of the great city for post-Stonewall America. Each book is a collection of the short chapters Maupin began publishing in the *San Francisco Chronicle* in May 1976 (the first volume appeared in 1978).[139] Their newspaper origin and their serial form evoke the feuilleton of early nineteenth-century Paris. Like the feuilleton, Maupin's tales were the products of an urban transformation fueled by immigration. Like the writers of those feuilletons, he offered to explain the new city emerging from the old. But for the late twentieth century, Maupin merged the story of the nineteenth-century city novel—featuring the young man from the provinces—with the story of the nineteenth-century women's novel—featuring the young woman seeking (or at least finding) a husband. The result, stories of more or less interchangeable young men and women moving to the city—from Cleveland, from Florida, from the political movements of the 1960s—for various combinations of lust and love, is Balzac with shorter sentences, more graphic sex, and fewer and less-refined cruelties. Almost everyone is looking for a man. Everyone becomes entangled in everyone else's stories.

Maupin had fun with the conventions of great city novels and the journalistic exposés of urban life they mirrored and fed. His cast is broadly divided between the city's business and social elite, on the one hand, and the young secretaries and waiters, the un- and underemployed, who provide his center of gravity, on the other. Uniting these social extremes, the romantic couple of the first volume consists of a transgender landlady (raised in a brothel) and a (dying) San Francisco–style captain of industry, the head of the city's premier advertising agency. The only family ties in this city are weak and/or hidden, and their revelation does not restore the social order: the gay husband of the socialite is unrepentant; the socialite is pregnant by a delivery boy; the landlady is the long-lost father of one of her tenants.

Maupin's *Tales of the City* series, though entertaining, was also limited by the conventions he was playing with. Key characters share either apartments or an apartment building, yet we hear very little about domestic life. Couples do form in the course of events, but they are established at the end of one book only to be sundered by disharmony or death before the beginning of the next volume, so that the universal pursuit of love can begin again. Walter Benjamin, reading Baudelaire, was sure of "the inconsequential nature of private life in the big city."[140] But if private life remains inconsequential, there can be no substantial reconstruction of "the public" or gender norms.[141]

Despite Maupin's apparent focus on the social margins, but consonant with the underlying structure of the literature of the great city (even transposed to the United States in the last quarter of the twentieth century), his tales actually focus on men, white people, and the middle class. The only substantial lesbian character in the early volumes decides she is really heterosexual, and her would-be lover, who appears to be black, turns out to have been a white woman passing, for circuitous reasons, for economic gain.[142] Everyone else, except for a couple of maids (one African American, one Vietnamese), an Asian American delivery boy, and his biracial children, is unequivocally white. All of Maupin's urban newcomers become financially comfortable without effort.

Maupin celebrates the sexualized city and the city as a site of emotional freedom. In *Tales of the City*'s romance of the gay community, middle-class white gay men (and eventually one or two lesbians) find a home. But even relationships among gay men are secondary. These novels' most enduring connections are friendships between gay men and straight women, and gay men and straight men. Even more clearly than Manuel Castells, Maupin presents middle-class white gay men offering community in the city to middle-class white heterosexuals.[143] This might seem like a more innovative outcome of the conjunctions of postmodern urban and queer life than Frances Fitzgerald's contemporaneous recognition of homosexuals as both the city's unconscious and its underworld; but it is an outcome just as clearly located in the history of the great city. It is, for the postmodern city, a familiar urban meaning.

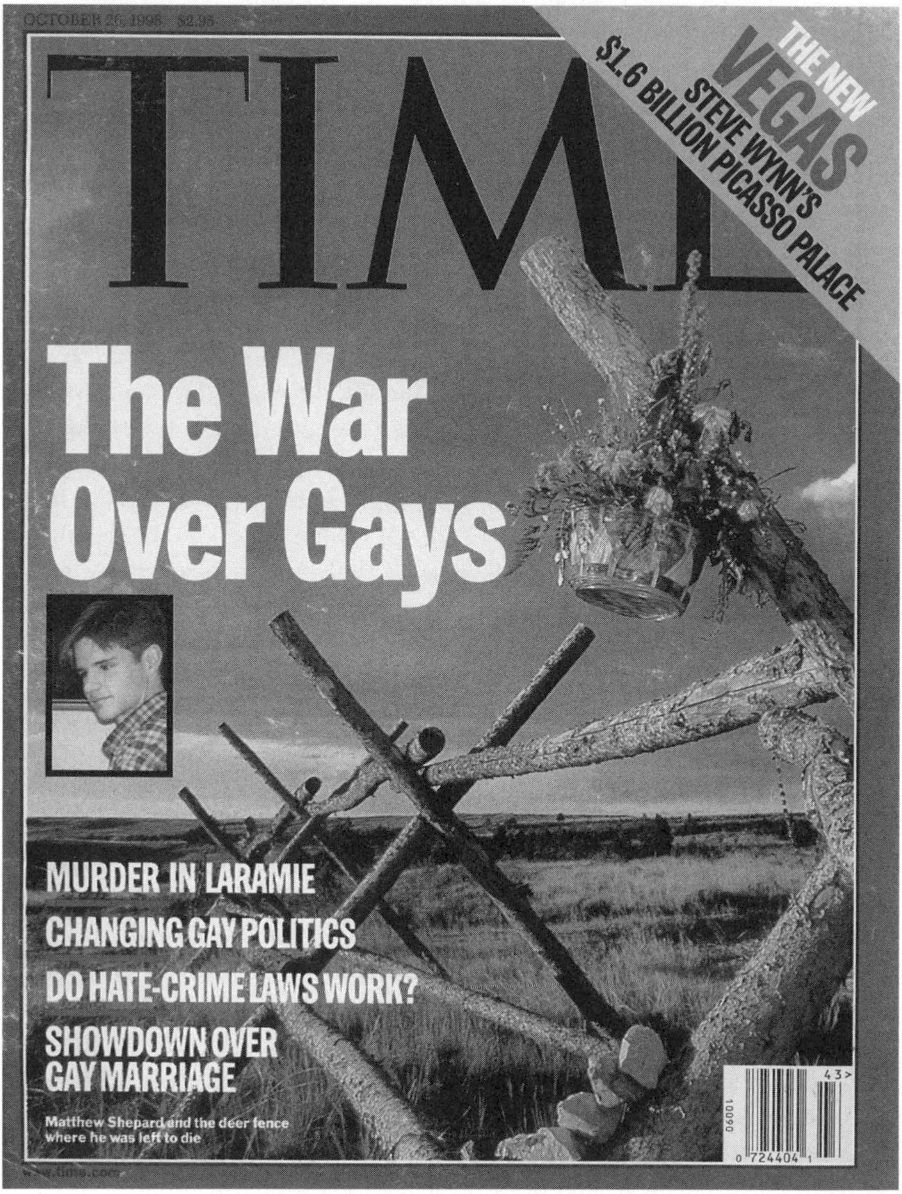

Cover of *Time*, October 26, 1998.

AFTERWORD

Queer in the Great City

SOMEWHERE

"Wyoming is a long, long way from Christopher Street." This, the opening line of a review of Beth Loffreda's *Losing Matt Shepard* (2000) in the *New York Times Book Review,* encapsulates the contrast between country and city invoked by almost all of the many journalists in the United States who reported on that young gay man's murder, in Wyoming, in 1998.[1] "Laramie is no thesis," Loffreda herself protests. "Laramie is no diagnosis. . . . Laramie didn't kill Matt."[2] Nevertheless, she begins her own discussion of local gay life by observing that "it isn't easy to be gay in Wyoming." And she goes on immediately to explain that being gay is not easy in Wyoming because Laramie is not a city—because there is no city in Wyoming. "[T]he wonderful thing about cities," she writes, quoting one of her gay informants, "is that 'you can get lost in the crowd but you can also find yourself in the crowd.'" But, she concludes, "[i]n Wyoming, crowds are an unlikely phenomenon."[3] The Shepard case and its consequences have been reprised, repeatedly, on stage and screen: each time the use of location as an organizing principle and source of explanation could not have been more explicit.[4]

Country and city were similarly contrasted in the United States throughout the accounts of the other high-profile queer murders of the 1990s. Brandon Teena's story, of the killing of a young transgender person living as a man, was retold in print and in documentary and feature films (including the Oscar Award–winning *Boys Don't Cry* [1999]) not only as a parable of gender and sexual transgression and their punishment but also as a lesson in the peculiar bleakness of rural Nebraska.[5] When Billy Jack Gaither was murdered in Sylacauga, Alabama, in February 1999, six months after Shepard's death, what apparently had to be explained, by newspaper and television journalists, was not why he died but why he had tried to live as a gay man in the small town in which he had grown up, instead of leaving as soon as he could for the freedom of the city.[6]

Many of the political battles over gay rights in the 1990s in the United States drew likewise on a country/city contrast. The struggle over Colorado's Amendment 2—an attempt to block civil rights protections for lesbian, gay, and queer people—was repeatedly cast as a contest in which the concerns of the "real," rural, Colorado were being undermined by the interests of the state's urban centers, which themselves had already been corrupted by an influx of immigrants from the cities of the East and West coasts.[7]

Sociologist Arlene Stein, in her study of "Timbertown," a small Oregon town bitterly divided by the 1993 campaign by the Oregon Citizen Alliance (OCA) to have antigay legal provisions enacted at local levels, describes the OCA deliberately fanning fears of a homosexuality identified with the sexual excess of San Francisco in widely circulated Christian Right videos such as *The Gay Agenda* (1992). As the timber industry on which the town had been built collapsed, longtime residents faced job insecurity and financial losses that disrupted their ability to fulfill conventional gender roles and expectations of family life. Stein traces their sense of being threatened by "outsiders": Californians arriving as retirees, aging hippies moving into town, Latinos coming to work at a local chicken factory. But all of these developments, the OCA implied, could be somehow dealt with by resisting the threat of homosexuality, always also the threat of the city. Preachers could "rail against cities and 'the gays, Asians, New Agers, and other undesirables' that populate them."[8]

Homosexuals were more visible in the United States in the 1990s in urban centers than in suburban, small-town, or rural locations, for all of the reasons and in all of the ways I have discussed throughout this book. And since Stonewall, urbanites throughout the nation had been more responsive to lesbian and gay concerns than other voters. In Colorado at the beginning of the 1990s, antidiscrimination ordinances that Amendment II would have overruled were already in place in Denver, Aspen, and Boulder.[9] In Oregon the OCA moved into action in small towns partly because voters in urban areas had resisted their efforts to institute antigay legislation at the state level. Nevertheless, as the editors of the national LGBT newsmagazine the *Advocate* felt compelled to observe on the first anniversary of Shepard's murder, "[G]ay men and lesbians lead" "precarious lives . . . even in the most sophisticated cities."[10] And there were lesbians and gay men living productive and integrated lives—as local business owners and teachers in local schools—in Stein's Timbertown.

In practice, neither actual urban gay visibility nor putative urban gay sympathy fully explains the U.S. media's commitment, at the end of the twentieth century, to presenting antigay violence as a product of rural locations. Nor does either explain concurrent antigay political campaigns that drew force from and contributed to urban/rural divisions, defining whichever place was being defended from the homosexual menace as fundamentally not urban.

When we are reminded that "Wyoming is a long, long way from Christopher Street," we are surely expected to understand this statement as self-evident. But why reach so far for a point of comparison? Why not cite Denver, a less resonant icon of urbanity than New York yet certainly a city, and much closer? Distance is, of course, the point. Wyoming and Christopher Street are defined by the terms of their coupling as distinct and very different places, the great distance between them a measure of that difference. Homosexuality and the city are united, in such invocations of Manhattan's Christopher Street, to signal the possibility of a gay life precluded in the country. By contrast, Wyoming, it seems, is Wyoming precisely because there are neither homosexuals nor cities there. By implication, there are no homosexuals *because* there are no cities.

Eliding as it does everything between the high plains and the urban center, such a statement radically simplifies the geography of the contemporary United States. What happened to the suburbs, the exurbs, the shopping malls, and the edge cities? Sprawl has vanished, as have postmodern metropolises without downtown centers and new urbanist developments with instant town squares.

Such a statement also radically simplifies the social map. After all, Christopher Street in 1998 was no longer either the only location or the key sign of gay New York. The young middle-class white men who once made Christopher Street gay had long since moved on to Chelsea, and had begun contemplating Harlem.[11] Conflicts that would persist throughout the next decade were already developing between the working-class and sometimes homeless black and Latino gay kids still walking the streets of Greenwich Village and local white residents, both gay and straight.[12] There were already many other lesbian, gay, and queer centers in New York City, each with its own combination of class, color, and gender, including the East Village; Greater Park Slope, in Brooklyn (from Brooklyn Heights to Prospect Heights); and Jackson Heights and Forest Hills/Kew Gardens, in Queens.[13] In the first decade of the new millennium, every New York City borough would begin to field its own annual gay pride parade. Even more to the point, there are many and complex lesbian, gay, and queer communities in other cities around the country. And there are lesbian, gay, and queer-identified individuals and networks in the nation's suburbs, exurbs, and new urbanist developments—even in Wyoming.[14]

Although it might seem self-evident that Wyoming is a long way from Christopher Street—or, in the words of a letter writer to the *Casper Star-Tribune* after Shepard's murder, Wyoming is "not San Francisco"—such statements must be seen as prescriptive rather than descriptive, and about time as well as place.[15] They draw on a fantasy of a simpler past when there was an uncorrupted countryside to be defended against a clearly bounded city. That city was an urban place partly because it contained a clearly bounded gay space, the location of which everyone knew, occupied by clearly defined gay people whom "we" could all recognize but didn't know and certainly were not related to. But once someone has to tell the world that Wyoming is not New York or San Francisco, such places are not indisputably different any longer. That someone is asserting a distinction that many fear is disappearing around them.

The effect of such statements is to assert the value of place itself, as well as to characterize a particular place and to "place" both homosexuals and cities. The country/city opposition can, after all, be invoked in support of either country or city. In the reporting of queer murders, the pattern works to the advantage of the city. Antigay violence is explained as a problem of backward rural areas. The freedom from responsibility and the sophistication of the up-to-date city are assured. In antigay political campaigns, however, those who contrast country and city values do so to the advantage of the country: rural probity and adherence to "traditional" values are presented as superior to urban decadence and abandonment of the past. But in both instances lines are drawn, a distinction is established, and geographic and social universes are simplified as the importance of place is reaffirmed.

Poster for *Boys Don't Cry*, Kimberly Peirce, director, 1999. Fox Searchlight.

What all of these developments indicate is that, by the late twentieth century, "homosexuals" had become markers of place. Both in the United States and internationally, what is particularly useful about this phenomenon is that we can be invoked both to confirm place differences *and* to demonstrate that such differences no longer exist. Queers can be called on, by their exclusion, to signal the significance of place. Place still matters; they are still murdering queers in the countryside of this country. But queers can also signal, by their presence, the insignificance of place. Place no longer matters. Not only are there same-sex couples in the suburbs of America these days (a sure sign of the end of suburban difference), but it is possible to be an American-style homosexual in almost any great city of our globalized world (a sure sign of the end of global difference).[16]

All of these assertions—even when they seem to contradict one another—share a common premise, namely, that it is possible to make a statement about place by making a statement about homosexuality. At the beginning of the 1990s, geographer David Harvey proposed that "the elaboration of place-bound identities has become more rather than less important in a world of diminishing spatial barriers to exchange, movement and communication."[17] But the absence or presence of lesbian, gay, or queer subjects in the countryside, in the suburbs, and in the city is not invoked in the kinds of statements I have cited in order to elaborate a place-bound identity. Rather, "homosexual," assumed to be a place-bound identity, is used by both pro-gay and anti-gay speakers—as well as speakers uninterested in homosexuality—to talk about place (both geographic and social) in a "world of diminishing spatial barriers" dominated by the postmodern flow of "ideas and ideologies, people and goods, images and messages, technologies and techniques."[18]

As urbanist Dolores Hayden has observed, "'Place' is one of the trickiest words in the English language, a suitcase so overfilled one can never shut the lid. It carries the resonance of homestead, [and of] location . . . as well as [of] a position in a social hierarchy. . . . Phrases like 'knowing one's place' or 'a woman's place' still imply both spatial and political meanings."[19] To discuss homosexuality in terms of geographic place—in terms of a country/city opposition—is also always to trade in assertions about social place as well. Even as antigay violence is explained as a rural problem, it is presented as an effect of homosexuals "out of place." Its victims can be seen as unwilling or unable to do what all good queers apparently must: flee for their lives to the bright lights of the big city. Shepard, Teena, and Gaither refused to accept the city as the only place in which they might be queer, and by doing so, they refused the social place prescribed for them, the place of the outcast from the "normal" life of the heartland and the family. To present their deaths as the result of their location—because they belonged both physically and socially elsewhere—is to insist not only that geographic place still matters but that social place still matters as well. Concomitantly, to assert the distinctness and value of small-town life—in contrast to the supposedly rootless lives of (urban) homosexuals—is to assert the value of a way of life in which everyone knows his or her place.

The homosexuality/city identification has been taken up by journalists, and in antigay political campaigns, to assert the value of place in the face of a changing social order and geography. By the same token, the social order and geography are changing in part because homosexuals and cities are changing, as recent debates among lesbians, gays, and queers and recent debates about cities attest. Within each of these debates, key arguments turn on the identification of homosexuals with cities. These arguments are concerned with two interrelated questions: Will "homosexual" remain a place-bound identity? Will cities remain distinctively urban places? These questions have been fused by the history I have just explored, in which the "difference" of homosexuals is confirmed, in part, by the "fact" that homosexuals live in cities, and the "difference" of cities is confirmed by the difference of their inhabitants, especially their visible gay populations. Both questions draw on the same underlying anxiety: Will cultural "difference" persist in a globalized world and, if so, in what forms?

A PLACE FOR US

The physical and social places of homosexuals had become less fixed, especially in the United States, by the end of the twentieth century, both because of the ongoing political work of gay advocates and lesbian feminists since the late 1960s advent of the gay and women's liberation movements, and because of the HIV/AIDS epidemic beginning in the 1980s. After the epidemic was dragged into the view of the "general public" in the United States, in the middle of that decade, by new generations of lesbian and gay activists and by media interest in the fates of celebrities, it brought gay men and lesbians unprecedented visibility. At first that visibility confirmed familiar patterns. But by the early 1990s, homosexuals could no longer be contained.

The epidemic initially confirmed the presence of gays in American cities, as well as deep-seated cultural fears of homosexuality as a form of sexual excess, an illness, and contagious. Maps showing rates of infection were
organized around urban centers—especially, at first, New York and San
Francisco—where local gay communities were devastated. The "innocent"
(those heterosexuals who contracted the virus through blood transfusions,
for example, whose illnesses were highly publicized) lived invariably in the
Midwest or the South.

As a result of the epidemic, two new variations on the narrative of gay
migration to the city were painfully developed: stories of sons returning
to the heartland to be cared for by their families, and stories of mothers
journeying to the coasts to nurse their sons in their adopted urban homes.
Again, the identification of homosexuality with the city was reiterated.

Among the wealth of artistic responses to the epidemic, Tony Kushner's
Pulitzer Prize–winning play *Angels in America* (1993–1994) received the
broadest public attention.[20] Kushner's play is set in New York City, and his

Silence = Death. ACT-UP demonstration, Philadelphia, 1992. Copyright Roger
Hallas.

homosexuals are familiar as well as familiarly place-bound. The play's gays are all male and the majority are white, although two are Jewish (Louis, a self-lacerating author surrogate, and Joe McCarthy's henchman Roy Cohn, the most publicly self-hating homosexual in post–World War II America), and there is, in a less prominent role, one African American, the nurse Belize. Everyone is educated. No one has financial worries. The women are nurses, angels, wives, and mothers. Through the story of the Mormon Joe Pitt, Kushner even includes the standard narrative of a young man who comes to terms with his homosexuality when he moves to the city, where he finds a male lover and himself. The work was widely recognized because it was both shocking and comforting. Kushner claimed "America" but did not challenge familiar views of queers or cities.

Nevertheless, the place of homosexuals had never been more publicly contested than it was in the 1990s in the United States. Gay men and lesbians had responded to the HIV/AIDS epidemic with unprecedented organizing efforts, with demands for city and federal government resources, educational campaigns, and the construction of new LGBT institutions and social services across the country. Meanwhile, a new generation of openly gay conservatives, taking advantage of new levels of gay visibility, tried to claim, as journalist Bruce Bawer ever-so-politely put it, "a place at the table."[21] Such claims, however carefully phrased, helped produce the battles that continue to be fought between pro- and antigay forces over social spaces such as the military, the church, and marriage, as well as geographic spaces such as Colorado, Vermont, Georgia's Cobb County, California, Oregon, Idaho, Hawaii, and Maine.[22] They also produced battles about place among lesbians, gays, and queers.

The historic identification of homosexuals with cities was as fundamental to those battles about place among lesbians, gays, and queers as it was for the antigay activists of the decade. In the antigay campaigns, broadly speaking, bad homosexuals were represented as living in bad cities. In the debates among lesbians, gays, and queers, there could, of course, be good as well as bad homosexuals. But that development required that there be homosexuals in the "country" as well as in the city, so that—from gay conservative perspectives—the good gays had a place to be.

Diane Hardy-Garcia offers a case in point. As chair of the Millennium March on Washington, in May 2000, Hardy-Garcia proffered a very clear example of what had by then become a paradigmatic move within lesbian/

gay/queer politics. She claimed (with the help of a reporter from the *New York Times*), that "the march was intended to show the generational and geographic range of the movement, its growing numbers of openly gay families and its ability to build coalitions." But her goal apparently depended on the contrast that immediately had to be drawn between all of these characteristics and the false "image" she had been working to erase, "that we were only an *urban* gay community."[23]

If from one perspective homosexuals required cities for our very existence, from another point of view homosexual diversity—generational and geographic, gay families and coalitions—seemed to depend on our distancing ourselves from our urban history. Ironically, by opposing families, generational and geographic range, and coalition to urban gay life, Hardy-Garcia's statement drew on and reinforced deeply familiar and very narrow understandings of homosexuality—and of urbanity—ostensibly in the service of constructing broader views. At the same time, the city remained her touchstone, even though her goal was to distance her constituency from urbanity and the forms of homosexuality that the city represents.

The move Hardy-Garcia attempted to make had already been repeatedly rehearsed in 1990s battles between gay conservatives and queer radicals over sex, marriage, and the future of gay life. On the "conservative" side, journalists like Michelangelo Signorile and Gabriel Rotello touted "deurbanization" as the only hope for gay men; to get gays out of the sexualized city was, they claimed, the only way to get them into meaningful lives, marriages, and families.[24] On the "radical" side, academics and journalists such as Michael Warner and Michael Bronski defended city life as the only source of an authentic and meaningful gay culture, politics, and community, one based in sexual freedom.[25]

That "homosexual" is a place-bound identity was assumed by both groups. The gay conservatives' emphasis on deurbanization implied that if homosexuals were going to expand their social place, they must also expand the physical space they occupied. They must move into "the country"—that is, the suburbs. (No one was actually advocating moving to the heartland.) Insofar as the suburbs represent no place, however, to send gays to the suburbs was also to try to spring homosexuals free of place, and thereby free of "homosexuality" itself. After all, in the United States, to be "normal" is to have no delimited place. Many of the young middle-class white gay men interviewed in a 2003 study of gay suburbanization explained their commitment to the suburbs as of a piece with their desire for indistinguishable selves and indistinguishable lives. They aspired to the status of "regular guys."[26] Such a lack of difference in gay lives was precisely what gay radicals feared.

The gay conservatives, however, depended on the popular identification of cities and homosexuality, just as Hardy-Garcia did, and they used that identification just as she did too, as a negative touchstone. They simplified and then rejected, but nevertheless consistently broadcast, conventional understandings of an "urban homosexuality." Where the radicals celebrated gay urban sexual cultures, the conservatives dramatized the misery of gay urban promiscuity to the exclusion of all other aspects of lesbian, gay, or queer city life. Women were, of course, peripheral to their stories. But there were also no couples and certainly no parents, no community centers, no choruses, no sports teams, no political groups, no professional networks, no self-help meetings, no religious gatherings, no marching bands, no archives, and no theater companies in their gay cities. Even gentrification, with its implication of a life beyond sex and partying, was erased. "The ghetto" was, however, repeatedly invoked. That is, the conservatives justified their call for deurbanization by intensifying their identification of what they represented as an old, unreformed gay life with the sex of the city, even as they touted a new gay life identified with marriage, family, and the suburbs.

The effect of this move was not so much to establish new places for lesbian, gay, and queer persons to occupy as to separate the "good" gays from the "bad" gays. What is key is that in the 1990s, in gay conservative rhetoric—and, as the place/marriage debates developed, in the queer radicals' rhetoric as well—the good gays and the bad gays were separated by their relation to the city. The gay conservative emphasis on the connection between the bad homosexual and the bad city contained the moral problem of homosexuality within city limits, whereas the virtues of the new, good gays could be demonstrated by their repudiation of the urban. At the same time, radicals increasingly insisted that gay difference depended on gay urbanization, and in their own version of the good/bad distinction, they could reject suburbanites as bad gays for their assumed assimilation.

This is to say that, despite their political differences, gay conservatives and radicals alike embraced and exploited the cultural equation of homosexuality and the city. They agreed, that is, that the city was key to the place

Lesbian resistance? "Suburban Subversion," in *Split-Level Dykes to Watch Out For*, by Alison Bechdel (Ithaca, N.Y.: Firebrand, 1998).

and meaning of homosexuality. Despite their different attitudes toward sex and sexuality, they even agreed on and further propounded the character of that city as, above all, sexual. This sexualized city would, of course, have been equally recognizable to those antigay activists who identified the San Francisco and New York they feared with public sexual excess—as indicated by the video clips of San Francisco gay pride parades they endlessly replayed and the specter of public school teachers armed with New York's Children of the Rainbow curriculum they endlessly invoked.[27] In other words, not only does the homosexuality/city equation have so much authority that it was agreed upon by gay and antigay activists alike, but it was taken up in the same very narrow terms by both groups.

Moreover, even while they were fundamentally opposed on the question of whether homosexuals should occupy a distinct social or physical place, the gay conservatives and queer radicals of the 1990s, like the journalists covering gay murders in the countryside and the antigay activists, needed a clear and stable barrier between the urban and the not-urban: the conservatives, to support their distinction between good and bad gays and to produce an uncontaminated alternative space in which they could pursue their vision of integration into the community of the normal; the radicals, to guarantee a space for a homosexuality that resisted assimilation, that would not be normalized but instead would produce its own distinctively lesbian/gay/queer communities.

SO THE CITY as a place as well as its homosexual populations were simplified by this reiteration of the gay/city equation. The suburbs lay in the background but were not elaborated, even by those who would send us there. There was, again, no faceless edge city, no featureless sprawl. And the "city" was an older city, not just clearly bounded but a place of street life, of people walking in public places, and of the encounters with strangers that result. It was, that is, the great city of Baudelaire or Engels, mid-nineteenth-century Paris and London or Manchester—which, though dramatically different, were each the highly sexualized province of elite male observers, to which they allude.[28] Moreover, just as the emphasis in this debate was on the great city that emerged in the nineteenth century, so it was on the subjects of that modern city (or the subjects of the literature of that city) as well: the elite male observers who wrote, and the denizens of the underworld they observed and wrote about.

Because of the contradictory social position of middle- and upper-class white gay men in the United States in the last decades of the twentieth century—culturally central by virtue of their class and race but marginalized by their sexuality—the white male academics and journalists contributing to this debate could fill both of the key roles of classic urban studies. As members simultaneously of the elite and of the underworld, they could be both the observers and the observed. (In that sense, they could most fully inhabit the paradoxical position, at both the margin and the center, to which Baudelaire, Benjamin, and their followers aspired.)

The participation of white women and women and men of color in these debates was, conversely, limited in part by the great city model. Pre–World War II urban sociology stressed the predominance of women in the city and the city's threat to male authority. Post–World War II American political discourse routinely presented cities as the province of ethnic and racial minorities. According to the actual demographics of most major U.S. cities, by the last decade of the twentieth century whites were often an urban minority.[29] Since the 1970s, lesbians and gay men of color, such as Melvin Dixon, Marlon Riggs, Cherríe Moraga, Cheryl Dunye, and Cheryl Clarke; and white lesbians, such as Rita Mae Brown, Marilyn Hacker, Sarah Schulman, and Rose Troche, have produced fiction, poetry, and films detailing their urban lives.[30] By the end of the 1990s, gay men of color, including literary critic Phillip Brian Harper and, especially, novelist and theorist Samuel Delany, in *Times Square Red, Times Square Blue*, were engaging in contemporary queer discussions of the city.

Delany's work, an explicit attempt to develop the gay/city identification, demonstrates the difficulties embedded in the "great city" paradigm. Simultaneously blurring and clarifying the conventions of great city studies, he identifies himself as a gay African American college professor from a family of professionals who goes out onto the street—the natural home of the economic, racial, ethnic, and sexual "lower" classes—to pursue his research. Sex is central to his project: the subject of his observations, a property of the subjects he is observing, and an axis of the relationship between himself as observer and his subjects. He connects the history of queer claims that cross-class sexual relationships are the hope of democracy and of the city, begun by Walt Whitman, to Jane Jacobs's *Death and Life of Great American Cities*, presenting the sexual encounters between men that he describes as models of the "contact" Jacobs identified. Contact, he emphasizes, is "fundamental to cosmopolitan culture . . . [and] quality of life."³¹ Nevertheless, his men having sex with men are a racially and class-mixed group, whereas the female figures in their city (women featured in porn films in Times Square theaters or hailed in sexual terms on Forty-second Street), like Baudelaire's *lesbiennes,* are only objects around which men negotiate their own racial, class, and sexual status.³²

Lesbians are consistently marginalized in arguments for gay urbanity that are focused on public sexual cultures, as the queer radicals' accounts have been. Within the great city, lesbianism, as the vice of whores, was seen as a product of public sexual cultures. But throughout the twentieth century, lesbians' bars, clubs, and other institutions were less numerous and visible than those of gay men. And by the 1990s, lesbians as a group were being relentlessly configured as naturally paired and domestically ideal (in contrast to sexually promiscuous urban gay men) by advocates of same-sex marriage and suburbanization. Gay conservatives offered images of lesbian domesticity to heterosexuals to defuse their fears of queers, and to gay men as a model to which they should aspire. Such women had no place within the great city.

If sex and street life were the overt terms of the identification of homosexuality and the city in the debates about place and same-sex marriage, the underlying terms of this discussion were artificiality and authenticity. The barrier between urban and not-urban, it was assumed by all, divides artifice from authenticity, although each "side" eagerly cast the other as enmeshed in an artificial world and in denial of the possibility of authenticity that their perspective alone offered. The gay conservatives represented gay urban life as a soulless sexual circus in contrast to the authentic pleasures of marriage and family in the suburbs. Radicals represented retreat from the city as retreat from an authentic gay life and social/political engagement to a mediated, artificial suburban world. Nevertheless, radicals and conservatives alike still had to grapple with the underlying association of homosexuality with artificiality, an association that could not be disentangled from the historic identification of homosexuality with the great city.

THE FUTURE OF CITIES

Clear distinctions between the city and the country, and concerns about artificiality and authenticity, taking the great city as a point of reference, were subjects central not only to lesbian/gay/queer debates about the future of homosexuals but also to the debates about the future of cities that began among urban commentators in the 1990s. Much recent discussion of the culture of cities has been shaped by anxiety about whether cities will persist as distinct places, as well as by the desire for such persistence. This, even as built environments so lacking in distinction that they can be described as "nonplace urban realms" proliferate, and the Internet, in theory at least, makes irrelevant the location of any individual with the resources to go online.[33] While Wyoming, Colorado, Vermont, and Oregon feared an encroaching homosexuality that was indistinguishable from an encroaching urbanity (how otherwise could civil unions threaten Vermont's status as an agricultural state?), New York and Los Angeles feared that their urbanity was being erased. Homosexuals appeared in urbanists' nightmares as well as in their utopian visions.

In recent discussions of cities, as in recent debates about the future of homosexuals, the identification of homosexuality with the city has been pivotal. Here too the equation of homosexuality and urbanity is played out in two apparently opposite ways, with gays presented as representatives of both simulated cities and authentic urbanity. But both possibilities depend upon the identification of homosexuals with the great city in particular, as well as on the persistence of that modern metropolis within analyses of postmodern urbanity.

One of the key anxieties accompanying the development of the modern city, traceable from the writings of Balzac in the 1830s and Engels in the 1840s to those of Simmel at the turn of the twentieth century, was that authentic human relations would not be possible in an urban setting because of the problem of legibility in the city, the necessary reliance on appearances in the rush of urban life, and the indifference to others generated by the crowd. Hence the identification of the city with artifice. Ironically, the modern city that produced this fear of artifice came to be seen, in retrospect, in turn-of-the-twenty-first-century discussions of the urban, as the site of an authentic, even quintessential, urbanity. As Elizabeth Wilson noted, in the 1990s "urbanists of various kinds drew on concepts of the good city . . . a nineteenth-century metropolis such as had been described and explored by Baudelaire and Benjamin," the city "of the *flaneur,* the pedestrian city, the city of many villages . . . cities of pleasure and civility."[34] This embrace of the great city model was, in part, a response to anxieties about urban artifice, about inauthentic persons and relations in the late twentieth century. It did not, however, allay those anxieties. They were instead dispersed into fear of a postmodern city inauthentic in itself, where the very buildings might be false—a city suburbanized, Disneyfied, malled, or theme-parked out of existence.

Representations of "the city" as a decentered postmetropolis, like Los Angeles; as a new urbanist development, like Seaside and Celebration, Florida; as a tidied-up and toned-down backdrop to the tourist trade, like Rudy Giuliani's New York; or as an interchangeable "global city" produced by the homogenizing flow of international capital—all reflect this fear of the loss of the city as a distinct place.[35] Simulation is central to the critiques of all of these urban developments: new urbanist communities mimic urbanism, we are told; New York has become a simulated version of itself, and Los Angeles a city of simulations.

This fear of artifice and yearning for authenticity constitute one axis along which recent lesbian/gay/queer debates and debates about the city have converged. Insofar as anxieties about the postmodern simulated city are an extension of anxieties about artificiality in the modern city, and insofar as homosexuals have long represented the artificial modern city, gays can appear as iconic residents of the simulated city. In a moment that has a peculiar resonance among the "friends of Dorothy," even as it restates the difference between city and heartland that is central to gay and urban identities, geographer Edward Soja introduces his discussion of Los Angeles as "simcity" with a famous line from The Wizard of Oz: "Toto, I've got a feeling we're not in Kansas anymore."[36] For sociologist Sharon Zukin, gay people offer a key example of the commodification of city culture.[37] What does the simulation of urbanity produce among the residents of Disney's new urbanist Celebration, according to cultural critic Andrew Ross, but fear of homosexuality?[38]

Iconic residents of the simulated city, gays can nevertheless, and simultaneously, function as a defense against artificiality. Because of their long association with the now "authentic" modern great city, they can serve as icons of an authentic urbanity. Thus, Ross begins his report on community in Celebration, Florida, with the gays of Celebration.[39] Art historian Rosalind Deutsche, countering Soja's analysis of Los Angeles as the model for our postmetropolitan future, bases her advocacy of a new, "reasonable urbanism" on a reading of a 1990 British gay novel, Neil Bartlett's Ready to Catch

Him Should He Fall. (Echoing Castells, Deutsche argues that gays model community, and so to create an urbanism that supports gay social life is to assert a standard of urban community.)⁴⁰ And the only optimistic sign in *Hollow City* (2000), Rebecca Solnit and Susan Schwartzenberg's account of San Francisco's real estate market run amok, is the gay candidate Tom Ammiano's mayoral campaign.⁴¹

In the United States, the role of gays in accounts of the city has, in fact, achieved a perfect incoherence. Gays are now being pursued by city governments and real estate developers alike precisely for their capacity to simulate, and thereby stimulate the revival of, an authentic (that is, modern) urbanism in postmodern cities. Their presence marks a place as properly urban and, it is predicted, that place then becomes a "city." This development even has its theoretician, social scientist Richard Florida.

Florida's work in *The Rise of the Creative Class* (2002) and *Cities and the Creative Class* (2005) has received widespread attention in the United States and internationally, in the media and from local governments as well as among economists, urban planners, and sociologists. An extraordinary amount of that attention has been paid to his references to gays.⁴² Rejecting "the greatest of the modern myths about cities . . . that *geography is dead,*" he insists that place matters.⁴³ Place matters, he argues, because it matters economically. But the economic potential of any given place, he proposes, depends on its social and cultural qualities. Places that offer a "community life" of interest to creative people will thrive economically, and such places, he claims, can be identified broadly by the presence of social bohemians and specifically by the presence of lesbians and gay men—a presence codified in his "gay index."⁴⁴ His model for the postindustrial city is one in which the queer radicals' insistence on a gay difference that depends on gay urbanity and the urbanists' identification of gays with both artifice and authenticity dovetail perfectly.

To support his analysis, Florida presents "the city" as the quintessential site of human creativity, offering as evidence a twentieth-century urban history that runs from the Chicago School's Robert Park to Jane Jacobs, and thereby makes clear his commitment to a great city model. But he focuses on gays as place makers not because of their own creativity—their roles as cultural or economic producers, always at least aspects of the romance of the gay community; for Florida, gays are place makers because they are

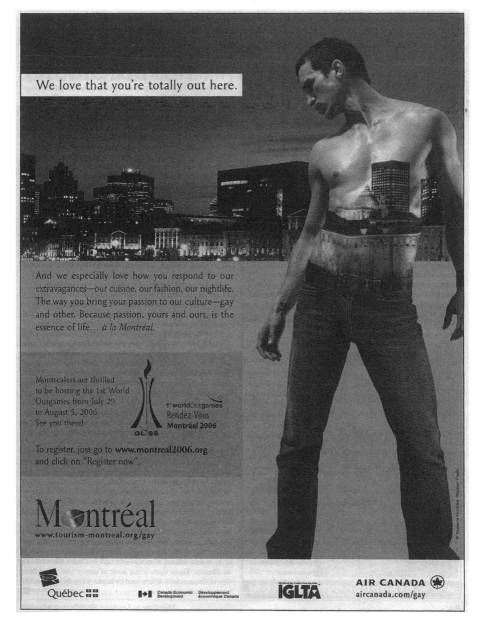

Our passions, whose culture? Advertisement, "We love that you're totally out here," 2006. http://www.tourism-montreal.org/gay.

the "*canaries* of the creative economy."[45] Gay presence is "a strong *signal* of a diverse, progressive environment," he argues. No longer political actors, that is, gays are an indicator of others' liberalism. No longer gentrifiers themselves, gays are "*harbingers* of redevelopment and gentrification in distressed urban neighborhoods." No longer consumers themselves, gays are "a *barometer* for a broad spectrum of amenities attractive to adults, especially those without children."[46] Florida is, in effect, systematizing the status of gays as markers of place that was laid out in 1990s media reports and political conflicts and reflected in LGBT and urbanists' debates. Gays have been transformed from urban saviors into pure signs of urbanity and, as such, signs of "the city's" potential for survival. Only truly urban cities, Florida argues, the kind occupied by gays, will persist as such, that is, as distinct places. By the same token, struggling cities can be revived only if they can become the kind of places his gays represent.[47]

Florida's analysis of gays as signs of urbanity exemplifies as well as illuminates not just a broad cultural development—the apotheosis of homosexuals as place markers—but also a specific pattern that can be traced through the past decade in the United States and internationally. After the City of Chicago set up rainbow-painted pylons on North Halsted Street in 1997 to mark out Boystown as a gay neighborhood, gay historian George Chauncey noted that this gesture gave evidence of Chicago's status as a "world-class city."[48] Invocations of the presence of gays as evidence of world-class-city status have also been central to the development of international gay tourist circuits. Gabriel Giorgi, for example, explains the marketing of Chueca as a new gay neighborhood in Madrid, as part of such a circuit. In Spain, "a democracy that still needs to demonstrate its strength and its resemblance to the older, so-called advanced democracies of the United States and northern Europe, gay visibility stands out as a symbol, a token of social tolerance and achieved freedom."[49] Similarly, in Sydney, Australia, the annual gay Mardi Gras festival, drawing tourists from around the world, has contributed to the reconstruction of that city "from an industrial port to a . . . global capital increasingly dependent . . . on an economy driven by consumption and leisure."[50] In Berlin, the mayor, Klaus Wowereit, a gay native son who came to power in 2001 and was reelected in 2006, in a city rapidly losing its industrial base, offered himself as an urban sign. Focusing Berlin's economic plans on tourism, he announced, "We are poor but sexy."[51]

THIS EVOLUTION OF gays from urban saviors to urban signs is not solely an effect of their ongoing identification with great cities and the recent embrace of great cities as models for authentic city life. Two other mutually reinforcing factors have contributed as well. One is the definitive recasting of the great city as a site of noneconomic values, as the city of the flaneur rather than industry, Paris rather than Manchester.[52] The other is an intensification of the association of gays with consumption.

Despite Manuel Castells's faith, expressed in the early 1980s, in the insulation of gays from the most powerful market forces, gay men were already being presented, in a 1972 issue of *Esquire*, as "the new artisans . . . always on the cutting edge of culture and urban living," with "child-free lives [that] allow them more time to pursue personal . . . and artistic interests."[53] This fantasy of gay urban life, Michael Bronski argues, was easily conflated with "the upscale consumerism of the 1970s and 1980s."[54] That conflation is now taken for granted. Geographer Richard Walker recently asserted both that "[g]ay liberation jump-started the yuppie era and its celebration of personal indulgence" in San Francisco in the 1970s, and that in the 1980s, "[t]he yuppie consumer culture . . . usher[ed] in . . . gay sensibilities in architecture, dress, and the arts."[55] In 2005, when sociologist Judith Stacey wanted to present contemporary Los Angeles as "the paradigmatic metropolis of postmodernism," she invoked both consumption and gays, each representing the other. "[N]o city better symbolizes sexual excess, consumer culture, and the antithesis of family values" and "no population" is more representative of this city, she writes, than "the gay male denizens who crowd the bars, beats, and boutiques of West Hollywood," Los Angeles' gay ghetto.[56]

Even lesbians are being inducted into equations of queers with consumption and cities. After a moment, early in the 1990s, when lesbianism was briefly chic, female couples began appearing in the lesbian and gay media at first, and in mainstream media more gradually, in advertisements for expensive goods. When New York City's lesbian magazine *GO!* was founded as an advertising vehicle in 2002, it blithely identified itself as "the cultural roadmap for the city girl." The magazine's audience was expected to know who a "city girl" was.[57]

But the most widely purveyed images of queer consumers remain images of moneyed white gay men, as in the Bravo cable television show *Queer Eye for the Straight Guy*, which flourished from 2002 to 2007. *Queer Eye for the*

Straight Guy confirmed that the "consumption" identified with this sub-group of gay men is not simply a matter of purchasing goods but purchasing goods with a veneer of style and culture, as *Esquire* had asserted gay men were peculiarly able to do three decades before.

This conflation of assumptions about gay men, consumption, and the city was encapsulated in the term "metrosexual," an import from Great Britain that first appeared there in the mid-1990s and quickly flared in the U.S. media after the turn of the twenty-first century. In itself, the term was a marketing ploy. A metrosexual was supposed to be a new type of man, a heterosexual with the style, the grooming habits, and the cultural capital (as well as the interest in shopping) ascribed to gay men. "Metro-" mediated between "homo-" and "hetero-"; the city representing the homosexual without sex, the homosexual as an accomplished consumer.[58]

Such a conflation of homosexuality, consumption, and the city has become so pervasive that LGBT hostility to the consumption-focused "gay life" now being sold to us all can take the form of hostility to the city. Thus, in *Gay and After* (1998), British queer critic Alan Sinfield labels what he rejects as the transnational post-Stonewall model of lesbian and gay life—founded on "the loving couple" as "the source of all meaning," and self-fulfillment at the expense of community ties—as "the metropolitan model" of homosexuality, which he identifies as a product of Anglo-American gay urban subcultures.[59] People who might otherwise see themselves as "gay" and "urban," like the men from the Philippines interviewed by Martin Manalansan in New York City in the 1990s for his study *Global Divas*, self-consciously reject "American gay urban life" despite having moved to U.S. cities to pursue their same-sex desires.[60] Reactions against popular images of gay urban life fuel gay men's journeys back and forth across urban/suburban and national borders, whether they are Americans who live in the suburbs of northern New Jersey and commute into New York City to pursue their "gay" lives, or Mexicans living in *zona rosa* in Mexico City, on the south side of Puerto Vallarta, or in Guadalajara, and traveling back and forth to Los Angeles.[61] Such reactions also justify the self-conscious commitment of many North American lesbians and gay men to suburban lives that they understand as less "gay" because they are not urban.

What has developed from the conflation of homosexuality, consumption, and cities is, in effect, a self-perpetuating system ensuring that the gays who are taken to represent modern urbanity in Chicago, Madrid, and Sydney remain a familiar moneyed, white, and male group. Reinforcing preexisting gender, racial, class, and national divisions among LGBT persons, this system at the same time continually emphasizes, to those it appears to favor, the hostility of the world in which they live, and so the possibility that they will be punished for their desires.

Hostility is, in fact, fundamental to the cultural usefulness of the homosexuals who represent modern urbanity in Chicago, Madrid, and Sydney—as well as that of the media gays of *Queer Eye for the Straight Guy* and the spectral homos hovering behind the metrosexual. The history of their oppression, as much as the incomes with which these men are credited, is where their value lies. Shopping requires money, or at least credit. Richard Florida is among the many who still cheerfully invoke the wealth of childless, male, same-sex households that supposedly allows them to "devote larger portions of their income to the purchase and development of amenities."[62] But the welcome these supposedly wealthy gays are offered in Chicago or Madrid or Sydney is equally based on the premise that they cannot expect to be accepted everywhere. Gay tourists, for example, are explicitly reminded by the cities and the companies seeking to profit from their travel that their sexuality is not accepted "at home": vacations can then be sold to them as necessary journeys to rare spaces of freedom.[63]

Hostility is also the premise of many of the urbanists who have recently posed gays as the hope of the city. Rosalind Deutsche, in her argument for a "reasonable urbanism" modeled on gay fiction, emphasizes the violence against gays that novelist Neil Bartlett describes in London in the 1980s.[64] Richard Florida's explanation for the role of gays as metropolitan signs is explicitly predicated on gay vulnerability. "As a group," he explains, "gays have been subject to a particularly high level of discrimination. Attempts by gays to integrate into the mainstream of society have met substantial opposition. To some extent, homosexuality represents the last frontier of diversity in our society, and thus a place that welcomes the gay community welcomes all kinds of people."[65] Canaries, after all, are kept in mines to die when the air goes bad, so that the miners might live.

THERE IS, MOST definitely, an asymmetrical relationship between the propositions that cities save gays, and that gays save cities. Lesbians and gay men continue to migrate to cities and to understand their sexualities as requiring urban life. When Keith Boykin, an African American gay man who became the director of the National Black Gay and Lesbian Leadership Forum, wrote about his own coming out in the mid-1990s, he spoke of "the gulf separating what I had become from what I had been. Raised in a simple, traditional family with suburban Midwestern values, I'd become a complex, untraditional urban dweller whose very existence challenged the conservative teachings of the Midwest."[66] Boykin saw his homosexuality as having turned him into an urbanite. Moreover, the family, the suburbs, and the Midwest he had left behind were separated from the city he had come to, not just by a gulf but also by active hostility.

Lesbians and gay men also continue to be described as the promise of the city, now including the cities of the American Midwest. As the *New York Times* reported in April 2005, a "recovery effort," "partly . . . led by . . . gay men and lesbians who have renovated neighborhoods and opened new businesses in recent years," has begun to take hold in St. Louis, which "lost half its population in the decades after World War II." That recovery effort is jeopardized however, by "history . . . myth . . . the deep divisions in Missouri politics, and . . . the even trickier terrain of sexual orientation." St. Louis was the lone source of dissent when its state voted overwhelmingly to ban same-sex marriage in 2004. Civic leaders still have to sell the "diversity" of the city to the rest of Missouri, even as they try to sell the state to the diverse "folks" they think they need to bring in to revitalize their city.[67]

The presentation of homosexuals as signs of urban life continues, meanwhile, to affirm mainstream assumptions about "gays and lesbians" as a white and well-off group. In the *New York Times* account of St. Louis, an assumed distinction between gays and African Americans is geographically marked: the city's "lesbian and gay" revitalization, we are told, is distinct from the "sagging brick houses" of the city's "black North End" neighborhood. Two recent films—*Flag Wars* (2003), a documentary about Columbus, Ohio, and *Quinceañera* (2006), fiction set in Echo Park, Los Angeles— criticize gentrifying white gays and lesbians for disrupting local black and Latino communities.[68] But there are no queers of color in *Flag Wars,* and in *Quinceañera,* where a young gay Latino is taken advantage of by an older gay white couple, the young man has no black or Latino queer compatriots. Furthermore, when Keith Boykin's home in Harlem and his fantasies of neighborhood redevelopment were written up in the *New York Times,* in 2005, no reference was made to his sexuality.[69]

Queers continue as well to be the subjects of city studies, including studies of each of the cities featured in this project: Paris, Los Angeles, Manchester, London, Chicago, New York, and San Francisco. Some of these studies
are among the richly detailed urban histories published since the early 1990s
by LGBT historians, anthropologists, and sociologists.[70] Others are among
the many examinations of "queer space" that began to appear in the mid-
1990s in conjunction with the development of queer theory.[71] Novelists still
write about gay and lesbian lives in those cities, as do University of Chicago sociologists. Offering elaborate portraits of queer urbanity, these works
resist the reduction of homosexuals to urban place markers, whether their
subjects are flânerie, as in Samuel Delany's *Times Square Red, Times Square
Blue* or Edmund White's *The Flâneur* (2001); sex, as in Edward O. Laumann
and his colleagues' Chicago study *The Sexual Organization of the City* (2004);
politics and institutions, as in Davina Cooper's *Sexing the City* (1994), on
London and Manchester, and Moira Rachel Kenney's *Mapping Gay L.A.*
(2001); or marriage and domestic life, as in Armistead Maupin's return

Souvenirs of New York City, 2007. Photograph by the author.

to his tales of San Francisco with *Michael Tolliver Lives* (2007).[72] Neverthe-less, the debates about homosexuality and about cities that have developed over the past two centuries persist in these recent works, as do their now-familiar terms—not only gentrification and the ghetto but also capital and vice, legibility, combination, attachment, public/private relations, the the-ater, and the street.

The "creative class" that Richard Florida's cities need to attract for their own economic survival is, being "creative," interested in more than just eco-nomic values. It is, in fact, the manifestation of other-than-economic values in urban settings that his "gay index" tracks. Gays not only give consumption a veneer of style but, at the same time, give cities increasingly turned over to consumption a veneer of authenticity. That veneer of authenticity rests, in the end, on the identification of homosexuals with the now-authentic great cities of the nineteenth century but also on the history of gay oppression. That history—with the possibility of enduring hostility that it conveys—connects homosexuals to what are, after style, the two other most highly prized noneconomic values in the postmodern city: "diversity" and "feeling."

As members of an oppressed minority, (wealthy, white, male) gays serve as evidence of urban diversity, however reassuringly familiar, even socially ideal, they might otherwise appear to be. Their oppression, moreover, secures their continuing identification with feeling. Their own feelings for each other, after all, are so intense as to lead them to defy social hostility. What is more, that intensity of feeling is supposedly carried over into their commitment to the city and to the communities that, in their flight from social hostility elsewhere, they journey to cities to seek.[73]

The romance of the gay community that developed in the 1970s among gays and urbanists out of the complex history of queer urbanity has been mainstreamed and eviscerated. Heterosexuals are moving not just into cit-ies these days but into what were once considered gay ghettos—Chelsea in New York City, Boystown in Chicago, the Castro in San Francisco—in pursuit of authentically urban experiences.[74] Meanwhile, San Francisco's Halloween parade, emblematic, in Manuel Castells's view, of the public cele-brations central to gays' creation of urban meaning, draws such huge crowds of outsiders that it was canceled in 2007, as a danger to its participants and the neighborhood.

The urban horrors of the great cities of the nineteenth century—or the post–World War II American city or New York City on the verge of collapse in the 1970s (choose your nightmare city)—have given way to urban amenities. At the same time, homosexuals have struggled to escape their status as horrors only to find themselves among the most desirable of those amenities. The cities in which gays now serve as signs of authentic urbanity may remain distinct places. But the experience of social difference those cities offer will be safely limited.

Notes

PREFACE

1. William Sharpe and Leonard Wallock, "From 'Great Town' to 'Nonplace Urban Realm': Reading the Modern City," in *Visions of the Modern City: Essays in History, Art, and Literature*, ed. William Sharpe and Leonard Wallock (Baltimore: Johns Hopkins University Press, 1987), 6.

2. Marcel Proust, *Remembrance of Things Past*, trans. C. K. Scott Moncrieff and Terence Kilmartin (1921; repr., New York: Vintage, 1981), 2:627, 628, 656.

3. Sharpe and Wallock, "From 'Great Town' to 'Nonplace Urban Realm,'" 6.

4. Historian George Mosse tells us, for example, that "[w]hen court cases concerning homosexuality were reported in the London press [in the nineteenth century], the analogy to the biblical cities of Sodom and Gomorrah was almost always drawn." George L. Mosse, *Nationalism and Sexuality: Respectability and Abnormal Sexuality in Modern Europe* (New York: Fertig, 1985), 32. For a copy of the *Hardwick* decision, see *"Bowers v. Hardwick,"* in *Reclaiming Sodom*, ed. Jonathan Goldberg (New York: Routledge, 1994), 117–42.

5. Mark S. McBride, quoted in Kevin Sack, "Gay Rights Movement Meets Big Resistance in S. Carolina," *New York Times*, July 7, 1998.

6. Ellen Goodman, "Once Liberal Vermont Surprisingly Divided," *Albany Times Union*, November 3, 2000.

7. Quoted in Carey Goldberg, "Marriage Law Roils Vermont Elections," *New York Times*, October 25, 2000. See also Carey Goldberg, "Vermont Residents Split over Civil Unions Law," *New York Times*, September 3, 2000.

8. Russell Johnson, quoted in James Dao, "Movement in the Pews Tries to Jolt Ohio," *New York Times*, March 27, 2005.

9. Charles Kaiser, *The Gay Metropolis, 1940–1996* (Boston: Houghton Mifflin, 1997), xii.

10. Emily Eakin, "The Cities and Their New Elite," *New York Times*, June 1, 2002; and Gabriel Giorgi, "Madrid *en Tránsito*: Travelers, Visibility, and Gay Identity," *GLQ: A Journal of Lesbian and Gay Studies* 8, nos. 1–2 (2002): 57–80.

11. Walt Whitman, "For You O Democracy," in *Leaves of Grass and Selected Prose,* ed. John Kouwenhoven (New York: Modern Library, 1950), 96.

12. Because lesbians were understood to be masculine women; gay men, feminine men; and gender transgression as both a sign and an explanation of same-sex desire, for most of the period I am discussing, gender-crossing is treated as an aspect of "homosexuality" rather than the source of a distinct "transgender" identification, as it has in some contexts come to be understood in recent decades. For an analysis of the variety of recent understandings of gender transgression, see David Valentine, *Imagining Transgender: An Ethnography of a Category* (Durham, N.C.: Duke University Press, 2007).

13. Richard Sennett, *The Fall of Public Man: On the Social Psychology of Capitalism* (New York: Vintage, 1978), 39.

14. Neil Smith, foreword to *The Urban Revolution,* by Henri Lefebvre, trans. Robert Bononno (Minneapolis: University of Minnesota Press, 2003), xix–xx. See also *State of World Population, 2007: Unleashing the Potential of Urban Growth* (New York: United Nations Fund for Population Activities, 2007).

15. Raymond Williams, "Metropolitan Perceptions and the Emergence of Modernism," in *The Politics of Modernism: Against the New Conformists,* ed. Tony Pinkney (London: Verso, 1997), 44.

1. LES LESBIENNES, OR THE CITY IN HISTORY

1. See Claude Pichois, *Baudelaire,* trans. Graham Robb (London: Hamilton, 1989), 125, 170.

2. T. S. Eliot would describe Baudelaire as "the greatest exemplar in *modern* poetry in any language," according to Pichois (ibid., vii).

3. See Pichois, *Baudelaire,* 232. The Sûreté publique is quoted on p. 224.

4. See Valerie Traub, "The Renaissance of Lesbianism in Early Modern England," *GLQ: A Journal of Lesbian and Gay Studies* 7, no. 2 (2001): 245–64, 249. See also "Men and Lesbianism," ed. Elisabeth Ladenson, special issue, *GLQ* 7, no. 3 (2001).

5. Pichois, *Baudelaire,* 233.

6. Charles Baudelaire, *Les Fleurs du mal,* trans. Richard Howard (Boston: Godine, 1982), 125.

7. Ibid., 130.

8. Charles Baudelaire, "The Painter of Modern Life," in *The Painter of Modern Life, and Other Essays,* trans. and ed. Jonathan Mayne, 2nd ed. (London: Phaidon, 1995), 13; hereafter cited parenthetically in text.

9. Walter Benjamin, *Charles Baudelaire: A Lyric Poet in the Era of High Capitalism,* trans. Harry Zohn (London: Verso, 1997), 90.

10. See Pichois, *Baudelaire,* 232.

11. Charles Baudelaire, "The Salon of 1846," in *Art in Paris, 1845–1862: Salons and Other Exhibitions Reviewed by Charles Baudelaire,* trans. and ed. Jonathan Mayne (London: Phaidon, 1965), 119.

12. See, for example, David Harvey, *Paris, Capital of Modernity* (New York: Routledge, 2003); and Edmund White, *The Flâneur: A Stroll through the Paradoxes of Paris* (New York: Bloomsbury, 2001).

13. Honoré de Balzac, *The Girl with the Golden Eyes*, in *History of the Thirteen*, trans. Herbert J. Hunt (New York: Penguin, 1974), 309; hereafter cited parenthetically in text.

14. A number of queer scholars have explored the history of the identification of sexual and racial "otherness" that emerged in the West over the course of the nineteenth century (notably in the new sexual sciences) and was developed in the twentieth century. See Siobhan Somerville, *Queering the Color Line: Race and the Invention of Homosexuality in American Culture* (Durham, N.C.: Duke University Press, 2000); and Jennifer Terry, *An American Obsession: Science, Medicine, and Homosexuality in Modern Society* (Chicago: University of Chicago Press, 1999).

15. Gold also procures the marquise's freedom from the consequences of her violent actions. After she murders Paquita in a jealous rage at her betrayal, she then pays the mother again, this time for her silence.

16. For discussions of Sand's lesbianism, and her relationship with Marie Dorval in particular, see Belinda Jack, *George Sand: A Woman's Life Writ Large* (New York: Knopf, 2000), 117, 222; 4, 204, 208, 350.

17. Joan DeJean, *Fictions of Sappho, 1546–1937* (Chicago: University of Chicago Press, 1989), 266.

18. See ibid., 354.

19. Parent-Duchâtelet, as a leading public hygienist of the first decades of the nineteenth century, "an expert in sewage and waste disposal" before he turned to the subject of prostitution, understood his new work as another means of cleansing the city. See Jill Harsin, *Policing Prostitution in Nineteenth-Century Paris* (Princeton: Princeton University Press, 1985), xv.

20. Moreover, because "[l]esbians have fallen to the last degree of vice to which a human creature can attain," they "require a most particular surveillance on the part of those who are charged with the surveillance of prostitutes, but more particularly on the part of persons to whom the direction of prisons dealing with these women is entrusted." Alexandre Parent-Duchâtelet, *La Prostitution dans la ville de Paris* (Paris: Bailliere, 1834), 1:170, quoted in Jean-Paul Aron and Roger Kempf, "Triumphs and Tribulations of the Homosexual Discourse," in *Homosexualities and French Literature: Cultural Contexts/Critical Texts*, ed. George Stambolian and Elaine Marks (Ithaca, N.Y.: Cornell University Press, 1979), 148.

21. Alexandre Parent-Duchâtelet, quoted in Richard von Krafft-Ebing, *Psychopathia Sexualis: A Medico-forensic Study*, trans. Harry E. Wedeck (1886–1903; repr., New York: Paperback Library, 1965), 608.

22. See Leslie Choquette, "Homosexuals in the City: Representations of Lesbian and Gay Space in Nineteenth-Century Paris," in *Homosexuality in French History and Culture*, ed. Jeffrey Merrick and Michael Sibalis (New York: Harrington Park, 2001), 163, 155.

23. Émile Zola, *Nana,* trans. Douglas Parmée (1880; repr., New York: Oxford University Press, 1992), 409; hereafter cited parenthetically in the text.

24. Zola had done his research, including a visit to Louise Taillandier's table d'hôte at 17 rue des Martyrs, clearly the model for Laure's. He was not pleased: "3 dining rooms. . . . In couples the women. . . . Mistresses of grave bourgeois who come to have fun. The girl dressed as a man. . . . An old slut, as soon as she finds a pretty novice, brings her here, and all the fat women woo her. Horrible fat women" (quoted in Choquette, "Homosexuals in the City," 153). He did not even bother to relocate Laure's from the rue des Martyrs and, as Leslie Choquette observes, hardly elaborated in the novel on his original notes.

25. Émile Zola, quoted in Robert Nye, *Masculinity and Male Codes of Honor in Modern France* (New York: Oxford University Press, 1993), 121.

26. Honoré de Balzac, *A Harlot High and Low,* trans. Rayner Heppenstall (New York: Penguin, 1970), 200. Hereafter cited parenthetically in the text.

27. According to Donald Olsen, this pattern has persisted: "[H]istorians and respectable scholars in general have usually concentrated on the pathological aspects of the modern city." Donald Olsen, *The City as a Work of Art: London, Paris, Vienna* (New Haven, Conn.: Yale University Press, 1986), 2. Sharon Marcus discusses the peculiar absence of the middle class from standard accounts of the city in *Apartment Stories: City and Home in Nineteenth-Century Paris and London* (Berkeley and Los Angeles: University of California Press, 1999).

28. See Stuart M. Blumin, "George G. Foster and the Emerging Metropolis," introduction to *New York by Gaslight, and Other Urban Sketches,* by George G. Foster, ed. Stuart M. Blumin (1850; repr., Berkeley and Los Angeles: University of California Press, 1990), 4.

29. Robert Bezucha, "Discourses on Misery," in *New History of French Literature,* ed. Denis Hollier (Cambridge, Mass.: Harvard University Press, 1989), 689.

30. G. W. M. Reynolds, quoted in Asa Briggs, *Victorian Cities* (1965; repr., Berkeley and Los Angeles: University of California Press, 1993), 62.

31. Foster, *New York by Gaslight,* 69.

32. In Buret's view the responsibility for this crisis lay directly with the new class of manufacturers: "In the mind of the owner, workers are not men but units of energy . . . rebellious instruments, and less economical than tools of iron and fire" (Eugène Buret, quoted in Bezucha, "Discourses on Misery," 691; ellipses in original).

33. Robert Vaughan, *The Age of Great Cities* (1842; repr., London: Woburn, 1969), 1.

34. "[N]o other urban settlement known [had] ever before grown so fast in so short a time" as nineteenth-century Paris and London. Richard Sennett, *The Fall of Public Man: On the Social Psychology of Capitalism* (New York: Vintage, 1978), 133.

35. Kingsley Davis, "The Urbanization of the Human Population," in *The City Reader,* ed. Richard T. LeGates and Frederic Stout (London: Routledge, 1996), 5.

36. Raymond Williams, *The Country and the City* (New York: Oxford University Press, 1973), 152.

37. Christine M. Boyer, *The City of Collective Memory: Its Historical Imagery and Architectural Entertainments* (Cambridge, Mass.: MIT Press, 1996), 280. See also Gareth Stedman Jones, *Outcast London: A Study in the Relationship between Classes in Victorian Society* (London: Oxford University Press, 1971).

38. See Olsen, *City as a Work of Art*; and Harvey, *Paris, Capital of Modernity*.

39. Baudelaire, *Les Fleurs du mal*, 90.

40. George Saintsbury, quoted in Briggs, *Victorian Cities*, 96.

41. Williams, *Country and the City*, 46.

42. A. Alison, *Principles of Population, and Their Connection with Human Happiness* (1840), 2:76, quoted in Friedrich Engels, *The Condition of the Working Class in England*, ed. Victor Kiernan (1845; repr., London: Penguin, 1987), 147.

43. See Walter Benjamin, "Paris—The Capital of the Nineteenth Century," in *Charles Baudelaire*, 155–76; and Briggs, *Victorian Cities*, 56.

44. Williams argued, from the perspective of the late twentieth century, that the growth of "the industrial cities . . . announced, even more decisively than the growth of capitals, the new character of the city and the new relations between city and country" while nevertheless rejecting what he describes as "the confusion which prevailed, in Dickens's time and beyond, between the idea of the city and the idea of industry" (*Country and the City*, 152, 153). His conviction that this was a confusion was based on a desire to account for the historic capitals. Although London and Paris burgeoned as economic centers and centers of manufacture (in ways different and at a different pace from the new industrial centers and from each other), they were not industrial cities. Richard Sennett, also in retrospect, points out that "[t]he greatest growth of population occurred in cities with few large scale industries; it occurred in the capitals," and that in fact "[c]apital cities of the industrial era were not industrial" (*Fall of Public Man*, 130, 136).

45. Engels, *Condition of the Working Class in England*, 146–47; hereafter cited parenthetically in the text.

46. Gustave Flaubert, quoted in Charles Bernheimer, *Figures of Ill Repute: Representing Prostitution in Nineteenth-Century France* (Cambridge, Mass.: Harvard University Press, 1989), 134.

47. "In the mid-nineteenth century the prostitute, as seller and merchandise in one, was seen as a symbol of modern life in the capitalist metropolis," according to Leslie Choquette, "Degenerate or Degendered? Images of Prostitution and Homosexuality in the French Third Republic," *Historical Reflections/Réflexions Historiques* 23, no. 2 (1997): 205.

48. Cesare Lombroso and Guglielmo Ferrero, *Criminal Woman, the Prostitute, and the Normal Woman*, trans. Nicole Hahn Rafter and Mary Gibson (Durham, N.C.: Duke University Press, 2004), 176; hereafter cited parenthetically in the text.

49. Ali Coffignon, quoted in Catherine van Casselaer, *Lot's Wife: Lesbian Paris, 1890–1914* (Liverpool: Janus, 1986), 11.

50. Havelock Ellis, *Studies in the Psychology of Sex*, vol. 1, pt. 4, Sexual Inversion (1897; repr., New York: Random House, 1936), 213.

51. Ibid., 215.

52. "A Tragedy Equal to the Most Morbid Imaginings of Modern French Romances," *Memphis Public Ledger,* January 26, 1892, cited in Lisa Duggan, *Sapphic Slashers: Sex, Violence, and American Modernity* (Durham, N.C.: Duke University Press, 2000), 181–82. Meanwhile, brothel owners of New Orleans were advertising lesbian scenes to their customers by touting the "many poses" of their "French models"; see Katy Coyle and Nadiene Van Dyke, "Sex, Smashing, and Storyville in Turn-of-the-Century New Orleans: Reexamining the Continuum of Lesbian Sexuality," in *Carryin' On in the Lesbian and Gay South,* ed. John Howard (New York: New York University Press, 1997), 64.

53. Elizabeth Wilson, "Forbidden Love," *Feminist Studies* 10, no. 2 (Summer 1984): 213.

54. Elizabeth Wilson, "Looking Backward, Nostalgia, and the City," in *Imagining Cities: Scripts, Signs, Memory,* ed. Sallie Westwood and John Williams (London: Routledge, 1997), 132–33.

55. Benjamin, *Charles Baudelaire;* hereafter cited parenthetically in the text.

56. As noted earlier, Jeanne Duval was apparently publicly named in *Les Lesbiennes de Paris* (see DeJean, Fictions of Sappho, 266). See also Elisabeth Ladenson, *Proust's Lesbianism* (Ithaca, N.Y.: Cornell University Press, 1999), 24.

57. Ladenson, *Proust's Lesbianism,* 22.

58. DeJean, *Fictions of Sappho,* 266–67, 275.

59. Baudelaire, *Les Fleurs du mal,* 123.

60. This is a joining in Baudelaire's work that Benjamin explicitly endorsed: "The correspondence between antiquity and modernity is the sole constructive conception of history in Baudelaire." Walter Benjamin, *The Arcades Project,* trans. Howard Eiland and Kevin McLaughlin (Cambridge, Mass.: Harvard University Press, 2002), 336 (J59a, 5).

61. In addition, Baudelaire, who desired to be read as a classical poet despite his commitment to contemporary art, is able to claim classical connections and classical credit with his *lesbiennes,* to construct a modern literature with classical authority, a literature simultaneously historically specific and ahistorical.

Christine Buci-Glucksmann proposes that in Baudelaire's writings, "the feminine constitutes one of the nineteenth-century's 'original historic forms' . . . an origin . . . where a 'prehistory' and a 'posthistory' . . . the archaic and the modern, are dialectically articulated. The feminine becomes the inevitable sign of a new historic regime of seeing and 'not-seeing,' of representable and unrepresentable," that is "characteristic of modernity: the cult of images, the secularization/sublimation of bodies, their ephemeral nature and reproducibility." Christine Buci-Glucksmann, "Catastrophic Utopia: The Feminine as Allegory of the Modern," *Representations* 14 (Spring 1986): 221. But it is not "the feminine" that achieves this, it is the lesbian specifically.

62. "The paradigm of the lesbian woman bespeaks the ambivalent position of 'modernity' vis-a-vis technological development," Benjamin observed in his notes as he was drafting his discussion of Baudelaire's interest (*Arcades Project,* 318 [J49a, 1]).

63. Baudelaire, "Salon of 1846," 118–19.

64. "It would be erroneous to assume that it ever occurred to Baudelaire to champion lesbians publicly in his writings," Benjamin explained. "He abandoned them to their doom, and they could not be saved" (*Charles Baudelaire*, 93). Baudelaire wrote to his lawyer during the trial of *Les Fleurs du mal*, "asking that the book be 'judged *as a whole*, and then a terrifying moral emerges'" (quoted in Pichois, *Baudelaire*, 228; Pichois's emphasis).

65. Balzac, *Girl with the Golden Eyes*, 326.

66. The flaneur also acquires an ancient history. "In the flaneur," Benjamin notes, "is reborn the sort of idler that Socrates picked out from the Athenian marketplace to be his interlocutor" (*Arcades Project*, 334 [J58a, 5]).

67. Benjamin, *Charles Baudelaire*, 55. Baudelaire identified the poet with the prostitute. "What is Art?" he asks, answering "Prostitution." Charles Baudelaire, *Intimate Journals*, trans. Christopher Isherwood (Hollywood: Marcel Rodd, 1947), 31. If the flaneur is a counterpart to the lesbian, he is also a counterpart to the poet.

68. Benjamin, *Arcades Project*, 347 (J66a, 6).

69. Baudelaire, "Painter of Modern Life," 9; emphasis in original.

70. Benjamin, *Arcades Project*, 267 (J21a, 4).

71. Baudelaire, *Les Fleurs du mal*, 97–98.

72. Walter Benjamin, "On Some Motifs in Baudelaire," in *Illuminations*, ed. Hannah Arendt, trans. Harry Zohn (New York: Schocken, 1969), 169–70.

73. Ibid., 170.

74. For a history of such readings of Proust's work, see Ladenson, *Proust's Lesbianism*.

75. Benjamin, *Charles Baudelaire*, 46.

76. Ibid., 93.

77. Benjamin, *Arcades Project*, 332 (J57, 9).

78. Baudelaire, *Les Fleurs du mal*, 97.

79. Ibid., 125.

2. Oscar Wilde in Los Angeles

1. See Mike Davis, *City of Quartz: Excavating the Future in Los Angeles* (New York: Vintage, 1992), 111.

2. Henry James, "The Figure in the Carpet," in *The Lesson of the Master, and Other Stories* (London: Lehmann, 1948), 157.

3. Aldo Rossi, *The Architecture of the City*, trans. Diane Ghirardo and Joan Ockman (Cambridge, Mass.: MIT Press, 1982), 13. Rossi's work was first published in Italian in 1966.

4. See, for example, Jeffrey Merrick, "'Brutal Passion' and 'Depraved Taste': The Case of Jacques-Francois Pascal," 85–86; Michael Sibalis, "The Palais-Royal and the Homosexual Subculture of Nineteenth-Century Paris," 119; and Leslie Choquette,

"Homosexuals in the City," 155; all in *Homosexuality in French History and Culture*, ed. Jeffrey Merrick and Michael Sibalis (New York: Harrington Park, 2001).

5. See George Chauncey, *Gay New York: Gender, Urban Culture, and the Making of the Gay Male World, 1890–1940* (New York: Basic Books, 1994).

6. Robert Park, "The City: Suggestions for the Investigation of Human Behavior in the Urban Environment," in *Classic Essays on the Culture of Cities*, comp. Richard Sennett (New York: Appleton-Century-Crofts, 1969), 91.

7. Oscar Wilde, *De Profundis*, in *The Soul of Man and Prison Writings*, ed. Isobel Murray (New York: Oxford University Press, 1999), 95.

8. See Alan Sinfield, *The Wilde Century: Effeminacy, Oscar Wilde, and the Queer Moment* (New York: Columbia University Press, 1994), 5; and Richard Ellmann, *Oscar Wilde* (New York: Knopf, 1988), 275–76.

9. Sinfield, *Wilde Century*, 3. See particularly Ed Cohen's account of the study of Wilde's appearance during the trial, in *Talk on the Wilde Side: Toward a Genealogy of a Discourse on Male Sexualities* (New York: Routledge, 1993).

10. Susan E. Gunter cites Leon Edel in her introduction to "'You Will Fit the Tighter into My Embrace!': Henry James's Letters to Jocelyn Persse," *GLQ: A Journal of Lesbian and Gay Studies* 7, no. 2 (2001): 336. See also Susan E. Gunter and Steven H. Jobe, eds., *Dearly Beloved Friends: Henry James's Letters to Younger Men* (Ann Arbor: University of Michigan Press, 2001); and Henry James, *Beloved Boy: Letters to Hendrik C. Andersen, 1899–1915*, ed. Rosella Mamoli Zorzi (Charlottesville: University of Virginia Press, 2004).

11. Henry James, quoted in Ellmann, *Oscar Wilde*, 179.

12. Henry James, quoted in Neill Matheson, "Talking Horrors: James, Euphemism, and the Spectre of Wilde," *American Literature* 71, no. 4 (December 1999): 713, 726.

13. Eve Kosofsky Sedgwick, *Epistemology of the Closet* (Berkeley and Los Angeles: University of California Press, 1990), especially chapter 4.

14. "Mayhew's brother Augustus wrote several novels of London life—*Kitty Lamere* (1855), *Paved With Gold* (1858), *The Finest Girl in Bloomsbury* (1861), and Henry collaborated with him on *The Greatest Plague of Life* (a lady's search for a servant, 1847), and *Living for Appearances* (1855)": Raymond Williams, *The Country and the City* (New York: Oxford University Press, 1973), 218.

15. Williams, *Country and the City*, 154.

16. Park, "City," 93. For studies of the literary connections and impact of the Chicago School of sociology, see Carla Cappetti, *Writing Chicago: Modernism, Ethnography, and the Novel* (New York: Columbia University Press, 1993); and Roderick A. Ferguson, *Aberrations in Black: Toward a Queer of Color Critique* (Minneapolis: University of Minnesota Press, 2004).

17. Havelock Ellis, *Studies in the Psychology of Sex*, vol. 1, pt. 4, *Sexual Inversion* (1897; repr., New York: Random House, 1936), chapter 4.

18. See Robert Duncan, "The Homosexual in Society" (1944), in *We Are Everywhere: A Historical Sourcebook in Gay and Lesbian Politics*, ed. Mark Blasius and

Shane Phelan (New York: Routledge, 1997), 230–33; and Jeannette Foster, *Sex Variant Women in Literature* (1956; repr., Baltimore, Md.: Diana Press, 1975).

19. Sedgwick, *Epistemology of the Closet*, 85.

20. Marcel Proust, *Cities of the Plain*, vol. 4 of *Remembrance of Things Past*, trans. C. K. Scott Moncrieff and Terence Kilmartin (1921; repr., New York: Vintage, 1981), 2:638.

21. On the city as a screen, see Anne Friedberg, *Window Shopping: Cinema and Modern Life* (Berkeley and Los Angeles: University of California Press, 1994); and Sue-Ellen Case, *The Domain-Matrix: Performing Lesbian at the End of Print Culture* (Bloomington: Indiana University Press, 1996).

22. Rossi, *Architecture of the City*, 57.

23. Kevin Lynch, *The Image of the City* (1960; repr., Cambridge, Mass.: MIT Press, 1997), 3.

24. Steven Marcus, *Engels, Manchester, and the Working Class* (1974; repr., New York: Norton, 1985), 176–77.

25. See, for example, the arguments of M. Christine Boyer, *The City of Collective Memory: Its Historical Imagery and Architectural Entertainments* (Cambridge, Mass.: MIT Press, 1996); Michael Sorkin, ed., *Variations on a Theme Park: The New American City and the End of Public Space* (New York: Hill & Wang, 1992); and Sharon Zukin, *The Cultures of Cities* (Cambridge, Mass.: Blackwell, 1995).

26. Raymond Williams points out the class specificity, and to that extent the fantasy, behind the image of the "knowable" rural community or small town, which was so often contrasted with the unknowable city as the nineteenth century progressed. "In the village as in the city there is division of labour, there is the contrast of social position, and . . . alternative points of view," Williams observed. "To be face-to-face in this world is already to belong to a class. No other community, in physical presence or in social reality, is by any means knowable" (*Country and the City*, 166).

27. Williams traces this association back to the writings of William Blake (ibid., 233).

28. Engels, *The Condition of the Working Class in England*, ed. Victor Kiernan (1845; repr., London: Penguin, 1987), 68–69.

29. For accounts of the period, and this literature, see Gareth Stedman Jones, *Outcast London: A Study in the Relationship between Classes in Victorian Society* (London: Oxford University Press, 1971); Boyer, *City of Collective Memory*; Judith Walkowitz, *City of Dreadful Delight: Narratives of Sexual Danger in Late-Victorian London* (Chicago: University of Chicago Press, 1992); and Seth Koven, *Slumming: Sexual and Social Politics in Victorian London* (Princeton: Princeton University Press, 2004).

30. Georg Simmel, "The Metropolis and Mental Life," in Sennett, *Classic Essays on the Culture of Cities*, 58, 59.

31. Ibid., 57.

32. Ibid.

33. Ibid., 53.

34. Georg Simmel, "The Metropolis and Mental Life" (alternate version), in *On Individuality and Social Forms: Selected Writings,* ed. Donald N. Levine (Chicago: University of Chicago Press, 1971), 336.

35. Simmel, "Metropolis and Mental Life" (in Sennett), 59.

36. Ibid., 57.

37. "Everywhere . . . Sodom, venal and threatening, exists . . . the invisible city" (my translation). André Raffalovich, quoted in Michael D. Sibalis, "Paris-Babylone/ Paris-Sodome: Images of Homosexuality in the Nineteenth-Century City," in *Images of the City in Nineteenth-Century France,* ed. John West-Sooby (Mooroka, Qld.: Boombana, 1999), 14.

38. Ellmann, *Oscar Wilde,* 299.

39. "The Decay of Lying," in *The Artist as Critic: Critical Writings of Oscar Wilde,* ed. Richard Ellmann (1969; repr., Chicago: University of Chicago Press, 1982), 297.

40. Ibid., 311. Wilde's example of a phenomenon made visible by art is London fogs, which the Impressionists were busy painting. "There may have been fogs for centuries in London," Wilde concedes. "But no-one saw them. . . . They did not exist till Art had invented them" (312).

41. Ibid., 309.

42. Ibid., 299.

43. Ibid.

44. Honoré de Balzac, *A Harlot High and Low,* trans. Rayner Heppenstall (New York: Penguin, 1970), 18; hereafter cited parenthetically in the text.

45. Honoré de Balzac, *Old Goriot,* trans. Marion Ayton Crawford (New York: Penguin, 1985), 34; hereafter cited parenthetically, as *Père Goriot,* in the text.

46. See Antony Copley, *Sexual Moralities in France, 1780–1980: New Ideas on the Family, Divorce, and Homosexuality* (London: Routledge, 1989), 24–25.

47. Honoré de Balzac, *The Girl with the Golden Eyes,* in *History of the Thirteen,* trans. Herbert J. Hunt (New York: Penguin, 1974), 377.

48. See Sibalis, "Palais-Royal and the Homosexual Subculture of Nineteenth Century Paris"; as well as William A. Peniston, "Pederasts, Prostitutes, and Pick-pockets in Paris of the 1870s," in Merrick and Sibalis, *Homosexuality in French History and Culture,* 169–88.

49. Honoré de Balzac, *Lost Illusions,* trans. Herbert J. Hunt (Harmondsworth, U.K.: Penguin, 1976), 655; hereafter cited parenthetically in the text.

50. Nicholas Dobelbower, "*Les Chevaliers de la girlande*: Cellmates in Restoration France," in Merrick and Sibalis, *Homosexuality in French History and Culture,* 131.

51. Moments before he kills himself, the imprisoned Lucien suddenly sees, in what Balzac labels a hallucination, both the prison yard with its contemporary inhabitants and medieval Paris at that same spot, "the Palais in all its primitive beauty" (*Harlot High and Low,* 403).

52. Vautrin makes this declaration at the gate of the Rastignacs' family home, in a moment that Proust's Baron du Charlus would later describe as "the *Tristesse*

d'Olympio of pederasty," referring to a poem by Victor Hugo about lost happiness. See Herbert J. Hunt, introduction to Balzac, *Lost Illusions*, x.

53. As the police file and catalog the secrets of others, they are themselves subject to a catalog Balzac offers of always legible urban types, in which the authorities and the criminals are joined. "Theft and the traffic in public prostitutes have much in common with the theatre, the police, the priesthood and the military," he proposes. "In these six conditions of life, the individual takes on an indelible character. He can no longer be other than he is." Theater is the sole "condition of life" among these six that does not need to be elaborated, perhaps because theater, with the possibilities it offers for making legible and for disguising, is the ground of connection between criminals and authorities. The authorities, Balzac explains, are visible to everyone: "The stigmata of the sacerdotal function are ineffaceable, and so are those of the soldiery." Criminals are visible to the authorities, "the prostitute and the thief, the murderer and the discharged prisoner, so easily recognized that, to their enemies, the spy and the constable, they are what his game is to the hunter; a colour, a smell, in short unmistakable *properties*" (*Harlot High and Low*, 444; emphasis in original). But Balzac concludes his discussion of legibility with a paradoxical assertion of "that profound understanding of disguise among the celebrities of the underworld" (444). Those with the greatest need to be concerned about their legibility, and about whose legibility "society" is most concerned, are somehow simultaneously ineffaceably legible but most accomplished at disguise.

54. Oscar Wilde, "The Critic as Artist: Part II," in *Plays, Prose Writings, and Poems*, ed. Isobel Murray (London: Dent/Everyman's Library, 1975), 35.

55. Oscar Wilde to Robbie Ross, *Selected Letters of Oscar Wilde*, ed. Rupert Hart-Davis (Oxford: Oxford University Press, 1979), 720.

56. Oscar Wilde, "Pen Pencil and Poison," in *Artist as Critic*, 338.

57. Oscar Wilde, *The Picture of Dorian Gray*, ed. Robert Mighall (1891; repr., New York: Penguin, 2003), 151, 144; hereafter cited parenthetically in the text.

58. The corollary to the novel's focus on physical legibility and the art of painting is Lord Henry Wotton's use of language. He is concerned not with physical legibility but with naming, which he rejects: "Names are everything. I never quarrel with actions. My one quarrel is with words" (ibid., 186).

59. Oscar Wilde, *An Ideal Husband*, in *An Ideal Husband, A Woman of No Importance* (New York: Boni & Liveright, 1919), 11.

60. Ibid., 43.

61. Ibid., 34.

62. Oscar Wilde, *The Importance of Being Earnest*, in *Plays, Prose Writings, and Poems*, 351.

63. Ibid., 352.

64. Ibid., 360.

65. Ibid., 382, 386, 390.

66. *The Picture of Dorian Gray* first appeared in *Lippincott's Magazine*, in 1890. The *Daily Chronicle* (London) described it suggestively as "unclean" and characterized

by "effeminate frivolity . . . studied insincerity . . . [and] theatrical cynicism." For both reviews, see the first appendix in Mighall's edition of *Picture of Dorian Gray*, 218, 217.

67. See Cohen, *Talk on the Wilde Side*, 161–62.

68. See Ellis, *Sexual Inversion*, 177.

69. Ibid., 173.

70. Ibid., 63.

71. Wilde, *De Profundis*, 77, 113.

72. *Daily Telegraph* (London), April 6, 1895, quoted in Cohen, *Talk on the Wilde Side*, 172.

73. Cohen, *Talk on the Wilde Side*, 166. This conflation of sexual and class anxieties was not only an English concern. The French were similarly convinced of the threat to the class structure posed by male homosexuality. In 1890 journalist Ali Coffignon lamented, in *Paris vivant: La Corruption á Paris*, "Le vice commun efface toutes les differences sociales; le maitre et le valet de chambre sont sur le meme pied; le millionaire et le va-nu-pieds fraternisent; le fonctionnaire et le repris de justice échangent leurs ignobles caresses" (The common vice obliterates all social differences; the master and the valet stand at the same level; the millionaire and the barefoot street urchin fraternize; the government worker and the criminal exchange their ignoble caresses [my translation]). Quoted in Sibalis, "Paris-Babylone/Paris-Sodome," 18.

74. In the 1890s Wilde would announce, "We are all of us more or less Socialists now-a-days," and would propose, "I think I am rather more than a Socialist. I am something of an Anarchist, I believe," while vaguely distancing himself from anarchist violence: "[O]f course, the dynamite policy is very absurd indeed" (quoted in Ellmann, *Oscar Wilde*, 121, 290).

75. Engels, *Condition of the Working Class in England*, 148.

76. Balzac presents Vautrin as a "man of the people in revolt against authority" (*Harlot High and Low*, 337), although such a description bears no relation to the details of his characterization.

77. Walt Whitman, "For You, O Democracy," in *Leaves of Grass, and Selected Prose*, ed. John Kouwenhoven (New York: Modern Library, 1950), 96.

78. Walt Whitman, "I Dream'd in a Dream," in *Leaves of Grass*, 107. Whitman offered deeply contradictory visions of the city, however. In 1870, in "Democratic Vistas," echoing Engels, he describes a city in which "the disease of the social body" is manifest in its disruption of sexual and gender norms. Describing New York and Brooklyn, he presents himself as only transiently seduced by "these hurrying, feverish, electric crowds of men, their complicated business genius, . . . and all this might, many-threaded wealth and industry concentrated here." Ultimately he rejects "the artificial," this "work of man" as opposed to "Nature," and distinguishes "the city" from "what is of the only real importance, [the] Personalities" of its citizens. In gendered terms, he asks, "Are there, indeed, *men* here worthy the name?

[*sic*] Are there athletes? Are there perfect women, to match the generous material luxuriance?" He then denounces "these cities, crowded with petty grotesques, malformations, phantoms ... [with] everywhere ... pervading flippancy and vulgarity, low cunning, infidelity—everywhere the youth puny, impudent, foppish, prematurely ripe—everywhere an abnormal libidinousness, unhealthy forms, male, female, painted, padded, dyed, chignon'd" ("Democratic Vistas," in *Leaves of Grass*, 468–69; emphasis in original). An "artificial city" of artificial persons, the disruption of proper masculinity and femininity, and "abnormal libidinousness" are all joined as if inevitably connected and condemned.

79. Edward Carpenter, *The Intermediate Sex* (1908), in *Selected Writings*, vol. 1, *Sex* (London: GMP, 1984), 218–19, quoting Walt Whitman.

80. Ibid. Reviewing Carpenter's *Chants of Labour: A Song Book of the People* in 1889, Wilde "praised the socialists for their conviction that art could help in the building up of an 'eternal city'" (quoted in Ellmann, *Oscar Wilde*, 291). Carpenter was already pursuing a vision of socialism "'not ... so much in its actual constructive programme' (though he agreed with that, and helped shape it), but rather because it 'enshrined a most glowing and vital enthusiasm towards the realisation of a new society'—one where beauty and creativity could emerge from the cellars and take possession of the world." Noel Greig (quoting Carpenter), introduction to Carpenter, *Sex*, 49.

81. Henry James, *The Princess Casamassima*, ed. Derek Brewer (New York: Penguin, 1987), 33; hereafter cited in the text.

82. Ellis, *Sexual Inversion*, 48.

83. Oscar Wilde, "The Soul of Man under Socialism," in Plays, Prose Writings, and Poems, 258, 288; hereafter cited in the text.

84. Linda Dowling, *Hellenism and Homosexuality in Victorian Oxford* (Ithaca, N.Y.: Cornell University Press, 1994), 35. After Wilde's trials, however, "it would be difficult to pronounce the word 'Hellenism' without an insinuating leer" (35).

85. Friedrich Engels to Karl Marx, quoted in Georg Lukács, *Realism in Our Time: Literature and the Class Struggle* (New York: Harper & Row, 1971), 131–32. Lukács commented approvingly that "[t]he personal, 'egotistic' interest in work should be seen in a wider ideological context. It is really part of the struggle for the development of a full human personality—an indispensable element in it, as Lenin recognized" (132). Wilde's "Soul of Man under Socialism," moreover, had its contemporary political adherents, becoming popular among revolutionaries in central and eastern Europe and in the United States; see Regenia Gagnier, *Idylls of the Marketplace: Oscar Wilde and the Victorian Public* (Stanford, Calif.: Stanford University Press, 1986), 20.

86. Wilde identifies journalism as the vehicle for this deplorable public demand for knowledge. Yet he contributed as an editor and writer to the late nineteenth-century spread of literacy and cheap newspapers in the West, on which he also drew to advance his own celebrity. The sensationalized reports of his trial that these

papers carried internationally were responsible for the extraordinarily broad cultural impact of his story. See Gagnier, *Idylls of the Marketplace,* for a discussion of Wilde's earlier courting of publicity; and Cohen, *Talk on the Wilde Side,* for an analysis of newspaper accounts of the trials.

87. Wilde, *De Profundis,* 138.

88. "London" (1888), in *Essays on London and Elsewhere* (1893), repr. in *The Portable Henry James,* ed. Morton Dauwen Zabel (New York: Viking, 1960), 523–24.

89. Oscar Wilde, quoted in Asa Briggs, *Victorian Cities* (1965; repr., Berkeley and Los Angeles: University of California Press, 1993), 356–57.

90. See Lloyd Lewis and Henry Justin Smith, *Oscar Wilde Discovers America* (1882; repr., New York: Harcourt, Brace, 1936), 247.

3. Perverts in Groups

1. Floyd Dell, *The Briary-Bush, a Novel* (New York: Knopf, 1921), 34.

2. See Kathryn Kish Sklar, *Florence Kelley and the Nation's Work,* vol. 1, *The Rise of Women's Political Culture, 1830–1900* (New Haven, Conn.: Yale University Press, 1995), 172.

3. Carl Sandburg, "Chicago," in *Chicago Poems,* quoted in Maureen A. Flanagan, *Seeing with Their Hearts: Chicago Women and the Vision of the Good City, 1871–1933* (Princeton, N.J.: Princeton University Press, 2002), 1.

4. Alain Locke, "The New Negro," introduction to *The New Negro: An Interpretation,* ed. Alain Locke (1925; repr., New York: Simon & Schuster, 1997), 5, 6.

5. See Mark Blasius and Shane Phelan, eds., *We Are Everywhere: A Historical Sourcebook in Gay and Lesbian Politics* (New York: Routledge, 1997), 134.

6. Richard von Krafft-Ebing, preface to the 1st ed. of *Psychopathia Sexualis: A Medico-forensic Study,* trans. Harry E. Wedeck (1886; repr., New York: Paperback Library, 1965), vii.

7. Random House "reissued [these editions] 'in a cheaper and more compact form,' no longer restricting their sale 'as hitherto, to professional readers.'" See Joseph Bristow, "Symonds's History, Ellis's Heredity: *Sexual Inversion,*" in *Sexology in Culture: Labelling Bodies and Desires,* ed. Lucy Bland and Laura Doan (Chicago: University of Chicago Press, 1998), 80.

8. The Vice Commission of the City of Chicago, *The Social Evil in Chicago: A Study of Existing Conditions with Recommendations by the Vice Commission of Chicago* (Chicago: Gunthorp-Warren Printing Co., 1911), 39; hereafter cited parenthetically in the text.

9. Lord Alfred Douglas explained in 1918, "To say that a man is an Oscar Wilde is to say—well, that he is a pervert" (*Times* [London], June 3, 1918), quoted in Lucy Bland, "Trial by Sexology: Maud Allan, *Salome,* and the 'Cult of the Clitoris' Case," in Bland and Doan, *Sexology in Culture,* 193.

10. Ironically, the solution proposed by the Vice Commission is that, rather than revealing what is hidden, they should not speak further of the subject, being

"doubtful . . . whether any spread of the actual knowledge of these practices is in any way desirable" (*Social Evil in Chicago*, 298). That is, those suspicious of deceit were committed to a cover-up.

11. See Mary Jo Deegan, *Jane Addams and the Men of the Chicago School, 1892–1918* (New Brunswick, N.J.: Transaction, 1990), 182, 207.

12. Ibid., 179–86.

13. See Ernest W. Burgess, "The Growth of the City: An Introduction to a Research Project," in *The City*, by Robert E. Park, Ernest W. Burgess, and Roderick D. McKenzie (1925; repr., Chicago: University of Chicago Press, 1984), 47. On the Chicago School, see Fred H. Matthews, *Quest for an American Sociology: Robert E. Park and the Chicago School* (Montreal: McGill-Queen's University Press, 1977); Martin Bulmer, *The Chicago School of Sociology: Institutionalization, Diversity, and the Rise of Sociological Research* (Chicago: University of Chicago Press, 1984); and Mary Jo Deegan, ibid., and *Race, Hull-House, and the University of Chicago* (Westport, Conn.: Praeger, 2002). Chicago School research on homosexuality is discussed by Gayle Rubin in "Studying Sexual Subcultures: Excavating the Ethnography of Gay Communities in Urban North America," in *Out in Theory: The Emergence of Lesbian and Gay Anthropology*, ed. Ellen Lewin and William L. Leap (Urbana: University of Illinois Press, 2002), 17–54. Data gathered by Chicago School sociologists and their students is used by David K. Johnson, in "The Kids of Fairytown: Gay Male Culture on Chicago's Near North Side in the 1930s," and by Allen Drexel, in "Before Paris Burned: Race, Class, and Male Homosexuality, 1935–1960," both in *Creating a Place for Ourselves: Lesbian, Gay, and Bisexual Community Histories*, ed. Brett Beemyn (New York: Routledge, 1997), 97–118 and 119–144, respectively.

14. Burgess, "Growth of the City," 47; and Louis Wirth, "Urbanism as a Way of Life," in *Classic Essays on the Culture of Cities*, ed. Richard Sennett (New York: Appleton-Century-Crofts, 1969), 148.

15. See James F. Short Jr., introduction to *The Social Fabric of the Metropolis: Contributions of the Chicago School of Urban Sociology*, ed. James F. Short Jr. (Chicago: University of Chicago Press, 1971), xxxix.

16. Robert Park, quoted in Donald N. Levine, introduction to *On Individuality and Social Forms: Selected Writings*, by Georg Simmel, ed. Donald N. Levine (Chicago: University of Chicago Press, 1971), l.

17. Louis Wirth, "A Bibliography of the Urban Community," in Park, Burgess, and McKenzie, *City*, 219.

18. Dell, *Briary-Bush*, 34.

19. Ibid., 33, 31–32. See also Marilee Lindemann on the meanings of "queer" in the 1920s, in *Willa Cather, Queering America* (New York: Columbia University Press, 1999).

20. See Jonathan Ned Katz, *Gay/Lesbian Almanac: A New Documentary* (New York: Harper & Row, 1983), 418–19. Katz quotes the Society for Human Rights, *Friendship and Freedom*. Gerber would later comment on Radclyffe Hall's *The Well of Loneliness*: "Had [Stephen Gordon] joined her own circle, which is large in every

metropolitan city and . . . chosen a homosexual girl as her partner, there would have been no morbid story"; quoted in Jonathan Ned Katz, *Gay American History: Lesbians and Gay Men in the U.S.A.*, rev. ed. (New York: Meridian, 1992), 405.

21. Johnson, "Kids of Fairytown," 100.

22. Ibid., 100–103.

23. See Drexel, "Before Paris Burned," 132.

24. Ibid., 133, 129.

25. Georg Simmel, "The Metropolis and Mental Life," in *Classic Essays on the Culture of Cities*, comp. Richard Sennett (New York: Appleton-Century-Crofts, 1969), 48; emphasis in original.

26. Burgess, "Growth of the City," 59.

27. See Asa Briggs, *Victorian Cities* (1965; repr., Berkeley and Los Angeles: University of California Press, 1993), 83.

28. Otto Ludwig Binswanger, *Die Pathologies und Therapie der Neurasthenie* (1896), cited in Sigmund Freud, "'Civilized' Sexual Morality and Modern Nervousness" (1908), in *Sexuality and the Psychology of Love*, ed. Philip Rieff (New York: Collier, 1963), 13.

29. Beard would be seen, by twentieth-century historians of psychiatry, as a precursor to Freud. See Charles E. Rosenberg, introduction to *American Nervousness: Its Causes and Consequences*, by George Beard (1881; repr., New York: Arno, 1972), i.

30. Beard, *American Nervousness*, 135–38.

31. Beard, quoted in Rosenberg, introduction, vii.

32. George Beard, *Sexual Neurasthenia: Its Hygiene, Causes, Symptoms, and Treatment* (1898; repr., New York: Arno, 1972), 101, 102.

33. Ibid., 102–3.

34. Ibid., 104, 103.

35. Ibid., 106, 107.

36. Krafft-Ebing, *Psychopathia Sexualis*, 6, 7.

37. Richard von Krafft-Ebing, quoted in Harry Oosterhuis, *Stepchildren of Nature: Krafft-Ebing, Psychiatry, and the Making of Sexual Identity* (Chicago: University of Chicago Press, 2000), 110.

38. Krafft-Ebing, *Psychopathia Sexualis*, 398, 590.

39. Beard, quoted in Rosenberg, introduction, vii.

40. Krafft-Ebing, *Psychopathia Sexualis*, 6.

41. Johann Ludwig Caspar, "perhaps the most famous authority on forensic medicine in mid-nineteenth century Germany," argued "that the extremes of luxury and poverty to be found in cities favored the practice of sexual deviance." George L. Mosse, *Nationalism and Sexuality: Respectability and Abnormal Sexuality in Modern Europe* (New York: Fertig, 1985), 29.

42. See Jennifer Terry, *An American Obsession: Science, Medicine, and Homosexuality in Modern Society* (Chicago: University of Chicago Press, 1999), 88. "The American physician John H. Girdner in his *New Yorkitis* (1901) discovered a communicable disease, a special kind of inflammation, as he called it, which resulted

from living in the big city. He found symptoms in 'nervousness and lack of direction of all muscular movements'" (Mosse, *Nationalism and Sexuality*, 137).

43. Charles Hughes, quoted in Terry, *American Obsession*, 74.

44. Havelock Ellis, *Studies in the Psychology of Sex*, vol. 1, pt. 4, *Sexual Inversion*
(1897; repr., New York: Random House, 1936), 351.

45. Ibid., 63. Iwan Bloch, a "Berlin physician and pioneer sexologist," argued in
his *Sexual Life of Our Time* (1906) that there were "'vibrations' emitted when men
and women tried to enter the modern age," and he identified the modern age with
"the temptations of the big city, ballrooms, dance floors, and cabarets" (see Mosse,
Nationalism and Sexuality, 38).

46. Freud, "'Civilized' Sexual Morality and Modern Nervousness," 11. There are
echoes here of the political concerns of Beard, Krafft-Ebing, and others; it sounds
as though the danger of urbanization is the class mobility it makes possible—the
too-rapid rise of urban newcomers from rural vigor to cultural attainment.

47. Ibid., 17, 18.

48. George L. Mosse, "Max Nordau and His Degeneration," introduction to
Degeneration, by Max Nordau (1892; repr., Lincoln: University of Nebraska Press,
1993), xiii, xiv.

49. Nordau, *Degeneration*, 43.

50. Ibid., 36.

51. Mosse, "Max Nordau and His Degeneration," v.

52. Nordau, *Degeneration*, 291. Nordau describes Baudelaire's "Femmes damnées"
as "dedicated to the worst aberration of degenerate women . . . the heroines of
unnatural vice" (44).

53. Ibid., 13.

54. See David Higgs, *Queer Sites: Queer Urban Histories since 1600* (New York:
Routledge, 1999), 190. John Addington Symonds had already insisted, in 1896, that
"the pulse" of "this passion" could be felt in "London, Paris, Berlin, Vienna, . . .
Constantinople, Naples, Teheran, and Moscow." John Addington Symonds, *A Problem in Modern Ethics: Being an Inquiry into the Phenomenon of Sexual Inversion*
(1896), in *Male Love: A Problem in Greek Ethics, and Other Writings*, ed. John Lau-
ritsen (New York: Pagan Press, 1983), 78–79.

55. See Mosse, *Nationalism and Sexuality*, 33, 32.

56. Wirth, "Bibliography of the Urban Community," 208.

57. Magnus Hirschfeld, *The Homosexuality of Men and Women*, trans. Michael
A. Lombardi-Nash (1913; repr., Amherst, N.Y.: Prometheus, 2000), 777; hereafter
cited parenthetically in the text.

58. See Edmund White, *Marcel Proust* (London: Weidenfeld & Nicolson, 1999).

59. Marcel Proust, *Cities of the Plain*, vol. 4 of *Remembrance of Things Past*, trans.
C. K. Scott Moncrieff and Terence Kilmartin (1921; repr., New York: Vintage, 1981),
2:637, 638; hereafter cited parenthetically in the text.

60. Georg Simmel, "Group Expansion and the Development of Individuality,"
in *On Individuality and Social Forms*, 254.

61. Edward Carpenter, *The Intermediate Sex* (1908), in *Selected Writings*, vol. 1, *Sex* (London: GMP, 1984), 217.

62. Sigmund Freud, "Certain Neurotic Mechanisms in Jealousy, Paranoia, and Homosexuality" (1922), in *Sexuality and the Psychology of Love*, 159. That Freud's homosexuals and his community are all male is made apparent by the three hypotheses he offers as explanations for this truism: that homosexual men see other men as potential love objects, not rivals; that homosexual men have conquered their natural rivalry with other men in favor of love; and that "social feeling [is] a sublimation of homosexual attitudes towards objects" (160).

63. Freud, "'Civilized' Sexual Morality and Modern Nervousness," 18.

64. Sigmund Freud, "The Psychogenesis of a Case of Homosexuality in a Woman" (1920), in *Sexuality and the Psychology of Love*, 145, 146.

4. City of Women

1. See Sarah Deutsch, *Women and the City: Gender, Space, and Power in Boston, 1870–1940* (New York: Oxford University Press, 2000), 104–14.

2. Henry James, *The Bostonians*, ed. Charles R. Anderson (1886; repr., New York: Penguin, 1986), 62 (emphasis in original); hereafter cited parenthetically in the text.

3. *The Complete Notebooks of Henry James*, ed. Leon Edel and Lyall H. Powers (New York: Oxford University Press, 1987), 19.

4. Oscar Wilde, "The Soul of Man under Socialism," in Plays, Prose Writings, and Poems, ed. Isobel Murray (London: Dent/Everyman's Library, 1975), 258.

5. Raymond Unwin, for example, a heterosexual disciple of Carpenter, went to Toynbee Hall, moved on to pursue his vision of a middle-class-oriented, cross-class community as a primary architect of the garden city movement, and concluded his career as a leading figure in British urban planning in the interwar decades. See Standish Meacham, "Raymond Unwin (1863–1940): Designing for Democracy in Edwardian England," in *After the Victorians: Private Conscience and Public Duty in Modern Britain*, ed. Susan Pedersen and Peter Mandler (New York: Routledge, 1994), 79–104.

6. See Standish Meacham, *Toynbee Hall and Social Reform, 1880–1914: The Search for Community* (New Haven, Conn.: Yale University Press, 1987).

7. Kathryn Kish Sklar, *Florence Kelley and the Nation's Work*, vol. 1, *The Rise of Women's Political Culture, 1830–1900* (New Haven, Conn.: Yale University Press, 1995), 174–75.

8. Ibid., 202.

9. Ibid., 192.

10. Deutsch, *Women and the City*, 109.

11. Florence Converse, *Diana Victrix* (1897), quoted in Lillian Faderman, *To Believe in Women: What Lesbians Have Done for America—A History* (Boston: Houghton Mifflin, 1999), 273.

12. Faderman, *To Believe in Women*, 141.

13. Jane Addams, *Twenty Years at Hull-House, with Autobiographical Notes* (1910; repr., New York: Penguin, 1998), 59, 60; hereafter cited parenthetically in the text.

14. Jane Addams to Ellen Gates Starr, quoted in Faderman, *To Believe in Women*, 120.

15. Faderman, *To Believe in Women*, 129.

16. Sklar, *Florence Kelley*, 192.

17. Shielding herself, Addams cites "an astute English visitor" who claimed that, despite their insistence on their own individuality, "all American cities seemed to him essentially alike and all equally the results of an industry totally unregulated by well-considered legislation" (*Twenty Years at Hull-House*, 129–30).

18. "The Settlement as a Factor in the Labor Movement" (originally published as chapter 10 of *Hull-House Maps and Papers*, by the Residents of Hull-House [1895]), in *The Jane Addams Reader*, ed. Jean Bethke Elshtain (New York: Basic Books, 2002), 47.

19. "Filial Relations" (originally published as chapter 3 of *Democracy and Social Ethics* [1902]), in Elshtain, *Jane Addams Reader*, 82.

20. Ibid., 82.

21. As Addams observes, "We are all more or less familiar with the results of isolation in rural districts; the Bronte sisters have portrayed the hideous immorality and savagery of the remote dwellers on the bleak moorlands of northern England; Miss Wilkins has written of the overdeveloped will of the solitary New Englander" (*Twenty Years at Hull-House*, 232).

22. Addams, "Filial Relations," 77, 86, 80.

23. Ibid., 78.

24. Addams, "Settlement as a Factor," 48–49.

25. "A Modern Lear" (1912), in Elshtain, *Jane Addams Reader*, 169.

26. Addams, "Filial Relations," 79.

27. Jane Addams, *The Spirit of Youth and the City Streets* (1909; repr., Urbana: University of Illinois Press, 1972), 47.

28. Talking about Lincoln, she also paralleled "the emancipation of the wage-worker" in the present with "the emancipation of the slave" in the recent past ("Modern Lear," 173).

29. Ibid., 171.

30. Jane Addams to Mary Rozet Smith, quoted in Faderman, *To Believe in Women*, 132. Faderman also quotes a series of letters between the couple from the mid-1890s: "'I bless you, dear, every time I think of you, which is all the time at present,' Jane wrote at the end of 1894. . . . After a visit with Jane before she was scheduled to go south with her family, Mary wrote, 'I came home with quite a glow at my heart. . . . You can never know what it is to me to have had you and to have you now.' Mary spoke in this same letter of being overcome by a 'rush of emotion . . . when I think of you'" (130).

31. Sklar, *Florence Kelley*, 373.

32. Addams, "Filial Relations," 76.

33. Jane Addams, "Contrasts in a Post-War Generation" (originally published as chapter 7 of *The Second Twenty Years at Hull-House, September 1909 to September 1929, with a Record of Growing World Consciousness* [1930]), in Elshtain, *Jane Addams Reader*, 296–97.

34. Jane Addams, *A New Conscience and an Ancient Evil* (1912; repr., Urbana: University of Illinois Press, 2002), 46.

35. Addams, "Contrasts in a Post-War Generation," 300.

36. Ibid., 300.

37. Ibid., 298.

38. Deutsch, *Women and the City*, 13–14.

39. British social investigator Beatrice Webb observed after an 1898 visit to Hull-House, "The residents consist in the main, of strong-minded energetic women, bustling about their various enterprises and professions, interspersed with earnest-faced self-subordinating and mild-mannered men who slide from room to room apologetically" (quoted in Sklar, *Florence Kelley*, 199).

40. See Mary Jo Deegan, *Jane Addams and the Men of the Chicago School, 1892–1918* (New Brunswick, N.J.: Transaction, 1990), 56.

41. Engels lived with Mary Burns from the mid-1840s until her death, in 1863, whereupon her sister Lizzie, who had kept house for them, took up Mary's role in his life. See Steven Marcus, *Engels, Manchester, and the Working Class* (1974; repr., New York: Norton, 1985), 43, 98–100.

42. In such works Addams attempted to explain the circumstances, the perspectives, and the needs of her subjects—whether young persons, prostitutes, or both—and the responsibility of the city to help rather than punish, with improved living conditions, education, and economic and cultural options. Her discussion of young people was the more successful in this regard.

43. See Joanne J. Meyerowitz, *Women Adrift: Independent Wage Earners in Chicago, 1880–1930* (Chicago: University of Chicago Press, 1988), 5, 8.

44. See ibid., 96–98; and Sklar, *Florence Kelley*, 197–98.

45. Addams was offered a position in the sociology department at the University of Chicago by Albion Small in 1913. See Deegan, *Jane Addams*, 5, 81.

46. On Addams's interactions with Mead and Thomas, see ibid., 105–41.

47. See ibid., 34–35.

48. Ibid., 167–89.

49. Robert E. Park, "Community Organization and Juvenile Delinquency," in *The City*, by Robert E. Park, Ernest W. Burgess, and Roderick D. McKenzie (1925; repr., Chicago: University of Chicago Press, 1984), 110–11.

50. Ibid., 107.

51. Ernest W. Burgess, "The Growth of the City: An Introduction to a Research Project," in Park, Burgess, and McKenzie, *City*, 47.

52. Ibid.

53. Ibid., 64–65.

54. Ibid., 59. Classic Chicago School studies include Louis Wirth's *The Ghetto* (1928), Harvey Warren Zorbaugh's *Gold Coast and Slum: A Sociological Study of Chicago's Near North Side* (1929), Paul G. Cressey's *The Taxi-Dance Hall: A Sociological Study in Commercialized Recreation and City Life* (1932), and Walter C. Reckless's *Vice in Chicago* (1933).

55. Park, "Community Organization and Juvenile Delinquency," 110.

56. Ibid., 104–5.

57. Burgess, "Growth of the City," 56.

58. Ernest W. Burgess, "Can Neighborhood Work Have a Scientific Basis?" in Park, Burgess, and McKenzie, *City*, 145.

59. Park, "Community Organization and Juvenile Delinquency," 100.

60. Ibid., 99; emphasis added.

61. Ibid., 108.

62. Robert E. Park, quoted in James F. Short Jr., introduction to *The Social Fabric of the Metropolis: Contributions of the Chicago School of Urban Sociology*, ed. James F. Short Jr. (Chicago: University of Chicago Press, 1971), xix.

5. Radclyffe Hall at the Chicago School

1. See Catherine van Casselaer, *Lot's Wife: Lesbian Paris, 1890–1914* (Liverpool: Janus, 1986), 50–61 passim.

2. Ibid., 113–14.

3. Karla Jay, *The Amazon and the Page: Natalie Clifford Barney and Renée Vivien* (Bloomington: Indiana University Press, 1988).

4. Gertrude Stein, *The Autobiography of Alice B. Toklas* (1933; repr., New York: Vintage, 1990), 82.

5. Gertrude Stein, *The Making of Americans; Being a History of a Family's Progress* (1925; repr., London: Peter Owen, 1968), 21.

6. Ernest W. Burgess, "The Growth of the City: An Introduction to a Research Project," in *The City*, by Robert E. Park, Ernest W. Burgess, and Roderick D. McKenzie (1925; repr., Chicago: University of Chicago Press, 1984), 47.

7. Ernest W. Burgess, "Can Neighborhood Work Have a Scientific Basis?" in Park, Burgess, and McKenzie, *City*, 144.

8. Radclyffe Hall, *The Well of Loneliness* (1928; repr., New York: Doubleday, 1990), 299, 406, 356; hereafter cited parenthetically in the text.

9. Robert E. Park, "The City: Suggestions for the Investigation of Human Behavior in the Urban Environment," in *Classic Essays on the Culture of Cities*, comp. Richard Sennett (New York: Appleton-Century-Crofts, 1969), 93; hereafter cited parenthetically in the text.

10. Louis Wirth, "A Bibliography of the Urban Community," in Park, Burgess, and McKenzie, *City*, 217.

11. Havelock Ellis, preface to Hall, *Well of Loneliness*, 6.

12. Robert Park, "The Urban Community as a Spatial Pattern and a Moral Order," in *The Urban Community: Selected Papers from the Proceedings of the American Sociological Society, 1925,* ed. Ernest W. Burgess (Chicago: University of Chicago Press, 1926), 6. These "villages" all have their "[d]istorted forms of sex behavior," according to Harvey Warren Zorbaugh, *Gold Coast and Slum: A Sociological Study of Chicago's Near North Side* (Chicago: University of Chicago Press, 1929), 100.

13. See Caroline F. Ware, *Greenwich Village, 1920–1930: A Comment on American Civilization in the Post-war Years* (1935; repr., Berkeley and Los Angeles: University of California Press, 1994), chaps. 6 and 8.

14. Where Addams saw family reconstruction, Wirth saw loss: "The transfer of industrial, educational, and recreational activities to specialized institutions outside the home has deprived the family of some of its most characteristic historical functions. . . . In cities mothers are more likely to be employed . . . marriage tends to be postponed, and the proportion of single and unattached people is greater. Families are smaller and more frequently without children than in the country." Louis Wirth, "Urbanism as a Way of Life" (1938), in *On Cities and Social Life,* ed. Albert J. Reiss Jr. (Chicago: University of Chicago Press, 1964), 80.

15. Ibid., 76.

16. Ibid., 75.

17. As Wirth would also point out, "Simmel . . . suggested" that "[t]he urban world puts a premium on visual recognition" (ibid., 73).

18. Ibid.

19. Nowhere in Hall's account of the city is there any mention of the street-oriented public sex scenes that are routinely the focus of descriptions of gay male urban life.

20. See my discussion of *The Social Evil in Chicago* and Dr. George Beard in chapter 3.

21. Park emphasizes this divided self as living in two worlds, "in both of which he is more or less of a stranger." Robert Park, "Human Migration and the Marginal Man," in *Classic Essays on the Culture of Cities,* comp. Richard Sennett (New York: Appleton-Century-Crofts, 1969), 141–42.

22. Ibid., 142.

23. Ibid., 141. Park cites "the Jew's" "pre-eminence as a trader and his keen intellectual interest, his sophistication, his idealism and lack of historic sense" (141).

24. Blanc is also a designer of "beautiful things—furniture, costumes, and scenery for ballets, even women's gowns if the mood was upon him" (Hall, *Well of Loneliness,* 352). Like Brockett, the only other significant gay male character in the novel, Blanc is associated with art, artifice, and the feminine.

25. Louis Wirth, "The Ghetto," in *On Cities and Social Life,* 85.

26. Moreover, "[t]he forces that underlie the formation and development of these areas bear a close resemblance to those at work in the ghetto" (ibid.).

27. Louis Wirth, "Consensus and Mass Communication," in *On Cities and Social Life,* 40.

28. Wirth, "Urbanism as a Way of Life," 75.

29. Ibid., 82.

30. Ibid., 75.

31. Ibid., 77.

6. Paris, Harlem, Hudson Street—1961

1. Jess Stearn, *The Grapevine: A Report on the Secret World of the Lesbian* (New York: Doubleday, 1964), 8.

2. Donald Webster Cory, *The Lesbian in America* (New York: MacFadden-Bartell, 1965), 67.

3. Kenneth Wherry, quoted in David K. Johnson, *The Lavender Scare: The Cold War Persecution of Gays and Lesbians in the Federal Government* (Chicago: University of Chicago Press, 2004), 2.

4. Kenneth Jackson, *Crabgrass Frontier: The Suburbanization of the United States* (New York: Oxford University Press, 1985), 243–44.

5. Betty Friedan, *The Feminine Mystique* (1963; repr., New York: Dell, 1983), 243. By contrast, Friedan observed, "[f]amilies where the wife intends to pursue a definite professional goal are less likely to move to the suburbs" (244). In the city, she explained, there were more jobs, educational opportunities, and child care options for women. She was also already arguing that the goal of this new insistence on a housebound suburban femininity was the escalation of women's commitment to consumption.

6. William H. Whyte Jr., "Are Cities Un-American?" in *The Exploding Metropolis*, ed. William H. Whyte Jr. (1958; repr., Berkeley and Los Angeles: University of California Press, 1993), 23–52; hereafter cited parenthetically in the text.

7. Whyte's effort to challenge the postwar reconstruction of the American landscape was "one of the crucial moments in the transformation of America," according to Sam Bass Warner Jr.: "[T]his manifesto is now the unexamined foundation of today's critical American urban writing." Sam Bass Warner Jr., foreword to Whyte, *Exploding Metropolis*, i, ii.

8. The suburbs had begun being sold as a moral refuge by the mid-nineteenth century. In the United States in the 1860s, developers were already insisting, as they wooed the well-off, that "the first city was built by the first murderer, and crime and vice and wretchedness have festered in it ever since." Through the 1930s, suburbs were touted to the wealthy as a means of achieving "moral control" over their environments. Jackson, *Crabgrass Frontier*, 70, 151.

9. William H. Whyte Jr., *The Organization Man* (New York: Doubleday Anchor, 1957), 414.

10. Acceding to the family orientation of the new "America," in "Are Cities Un-American?" Whyte tries to argue in favor of cities on the grounds that they are better settings than suburbs for raising children, because of the urban presence of "all kinds of people, colored and white, old and young, poor and rich" (40). But he

quickly concedes that economics as well as the "social drive" make the city unappealing for the families that couples produce (28).

11. Thomas Bender describes the antiurban strains in American culture in *Toward an Urban Vision: Ideas and Institutions in Nineteenth-Century America* (1975; repr., Baltimore: The Johns Hopkins University Press, 1982).

12. Elaine Tyler May, *Homeward Bound: American Families in the Cold War Era* (New York: Basic Books, 1988), 10.

13. See David M. Oshinsky, *A Conspiracy So Immense: The World of Joe McCarthy* (New York: Free Press, 1983), 66–71. See also Rosalyn Baxandall and Elizabeth Ewen, *Picture Windows: How the Suburbs Happened* (New York: Basic Books, 2000), 90, 97.

14. Dolores Hayden, *Building Suburbia: Green Fields and Urban Growth, 1820–2000* (New York: Pantheon, 2003), 130.

15. Oshinsky, *Conspiracy So Immense*, 69–70.

16. William Levitt, quoted in Baxandall and Ewen, *Picture Windows*, 105.

17. William Levitt, quoted in Hayden, *Building Suburbia*, 135.

18. The House Un-American Activities Committee was set up in 1938 by conservatives hostile to the vision of public life, and state responsibility for that public life, played out in Roosevelt's New Deal. Though charged with investigating "un-American propaganda," it "devot[ed] most of its efforts to exposing alleged communist influence in CIO unions and New Deal agencies" (Ellen Schrecker, *Many Are the Crimes: McCarthyism in America* [Boston: Little Brown, 1998], 90–91). This battle was delayed by the war, but HUAC was made a permanent committee in 1945, and conservative hostility to the New Deal, focusing on communist threats, reemerged rapidly as a political force in the later 1940s.

Antihomosexual sentiment had been deeply embedded in the earliest attacks on Roosevelt's programs, in charges that a government run by an effete elite aimed to sap the rugged independence of real Americans and feminize the nation: "[C]ritics believed that as government bureaucracy increased, individual responsibility and determination declined. Socialism made citizens lazy and stunted their independence" (Johnson, *Lavender Scare*, 95). There were also, of course, more personal attacks: "Information is accumulating," conservative journalist Westbrook Pegler wrote in June 1950, "which shows that perversion has been so kindly regarded in the New Deal cult as to amount to a characteristic of that administration." The conflation of loss of independence with feminization and feminization with homosexuality enabled a moral attack on the New Deal. Thus, according to Senator Thomas Pryer Gore (D-Okla.), the New Deal had "spoiled the character and the morals, spoiled the souls of millions of people" (quotes from Johnson, *Lavender Scare*, 97, 95).

In the month that McCarthy began his campaign, February 1950, deputy undersecretary John Peurifoy, while appearing before a congressional committee in order to deny that the State Department "employed any actual Communists," admitted that ninety-one homosexuals had been identified as security risks and purged (Johnson, *Lavender Scare*, 1).

19. Joseph McCarthy, quoted in Johnson, *Lavender Scare,* 36.

20. *Employment of Homosexuals and Other Sex Perverts in Government,* 81st Cong., 2nd sess., S. Rep. 241 (Washington, D.C.: Government Printing Office, 1950); reprinted in *We Are Everywhere: A Historical Sourcebook in Gay and Lesbian Politics,* ed. Mark Blasius and Shane Phelan (New York: Routledge, 1997), 241–51.

21. The connections between postwar understandings of homosexuals and communists were first laid out by John D'Emilio, in "The Homosexual Menace: The Politics of Sexuality in Cold War America," in *Passion and Power: Sexuality in History,* ed. Kathy Peiss and Christina Simmons (Philadelphia: Temple University Press, 1989), 226–40, and have since been extensively explored by Johnson in *Lavender Scare.*

22. See Ronald Bayer, *Homosexuality and American Psychiatry: The Politics of Diagnosis* (Princeton: Princeton University Press, 1987), 39.

23. Joseph McCarthy, quoted in Schrecker, *Many Are the Crimes,* 152.

24. "Employment of Homosexuals," 244.

25. J. Howard McGrath, quoted in Schrecker, *Many Are the Crimes,* 144.

26. Quoted by Johnson, in *Lavender Scare,* 36.

27. Irving Bieber, in 1962, quoted in Bayer, *Homosexuality and American Psychiatry,* 30.

28. Richard Hauser, *The Homosexual Society* (1962; repr., London: Mayflower Dell 1965), 115.

29. Jack Lait and Lee Mortimer, *Washington Confidential* (New York: Dell, 1951), 120.

30. J. Edgar Hoover, quoted in Schrecker, *Many Are the Crimes,* 151.

31. Lait and Mortimer, *Washington Confidential,* 130.

32. Jack Lait and Lee Mortimer, *New York: Confidential! The Lowdown on Its Bright Life,* rev. ed. (New York: Dell, 1951), 104. Homosexuals and communists were also identified with African Americans through their shared association with improper relations. African Americans and homosexuals were linked as a source of sexual threat because of the dominant vision of both groups as sexually excessive, a vision codified in the sexual science that emerged in the late nineteenth century to describe the "lower races," as well as the "lower classes" and the perverts, as lacking sexual control (Jennifer Terry, *An American Obsession: Science, Medicine, and Homosexuality in Modern Society* [Chicago: University of Chicago Press, 1999]). This assumption provided a basis for the belief that African Americans as well as homosexuals were committed to boundary crossing: the sexual excessiveness of homosexuals would lead to sex across class and racial barriers, and the sexual excessiveness of African Americans would lead to miscegenation. The proper masculinity of black men and the proper femininity of black women were also continuously under attack, as in Daniel Patrick Moynihan's *The Negro Family: A Case for National Action* (1965), which led to the charge that African Americans, like homosexuals and communists, could not construct proper families.

The other group identified as un-American and urban, along with homosexuals and communists, was Jews. As we have seen, Robert Park saw Jews as prime candidates for the status of his representative urban "marginal man"; Jews were described in the 1930s, by the Chicago School's Ernest Burgess, as "an urban people"; and in the United States of the 1950s, they were identified with communism. In addition, Jews had long been represented by outsiders as inappropriately gendered—the men too feminine, the women too masculine—and so as having improper family structures. See, for example, Daniel Boyarin, *Unheroic Conduct: The Rise of Heterosexuality and the Invention of the Jewish Man* (Berkeley and Los Angeles: University of California Press, 1997).

33. Johnson, *Lavender Scare*, 33.

34. Lait and Mortimer, *Washington Confidential*, 126, 116.

35. Arthur M. Schlesinger Jr., *The Vital Center: The Politics of Freedom* (Boston: Houghton Mifflin, 1949), 127.

36. Lait and Mortimer, *Washington Confidential*, 116, 121. In practice the Communist Party in America was actually hostile to homosexuality. And although there was some crossing of racial boundaries among queers (whites at drag balls or bars in black communities, and blacks in white social settings), there is evidence from large and small cities alike—including New York, Chicago, Washington, Buffalo, and Birmingham—of very distinct black and white gay and lesbian social groupings. See, for example, George Chauncey, *Gay New York: Gender, Urban Culture, and the Makings of the Gay Male World, 1890–1940* (New York: Basic Books, 1994); Allen Drexel, "Before Paris Burned: Race, Class, and Homosexuality on the Chicago South Side, 1935–1960," Brett Beemyn, "A Queer Capital: Race, Class, Gender, and the Changing Social Landscape of Washington's Gay Communities, 1940–1955," and John Howard, "Place and Movement in Gay American History: A Case from the Post–World War 2 South," in *Creating a Place for Ourselves: Lesbian, Gay, and Bisexual Community Histories*, ed. Brett Beemyn (New York: Routledge, 1997); and Elizabeth Lapovsky Kennedy and Madeline D. Davis, *Boots of Leather, Slippers of Gold: The History of a Lesbian Community* (New York: Routledge, 1993). James Baldwin later described the difficulties of his own life as one of three black men—he hypothesized—in what he called the "alabaster" Greenwich Village of the 1940s, in "Freaks and the American Ideal of Manhood" (1985), in *Collected Essays*, ed. Toni Morrison (New York: Library of America, 1998), 814–29. Poet and activist Audre Lorde described Communist Party hostility to homosexuals in New York City in the 1950s. She also observed that although the only place in the city where black and white women were interacting was among the "gay girls" of the Village, the few black women present downtown were still subject to racist assumptions. See Audre Lorde, *Zami: A New Spelling of My Name* (Trumansburg, N.Y.: Crossing, 1982).

37. Jacob Riis, *How the Other Half Lives* (1890), quoted in Daniel Seligman, "The Enduring Slums," in Whyte, *Exploding Metropolis*, 114–15.

38. Seligman, "Enduring Slums," 115.

39. See Deborah Epstein Nord, "The Social Explorer as Anthropologist: Victorian Travellers among the Urban Poor," in *Visions of the Modern City: Essays in*

History, Art, and Literature, ed. William Sharpe and Leonard Wallock (Baltimore: The Johns Hopkins University Press, 1987), 122–34.

40. Friedrich Engels, *The Condition of the Working Class in England,* ed. Victor Kiernan (1845; repr., London: Penguin, 1987), 124.

41. W. E. B. Du Bois, *The Philadelphia Negro: A Social Study* (1899; repr., Philadelphia: University of Pennsylvania Press, 1996), 74, 75.

42. Seligman, "Enduring Slums," 117, 114. Seligman can then reframe the problem of slums as slum dwellers' "hamper[ing]" of "the social advance of the whole Negro community." This formulation erases white racism and reidentifies "slums" with "Negroes." Though they "encounter" "racial hostility," which in part accounts for their continuing poverty, they also "aggravate racial tensions." Nevertheless, "slum formation is not primarily a matter of race; it is the impoverished rural background of the immigrants that counts" (114).

43. Ibid., 124–25. The nonwhite newcomers can be blamed. Seligman quotes a Negro "leader," unidentified, who speaks against new immigrants from "the farm," single men who get "into trouble" because they are not ready for city life, "can't read or write much, and . . . [have] no morals at all" (117).

44. Ibid., 115.

45. Alfred C. Kinsey, *Sexual Behavior in the Human Male* (Philadelphia: Saunders, 1948), 458.

46. Ibid., 457. According to Kinsey, organization requires that homosexuals make themselves legible: "[I]t is this city group which exhibits all the affectations, the mannerisms, the dress, and the displays which the rest of the population take to be distinctive of all homosexual persons, even though it is only a small fraction of the males with homosexual histories who ever display such characteristics" (457).

47. See Robert A. M. Stern, Thomas Mellins, and David Fishman, *New York 1960: Architecture and Urbanism between the Second World War and the Bicentennial* (New York: Monacelli, 1995), 46.

48. For example, Marshall Berman reads Jacobs as a modernist in *All That Is Solid Melts into Air: The Experience of Modernity* (New York: Penguin, 1988), 314. Deborah L. Parsons describes Jacobs as postmodern in *Streetwalking the Metropolis: Women, the City, and Modernity* (New York: Oxford University Press, 2000), 8. Jacobs is most often claimed for the antimodern or traditionalist camp in discussions of New Urbanism.

49. See Andres Duany, Elizabeth Plater-Zyberk, and Jeff Speck, *Suburban Nation: The Rise of Sprawl and the Decline of the American Dream* (New York: North Point, 2000), 264.

50. Jane Jacobs, *The Death and Life of Great American Cities* (1961; repr., New York: Vintage, 1992), 21; hereafter cited parenthetically in the text.

51. In Mumford's frequently cited review of *The Death and Life of Great American Cities,* he was predictably hostile to Jacobs's advocacy of urban density as the necessary basis for an equally necessary urban complexity. "Home Remedies for

Urban Cancer," in *The Lewis Mumford Reader,* ed. Donald L. Miller (New York: Pantheon, 1986), 184–200.

52. Robert A. Caro, *The Power Broker: Robert Moses and the Fall of New York* (New York: Vintage, 1975).

53. Contemporary gay writers who have drawn on Jacobs's work include historians George Chauncey, in *Gay New York,* and Marc Stein, in *City of Sisterly and Brotherly Loves: Lesbian and Gay Philadelphia, 1945–1972* (Chicago: University of Chicago Press, 2000); geographer David Higgs, in *Queer Sites: Gay Urban Histories since 1600* (London: Routledge, 1999); and journalists and essayists Michael Bronski, in *Beyond the Pleasure Principle: Sex, Backlash, and the Struggle for Gay Freedom* (New York: St. Martin's, 1998), Samuel R. Delany, in *Times Square Red, Times Square Blue* (New York: New York University Press, 1999), and Patrick Moore, in *Beyond Shame: Reclaiming the Abandoned History of Radical Gay Sexuality* (Boston: Beacon, 2004).

54. William H. Whyte Jr., "C. D. Jackson Meets Jane Jacobs," preface to Whyte, *Exploding Metropolis,* xv–xvii.

55. For an account of Moses's plans and the opposition with which they were met, see Stern, Mellins, and Fishman, *New York 1960,* 247–50, 259–63.

56. James Baldwin, "Fifth Avenue, Uptown: A Letter from Harlem," from *Nobody Knows My Name* (1961), in *Collected Essays,* 170, 174.

57. Ibid., 179.

58. James Baldwin, "On the Painter Beauford Delaney" (1965), in *Collected Essays,* 720.

59. James Baldwin, *No Name in the Street* (1972), in *Collected Essays,* 366; emphasis in original.

60. Consequently, Philadelphia's Washington Square was "torn up, closed . . . and redesigned" in the mid-1950s, scattering all users. Jacobs explains that low-status persons and uses are not destructive, that is, they do not drive out higher-status persons and uses: "People or uses with less money . . . less choice or less open respectability move into already weakened areas of cities, neighborhoods that are no longer coveted by people with the luxury of choice" (*Death and Life of Great American Cities,* 98). Nevertheless, these "perverts" were clearly not "welcome users" in her view.

61. Jacobs's other two repeated examples were the North End of Boston and Back of the Yards, Chicago.

62. See Stein, *City of Sisterly and Brotherly Loves,* 87.

63. See Nan Alamilla Boyd, *Wide Open Town: A History of Queer San Francisco to 1965* (Berkeley and Los Angeles: University of California Press, 2003), 69, 75.

64. Johnson, *Lavender Scare,* 60.

65. See Chauncey, *Gay New York,* 227, 244; and Caroline F. Ware, *Greenwich Village, 1920–1930: A Comment on American Civilization in the Post-war Years* (1935; repr., Berkeley and Los Angeles: University of California Press, 1994), 105–27, 235–67.

66. Ware, *Greenwich Village, 1920–1930*, 237.

67. Lait and Mortimer, *New York: Confidential!*, 65–66.

68. Chauncey, *Gay New York*, 246.

69. See Baldwin, "Freaks and the American Ideal of Manhood," 821–23.

70. James Baldwin, "The American Dream and the American Negro," originally published in *New York Times Magazine*, March 7, 1965, in *Collected Essays*, 718.

71. Caro, *Power Broker*, 968.

72. James Baldwin, *Go Tell It on the Mountain* (1953; repr., New York: Dell, 1985), 19; hereafter cited parenthetically in the text.

73. James Baldwin, *Giovanni's Room* (1956; repr., New York: Random House, Delta, 2000), 20; hereafter cited parenthetically in the text.

74. James Baldwin, *Another Country* (1962; repr., New York: Vintage, 1993), 203; hereafter cited parenthetically in the text.

75. David's history lesson in Paris, in *Giovanni's Room,* is the most explicitly sexual in Baldwin's early fiction. He learns there that he must acknowledge his own sexual past. "I repent now," he tells us, "for all the good it does—one particular lie among the many lies I've told, told, lived, and believed . . . the lie which I told to Giovanni . . . that I had never slept with a boy before" (6). He repents this "lie" because his refusal to acknowledge his own history—that is, his own homosexuality—has destroyed his relationship with Giovanni, whom he loves, and has destroyed Giovanni himself.

76. James Baldwin, "A Question of Identity," from *Notes of a Native Son* (1955), in *Collected Essays*, 93.

77. Ibid., 100.

78. James Baldwin, "The Discovery of What It Means to Be an American," from *Nobody Knows My Name*, in *Collected Essays*, 140.

79. Baldwin, *No Name in the Street*, 373. The black American protagonist of Baldwin's story "This Morning, This Evening, So Soon" (in *Going to Meet the Man* [1965; repr., New York: Vintage, 1993]), preferring Paris to New York, explains that the French capital was "a place where people were too busy with their own lives, *their private lives*, to make fantasies about mine, to set up walls around mine" (175; emphasis in original).

80. Baldwin, *No Name in the Street*, 376.

81. Baldwin, "Question of Identity," 93.

82. James Baldwin, "Alas, Poor Richard," from *Nobody Knows My Name*, in *Collected Essays*, 249.

83. James Baldwin, "My Dungeon Shook: Letter to My Nephew," from *The Fire Next Time* (1963), in *Collected Essays*, 292.

84. James Baldwin, "Preservation of Innocence," in *Collected Essays*, 595.

85. James Baldwin, "Notes for a Hypothetical Novel: An Address," from *Nobody Knows My Name*, in *Collected Essays*, 223.

86. Baldwin, "Fifth Avenue, Uptown," 179.

87. Caro, *Power Broker*, 967.

88. See Estelle B. Freedman, "'Uncontrolled Desires': The Response to the Sexual Psychopath, 1920–1960," in Peiss and Simmons, *Passion and Power*, 213. See also John Gerassi, *The Boys of Boise: Furor, Vice, and Folly in an American City* (New York: Collier, 1966); and Neil Miller, *Sex-Crime Panic: A Journey to the Paranoid Heart of the 1950s* (Los Angeles: Alyson, 2002).

89. J. Paul de River, *The Sexual Criminal* (1949), quoted in Freedman, "'Uncontrolled Desires,'" 214.

90. Freedman, "'Uncontrolled Desires,'" 213–14.

91. James Baldwin, "The Harlem Ghetto," from *Notes of a Native Son*, in *Collected Essays*, 53.

92. Baldwin, "Fifth Avenue, Uptown," 174.

93. Ibid., 170–71.

94. In Baldwin's later work he replicates and complicates Jacobs's lessons here; threat and safety are racialized, but they are also complicated by the difficulties of family relationships. Baldwin describes himself as a thirteen-year-old boy crossing Fifth Avenue at Forty-second Street, on his way to the New York Public Library, when "the cop in the middle of the street muttered as I passed him, 'Why don't you niggers stay uptown where you belong?'" ("Down at the Cross: Letter from a Region in My Mind," from *Fire Next Time*, 298). In his last novel, *Just above My Head* (1979), residents coming out of their houses in a black neighborhood of Atlanta save the lives of a group of young northern black men threatened by whites who are strangers in that part of town. In *Tell Me How Long the Train's Been Gone* (1968), his protagonist, as a small black boy in New York City, gets lost on the subway and attaches himself in desperation to a black man he sees there, not knowing where he is and afraid of the white adults who are ignoring him. The man returns him to his neighborhood. But the child became lost because he was fleeing his family; he asks the stranger who rescues him to become his father and take him home, because he is afraid of his own father's home.

95. David's father, tired and withdrawn from his son when the family is home alone together, is "boyish and expansive" on social occasions, "handling all the men as though they were his brothers, and flirting with all the women" (*Giovanni's Room*, 12). His aunt is "always overdressed, overmade-up . . . with too much jewelry everywhere, clanging and banging," and "flirt[ing] with the men in a strange, nerve-wracking kind of way" (11–12).

96. It was not until his later novels, especially *Just above My Head*, that Baldwin would describe gay men who are accepted by their families.

97. Baldwin's white protagonist and narrator in *Giovanni's Room*, David, whose "ancestors conquered a continent," whose "blond hair gleams," and who has a "face . . . like a face you have seen many times," wants above all to be secure, which means in his experience to be unexceptional, in order to be an American of his moment (3). He lives in a conceptual universe cleanly divided between the home and the nation. The home and the nation are, moreover, inextricable from one another. The only way to secure one's place in the home, and so by extension in the

nation (and vice versa)—in fact, the only way to secure a place for oneself at all—is by properly performing the gender and sexual roles one has been assigned.

98. Baldwin, "Preservation of Innocence," 597.

99. Eric's first love is LeRoy, a slightly older black boy. LeRoy has to explain to the oblivious Eric that, as he is not the son of a wealthy man and has obligations to his family, he will not be going north. But LeRoy also tells him, "You *better* get out of this town. Declare, they going to lynch you before they get around to me" (*Another Country*, 206; emphasis in original).

100. Baldwin, *No Name in the Street*, 385.

101. Jacobs invokes the familiar contrast between the city and "small settlements [in which] everyone knows your affairs" (*The Death and Life of Great American Cities*, 58).

102. Before David's first sexual (and homosexual) experience, he is happy in public, taking an evening walk "down the dark, tropical Brooklyn streets . . . with all the world's grownups, it seemed, sitting shrill and dishevelled on the stoops and all the world's children on the sidewalks or in the gutters or hanging from fire escapes, with my arm around Joey's shoulder. I was proud, I think, because his head came just below my ear" (*Giovanni's Room*, 7).

103. Baldwin, "Harlem Ghetto," 50.

104. James Baldwin, "East River, Downtown: Postscript to a Letter from Harlem," from *Nobody Knows My Name*, in *Collected Essays*, 185; emphasis in original.

105. Ibid.

106. Baldwin, *No Name in the Street*, 386.

107. In *The Power Broker*, Robert Caro describes in detail the path of many different postwar "urban renewal" projects in New York City and the desperate attempts of local people to resist the destruction of their neighborhoods.

108. St. Clair Drake and Horace R. Cayton, *Black Metropolis: A Study of Negro Life in a Northern City*, rev. ed. (New York: Harper & Row, 1962), 795–96.

109. Seligman, "The Enduring Slums," 50.

110. Baldwin, "Harlem Ghetto," 51.

111. James Baldwin, "Nobody Knows My Name: A Letter from the South," from *Nobody Knows My Name*, in *Collected Essays*, 197.

112. Baldwin, "Fifth Avenue, Uptown," 173, 174.

113. Ibid., 177; emphasis in original.

114. Baldwin, "Discovery of What It Means," 141.

115. James Baldwin, "A Fly in Buttermilk," from *Nobody Knows My Name*, in *Collected Essays*, 187.

116. James Baldwin, introduction to *Nobody Knows My Name*, in *Collected Essays*, 135.

117. The relentless separation of housing from economic uses and the structure of employment for men and women in the mid-twentieth century ensured that children encountered adult men rarely in the course of the day, Jacobs argued, if there was the "full employment" such housing schemes presumed. Planning for

all of these structures was routinely organized around gender segregation, "aim[ed] at filling the presumed daily needs of impossibly vacuous housewives and preschool tots" (*Death and Life of Great American Cities*, 83). But, as Jacobs pointed out, mothers and small children alone cannot sustain public spaces.

118. Baldwin, "Fifth Avenue, Uptown," 175.

119. In an essay on André Gide written at the same time as *Giovanni's Room*, Baldwin expressed, if indirectly, great anxiety about the group life of homosexuals. "The really horrible thing about the phenomenon of present-day homosexuality," he wrote, "is that today's unlucky deviate can only save himself by the most tremendous exertion of all his forces from falling into an underworld in which he never meets either men or women, where it is impossible to have either a lover or a friend, where the possibility of genuine human involvement has altogether ceased." "The Male Prison," from *Nobody Knows My Name*, in *Collected Essays*, 234.

120. In *Another Country*, Baldwin observes, similarly, that "behind affection, came all the winds of fear" (212).

121. Jacobs implies that each neighborhood has a complex specificity, that neighborhoods cannot be seen as simply manifestations of groups: "In this [local residents] are correct, for the multitude of relationships and public characters that make up an animated city street neighborhood are always unique, intricate and have the value of an unreproducible original" (*Death and Life of Great American Cities*, 279).

7. City of Feeling

1. Goffman cites Robert Park's *Race and Culture*, proposing that "everyone is always and everywhere, more or less consciously, playing a role. . . . It is in these roles that we know each other; it is in these roles that we know ourselves." Erving Goffman, *The Presentation of Self in Everyday Life* (New York: Doubleday Anchor, 1959), 19.

2. Ibid., 72.

3. Erving Goffman, *Stigma: Notes on the Management of Spoiled Identity* (1963; repr., New York: Simon & Schuster, 1986), 88, 111, 116. Goffman's work has been extensively taken up in LGBT scholarship, from Esther Newton, in *Mother Camp*, and Martin Levine, in *Gay Macho*, in the 1970s, to Eve Kosofsky Sedgwick in the 1990s.

4. Both Lofland and Sennett situate their analyses in the context of broad historical overviews of the development of modern cities. Lofland cites a new recognition of understandings of "public space" as crucial to "understanding the dynamics of city living." Lyn Lofland, *A World of Strangers: Order and Action in Urban Public Space* (Prospect Heights, Ill.: Waveland, 1973), xiii. Sennett argues for the need to recognize emotion and a "new search for values." Richard Sennett, introduction to *Classic Essays on the Culture of Cities*, comp. Richard Sennett (New York: Appleton-Century-Crofts, 1969), 19. See also Stephan Thernstrom and Richard Sennett, eds.,

Nineteenth-Century Cities: Essays in the New Urban History (New Haven: Yale University Press, 1969), vii.

5. Lofland, *World of Strangers*, 3. Lofland's study was based on a research project begun in Ann Arbor and Detroit, Michigan, and concluded in San Francisco, from 1965 to 1970 (x).

6. Richard Sennett, *The Fall of Public Man: On the Social Psychology of Capitalism* (New York: Vintage, 1978), 39.

7. Lofland, *World of Strangers*, 99.

8. Sennett, *Fall of Public Man*, 39. Despite his emphasis on theater, Sennett explicitly rejected what he called "the Goffman school" of sociology (35–36).

9. Lofland, *World of Strangers*, 177–78; emphasis in original.

10. Ibid., 82. Lofland qualifies her focus on place later in her book, conceding that "the skilled city dweller utilizes appearential *and* locational *and* behavioral clues to make identifications—each piece of information reinforcing, correcting, or adding to the other" (97; emphasis in original).

11. Sennett, *Fall of Public Man*, 48, 59–60.

12. Ibid., 51.

13. It is, after all, because Sennett's special strangers are "lone rather than in family clusters" that they are not "divisible into ethnic, economic, or racial types." That is, family is what attaches people to (ethnic, economic, or social) groups, and residential patterns confirm the connection (ibid., 52).

14. Goffman, *Presentation of Self*, 74–75; emphasis in original. Goffman also drew examples from the feminist studies of Simone de Beauvoir and Mirra Komarovsky.

15. Ibid., 35–36.

16. Lofland, *World of Strangers*, 82.

17. Sennett, *Fall of Public Man*, 7.

18. Ibid., 15–16.

19. Ibid., 7.

20. Susan Sontag, "Notes on 'Camp'" (1964), in *Against Interpretation, and Other Essays* (1966; repr., New York: Octagon, 1986): 277; hereafter cited parenthetically in the text.

21. Esther Newton, *Mother Camp: Female Impersonators in America* (1972; repr., Chicago: University of Chicago Press, 1979).

22. Ibid., 22; hereafter cited parenthetically in the text.

23. Consequently, pace Sontag, "'camp taste' . . . is synonymous with homosexual taste" (ibid., 105).

24. Goffman, *Stigma*, 23.

25. This image can be traced from Donn Teal's *The Gay Militants* (New York: Stein & Day, 1971) to Martin Duberman's *Stonewall* (New York: Plume, 1994) and Nigel Finch's 1995 film of Duberman's book, also titled *Stonewall* (DVD, BBC Warner, 2008).

26. See Marc Stein, *City of Sisterly and Brotherly Loves: Lesbian and Gay Philadelphia, 1945–1972* (Chicago: University of Chicago Press, 2000), 190. See also John

D'Emilio, *Sexual Politics, Sexual Communities*, 2nd ed. (Chicago: University of Chicago Press, 1998); and Nan Alamilla Boyd, *Wide Open Town: A History of Queer San Francisco to 1965* (Berkeley and Los Angeles: University of California Press, 2003).

27. See D'Emilio, *Sexual Politics, Sexual Communities*; Boyd, *Wide Open Town*; Stein, *City of Sisterly and Brotherly Loves*; and Moira Rachel Kenney, *Mapping Gay L.A.* (Philadelphia: Temple University Press, 2001).

28. For discussions of such self-transformations, and activists' accompanying costumes, see Arnie Kantrowitz, "Letter to a Queer Generation" (1992), in *We Are Everywhere: A Historical Sourcebook in Gay and Lesbian Politics*, ed. Mark Blasius and Shane Phelan (New York: Routledge, 1997), 812–17; and Karla Jay, *Tales of the Lavender Menace: A Memoir of Liberation* (New York: Basic Books, 1999).

29. Coming out also, in practice, sometimes heightened the reliance of those who came out on the group, if their decision evoked the hostility of their families, employers, and heterosexual friends, or revealed to them their own anger at their families, employers, and heterosexual friends. See Kantrowitz, "Letter to a Queer Generation."

30. Evelyn Hooker, "The Homosexual Community" (1961), in *The Same Sex: An Appraisal of Homosexuality*, ed. Ralph W. Weltge (Philadelphia: Pilgrim, 1969), 27, 29. Hooker's study was based in Los Angeles.

31. Ibid., 29.

32. Ibid., 28.

33. Quoted in Boyd, *Wide Open Town*, 200.

34. Frances Fitzgerald, *Cities on a Hill: A Journey through Contemporary American Cultures* (New York: Simon & Schuster, 1986), 29.

35. Weston highlights the importance of cultural texts prompting this migration: novels, television, and film. Much of the autobiography and the fiction produced by gay liberation, the women's movement, and lesbian feminism features accounts of moving to the city. See Kath Weston, "Get Thee to a Big City: Sexual Imaginary and the Great Gay Migration," in *Long Slow Burn: Sexuality and Social Science* (Routledge: New York, 1998), 29–56.

36. Historian Jeffrey Weeks concurred in retrospect: "[T]he main impact of the new gay sense of purpose and militancy over the two decades after 1969 was not the revolutionary transformation of society but a vast expansion of the lesbian and gay world." Jeffrey Weeks, introduction to *Homosexual: Oppression and Liberation*, by Dennis Altman (New York: New York University Press, 1993), 10.

37. Rita Mae Brown, *Rubyfruit Jungle* (New York: Daughters, 1973); Andrew Holleran, *Dancer from the Dance* (New York: Plume, 1986).

38. Brown, *Rubyfruit Jungle*, 120.

39. Both protagonists come out, then, but they do so only after being pushed, or out of despair. Neither fiction refers to the new political movement, except for Holleran's very shadowy depiction of a gay pride demonstration at the conclusion of *Dancer from the Dance*.

40. Brown, *Rubyfruit Jungle*, 136.

41. Molly spends a lot of time in the novel refusing to prostitute herself. By Brown's second novel, *In Her Day* (1976), her social scheme has become complicated enough to include middle-class college professors and young political activists. Prostitution is less often evoked.

42. Holleran's Malone ends up supporting himself by prostitution and being offered for sale, by his mentor, to a young millionaire.

43. Holleran, *Dancer from the Dance*, 18, 17.

44. Brown, *Rubyfruit Jungle*, 133.

45. Holleran, *Dancer from the Dance*, 176. When the novel was published in France, in 2007, it was fittingly titled *Le Danseur de Manhattan*.

46. Louis Wirth, *The Ghetto* (Chicago: University of Chicago Press, 1928), 20.

47. Ibid., 26.

48. Ibid., 21.

49. Ibid., 5, 20, 8, 287.

50. Joe W. Trotter, "African Americans in the City: The Industrial Era, 1900–1950," in *New African American Urban History,* ed. Kenneth W. Goings and Raymond A. Mohl (Thousand Oaks, Calif.: Sage, 1996), 305–8, 308.

51. The "homosexual world," and later the "gay world" and the "gay life," had been common terms for homosexual social life in the United States since early in the twentieth century. The term "ghetto" used in relation to gays seems to have emerged during the 1960s. In "The Homosexual Ghetto?" for the Daughters of Bilitis publication the *Ladder*, in 1965, Leo Ebreo pointed to parallels in the terms of Jews' and gays' pursuit of assimilation and resistance to political activity: the insistence of so many that "I'm not that Jewish!" or "I'm not that homosexual!" Homophile activists were being accused by others of trying to put homosexuals in a ghetto, which "the 'assimilated' homosexual, from his troglodyte perspective, may imagine [as] an assembly of campy ballet dancers and hair dressers." At the same time, political activity on behalf of gays was justified when "[t]here is already something of a ghetto pattern for homosexuals, because of the pressures put on them to confine themselves to certain vocations where they are 'expected' and to isolate themselves." Finally, as Carl Wittman would later do, Ebreo described the closet as a form of ghetto: "The homosexual who 'passes' is often in a ghetto composed of one person, sometimes of two." Leo Ebreo, "The Homosexual Ghetto?" (1965), repr. in Blasius and Phelan, *We Are Everywhere*, 340, 341, 342.

52. Teal, *Gay Militants*, 111.

53. Carl Wittman, "Refugees from Amerika: A Gay Manifesto," in *Out of the Closets: Voices of Gay Liberation,* ed. Karla Jay and Allen Young (1972; repr., New York: New York University Press, 1992), 330.

54. Ibid., 334.

55. Ibid., 330. Echoing Wittman by linking the ghetto with oppression, at the opening of *The Gay Militants* Don Teal describes Greenwich Village as "the nation's second largest gay ghetto" (17). But gays who rejected gay liberation could do so by claiming the ghetto: "I don't even find the gay ghetto particularly repressed or

persecuted," wrote David McReynolds, "Notes for a More Coherent Article," *WIN*, November 15, 1969, 14, quoted in Teal (75).

56. In the 1970s, there were also, of course, groups of gay men ("radical faeries" and others) and lesbians (lesbian feminist separatists and others) who self-consciously abandoned the city, choosing often-communal rural lives—as did members of the broader back-to-the-land movement of the day. See Arlene Stein, *The Stranger Next Door: The Story of a Small Town's Battle over Sex, Faith, and Civil Rights* (Boston: Beacon, 2001), 43–47. The great gay migration to the city was also accompanied by a broader middle-class heterosexual return to the cities. See Manuel Castells, *The City and the Grassroots: A Cross-Cultural Theory of Urban Social Movements* (Berkeley: University of California Press, 1983).

57. Weston, "Get Thee to a Big City," 34.

58. Ibid., 32.

59. Ibid., 41.

60. Ibid., 49.

61. In both Brown's and Holleran's novels, the protagonists are white and conventional in their gendered behaviors. But in both works, confirming the status of drag queens as representative homosexuals and city people, those protagonists are introduced to urban gay life by strikingly effeminate men. In *Rubyfruit Jungle,* the first person Molly meets in New York is Calvin, a flaming queen who shows her the ropes before leaving to try his luck in San Francisco. In *Dancer from the Dance,* Malone is taken up by the flamboyant Sutherland, who guides him through gay Manhattan. Brown's Calvin is also African American, to complete his status as a representative of the urban. In *Dancer from the Dance,* in the tradition of Walt Whitman and Edward Carpenter, Holleran insists on the democratic impulse of desire between men. But this generally means that the white men he describes desire Italians or Puerto Ricans. That Italian or Puerto Rican men might have their own desires remains a peripheral possibility.

62. Fitzgerald, *Cities on a Hill,* 34–35, 60, 116.

63. *Tongues Untied,* directed by Marlon Riggs (Frameline, 1990).

64. Weston, "Get Thee to a Big City," 51.

65. The divisions between these stages were not sharp, however: gay commentators in the 1970s and 1980s, such as Altman and White, were committed to the principles of the gay liberation movement if not also activist, and even heterosexual commentators such as Castells and Fitzgerald were sympathetic to the movement in different degrees.

66. According to Marcus Overseth, "The barscene in San Francisco is at once a refuge and a nirvana for Plasticgays from every crossroads hamlet in Amerika." Marcus Overseth, "Grows Rapidly: What Kind of People?" *San Francisco Free Press,* December 7–21, 1969, quoted in Teal, *Gay Militants,* 56.

67. Dick Leitsch, "Homosexuals Don't Really Exist," *GAY,* April 27, 1970, quoted in Teal, *Gay Militants,* 78.

68. Dennis Altman, *The Homosexualization of America: The Americanization of the Homosexual* (Boston: Beacon, 1982), 238.

69. Altman, *Homosexual*, 238.

70. Altman, *Homosexualization of America*, 32.

71. Edmund White, *States of Desire: Travels in Gay America* (New York: Dutton, 1983), 299, 321. White's reports were originally written for and published in the most successful gay cultural magazine of the 1970s and 1980s, which was called *Christopher Street* after gay Greenwich Village's main drag.

72. Ibid., 261, 265. For a more recent example of the neutral use of "ghetto," see Gayle S. Rubin, "The Miracle Mile: South of Market and Gay Male Leather, 1962–1997," in *Reclaiming San Francisco: History, Politics, Culture*, ed. James Brook, Chris Carlsson, and Nancy J. Peters (San Francisco: City Lights, 1998), 247–72.

73. Martin P. Levine, *Gay Macho: The Life and Death of the Homosexual Clone*, ed. Michael S. Kimmel (New York: New York University Press, 1998), 32. Levine cites, among other sources, the 1968 Kerner Commission report on the urban riots that had erupted across the United States in the mid-1960s. For a more recent example of rejection of the term "ghetto," see Robert W. Bailey, *Gay Politics, Urban Politics: Identity and Economics in the Urban Setting* (New York: Columbia University Press, 1999).

74. Levine, *Gay Macho*, 32.

75. Altman, *Homosexualization of America*, 31.

76. Altman, *Homosexual*, 51.

77. Castells, *City and the Grassroots*, 157–58.

78. Altman, *Homosexualization of America*, 32.

79. Castells, *City and the Grassroots*, 139.

80. Ibid., 161.

81. Ibid., 139, 156.

82. White, *States of Desire*, 62.

83. Altman, *Homosexualization of America*, 32.

84. Castells, *City and the Grassroots*, 160.

85. Ibid.

86. Ibid., 161.

87. Ibid., 160–61.

88. White, *States of Desire*, 61. White explains in an afterword that his travels through the cities of gay America have turned him into a socialist in the Whitman—which is to say also the Edward Carpenter and the Jane Addams—mold.

89. See also Lawrence Knopp's discussion of the ways in which gay men submerged their sexual identity within a presentation of themselves as committed to urban preservation. Lawrence Knopp, "Gentrification and Gay Neighborhood Formation in New Orleans: A Case Study," in *Homo Economics: Capitalism, Community, and Lesbian and Gay Life*, ed. Amy Gluckman and Betsy Reed (New York: Routledge, 1997), 45–63.

90. In practice, however, Bostonian homosexuality, being more progressive, was less ghettoized. Washington homosexuality, being more conservative—more hostile to the "ghetto" as an idea—coincided with a more developed gay ghetto.

91. In San Francisco, Tom Ammiano observed, in 1988, "When gay people take over a neighborhood, they call it gentrification. When straight people take over a neighborhood, they call it a renaissance" (quoted in Rubin, "Miracle Mile," 263).

92. Weston, "Get Thee to a Big City."

93. White, *States of Desire,* 62.

94. As gay liberationists and lesbian feminists had observed, however, "heterosexual" is a public sexual identity, ratified by the state with marriage. Goffman had already bound sexuality to public life. He made clear his sense of the public nature of what is conventionally deemed private, including sexual behavior, in *Stigma.* "[W]hether we interact with strangers or intimates," he observes, "the finger tips of society have reached bluntly into the contact, even here putting us in our place." His example is marriage and, in that setting, "wives." "Unique historically entangled features are likely to tint the edges of our relation to this person," he concedes, but "still, at the center is a full array of socially standardized anticipations . . . for example, that she will look after the house, entertain our friends, and be able to bear children. She will be a good or a bad wife, and be this relative to standard expectations, ones that other husbands in our group have about their wives too." He concluded, "Surely it is scandalous to speak of marriage as a particular relationship" (53).

95. Two decades later, in *Flesh and Stone,* Sennett would come to focus on the experience of the body as the hope of the city: "[U]rban experiences take form largely from the ways people experience their own bodies. For people in a multicultural city to care about one another . . . we have to change the understanding we have of our own bodies. We will never experience the difference of others until we acknowledge the bodily insufficiencies in ourselves." He ends that book with a discussion of Jane Jacobs, and of Greenwich Village as an urban ideal, but notes only that the Village includes "a large homosexual community." Richard Sennett, *Flesh and Stone: The Body and the City in Western Civilization* (New York: Norton, 1994), 370, 356.

96. Sennett made it clear that women's urban experience was an entirely other question he need only parenthetically address, but he suggested the key to that difference was women's lack of freedom on the streets, because for women the city was always a source of moral compromise, which is to say, a sexual threat. See Sennett, *Fall of Public Man,* 23.

97. White, *States of Desire,* 284, 285; emphasis in original.

98. Castells, *City and the Grassroots,* 167.

99. Ibid., 157.

100. Dr. David Reuben's *Everything You Always Wanted to Know about Sex, but Were Afraid to Ask* (New York: McKay, 1969), however, in which lesbianism is discussed under the rubric of prostitution, suggests the persistence of that association.

101. Valerie Taylor, *The Girls in 3-B*, (1959; repr., New York: Feminist Press, 2003). See also the novels of Paula Christian. The urbanity of lesbians was emphasized at midcentury, from (even the title of) a rare anthology of fiction, scientific comment, and memoir, Ann Aldrich's edited *Carol in a Thousand Cities* (1960), to the details of the social studies of the period, such as Donald Webster Cory's *The Lesbian in America* (1965).

102. For an account of lesbian life in San Francisco prior to Stonewall, see Boyd, *Wide Open Town*. For a discussion of lesbian settings in San Francisco in the 1970s and 1980s, see Sasha G. Lewis, *Sunday's Women: Lesbian Life Today* (Boston: Beacon, 1979); and Susan Stryker and Jim Van Buskirk, *Gay by the Bay: A History of Queer Culture in the San Francisco Bay Area* (San Francisco: Chronicle, 1996), 99–100. For other cities, see Kenney, *Mapping Gay L.A.*; and Becki L. Ross, *The House That Jill Built: A Lesbian Nation in Formation* (Toronto, Ont.: University of Toronto Press, 1995).

103. See Kenney, *Mapping Gay L.A.*; and Michael Bronski, *The Pleasure Principle: Sex, Backlash, and the Struggle for Gay Freedom* (New York: St. Martin's, 1998), 154–57.

104. Alan P. Bell and Martin S. Weinberg, *Homosexualities: A Study of Diversity among Men and Women* (New York: Simon & Schuster, 1978), 235.

105. Ettore's city being London in the 1970s, many of the households making up the lesbian ghetto she studied were squatters in working-class neighborhoods. E. M. Ettore, *Lesbians, Women, and Society* (London: Routledge & Kegan Paul, 1980). The American study of lesbian community from this period, sociologist Susan Krieger's *The Mirror Dance*, also focused on a self-consciously political group, but in a medium-sized midwestern college town. Susan Krieger, *The Mirror Dance: Identity in a Women's Community* (Philadelphia: Temple University Press, 1983).

106. Lewis, *Sunday's Women*, 6.

107. Ibid., 156. In San Francisco's lesbian world, Lewis cites bars and clubs and women cruising as well as political gatherings.

108. Adrienne Rich, "Twenty-One Love Poems," no. 19, in *The Dream of a Common Language: Poems, 1974–1977* (New York: Norton, 1978), 34.

109. Altman, *Homosexualization of America*, 31.

110. Fitzgerald, *Cities on a Hill*, 34–35.

111. Fitzgerald's observation that lesbians "appeared in large numbers only on Gay Freedom Day" suggests that lesbians were visible to some of these observers only when they congregated with men, that is, on the street (ibid., 35).

112. Castells, *City and the Grassroots*, 140.

113. Harry Britt, quoted in ibid, 138.

114. Castells, *City and the Grassroots*, 167.

115. Altman, *Homosexualization of America*, 31.

116. Castells, *City and the Grassroots*, 167.

117. Altman, *Homosexualization of America*, 31.

118. Castells, *City and the Grassroots*, 162.

119. See John D'Emilio, "Capitalism and Gay Identity," in *The Lesbian and Gay Studies Reader*, ed. Henry Abelove, Michèle Barale, and David Halperin (New York: Routledge, 1993), 467–76; Jeffrey Weeks, *Coming Out: Homosexual Politics in Britain from the Nineteenth Century to the Present* (1977; repr., London: Quartet, 1979); and Henning Bech, *When Men Meet: Homosexuality and Modernity* (1987), trans. Teresa Mesquit and Tim Davies (Chicago: University of Chicago Press, 1997).

120. Bech, *When Men Meet*, 98, 99.

121. Castells, *City and the Grassroots*, 163.

122. Ibid., 166, 167.

123. Ibid., 167.

124. Michel Foucault, "Friendship as a Way of Life," *Foucault Live (Interviews, 1961–1984)*, trans. John Johnston, ed. Sylvère Lotringer (New York: Semiotext[e], 1996), 310, 308. Martin Levine describes friendship as the central bond among the gay "clones" of the 1970s and early 1980s (*Gay Macho*). As the narrator observes in Andrew Holleran's *Dancer from the Dance*, "[O]f all the bonds between homosexual friends, none was greater than that between the friends who danced together. The friend you danced with, when you had no lover, was the most important person in your life; and for people who went without lovers for years, that was all they had" (111–12).

125. White, *States of Desire*, 286.

126. Bech, *When Men Meet*, 115.

127. Ibid., 154. Bech acknowledges gay friendship and networks, citing White, but sees them as less secure, and therefore less a mitigation of isolation, than the family left behind. In fact, he is so committed to the contradictions of perverts in groups that although he does admit that urban residence is "conducive" to gay urban life, and moreover that "in urban living" the "*potentialities* of community and opportunity" are "often just as important as actualization itself," still, "in order for a homosexual neighborhood to actualize, the individuals will in any case have to leave their dwellings and enter the city or other people's places" (116; emphasis in original).

128. As Robert Park observed in the 1920s, "It is the incompetent persons . . . who still maintain an interest . . . in the local communities of our great cities. Women, particularly women without professional training . . . immigrants who are locally segregated . . . [and c]hildren . . . who necessarily live close to the ground." Robert Park, "Community Organization and the Romantic Temper," in *The City*, by Robert E. Park, Ernest W. Burgess, and Roderick D. McKenzie (1925; repr., Chicago: University of Chicago Press, 1984), 113.

129. Castells, *City and the Grassroots*, 152.

130. Levine, *Gay Macho*.

131. Bech, *When Men Meet*, 136.

132. When discussions of lesbian and gay domestic life (often based in San Francisco) began to appear, in the 1990s, they were the work either of lesbians, such as anthropologist Kath Weston, *Families We Choose: Lesbians, Gays, Kinship* (New

York: Columbia University Press, 1991), or of gay men who began by describing their experience of their mothers' domestic burdens, as in sociologist Christopher Carrington, *No Place like Home: Relationships and Family Life among Lesbians and Gay Men* (Chicago: University of Chicago Press, 1999).

133. Fitzgerald, *Cities on a Hill,* 31, 32.

134. Castells, *City and the Grassroots,* 139.

135. Ibid., 163, 162.

136. For a recent reference to this mantra, see Michael Sorkin, "Variations on a Theme Park," introduction to *Variations on a Theme Park: The New American City and the End of Public Space,* ed. Michael Sorkin (1992; repr., New York: Hill & Wang, 1999), xv.

137. Robert E. Park, "The City: Suggestions for the Investigation of Human Behavior in the Urban Environment," in *Classic Essays on the Culture of Cities,* comp. Richard Sennett (New York: Appleton-Century-Crofts, 1969), 101.

138. Marshall Berman, *All That Is Solid Melts into Air: The Experience of Modernity* (New York: Penguin, 1982), 171, 165, 316.

139. That first volume, *Tales of the City,* was followed by *More Tales of the City* (1980), *Further Tales of the City* (1982), *Babycakes* (1984), *Significant Others* (1987), and *Sure of You* (1989). The first three volumes were also made into a public television series. In 2007, Maupin published a concluding volume, *Michael Tolliver Lives.*

140. Walter Benjamin, *Charles Baudelaire: A Lyric Poet in the Era of High Capitalism,* trans. Harry Zohn (London: Verso, 1997), 46.

141. A pedophile falls to his death in San Francisco Bay at the end of the first volume, so that it is also clear that there are limits to the sexual permissiveness of this city, and this series.

142. Mona Ramsey, the erstwhile lesbian, reappears later as a lesbian again, female sexuality being, as Balzac (among others) has told us, variable. There are no consistently lesbian characters with significant roles until the third volume, and no more than the one couple who appear then, until the fifth volume.

143. Maupin later explained that his editor at the *Chronicle* kept a chart of gay and straight characters to ensure that the proportion of gays in the stories was not greater than what he understood to be the proportion of gays in the city. Armistead Maupin, "I Aspired to Be Anna Madrigal," interview by Stanley Ely, *Harvard Gay and Lesbian Review* (Winter 1998): 8.

Afterword

1. Laura Manserus, "Murder in Laramie," review of *Losing Matt Shepard,* by Beth Loffreda, *New York Times Book Review,* October 27, 2000, 37. The multitude of responses to the case that focused on location included Steve Lopez, "To Be Young and Gay in Wyoming," *Time,* October 26, 1998, 38–40; JoAnn Wypijewski, "A Boy's Life," *Harper's Magazine,* September 1999, 61–74; and Donna Minkowitz, "Love and Hate in Laramie," *Nation,* July 12, 1999, 18.

2. Beth Loffreda, *Losing Matt Shepard: Life and Politics in the Aftermath of Anti-gay Murder* (New York: Columbia University Press, 2000), x.

3. Ibid., 63.

4. See, for example, Moisés Kaufman's play *The Laramie Project* (2000), which Kaufman also directed for a film aired on HBO in 2002 (DVD, HBO Home Video); the NBC made-for-television movie *The Matthew Shepard Story,* directed by Roger Spottiswoode (2002); and the documentary *Laramie Inside Out,* directed by Beverly Seckinger (New Day Films, 2006).

5. See *The Brandon Teena Story,* directed by Susan Muska and Gréta Olafsdóttir (Zeitgeist Films, 1998); *Boys Don't Cry,* DVD, directed by Kimberly Peirce (20th Century Fox Home Entertainment, 1999); and Judith Halberstam, *In a Queer Time and Place: Transgender Bodies, Subcultural Lives* (New York: New York University Press, 2005).

6. See, for example, David Firestone, "Murder Reveals Double Life of Being Gay in Rural South," *New York Times,* March 6, 1999. Firestone begins, "The closets that people build in small, severe towns like this one are thick and difficult to penetrate," going on to explain that "Mr. Gaither would have probably escaped Sylacauga, like most gay people who grow up here, but was too devoted to his parents to contemplate leaving." He sees no contradiction in also citing a friend of Gaither's who observes that "there were about 100 gay people in town." (They were also all presumably devoted children.) The PBS *Frontline* report "Assault on Gay America: The Life and Death of Billy Jack" (February 15, 2000, transcript no. 1181K) includes interviews with local people as well as Gaither's brother and sister, who all claim to have known that Gaither was gay: "[P]eople would walk up and say, 'Is he gay?' And we'd say 'Yeah.' If they walked over to Billy Jack, and they say 'Are you gay?' he'd say, 'Yes, and I love it.' We accepted him like one of the girls, and he enjoyed that" (1). Gaither's sister, a lesbian, lives in Sylacauga with her partner. Nevertheless, the report concludes ominously, "Sylacauga is still not an easy place to be openly gay" (20).

7. For accounts of the Colorado conflict, see Chris Bull and John Gallagher, *Perfect Enemies: The Religious Right, the Gay Movement, and the Politics of the 1990s* (New York: Crown, 1996); and Didi Herman, *The Anti-gay Agenda: Orthodox Vision and the Christian Right* (Chicago: University of Chicago Press, 1997).

8. Arlene Stein, *The Stranger Next Door: The Story of a Small Community's Battle over Sex, Faith, and Civil Rights* (Boston: Beacon, 2001), 231. *The Gay Agenda* was produced by the Antelope Valley Springs of Life Ministry, Lancaster, Calif., in 1992.

9. See Bull and Gallagher, *Perfect Enemies,* 104.

10. "Matthew Shepard One Year Later," *Advocate,* October 12, 1999, 36.

11. Fall 2001 reports in both the *New York Times* and the *Village Voice* described the move of young, white, middle-class gay men to Harlem. See "Gay White Pioneers, on New Ground," *New York Times,* November 19, 2000. By spring 2007, this same group was apparently relocating to Hell's Kitchen. See David Shaftel, "Under the Rainbow," *New York Times,* March 25, 2007.

12. See Steven Kurutz, "The Kids of Christopher Street," *New York Times*, October 1, 2006. See also Michael Warner, *The Trouble with Normal: Sex, Politics, and the Ethics of Queer Life* (New York: Free Press, 1999).

13. For data, see Robert W. Bailey, *Gay Politics, Urban Politics: Identity and Economics in the Urban Setting* (New York: Columbia University Press, 1999), 230.

14. See, for example, Rosalyn Baxandall and Elizabeth Ewen, *Picture Windows: How the Suburbs Happened* (New York: Basic Books, 2000), 223; Andrew Ross, *The Celebration Chronicles: Life, Liberty, and the Pursuit of Property Value in Disney's New Town* (New York: Ballantine, 1999), 198–202; and Loffreda, *Losing Matt Shepard*, chapter 3. See also collections of personal narratives about gay rural life and hometowns, such as John Preston, ed., *Hometowns: Gay Men Write about Where They Belong* (New York: Dutton, 1991); and narratives of odysseys across North America in which the authors "discover" that "we" are everywhere, such as Edmund White, *States of Desire: Travels in Gay America* (New York: Dutton, 1983), Neil Miller, *In Search of Gay America: Women and Men in a Time of Change* (New York: Atlantic Monthly Press, 1989), Frank Browning, *The Culture of Desire: Paradox and Perversity in Gay Lives Today* (New York: Vintage, 1994), and Lindsy Van Gelder and Pamela Robin Brandt, *The Girls Next Door: Into the Heart of Lesbian America* (New York: Simon & Schuster, 1996).

15. Quoted in Loffreda, *Losing Matt Shepard*, 64.

16. Each of these arguments has been advanced, in recent years, in the United States or in relation to the United States. On the topic of gays in suburbia, see the *New York Times Magazine* issue titled "The Suburban Nation," April 9, 2000. See also Michael Schwirtz and Joshua Yaffa, "A Clash of Cultures at a Square in Moscow," *New York Times*, July 11, 2007.

17. David Harvey, "From Space to Place and Back Again: Reflections on the Condition of Postmodernity," in *Mapping the Futures: Local Cultures, Global Change*, ed. Jon Bird et al. (London: Routledge, 1993), 4.

18. Arjun Appadurai, "Grassroots Globalization and the Research Imagination," *Public Culture* 12, no. 1 (Winter 2000): 5.

19. Dolores Hayden, *The Power of Place: Urban Landscapes as Public History* (Cambridge, Mass.: MIT Press, 1996), 15–16. Hayden later invokes "the territories of . . . gay and lesbian communities," among others, as examples of "the interplay between the social and spatial" (23).

20. Tony Kushner, *Angels in America: A Gay Fantasia on National Themes*, 2 vols. (New York: Theatre Communications Group, 1993–1994). After initial performances on both coasts, the play toured the nation. It was also staged by theater groups in smaller cities and on college campuses around the country, where it served alternately as a magnet for local antigay campaigns or as a symbol of local resistance to antigay sentiment. (See Kaufman, *Laramie Project*.) Finally, a film version of *Angels in America*, directed by Mike Nichols, was aired on HBO in 2003 (DVD, Warner Home Video/HBO, 2004).

21. Bruce Bawer, *A Place at the Table: The Gay Individual in American Society* (New York: Poseidon, 1993).

22. Bull and Gallagher, *Perfect Enemies,* and Herman, *Anti-gay Agenda,* offer detailed accounts of many of these political battles.

23. Robin Toner (in part, quoting Diane Hardy-Garcia), "A Gay Rights Rally over Gains and Goals," *New York Times,* May 1, 2000.

24. Michelangelo Signorile, *Life Outside: The Signorile Report on Gay Men; Sex, Drugs, Muscles, and the Passages of Life* (New York: HarperCollins, 1997); Gabriel Rotello, *Sexual Ecology: AIDS and the Destiny of Gay Men* (New York: Dutton, 1997). Signorile admits there are couples in the city, but they do not appear in his discussions. Bruce Bawer opened his argument, in *A Place at the Table,* with the image of a teenage boy—white, middle-class, protected, suburban-bred—on the verge of corruption by a flood of sexual images as he hesitates over the purchase of a gay paper at a newsstand in Grand Central Station, portal to the most corrupting city of all. This young man would be saved from such corruption, Bawer implies, if he were allowed to claim the social "place" he was born to.

25. Michael Warner, *Trouble with Normal*; Michael Bronski, *The Pleasure Principle: Sex, Backlash, and the Struggle for Gay Freedom* (New York: St. Martin's, 1998). See also Dangerous Bedfellows Collective [Ephan Glenn Colter et al.], eds., *Policing Public Sex: Queer Politics and the Future of AIDS Activism* (Boston: South End, 1996); and William L. Leap, ed., *Public Sex/Gay Space* (New York: Columbia University Press, 1999).

26. See Wayne H. Brekhus, *Peacocks, Chameleons, Centaurs: Gay Suburbia and the Grammar of Social Identity* (Chicago: University of Chicago Press, 2003). For a recent account of the suburbs as "no place," see James Howard Kunstler, *The Geography of Nowhere: The Rise and Decline of America's Man-Made Landscape* (New York: Simon & Schuster, 1993).

27. Gay pride parades and the Children of the Rainbow curriculum are both invoked, for example, in Stephen Bransford's defense of the advocates of Amendment 2, *Gay Politics vs. Colorado and America: The Inside Story of Amendment 2* (Cascade, Colo.: Sardis, 1994). That the Rainbow curriculum contained fewer than two pages on homosexuality and was never instituted seems to be irrelevant to antigay concerns. See also Arlene Stein, *Stranger Next Door,* 132–33. Marshall Berman proposed, in the midst of talking about the reconstruction of New York City's Times Square, that there was "a puritanical complex that intertwines fear of sex with fear of the city itself. This complex goes back a long way: we can find it at the very end of the Bible, in the book of Revelation, in the portrayal of the Great Whore Babylon. When God destroys her, the book says, all urban activities—trade, commerce, crafts, music—come to an abrupt end." Marshall Berman, "Signs of the Times," *Dissent* 44, no. 4 (Fall 1997): 81.

28. Steven Marcus discusses Engels's sexual relationship with the woman who guided him through working-class Manchester, in *Engels, Manchester, and the Working Class* (New York: Norton, 1985). Elizabeth Wilson credits Benjamin with "acknowledg[ing] the sexual, and sexually dubious, aspect of loitering and looking, most famously articulated in Charles Baudelaire's poem 'A Une Passante.'" Elizabeth

Wilson, "Nostalgia and the City," in *Imagining Cities: Scripts, Signs, Memory*, ed. Sallie Westwood and John Williams (New York: Routledge, 1997), 136.

29. "By 1990, New York had a white population of only 38%," with whites "outnumbered by African-Americans, Latinos and Asian Americans who comprised 61% of the city, including both long-term residents and new immigrants. (Across the nation, the top ten cities show similar changes, from about 70 percent white in 1970 to less than 40 percent in 1990.)" Hayden, *Power of Place*, 6.

30. In the 1990s, lesbian and feminist critics worked to reconceive women's roles in the city by proposing a female or a specifically lesbian flaneur, or reevaluating women's role in the history of urban consumption. See Michèle Aina Barale on Ann Bannon, in "Queer Urbanities: A Walk on the Wild Side," in *Queer Diasporas*, ed. Cindy Patton and Benigno Sánchez-Eppler (Durham, N.C.: Duke University Press, 2000), 204–14; and Sally R. Munt's lesbian flaneur in *Heroic Desire: Lesbian Identity and Cultural Space* (New York: New York University Press, 1998). Dianne Chisholm integrated lesbians into her vision of queer urban possibilities in *Queer Constellations: Subcultural Space in the Wake of the City* (Minneapolis: University of Minnesota Press, 2005).

31. Samuel R. Delany, *Times Square Red, Times Square Blue* (New York: New York University Press, 1999), 198–99, xviii.

32. Delany begins and ends *Times Square Red, Times Square Blue* on the street—Forty-second Street—at the stand of Ben, an African American shoeshine man who spends his day, when not working on shoes, importuning women of all colors who walk past. Delany explains this as a tactic: Ben, he claims, is asserting his own status, and when the women are accompanied by men, Ben maneuvers those men into having their shoes shined in order to reassert *their* superiority. Delany notes, however, that the women—especially women not with men—whether they are walking singly or in groups, are not pleased by Ben's comments; and that Ben makes a very good living and has a wife and elaborated family life at home. Unfortunately, this admiring story puts women both into use and out of the real picture, depicted as uncomfortable without men on the street—while the wife remains presumably secure at home. The only woman who appears as a distinct person in Delany's narrative—Ana, whom he takes on a tour of the theaters because she is curious—later confesses that she was "scared to death" in the places he sees as so appealing. He does not ask her why.

33. On "nonplace urban realms," see William Sharpe and Leonard Wallock, "From 'Great Town' to 'Nonplace Urban Realm,'" in *Visions of the Modern City: Essays in History, Art, and Literature*, ed. William Sharpe and Leonard Wallock (Baltimore: The Johns Hopkins University Press, 1987), 1–50. For a survey of responses to the possibilities of the Internet, see Stephen Graham, "Imagining the Real-Time City: Telecommunications, Urban Paradigms, and the Future of Cities," in Westwood and Williams, *Imagining Cities*, 31–49.

34. Wilson, "Nostalgia and the City," 133.

35. On Los Angeles, see Edward W. Soja, *Postmetropolis: Critical Studies of Cities and Regions* (Oxford: Blackwell, 2000). On the new urbanism and Celebration,

Florida, see Peter Katz, ed., *The New Urbanism: Toward an Architecture of Community* (New York: McGraw-Hill, 1995); Andres Duany, Elizabeth Plater-Zyberk, and Jeff Speck, *Suburban Nation: The Rise of Sprawl and the Decline of the American Dream* (New York: North Point, 2000); and Ross, *Celebration Chronicles*. On New York as backdrop, see Michael Sorkin, ed., *Variations on a Theme Park: The New American City and the End of Public Space* (1992; repr., New York: Hill & Wang, 1999); M. Christine Boyer, *City of Collective Memory: Its Historical Imagery and Architectural Entertainments* (Cambridge, Mass.: MIT Press, 1996); and Sharon Zukin, *The Cultures of Cities* (Oxford: Blackwell, 1995). On global cities, see Zukin, *Cultures of Cities*; and Saskia Sassen, *The Global City: New York, London, Tokyo* (Princeton N.J.: Princeton University Press, 1991).

36. Edward W. Soja, "Inside Exopolis: Scenes from Orange County," in Sorkin, *Variations on a Theme Park*, 94.

37. Zukin, *Cultures of Cities*, 263–64.

38. Ross, *Celebration Chronicles*, 114–15.

39. Ibid., 198.

40. Rosalind Deutsche, "Reasonable Urbanism," in *Giving Ground: The Politics of Propinquity*, ed. Joan Copjec and Michael Sorkin (New York: Verso, 1999), 175.

41. Rebecca Solnit and Susan Schwartzenberg, *Hollow City: The Siege of San Francisco and the Crisis of American Urbanism* (New York: Verso, 2000).

42. "[I]n my 400-plus page book *The Rise of the Creative Class*, which is filled with . . . arguments, sub-theses, graphs, charts, [and] anecdotes . . . the part that drew the most attention was about seven pages long, and it was about gays. People have come out in droves, accusing me of 'promoting a gay agenda' or . . . 'undermining the tenets of Judeo-Christian society,'" Richard Florida explains. Quoted in Patrick Letellier, "Success Depends on Gays," *Advocate*, June 7, 2005, 22.

43. Richard Florida, *Cities and the Creative Class* (New York: Routledge, 2005), 28; emphasis in original.

44. Ibid., 29. Florida's "gay index" ranks cities according to their "gayness," based on demographic and other statistical data.

45. Ibid., 131; emphasis in original.

46. Ibid.; emphases added.

47. Cities seem to be embracing Florida's lesson, as he has been hired to consult in Providence; Memphis; Indianapolis; and Bellevue, Washington. See Emily Eakin, "The Cities and Their New Elite," *New York Times*, June 1, 2002.

48. Chauncey was speaking in *Chicago* magazine, June 1998; quoted in Marcel Acosta and Jeffrey Hinkle, "Branding Queer Identity: Chicago's North Halstead District," *Planners Network*, no. 146 (March–April 2001): 13.

49. Gabriel Giorgi, "Madrid *en Tránsito*: Travelers, Visibility, and Gay Identity," *GLQ: A Journal of Gay and Lesbian Studies* 8, nos. 1–2 (2002): 61. As Giorgi notes, such marketing "becomes an instance of historical and political validation" (61).

50. Kevin Markwell, "Mardi Gras Tourism and the Construction of Sydney as an International Gay and Lesbian City," *GLQ: A Journal of Lesbian and Gay Studies* 8, nos. 1–2 (2002): 82.

51. Klaus Wowereit, quoted in Mark Landler, "Berlin Mayor, Symbol of Openness, Has National Appeal," *New York Times*, September 23, 2006.

52. Manchester, that emblematic industrial city, has itself now been reconstructed, in paradigmatic postmodern fashion, as a hip new center for leisure and consumption, a process that began in the mid-1980s with the development of its downtown gay "Village." The city was, consequently, of particular interest to LGBT geographers developing analyses of "queer space" in the 1990s. See, for example, Stephen Quilley, "Constructing Manchester's 'New Urban Village': Gay Space in the Entrepreneurial City," in *Queers in Space: Communities, Public Places, Sites of Resistance*, ed. Gordon Brent Ingram, Anne-Marie Bouthillette, and Yolanda Retter (Seattle: Bay Press, 1997), 283.

53. "The Pleasure Seekers," *Esquire*, February 1972, quoted in Bronski, *Pleasure Principle*, 154.

54. Ibid., 155.

55. Richard A. Walker, "An Appetite for the City," in *Reclaiming San Francisco: History, Politics, Culture*, ed. James Brook, Chris Carlsson, and Nancy J. Peters (San Francisco: City Lights, 1998), 12, 15.

56. Judith Stacey, "The Families of Man: Gay Male Intimacy and Kinship in a Global Metropolis," *Signs* 30, no. 3 (Spring 2005): 1914, 1915.

57. There are still significant numbers of lesbians living even within urban neighborhoods usually identified with gay men, just as there were lesbians in the gay ghettos of the 1970s. According to Robert Bailey, "women are less 'ghettoized'— or, stated more positively, although the peak concentrations of gay men and women overlap, women are more likely to be integrated into a broader range of neighborhoods in the city" (*Gay Politics, Urban Politics*, 76). But he notes that Castells, in his influential study of San Francisco, "underestimated the presence and role of women, both individually and as a spatially defined community, among the concentrations of sex-identified residents in urban areas dominated by gay men. . . . At their peak concentration, two coterminous, sexually defined communities exist" (77). Studies mapping the different urban residential patterns of lesbians and gay men include Anne-Marie Bouthillette, "Queer and Gendered Housing: A Tale of Two Neighborhoods in Vancouver," and Elsie Jay, "Domestic Dykes: The Politics of In-difference," in Ingram, Bouthillette, and Retter, *Queers in Space*, 213–32 and 163–68, respectively.

58. See, for example, Warren St. John, "Metrosexuals Come Out," *New York Times*, June 22, 2003; and William Safire, "The Way We Live Now," *New York Times Magazine*, December 7, 2003, 30.

59. Alan Sinfield, *Gay and After* (London: Serpent's Tail, 1998), 70, 103.

60. Martin F. Manalansan IV, *Global Divas: Filipino Gay Men in the Diaspora* (Durham, N.C.: Duke University Press, 2003), 22, 23.

61. See Brekhus, *Peacocks, Chameleons, Centaurs*, 68, 88; and Lionel Cantú, "*De Ambiente*: Queer Tourism and the Shifting Boundaries of Mexican Male Sexualities," in "Queer Tourism: Geographies of Globalization," ed. Jasbir Kaur Puar, special issue, *GLQ: A Journal of Lesbian and Gay Studies* 8, nos. 1–2 (2002): 139–66.

62. Florida, *Cities and the Creative Class,* 189. For an assessment of the myth of gay affluence, see M. V. Lee Badgett, *Money, Myths, and Change: The Economic Lives of Lesbians and Gay Men* (Chicago: University of Chicago Press, 2001).

63. See the discussions of marketing in Giorgi, "Madrid"; and Jasbir Kaur Puar, "Circuits of Queer Mobility: Tourism, Travel, and Globalization," in Puar, "Queer Tourism," 101–38.

64. Deutsche, "Reasonable Urbanism," 186. Deutsche is discussing Neil Bartlett, *Ready to Catch Him Should He Fall* (New York: Dutton, 1990).

65. Florida, *Cities and the Creative Class,* 41.

66. Keith Boykin, *One More River to Cross: Black and Gay in America* (New York: Anchor, 1996), 23.

67. Kirk Johnson, "For St. Louis, Great Expectations but a Slow-Rolling Renaissance," *New York Times,* April 8, 2005.

68. *Flag Wars,* DVD, directed by Linda Goode Bryant and Laura Poitras (2003; Zeitgeist Films, 2007); *Quinceañera,* DVD, directed by Richard Glatzer and Wash Westmoreland (2006; Sony Pictures, 2007). Lesbians figure alongside gay men in both of these films, though in *Flag Wars* a lesbian realtor plays a central role, whereas in *Quinceañera* the lesbian, a minor figure, agrees to rent to the Latino family being thrown out of their home by a white gay male couple.

69. See Josh Barbanel, "Harlem (Housing Woes) on His Mind," *New York Times,* July 10, 2005. Familiar patterns of thought about the city even curtail self-conscious efforts to challenge the assumption that all urban homosexuals are white. When, for example, Manalansan writes about the "violent struggles around urban space by queers of color," he focuses on the street and his queers are still all male. Moreover, despite his testimony to the many kinds of violence exerted to control the presence of queers of color in a New York City shaped by gentrification and post-9/11 policing, he still endorses "the city" as a "sign of desire." "[C]ities still hold the promise of redemption," he writes. "For many queers, urban space offers some semblance of a possible democratic future." "The city" continues to hold on to its reputation as the savior of gays. Martin F. Manalansan IV, "Race, Violence, and Neoliberal Spatial Politics in the Global City," *Social Text,* nos. 84–85 (2005): 142, 153.

70. These studies have been central to the development of LGBT studies as a field. See, for example, George Chauncey, *Gay New York: Gender, Urban Culture, and the Makings of the Gay Male World, 1890–1940* (New York: Basic Books, 1994); Elizabeth Lapovsky Kennedy and Madeline D. Davis, on Buffalo, N.Y., in *Boots of Leather, Slippers of Gold: The History of a Lesbian Community* (New York: Routledge, 1993); Marc Stein, *City of Sisterly and Brotherly Loves: Lesbian and Gay Philadelphia, 1945–1972* (Chicago: University of Chicago Press, 2000); Nan Alamilla Boyd, *Wide Open Town: A History of Queer San Francisco to 1965* (Berkeley and Los Angeles: University of California Press, 2003); Gary L. Atkins, *Gay Seattle: Stories of Exile and Belonging* (Seattle: University of Washington Press, 2003); Matthew Houlbrook, *Queer London: Perils and Pleasures in the Sexual Metropolis, 1918–1957* (Chicago:

University of Chicago Press, 2005); Lillian Faderman and Stuart Timmons, *Gay L.A.: A History of Sexual Outlaws, Power Politics, and Lipstick Lesbians* (New York: Basic Books, 2006); and Daniel Hurewitz, *Bohemian Los Angeles and the Making of Modern Politics* (Berkeley and Los Angeles: University of California Press, 2007).

71. Queer-space projects, often led by geographers, focused on sex and politics, examined the identification of gays with consumption, and placed increasing emphasis on gender, race, and class as factors in conceptions of sexuality and the use of space. Key works in the development of queer-space analyses include such collections as David Bell and Gill Valentine, eds., *Mapping Desire: Geographies of Sexualities* (New York: Routledge, 1995); Ingram, Bouthillette, and Retter, *Queers in Space*; and Richard Phillips, Diane Watt, and David Shuttleton, eds., *De-centring Sexualities: Politics and Representation beyond the Metropolis* (London: Routledge, 2000).

72. See Edmund White, *The Flâneur: A Stroll through the Paradoxes of Paris* (New York: Bloomsbury, 2001); Edward O. Laumann et al., eds., *The Sexual Organization of the City* (Chicago: University of Chicago Press, 2004); Davina Cooper, *Sexing the City: Lesbian and Gay Politics within the Activist State* (London: Rivers Oram, 1994); Moira Rachel Kenney, *Mapping Gay L.A.: The Intersection of Place and Politics* (Philadelphia: Temple University Press, 2001); and Armistead Maupin, *Michael Tolliver Lives* (New York: HarperCollins, 2007).

73. Political scientist Robert Bailey, in *Gay Politics, Urban Politics,* uses the association of gays with feeling to argue for adding emotion, expressed through the desire for community demonstrated by identity politics, to purely economic analyses of city life. Jane Jacobs observed in the 1990s that "what people call gay ghettos" "really show evidence of people caring for the area and the community and each other." *XTRA!* (Toronto), October 9, 1997, 13, quoted in David Higgs, *Queer Sites: Gay Urban Histories since 1600* (London: Routledge, 1999), 7.

74. See Kate Zernike, "The New Couples Next Door, Gay and Straight," *New York Times,* August 24, 2003; Motoko Rich, "Edged Out by the Stroller Set," *New York Times,* May 27, 2004; and Patricia Leigh Brown, "Gay Enclaves Face Prospect of Being Passé," *New York Times,* October 30, 2007.

Index

Abbott, Berenice, 142, 157, 160

Addams, Jane, xv, 99, 110–38, 142–44, 152, 161, 163, 165–66, 205, 261, 266, 337n88; *Democracy and Social Ethics*, 120, 123; *Hull-House Maps and Papers*, 130–34; *A New Conscience and an Ancient Evil*, 131; *The Second Twenty Years at Hull-House*, 125; *The Spirit of Youth and the City Streets*, 131; *Twenty Years at Hull-House*, 115–37

Advise and Consent, xvi

Aldrich, Ann, 339n101

Altman, Dennis, 243, 247–50, 262, 264

Amendment 2, 274, 314n27

Ammiano, Tom, 290

Amsterdam, 103

Anderson, Margaret, 142

Angels in America (Kushner), 280–81, 343n20

artifice, 7–10, 12, 14, 20, 33, 44–45, 49, 138, 153–54, 226–29, 287–88, 289

"attachment," 169–218, 254, 257, 265, 267, 298. *See also* "combination"

Bailey, Robert, 337n73, 347n57, 348n73

Balch, Emily Greene, 124–25

Baldwin, James, xv, 182–218, 221, 257, 266, 269, 329n79, 332n119; *Another Country*, 183, 191, 201, 203, 206–8, 214–17, 331n99; "Fifth Avenue Uptown," 195, 200; *The Fire Next Time*, 194, 330n94; *Giovanni's Room*, 183, 190–91, 201–2, 206–7, 210, 216–18, 237, 238, 329n75, 330n95, 330n97, 331n102; *Go Tell It on the Mountain*, 183, 190, 191, 201–3, 206, 212; "The Harlem Ghetto," 183, 194, 200, 211; *Just above My Head*, 330n94, 330n96; *Nobody Knows My Name*, 183, 184, 195, 200, 207, 212; *Notes of a Native Son*, 183, 200; "Preservation of Innocence," 194; *Tell Me How Long the Train's Been Gone*, 330n94

Balzac, Honoré de, 14, 18, 21, 22, 24–25, 48, 51–59, 79, 92, 104, 152, 154, 174, 177, 193, 223, 270, 288; *The Girl with the Golden Eyes*, 5–10, 12, 30, 34, 46, 52, 54, 57, 178; *A Harlot High and Low*, 51–59, 60, 69, 178, 310n51, 311n53; *Lost Illusions*, 53, 54, 58; *Père Goriot*, 53, 54, 55, 69

Barnes, Djuna, 142

Barney, Natalie Clifford, 141–42

Bartlett, Neil, 289–90, 295

Bates, Katherine Lee, 114

Baudelaire, Charles, 25, 26, 37, 40–42, 93, 98, 128–31, 152, 254, 258, 265, 269,

270, 285, 286, 287, 306n60, 306n61, 307n67; on Balzac, 51; on the flaneur, 30–34, 47, 129–30, 138, 227, 288; *Les Fleurs du mal,* 3–7, 10, 18, 26–34; "The Painter of Modern Life," 4

Bawer, Bruce, 281, 344n24

Beach, Sylvia, 142

Beard, Dr. George, 95, 162, 169, 316n29; *American Nervousness,* 93–94, 258; *Sexual Neurasthenia,* 93–94

Bech, Henning, 265–66, 268, 340n127

Bechdel, Alison, 284

Beebo Brinker (Bannon), xviii

Bender, Thomas, 42

Benjamin, Walter, xv, 39–40, 254, 269, 286; on Baudelaire, 4–6, 25–34, 40, 129, 258, 265, 270, 306n60, 306n62, 307n64, 307n67; on the flaneur, 30–34, 138, 288, 307n66; on Paris, 19, 25

Berlin, xii, xv, 49, 103, 106, 292

Berman, Marshall, 42, 269–70, 344n27

Birmingham, 18, 47

Bloch, Iwan, 317n45

Boas, Franz, 146

Booth, Charles, 17, 131

Boston, 111, 115, 185, 209, 232, 246, 252, 253

Boston marriage, 111–13, 124

Bowers v. Hardwick, xi

Boykin, Keith, 295–96

Boys Don't Cry, 273, 277

Boys in the Band, 225

Briggs, Asa, 19

Britt, Harry, 264

Bronski, Michael, 282, 293

Brooks, Romaine, 142

Brown, Rita Mae, 235–37, 261, 286, 334n39, 335n41, 336n61

Bryher, 142

Buci-Glucksmann, Christine, 306n61

Buret, Eugène, 17, 304n32

Burgess, E. W., 89, 92, 135–36, 144–45, 147

Burnham, Daniel, 189

Burns, Mary, 131

camp, 226–29, 256

capital, xv, 18–24, 29, 68–79, 112–25, 209, 214–18, 254, 265, 269, 290–99

Carpenter, Edward, 69–70, 100, 107–8, 109, 113, 117, 118, 124, 313n80, 336n61, 337n88

Caspar, Johann Ludwig, 316n41

Castells, Manuel, 243–44, 248–54, 255, 258–60, 263–70, 290, 293, 298, 347n57

Cayton, Horace R., 210, 240

Chauncey, George, 292

Chicago, xv, xvii, 90–91, 115–39, 141–44, 145, 169, 188–89, 191, 210, 212, 230, 233, 252; Boystown, 292, 298; as a "shock city," 83–85; as a "world-class city," 292, 294–95, 297

Chicago School sociology, 42, 88–89, 91, 92, 133–38, 144–66, 185, 188, 315n13

Chicago Vice Commission, 86–89, 99, 162, 227, 314n10

Christopher Street, 255, 337n71

civil unions, xiv, 288. *See also* same-sex marriage

Clarke, Cheryl, 286

Coffignon, Ali, 11, 24, 312n73

Cohen, Ed, 68

Colette, 141

Colorado, 274, 281, 288; Aspen, 274; Boulder, 274; Denver, 232, 274, 275

Coman, Katherine, 114

"combination," 117–38, 155–66, 172–73, 175–81, 210–18, 230–42, 254. *See also* "attachment"

Constantinople, 103

Converse, Florence, 115

Cooper, Davina, 297

Cory, Donald Webster, 169, 339n101

Courbet, Gustave, 10, 11

crime, 22–24, 50–59, 68, 92, 186, 198–199, 206, 239, 265

cross-class interactions, 14–17, 30–31,
    48–49, 68, 71–75, 103–4, 107, 112–15,
    124, 130–31, 174–75

Davis, Mike, 44
Davray, Jules, 11
de Gourmont, Remy, 141
DeJean, Joan, 26
Delany, Beauford, 185, 187
Delany, Samuel, xv, 286–87, 297,
    345n32
Dell, Floyd, 83, 90, 145
D'Emilio, John, 264–65
Detroit, 232, 240
Deutsch, Sarah, 128
Deutsche, Rosalind, 289–90, 295
Dickens, Charles, 42, 194
Dixon, Melvin, 286
Doré, Gustave, 45, 48
Douglas, Lord Alfred, 38, 314n9
drag queens, 91, 228–30
Drake, St. Clair, 210, 240
Dreier, Mary, 114–15
Du Bois, W. E. B., 178
Duncan, Robert, 43
Dunye, Cheryl, 286
Dusseldorf, 103
Duval, Jeanne, 10, 26

Ellis, Havelock, 24, 42–43, 66–67, 84,
    85, 96, 109, 117, 146, 169
Engels, Friedrich, xv, 17, 19, 21, 24, 46,
    47, 69, 76–77, 130–31, 151, 156, 174,
    178, 285, 288, 344n28
Ettore, E. M., 261, 339n105

family, 7, 14, 21–22, 72–73, 77, 94, 95,
    107–8, 119–23, 136–37, 151, 156–57, 171,
    174, 179–80, 194–203, 209, 223–24,
    232, 274, 282, 287, 322n14
Fiacre, Louis, 11
Finnie, Alfred, 91
Fitzgerald, Frances, 233, 241, 242–43,
    246, 262, 264, 268, 271

Flag Wars, 296
flaneur, the, 30–34, 47, 67, 71, 101,
    129–30, 138, 205, 227, 288, 293, 297,
    307n66, 345n30
Flanner, Janet, 142, 157
Flaubert, Gustave, 22
Florida, 270; Celebration, 45, 289;
    Miami, 233; Seaside, 289
Florida, Richard, 290–92, 295, 298,
    346n42, 346n47
Foster, George, 16–17, 175
Foster, Jeannette, 43
Foucault, Michel, 267
Freud, Sigmund, 96–97, 108–9, 117, 124,
    163, 317n46, 318n62
Friedan, Betty, 170, 323n5

Gaither, Billy Jack, 272, 278, 342n6
Garland, Judy, 230
Gautier, Théophile, 5
Gay Agenda, The, 274
gay clones, 246
gay index, the, 290, 298
gay liberation, 43, 125, 143, 229, 230–35,
    240–42, 243–44, 261, 266, 279,
    336n65, 338n94
gay pride parades, 234, 236, 239, 264,
    268, 276, 285, 334n39, 339n111,
    344n27; Millennium March, 281–82;
    protests, 264, 280
gentrification, xv, 242, 249–53, 257, 266,
    283, 292, 296
Gerber, Henry, 90, 230, 315n20
ghetto, the, xv, 165, 209, 210–12, 221,
    238–53, 262–63, 283, 298, 322n26,
    335n51, 335n55, 338n90, 347n57
Giorgi, Gabriel, 292
Girdner, John H., 316n42
Giuliani, Rudolph, 289
Goffman, Erving: The Presentation of
    Self in Everyday Life, 222, 224, 332n1;
    Stigma, 222, 229, 332n3, 338n94
Gomorrah, xii, 180–81
Great Migration, 84, 183, 235

Guadalajara, 294
Guys, Constantin, 4, 7

Hacker, Marilyn, 286
Hall, Radclyffe, xv, 91, 99, 109, 140–66, 206, 235, 238, 267, 322n24
Hamburg, 103
Hardy-Garcia, Diane, 281–82, 283
Harper, Phillip Brian, 286
Harvey, David, 6, 25, 42, 278
Haussmann, Baron, 18
Hayden, Dolores, 278
H.D., 142
Heap, Jane, 142
Hirschfeld, Magnus, 99–109, 117, 124, 155, 165–66, 177, 233, 267
history, 20–34, 181–94, 223–24, 254–59, 268–69, 287–90
HIV/AIDS epidemic, 243, 253, 279–81
Holleran, Andrew, 235–37, 334n39, 336n61, 340n124
home, 21–22, 101, 125–33, 161, 171, 179, 180, 205, 217, 228, 241, 264, 266–68, 270, 295
homophile movement, 230
Hooker, Evelyn, 233
Hoover, J. Edgar, 175
Howard, Ebenezer, 188

Jackson, Kenneth, 170, 323n8
Jacobs, Jane, xiv, 181–218, 221, 254, 257, 265, 266, 268, 269, 286, 290, 328n60, 349n73, 331n117, 332n121
James, Henry, 37–41, 44, 45, 50, 57, 80; *The Bostonians*, 111–12, 123, 125–26, 253, 258; *The Princess Casamassima*, 70–75, 79
Jefferson, Thomas, 172
Jerrold, Blanchard, 48

Kaiser, Charles, xiv–xv
Kelley, Florence, 130, 133
Kellor, Frances, 114–15
Kenney, Moira Rachel, 297

Killing of Sister George, The, 220
Kinsey, Alfred, 180, 327n46
Knopp, Lawrence, 337n89
Krafft-Ebing, Richard von, 84, 85, 94–96, 98, 146, 169
Krieger, Susan, 339n105
Krier, Leon, 25
Kushner, Tony, 280–81

La Fontaine, Jean de, 5
Lait, Jack, 175, 177, 187
Lamartine, Alphonse, 5
Laumann, Edward O., 297
Le Corbusier, 189
Leeds, 18, 47
legibility, 41, 44–50, 54–68, 70–75, 78–80, 85–88, 96, 103–7, 157–58, 175–76, 206–7, 221, 222–25, 232, 256
Leicester, 21
lesbian feminism, 43, 243, 261–63, 267, 336n56, 338n94
Lesbos, 27, 35, 98
Levine, Martin, 243, 246, 266, 340n124
Levitt, William, 173
Lewis, Sasha G., 262
Locke, Alain, 84
Loffreda, Beth, 273
Lofland, Lyn, 223–25, 254, 332n4, 333n10
Lombroso, Cesare, 22, 23
London, xii, xv, xvii, 16–20, 42, 45, 47, 48, 59, 63–66, 70–75, 79, 89, 103, 113, 115, 141, 145, 147–48, 154, 158, 178, 188, 268, 285, 297; East End, 76, 178; West End, 63, 76
Los Angeles, xvii, 36–39, 41, 44–46, 80, 232, 233, 247, 288, 289, 297; Echo Park, 296; Hollywood, 191; West Hollywood, 80, 242, 293
Louys, Pierre, 141
Lowie, Robert, 146
Lynch, Kevin, 45–46

Madrid, xiv, 292, 294–95
Manalansan, Martin F., IV, 294, 348n69

Manchester, xv, xvi, 18–20, 46, 47, 83, 133, 178, 285, 293, 297, 347n52
Marcus, Sharon, 304n27
Marcus, Steven, 46, 344n28
Martineau, Louis, 11
Marx, Karl, 76–77
Maupin, Armistead, 270–71, 297, 341n143
May, Elaine Tyler, 172
Mayhew, Henry, 17, 42, 178, 308n14
McCarthy, Joseph, 172–75, 324n18
Mead, George Herbert, 133, 135
Mearns, Andrew, 48
Memphis, xv, 24
Mendes, Catulle, 11
metrosexual, 294
Mexico City, xvi, 294
migration, xiv, 17, 84, 113, 142, 148, 178–79, 228; the Great Gay Migration, 235, 241. *See also* Great Migration
Milk, Harvey, 264
Mogador, Celeste, 11
Moll, Albert, 22
Montreal, 291
Moraga, Cherríe, 286
Mortimer, Lee, 175, 177, 187
Moses, Robert, 181–82, 189, 331n107
Mosse, George, 97–98, 301n4
Mumbai, xvi
Mumford, Lewis, 42, 181–82, 189, 327n51
Munich, 103
Musset, Alfred de, 5

nature, 7–9, 20–24, 124, 151–55, 226–30, 254. *See also* artifice
Nebraska, 273
New Orleans, 233, 306n52
Newton, Esther, 226, 228–30, 233
new urbanism, 46, 181
New York City, xvii, 16–17, 38, 140, 147, 154, 181–218, 230, 233, 235, 238, 240, 244, 246, 252, 259, 262, 268, 280, 285, 288, 289, 294, 297; Brooklyn, 210; Chelsea, 275, 298; Christopher Street, 273, 275, 276; demographics, 345n29; East Village, 276; Forest Hills/Kew Gardens, 276; Greater Park Slope, 276; Greenwich Village, 181–85, 187, 213, 230, 242, 246, 276, 338n95; Harlem, 183–84, 187, 190, 200–201, 211, 212, 213, 275, 296; Jackson Heights, 276; Times Square, 45, 287, 344n27
Nordau, Max, 97–98, 169, 258

Ohio: Cleveland, 240, 270; Columbus, 296
Olsen, Donald, 304n27
Oregon, 274, 281, 288

Parent-Duchâtelet, Alexandre, 10–11, 12, 22, 88, 303n19, 303n20
Paris, xii, xvii, 2, 6–34, 38, 41, 103, 106, 141–63, 183, 184–85, 188, 191–94, 237, 268, 270, 285, 293, 297
Park, Robert, xv, 38, 42, 89, 135–38, 144–65, 172, 178, 185, 187, 205, 227, 240, 269, 290, 332n1, 340n128
Petrograd, xii
Philadelphia, 178, 186–87, 232, 252
place, xviii, 273–87, 290–92, 297–99
prostitution, 10–14, 21–22, 86, 88, 129, 131, 260, 305n47, 307n67, 335n41, 335n42, 338n100
Proust, Marcel, xii, 26, 32–33, 44, 100–109, 117, 155, 165–66, 178, 267
public/private, 7–8, 49–50, 77–79, 118–23, 180, 203–8, 259–63, 338n94
Puerto Vallarta, 294
Pullman, George M., 121–23

Queer Eye for the Straight Guy, 293–94, 295
queer space, 297, 347n52, 349n71
queer theory, 43, 297
Quinceañera, 296

racialized city, the, 8–9, 83–84, 91, 96, 113, 130, 136, 147, 163–65, 172, 175, 177–79, 190–91, 193, 194–218, 228, 238–53, 259–60, 271, 286–87, 293–95, 296, 298, 325n32, 326n36, 327n42, 336n61
Raffalovich, André, 50
Reynolds, G. M. W., 16
Rich, Adrienne, 262, 267
Riggs, Marlon, 286; *Tongues Untied*, 242, 248
Riis, Jacob, 177
Rome, 17, 18, 24, 103
Ross, Andrew, 289
Ross, Robbie, 38, 50, 59, 238
Rossi, Aldo, 35, 45, 80
Rotello, Gabriel, 282

Saintsbury, George, 18
same-sex marriage, xiv, 282–83. *See also* civil unions
Sand, George, 5, 10
San Francisco, xvii, 187, 191, 210, 232, 233, 240, 242, 244, 247, 249–52, 258–59, 262–71, 276, 280, 285, 290, 293, 297; the Castro, 241, 249, 262–64, 298
São Paolo, xvi
Sappho, 140
Sassen, Saskia, 252
Schlesinger, Arthur, Jr., 177
Schrecker, Ellen, 324n18
Schulman, Sarah, 286
Schwartzenberg, Susan, 290
Scudder, Vida, 114
Seattle, 210
Sedgwick, Eve Kosofsky, 39, 44
Seligman, Daniel, 177–79, 210, 327n42, 327n43
Sennett, Richard, xv–xvi, 25, 42, 254, 304n34, 305n44, 332n4, 338n95; *The Fall of Public Man*, 222–26, 258–59, 333n13, 338n96
settlement house movement, 76, 112–38, 261

Seville, 24
Sheffield, 18
Shepard, Matthew, 273–74, 275, 276, 278
Signorile, Michelangelo, 282
Simmel, Georg, 104, 135, 144, 156, 205, 288; "The Metropolis and Mental Life," xv, 49–50, 75–76, 89, 91–92, 105, 227
Sims, George, 48
Sinfield, Alan, 39, 294
Sklar, Kathryn Kish, 114
Smith, Mary Rozet, 115–17, 123, 319n30
Social Evil in Chicago, The (Chicago Vice Commission), 86–89, 99, 162, 227, 314n10
Sodom, xii, 98, 180–81
Soja, Edward, 44, 289
Solano, Solita, 160
Solnit, Rebecca, 290
Somerville, Siobhan, 303n14
Sontag, Susan, 226–28, 233, 256
Stacey, Judith, 293
Star, Ellen Gates, 115, 123, 126
Stearn, Jess, 169, 177
Steffens, Lincoln, 84
Stein, Arlene, 274, 336n56
Stein, Gertrude, 142–43
St. Louis, 296
Stonewall, 230, 241, 242, 243, 247, 253, 267, 270
Stonewall, 251
strangers, xvi, 194–208, 222–26, 322n21; *Strange Brother*, 90, 197; *Strange Sisters*, 204
street, the, 101, 129–30, 196–98, 263–64, 287. *See also* flaneur, the
Sue, Eugene, 16, 175
Sydney, 292, 294–95
Sylacauga, Alabama, 274
Symonds, John Addington, 43, 317n54

Tardieu, Ambroise, 11
Taxil, Leo, 11
Taylor, Valerie, 261

Teena, Brandon, 273, 278
Terry, Jennifer, 303n14
theater: the city as, 58, 221–30, 232, 256, 258–63
Thebes, 17
Thomas, W. I., 42, 89, 133, 135
Toklas, Alice B., 142
Toulouse-Lautrec, Henri de, 3, 12, 32, 140
tourism, 292, 295
Troche, Rose, 286

Ulrichs, Karl, 84, 94
Unwin, Raymond, 318n5

Vaughan, Robert, 17
Vermont, xiii, 281, 288
vice, xv, 2–34, 57–58, 85–88, 92–98, 129, 131, 136, 153, 179, 183, 190, 198, 254, 265, 270
visibility. *See* legibility
Vivien, Renée, 142

Walker, Richard, 293
Walpole, Hugh, 39
Ware, Caroline F., 187
Warner, Michael, 282
Washington, D.C., 39, 175, 187, 232, 246, 252, 253
Webb, Beatrice, 320n39
Weeks, Jeffrey, 265, 334n36
Weston, Kath, 235, 241–42, 334n35
Wherry, Kenneth, 169
White, Edmund, 6, 226, 243–46, 250–53, 257–59, 267, 297, 337n88
Whitman, Walt, 42, 43, 70, 118, 145, 286, 312n78, 336n61, 337n88; "For You O Democracy," xv, 69; "I Dream'd in a Dream," 69

Whyte, William, Jr.: *The Exploding Metropolis*, 171–72, 177–81, 323n7, 323n10; *The Organization Man*, 171
Wilde, Oscar, xv, 36–80, 101, 118, 142, 143, 206, 207, 226, 259, 313n80, 313n86; "Decay of Lying," 59, 66; *De Profundis*, 79; *An Ideal Husband*, 63–64; *The Importance of Being Earnest*, 63–66; *Lady Windermere's Fan*, 63; "Pen Pencil and Poison," 59–60; *Picture of Dorian Gray*, 60–63, 66, 311n58; "Soul of Man under Socialism," 70–71, 75–79, 98, 112, 310n40, 313n85; *A Woman of No Importance*, 63
Williams, Raymond, xvi, 18, 42, 47, 305n44, 309n26, 309n26
Wilson, Elizabeth, 25, 31, 42, 269, 288, 344n28
Wirth, Louis, 89, 99, 145, 151, 156, 165–66, 172, 243, 322n14; *The Ghetto*, 238–39
Wittman, Carl, 240–41, 242, 249
women's liberation movement, 125, 230, 261, 267, 279
Woods, Robert, 134
Worpole, Ken, 25
Wowereit, Klaus, 292
Wright, Richard, 194
Wyoming, 273, 275–76, 288; Laramie, 273

Zola, Émile, 21, 22, 24–25, 34, 48, 98, 131, 145, 304n24; *Nana*, xv, 5, 12–14, 258
Zukin, Sharon, 289

Julie Abraham is a professor of literature and LGBT studies at Sarah Lawrence College. She is the author of *Are Girls Necessary? Lesbian Writing and Modern Histories* (Minnesota, 2009) and the editor of *Diana: A Strange Autobiography.* Her reviews have appeared in the *Nation* and the *Women's Review of Books.*